BLACKSTONE'S GUIDE TO

The Civil Partnership Act 2004

Nichola Gray and Dominic Brazil

OXFORD
UNIVERSITY PRESS

OXFORD

UNIVERSITY PRESS

Great Clarendon Street, Oxford OX2 6DP

Oxford University Press is a department of the University of Oxford.
It furthers the University's objective of excellence in research, scholarship,
and education by publishing worldwide in

Oxford New York

Auckland Cape Town Dar es Salaam Hong Kong Karachi
Kuala Lumpur Madrid Melbourne Mexico City Nairobi New Delhi
Shanghai Taipei Toronto

With offices in

Argentina Austria Brazil Chile Czech Republic France Greece
Guatemala Hungary Italy Japan South Korea Poland Portugal
Singapore Switzerland Thailand Turkey Ukraine Vietnam

Oxford is a registered trade mark of Oxford University Press
in the UK and in certain other countries

Published in the United States
by Oxford University Press Inc., New York

British Library Cataloguing in Publication Data

Data available

Library of Congress Cataloging in Publication Data

Gray, Nichola.
Blackstone's guide to the Civil Partnership Act 2004 / Nichola Gray
and Dominic Brazil.
     p. cm.
Includes bibliographical references and index.
ISBN 0-19-928570-5 (acid-free paper)
   1. Civil unions—Law and legislation—Great Britain.   2. Gay couples—Legal status,
laws, etc.—Great Britain.   3. Great Britain. Civil Partnership Act 2004   I. Title:
Civil Partnership Act 2004.   II. Brazil, Dominic.   III. Title.
   KD771.G72   2005
   346.4101'68—dc22

                                                                              2005011128

Typeset by RefineCatch Limited, Bungay, Suffolk
Printed in Great Britain
on acid-free paper by
Biddles Ltd., King's Lynn

ISBN 0-19-928570-5   978-0-19-928570-9

1 3 5 7 9 10 8 6 4 2

Preface

The Civil Partnership Act 2004 is a ground breaking Act which enables gay and lesbian couples to enter into a 'civil partnership'—a formal legal relationship akin to marriage. The purpose of the Act is to remedy discrimination in existing legislation against gay and lesbian couples. It provides civil partners with the same rights and obligations as spouses. It also provides same sex couples who do not register as civil partners with the same rights and obligations as unmarried, opposite sex partners.

The Guide has been written with the practising lawyer in mind. Many parts of the 2004 Act mirror existing statutory provisions (for example, the Matrimonial Causes Act 1973) and will be familiar to family lawyers. Reference is made throughout the Guide to mirror provisions wherever they exist in other statutes. This will enable practitioners to consider a wealth of relevant case law which it has not been possible to include within this Guide. The 2004 Act is a substantial statute. It makes amendments to myriad other statutes ranging from the Sexual Offences Act 2003 to the Dentists Act 1984. It has not been possible to address every change made by the 2004 Act; instead the Guide focuses upon those changes which are likely to be of most interest to practitioners.

The 2004 Act received Royal Assent on 18 November 2004. The government has announced that the 2004 Act will come into force on 5 December 2005. A great deal of subordinate legislation will be required in order to give effect to the 2004 Act. At the date of writing this Guide, no such regulations have been made.

The law is stated as at 1 February 2005. Please note that the copy of the Act contained in this Guide omits any sections and schedules which refer to Scottish or Northern Irish Law, as follows: ss 85–209, 225–232, 248, 252, Schs 10–19, 22, Pts 3 and 4 of Sch 23, Pts 2, 5, 6, 9, 10, 12 and 15 of Sch 24, Schs 28 and 29.

Nichola Gray
Dominic Brazil

Contents—Summary

Contents

Contents

Table of Cases

Tables of Primary Legislation

EC Legislation

Table of Secondary Legislation

Table of Acronyms

CPA 2004   Civil Partnership Act 2004
DPMCA 1978   Domestic Proceedings and Magistrates' Courts Act 1978
FAA 1976   Fatal Accidents Act 1976
FLA 1996   Family Law Act 1996
IPFDA 1975   Inheritance (Provision for Family and Dependants) Act 1975
MCA 1973   Matrimonial Causes Act 1973
MFPA 1984   Matrimonial and Family Proceedings Act 1984
SSCBA 1992   Social Security Contributions and Benefits Act 1992

1

INTRODUCTION

A. ARTICLE 14, EUROPEAN CONVENTION FOR THE PROTECTION OF HUMAN RIGHTS AND FUNDAMENTAL FREEDOMS, 1950

Historically, same sex partners have faced a number of legal disadvantages **1.01** compared with married couples and unmarried opposite sex partners. A number of statutes discriminated against same sex couples by limiting the definition of a 'couple' to individuals who lived together as 'husband and wife'. The Family Law Act 1996, s 62(1), for example, originally defined 'cohabitants' as 'a man and a woman who were living together as husband and wife', thus limiting the ability of same sex partners to apply for occupation orders in relation to the partnership home.

Discrimination against lesbian and gay couples also permeated judicial **1.02** pronouncements. In *Re P (A Minor) (Custody)*[1] for example, where a father appealed against a custody order which had been made in favour of a lesbian mother, Watkins LJ opined:

This is neither the time nor the place to moralize about sexual deviance and its consequences by those whose practise it, but the possible effect on a young child living in proximity to that practice is of crucial importance to that child and to the public interest. I accept that it is not right to say that a child should in no circumstances live with a mother who is carrying on a lesbian relationship with a woman who is also living with her, but I venture to suggest that it can only be countenanced by the courts when it is driven to the conclusion that there is in the interests of the child no acceptable alternative form of custody.

---

[1] [1983] 4 FLR 401, CA.

1.03 The introduction of the Human Rights Act 1998 heralded both a statutory and a judicial change towards discrimination against same sex partners. Article 14 of the European Convention for the Protection of Human Rights and Fundamental Freedoms, 1950 prohibits discrimination against individuals in the enjoyment of Convention rights:

Article 14—Prohibition of discrimination

The enjoyment of the rights and freedoms set forth in this Convention shall be secured without discrimination on any ground such as sex, race, colour, language, religion, political or other opinion, national or social origin, association with a national minority, property, birth or other status.

1.04 Section 3 of the Human Rights Act 1998 requires the court to interpret, as far as possible, primary and subordinate legislation in a way which is compatible with Convention rights. Thus, in *Ghaidan v Godin-Mendoza*,[2] the House of Lords interpreted the phrase 'a person who was living with the original tenant as his or her wife or husband' in the Rent Act 1977 to include a member of a same sex couple in order to ensure compatibility with Convention rights.

1.05 The sentiments expressed by Baroness Hale in *Ghaidan v Godin-Mendoza* contrast starkly with the views stated by Watkins LJ in *Re P* two decades earlier:

Homosexual couples can have exactly the same sort of inter-dependent-couple relationship as heterosexuals can. Sexual 'orientation' defines the sort of person with whom one wishes to have sexual relations. It requires another person to express itself. Some people, whether heterosexual or homosexual, may be satisfied with casual or transient relationships. But most human beings eventually want more than that. They want love. And with love they often want not only the warmth but also the sense of belonging to one another which is the essence of being a couple. And many couples also come to want the stability and permanence which go with sharing a home and a life together, with or without the children who for many people go to make a family. In this, people of homosexual orientation are no different from people of heterosexual orientation.

. . . Any difference in treatment is based upon their sexual orientation. It requires an objective justification if it is to comply with Art 14. Whatever the scope for a 'discretionary area of judgment' in these cases may be, there has to be a legitimate aim before a difference in treatment can be justified.

1.06 The margin of appreciation in relation to Article 14 (ie the discretion to depart from the article on the grounds of public policy) is narrow. There must be 'convincing and weighty reasons' to justify a different treatment on the grounds of sexual orientation.[3]

1.07 Prior to the Civil Partnership Act 2004, statutory discrimination against same sex couples was remedied in a number of discrete areas. Thus, the Adoption and Children Act 2002 expressly enabled same sex couples to apply for adoption orders. The Domestic Violence, Crime and Victims Act 2004 redefined 'cohabit-

---

[2] [2004] UKHL 30, [2004] 2 FLR 600, HL.
[3] *Karner v Austria* Application 400016/98, [2003] 2 FLR 623, ECHR.

ants' for the purposes of the Family Law Act 1996 to include same sex couples, thereby enabling same sex partners to apply for occupation orders.

Statutory recognition for transsexuals was provided by the Gender Recognition Act 2004 which enabled transsexuals who obtained full gender recognition certificates to marry someone of the opposite gender to his/her acquired gender.[4]   **1.08**

On 30 June 2003, the Department for Trade and Industry published a consultation document entitled 'Civil Partnership: A framework for the legal recognition of same sex couples' which detailed the government's intention to introduce a Bill to create a new form of legal relationship between same sex couples. Following a turbulent passage through the House of Lords, the Civil Partnership Bill received Royal Assent on 18 November 2004. A great deal of secondary legislation will be required in order to give effect to the provisions of the Civil Partnership Act 2004. The government has announced that the 2004 Act will come into force on 5 December 2005.   **1.09**

The extent to which lesbian and gay couples will take up the opportunity of entering into civil partnerships is unclear. In its consultation document, the Department for Trade and Industry estimated that 5 per cent of the population of Great Britain was lesbian, gay or bisexual. Based upon the experience of similar schemes in Denmark, Sweden, Norway and the Netherlands, the rate of civil partnership registration is likely to be 10 per cent of the marriage rate in the heterosexual population (the 'low take-up scenario'). Alternatively, if the proportion of civil partnership registration in the lesbian, gay and bisexual population is the same as the proportion of marriages in the heterosexual population, 33 per cent of lesbian, gay and bisexual partners are likely to enter into civil partnerships (the 'high take-up scenario'). Within ten years of the implementation of the 2004 Act, the number of civil partnerships is therefore estimated to be between 22,000 and 310,000, depending upon the rate of take-up.   **1.10**

B. AN OVERVIEW OF THE CIVIL PARTNERSHIP ACT 2004

According to the explanatory notes which accompany the Civil Partnership Act 2004:   **1.11**

The purpose of the Civil Partnership Act is to enable same sex couples to obtain legal recognition of their relationship by forming a civil partnership.

In order to register as civil partners, two individuals must: **1.12**

(a) be of the same sex;

(b) not already be lawfully married or parties to an existing civil partnership;

---

[4] Remedying the declaration of incompatibility of Matrimonial Causes Act 1973, s 11(c) with Arts 8 and 12 made in *Bellinger v Bellinger* [2003] UKHL 21, [2003] 2 AC 467, HL.

(c) be over the age of 18 (or have the consent of 'appropriate persons' if aged 16 or 17).

1.13 The 2004 Act establishes a system of registration of civil partnerships, provides for the legal separation of the civil partners and the dissolution and annulment of civil partnerships by court order. The 2004 Act closely resembles the provisions governing the creation and dissolution of marriages.

1.14 The intention of the 2004 Act is that civil partners should have the same status, rights and obligations as married couples. There is, however, no general prohibition against discrimination on the grounds of sexual orientation contained in the 2004 Act. Instead, the 2004 Act aims to remedy discrimination by creating fresh rights and obligations and by amending existing discriminatory legislation.

1.15 Although the explanatory notes give the impression that the ambit of the 2004 Act is limited to those individuals who register as civil partners, the Act also makes numerous amendments to existing statutes to ensure that same sex partners who choose not to register as civil partners receive the same treatment as unmarried opposite sex couples.

1.16 The key changes that are made by the 2004 Act and which are addressed in this Guide are:

(a) **Creation and dissolution of civil partnerships**: the 2004 Act closely resembles the provisions in relation to married couples contained in the Marriage Acts 1949 to 1986 and the Matrimonial Causes Act 1973. There is, however, no provision comparable to adultery as a ground for dissolution. References to sexual conduct, whether in relation to the validity or dissolution of a civil partnership, are notably absent from the 2004 Act.

(b) **Recognition of foreign civil partnerships and foreign dissolution orders**: a number of foreign jurisdictions already have schemes which recognize same sex relationships. The 2004 Act provides for foreign civil partnerships to be recognized in England and Wales in defined circumstances. It also mirrors the provisions of the Family Law Act 1986 (in relation to marriages) by defining the circumstances in which foreign dissolution orders of civil partnerships will be recognized.

(c) **Financial relief in the High Court, county court and magistrates' court**: Schedules 5, 6 and 7 to the 2004 Act enable civil partners to make financial claims against each other in the same way as spouses. The provisions mirror those contained in the Matrimonial Causes Act 1973, the Domestic Proceedings and Magistrates' Courts Act 1978 and the Matrimonial and Family Proceedings Act 1984.

(d) **Wills, intestacy, family provision and fatal accident claims**: the 2004 Act amends the Wills Act 1837 so that the registration and dissolution of a civil partnership will have the same effect upon the civil partners' wills as the formation and dissolution of a marriage upon spouses' wills. The rules of intestacy are amended so that civil partners receive the same treatment as spouses under those rules. The Inheritance (Provision for Family and Dependants) Act 1975 and the Fatal Accidents Act 1976 are also amended so that civil partners are able to make claims on the same basis as spouses. The amendments also benefit unregistered same sex partners who will, in future, be treated on the same basis as unmarried opposite sex couples.

(e) **Succession to and transfer of tenancies**: the 2004 Act provides for equality of treatment between spouses and civil partners and between unmarried opposite sex couples and unregistered same sex couples in relation to succession to tenancies and repossession proceedings. The 2004 Act also amends Sch 7 to the Family Law Act 1996 to enable civil partners to apply for a transfer of the tenancy of the civil partnership home in the same way that spouses may apply for a transfer of the tenancy of the matrimonial home. A purposive interpretation of the amendments will enable unregistered same sex partners to apply for transfers of tenancies on the same basis as unmarried opposite sex couples.

(f) **Children**: the 2004 Act enables civil partners to apply for residence and contact orders without the leave of the court and to apply for parental responsibility in relation to a child of the family. The 2004 Act also enables civil partners to make applications for financial relief for children of the family under Sch 1 to the Children Act 1989.

(g) **Domestic violence**: the 2004 Act amends the Family Law Act 1996 and grants civil partners rights of occupation ('home rights') of the civil partnership home in the same way that spouses have rights of occupation of the matrimonial home. The amendments enable civil partners to apply for occupation orders on the same basis as spouses and for unregistered same sex partners to apply on the same basis as unmarried opposite sex couples.

(h) **Social security benefits**: the 2004 Act makes amendments to various statutes governing social security and tax credits so that civil partners are treated in the same way as spouses. Unregistered same sex couples will also be treated as a single family unit in the same way that unmarried opposite sex partners are treated as a single entity.

(i) **Pensions**: the 2004 Act makes various amendments in relation to the basic state pension and SERPS/S2P so that, in general terms, civil partners are treated in the same way as widowers (rather than widows). The 2004 Act does not, however, require private pension schemes to alter their rules in order to eliminate discrimination against civil partners or unregistered same sex couples.

2

THE CREATION OF A CIVIL PARTNERSHIP

A. ELIGIBILITY

Section 3 of the 2004 Act contains the eligibility criteria for individuals who **2.01** wish to register as civil partners. Two individuals are eligible to register as civil partners of each other if:

(a) they are of the same sex;

(b) neither is already a civil partner or lawfully married;

(c) they are both over the age of 18;[1]

(d) they are not within the prohibited degrees of relationship.

An individual who is 16 or 17 may still be registered as a civil partner if either: **2.02**

(a) the consent of 'appropriate persons' is obtained;[2] or

---

[1] Over 16 in Scotland.
[2] CPA 2004, s 4(1).

7

(b) the individual had previously entered into a civil partnership with another individual who subsequently died.[3]

1. Prohibited Degrees of Relationship

2.03 Schedule 1 to the 2004 Act contains lists of those degrees of relationship which are prohibited and which therefore preclude the registration of a civil partnership. The degrees of relationship which are prohibited between potential civil partners mirror those degrees of relationship which are prohibited between potential spouses by the Marriage Acts 1949 to 1986. The prohibitions are divided into two categories:

(a) absolute prohibition if one of the individuals is related to the other in the manner set out in Table 1 (kindred); and

(b) qualified prohibition if one of the individuals falls within the lists in Tables 2 and 3 (affinity) in relation to the other.

2.04 The relationships referred to in Tables 2 and 3 are replicated in the Marriage Act 1949 by virtue of amendments made by the 2004 Act.[4] Thus, affinity through civil partnership may prevent individuals from marrying. If one of the parties to a marriage is already a civil partner, the marriage will be void.[5]

TABLE 1. Kindred

Adoptive or former adoptive child
Adoptive or former adoptive parent
Parent
Child
Grandparent
Grandchild
Parent's sibling or half-sibling
Sibling or half-sibling
Sibling's or half-sibling's child

TABLE 2. Affinity

Child of former civil partner
Child of former spouse
Former civil partner of grandparent
Former civil partner of parent
Former spouse of grandparent
Former spouse of parent
Grandchild of former civil partner
Grandchild of former spouse

---

[3] ibid, s 4(3).
[4] Marriage Act 1949, s 1, Sch 1 as amended by CPA 2004, Sch 27, paras 13–17.
[5] MCA 1973, s 11 as amended by CPA 2004, Sch 27, para 40.

TABLE 3. Affinity

Relationship	Relevant deaths
Former civil partner of child	The child The child's other parent
Former spouse of child	The child The child's other parent
Parent of former civil partner	The former civil partner The former civil partner's other parent
Parent of former spouse	The former spouse The former spouse's other parent

2. Exceptions to Qualified Prohibition in Table 2

A civil partnership may still be registered if the relationship is within Table 2 if:[6] **2.05**

(a) both individuals have reached the age of 21; and

(b) the younger of them has not, at any time before reaching the age of 18, been a child of the family of the other (ie has lived in the same household and been treated as a child of the family of the other).[7]

Individuals falling within Table 2 must produce evidence to the registration **2.06** authority that they have both reached the age of 21 and must each provide a declaration (recorded in the register) specifying their relationship and declaring that the younger has not been treated as a child of the family of the elder.

In lieu of such evidence and personal declarations, the proposed civil partners **2.07** may seek a declaration from the High Court[8] confirming their ages and the fact that the younger has not been treated as a child of the family of the elder.

If it is alleged that a false declaration has been made by the proposed civil **2.08** partners, a third party may prevent the issue of a civil partnership schedule by lodging a signed statement to that effect with the registration authority.[9] The authority is then prohibited from issuing the schedule until the proposed civil partners have obtained the necessary declaration from the High Court.

3. Exceptions to Qualified Prohibition in Table 3

A civil partnership may still be registered if the relationship falls within Table 3 **2.09** if:[10]

(a) both individuals have reached the age of 21; and

(b) the persons listed in column 2 are dead.

---

[6] CPA 2004, Sch 1, para 5(1).
[7] ibid, s 75(3).
[8] ibid, Sch 1, para 7.
[9] ibid, Sch 1, para 6.
[10] ibid, Sch 1, para 9(2).

2.10 Unlike individuals falling within Table 2, individuals falling within Table 3 are not required to provide any declaration as to their age or affinal relationship. They must, however, produce evidence that they have both reached the age of 21 and that the persons listed in column 2 are dead.

4. The Consent of 'Appropriate Persons' for 16 and 17 Year Olds

2.11 Schedule 2 to the 2004 Act contains details of the 'appropriate persons' who must give consent to the registration of a civil partnership involving a 16 or 17 year old who is not a surviving civil partner. In ordinary cases, the parents of the individual, if they have parental responsibility, must both give consent and each guardian (if any) of the individual must give consent. If a residence order is or was in force immediately before the individual attained the age of 16, each of the persons with whom the individual lived as a result of the order must give consent.

2.12 The 2004 Act also defines the 'appropriate persons' who must give consent where there is a special guardianship order, care order, placement order and where an adoption agency has been authorized to place the individual for adoption.

2.13 If an 'appropriate person' refuses to give his/her consent, the court may, on application, give its consent on behalf of the appropriate person whether the registration takes place under the standard procedure[11] or under the special procedure.[12]

2.14 An 'appropriate person' may, unless the court has given consent on his/her behalf,[13] also prevent the issue of a civil partnership schedule or Registrar General's licence by giving a written notice, to any registration authority, that he forbids its issue.[14] Such notice must specify the name of the person giving it, his/her place of residence, and his/her relationship to the child which enables him/her to forbid the issue of the civil partnership schedule or Registrar General's licence.[15]

2.15 The effect of such a notice from an 'appropriate person' is to render the notice of proposed civil partnership void.[16] The fact that the issue of a civil partnership schedule or Registrar General's licence has been forbidden must be recorded in the register.[17] The failure to obtain the consent of 'appropriate persons' does not in itself render a civil partnership void unless a notice forbidding the issue of the civil partnership schedule or Registrar General's licence has actually been given.[18]

---

[11] ibid, Sch 2, para 4.
[12] ibid, Sch 2, para 10(5).
[13] ibid, Sch 2, paras 6(6) & 12.
[14] ibid, Sch 2, paras 6(2) & 12.
[15] ibid, Sch 2, paras 6(3) & 12.
[16] ibid, Sch 2, paras 6(5) & 12.
[17] ibid, Sch 2, paras 6(4) & 12.
[18] ibid, s 52(1).

The consent of an 'appropriate person' may be dispensed with if that person **2.16** is absent, inaccessible or under a disability. The procedure for dispensing with such consent differs between the standard and special procedures and is addressed later.

B. REGISTRATION OF A CIVIL PARTNERSHIP

There are three procedures by which a civil partnership may be registered: **2.17**

(a) the standard procedure;

(b) the modified standard procedure for house-bound, detained and non-resident persons;

(c) the special procedure for those cases in which an individual is seriously ill and is not expected to recover.

A civil partnership is created (and regarded as having been registered) at the **2.18** moment at which each of the proposed civil partners signs a 'civil partnership document' in the presence of a civil partnership registrar and two witnesses.[19] In the case of the standard (and modified) procedure the document which must be signed is known as a 'civil partnership schedule'.[20] In the case of the special procedure, the document which must be signed is the Registrar General's licence.[21]

Whichever procedure is adopted, the place of registration (at which the **2.19** civil partnership document is actually signed) must be in England or Wales and must not be in religious premises.[22] No religious service is permitted to take place during the signing of the civil partnership document.[23] In the case of the standard (and modified) procedure only, the place of registration must also be open to the public and must be agreed with the registration authority.[24]

C. THE STANDARD PROCEDURE

There are four stages to the registration of a civil partnership under the standard **2.20** procedure:

(a) both of the proposed civil partners give notice of a proposed civil partnership

---

[19] ibid, s 2(1).
[20] ibid, s 7(1)(b).
[21] ibid, s 7(1)(a).
[22] ibid, s 6(1).
[23] ibid, s 2(5).
[24] ibid, s 6(3).

to a registration authority (a local council)[25] which then publicizes the relevant information;

(b) a waiting period of 15 days during which the notices are publicized;

(c) the issue of a civil partnership schedule by the registration authority at the request of one or both of the proposed civil partners;

(d) registration of the civil partnership (by both partners signing the civil partnership schedule) within 12 months.

2.21   In order to register under the standard procedure, both of the proposed civil partners must have resided in England or Wales for at least seven days immediately before giving a notice of proposed civil partnership and must fulfil the eligibility criteria.[26]

1. Notice of Proposed Civil Partnership

2.22   The first stage of the standard procedure requires notices of proposed civil partnership to be given by the prospective civil partners. Each of the proposed civil partners must give a notice of proposed civil partnership which must include a declaration signed in the presence of an authorized person at the registration authority confirming:[27]

(a) that there is no impediment of kindred or affinity or other lawful hindrance to the formation of the civil partnership;

(b) that each of them has had a usual place of residence in England or Wales for at least seven days immediately before giving the notice;

(c) if one of the proposed civil partners is 16 or 17 (and is not a surviving civil partner), that the consent of each appropriate person has either been obtained or has been dispensed with or that the court has given its consent or that no person exists whose consent is required;[28]

(d) if one of the proposed civil partners is subject to immigration control (ie is not a European Economic Area national or has obtained or requires leave to enter or remain in the UK) that the qualifying condition in Sch 23, para 2 is fulfilled.[29]

2.23   The notice must also state the place at which the registration will take place[30] and must contain such other information as may be prescribed by regulations.

2.24   It is not necessary for the proposed civil partners to give the notices on the same day.

---

[25] ibid, s 28.
[26] ibid, s 8(1)(b).
[27] ibid, s 8(4).
[28] ibid, Sch 2, para 5.
[29] ibid, Sch 23, para 5.
[30] ibid, s 6(1)(c).

The registration authority may require any person giving notice of a proposed 2.25
civil partnership to provide:

(a) 'specified evidence' (evidence of name, age, dissolution of prior civil partnership or marriage, nationality or residence) in relation to that person; or,
in exceptional circumstances, in relation to that person's proposed civil
partner also;[31]

(b) if the consent of an appropriate person is required, written evidence that the
consent has in fact been given.[32]

If an appropriate person refuses his/her consent, the court may, on application, 2.26
give its consent on behalf of that person.[33]

Where the consent of a person cannot be obtained because he/she is absent, 2.27
inaccessible or under a disability:

(a) the registration authority must dispense with his/her consent if there is
another person whose consent is also required;[34]

(b) if no other person's consent is required, the Registrar General may dispense
with the need for consent or the court[35] may, on application, consent to the
child registering as a civil partner.[36]

Following the receipt of a notice of proposed civil partnership, the registration 2.28
authority must:

(a) record in the register the fact that a notice has been received, the
information in it and the fact that the necessary declarations have been
attested;[37]

(b) publicize the name of the person giving the notice, the name of that person's
proposed civil partner and any other information prescribed by regulations.[38] The Registrar General and any registration authority in whose area
the registration will take place or in whose area either of the proposed civil
partners has resided for the preceding seven days must also publicize this
information.

---

[31] ibid, s 9.
[32] ibid, Sch 2, para 7.
[33] ibid, Sch 2, para 4.
[34] ibid, Sch 2, para 3(2).
[35] County court or magistrates' court in the district area or local justice area in which the applicant or respondent resides or the High Court: ibid, Sch 3, para 15(1).
[36] ibid, Sch 2, para 3(3).
[37] ibid, s 8(3).
[38] ibid, s 10(1).

2. The Waiting Period

2.29 The second stage of the standard procedure is a 'waiting period' which follows the receipt by the registration authority of a notice of proposed civil partnership. This 'waiting period':[39]

(a) begins on the day after the notice is recorded in the register; and

(b) ends at the end of a 15 day period beginning with that day.

2.30 The Registrar General has the power to shorten the waiting period to such period as he considers appropriate if there are 'compelling reasons because of the exceptional circumstances of the case'.[40]

2.31 The purpose of this 'waiting period' is to enable third parties to object to the issue of the civil partnership schedule. A notice of objection, which may be given to any registration authority, must:[41]

(a) state the objector's place of residence and the ground of objection; and

(b) be signed by or on behalf of the objector.

2.32 Following receipt of a notice of objection, the registration authority must record in the register the receipt of the notice of objection and the information contained in it.[42]

2.33 The receipt of a notice of objection prevents the issue of a civil partnership schedule until such time as either:[43]

(a) the registration authority which first received the notice of proposed civil partnership has investigated the objection and has satisfied itself that the objection should not prevent the issue of a civil partnership schedule; or

(b) the objection is withdrawn.

2.34 There is a right of appeal to the Registrar General if the registration authority, having investigated the objection, refuses to issue a civil partnership schedule.[44]

2.35 If an objector's grounds of objection are declared, by the Registrar General, to be frivolous, the objector is liable for the costs of the proceedings before the Registrar General and for damages payable to the proposed civil partner to whom the objection related.[45]

---

[39] ibid, s 11.
[40] ibid, s 12.
[41] ibid, s 13(2).
[42] ibid, s 14(3).
[43] ibid, s 15(4).
[44] ibid, s 16.
[45] ibid, s 17.

3. The Issue of the Civil Partnership Schedule

The third stage of the standard procedure is the issue of a civil partnership 2.36
schedule. As soon as the waiting period, in relation to each notice, has expired,
the registration authority in whose area the proposed registration is to take place
has a duty[46] to issue a civil partnership schedule at the request of one or both of
the proposed civil partners unless:

(a) the registration authority is not satisfied that there is no lawful impediment
to the issue of a civil partnership schedule;[47] or

(b) a notice of objection has been received; or

(c) if one of the proposed civil partners is 16 or 17 and the issue of a civil
partnership schedule has been forbidden by an appropriate person.[48]

There is a right of appeal to the Registrar General[49] in the event that the 2.37
registration authority considers there to be a lawful impediment. If the representation made to the registration authority as to the impediment is declared to be
frivolous,[50] provision is made for the payment of costs and damages.

If one of the proposed civil partners is 16 or 17, the civil partnership schedule 2.38
must contain a statement that its issue has not been forbidden by an appropriate
person.[51]

4. Registration of the Civil Partnership

The fourth and final stage of the standard procedure is the registration of the 2.39
civil partnership. The civil partnership is created and registered by each of the
proposed civil partners signing a civil partnership schedule in the presence of a
civil partnership registrar and two witnesses[52] in the 12 month period beginning
with the day on which the notices of proposed civil partnership were recorded
(or the day on which the earlier notice was recorded, if the notices were recorded
on different days).[53]

If the civil partnership is not registered within the 12 month period, the 2.40
notices of proposed civil partnership and the civil partnership schedule are
void.[54]

The 2004 Act makes no provision for any particular form of words to be used 2.41
during the registration process. On the contrary, the registration process is a

---

[46] ibid, s 14(1).
[47] ibid, s 14(3).
[48] ibid, Sch 2, para 8.
[49] ibid, s 15(1)(b).
[50] ibid, s 16(2) & (3).
[51] ibid, Sch 2, para 9.
[52] ibid, s 2(1).
[53] ibid, s 17.
[54] ibid, s 17(3).

purely written process in the presence of two witnesses and a civil partnership registrar. The absence of any provision for spoken words in the 2004 Act is intentional. Local authorities will, however, be free to offer ceremonies which would include spoken words.

D. THE PROCEDURE FOR HOUSE-BOUND, DETAINED AND NON-RESIDENT PERSONS

1. House-bound Persons

2.42 The 2004 Act mirrors the Marriage Act 1983 in enabling house-bound and detained persons to register as civil partners at the place where one of them is usually resident or detained. For the purposes of the 2004 Act, an individual is 'house-bound' if his/her registered medical practitioner provides a statement confirming that the individual ought not to move or be moved because of illness or disability and that this is likely to be the case for the following three months.[55]

2.43 Provided they fulfil the eligibility criteria, the 2004 Act enables two individuals to be registered as civil partners of each other at the place where one of them is house-bound. The standard procedure applies, but with the following modifications:[56]

(a) each notice of proposed civil partnership must be accompanied by a medical statement from the registered medical practitioner (the receipt of which must be recorded in the register) which has been made not more than 14 days before the notice of proposed civil partnership is recorded in the register;

(b) the civil partnership schedule must be signed by the proposed civil partners within three months (instead of 12) of the day on which the notices of proposed civil partnership were recorded; or, if they were not recorded on the same day, within three months of the day on which the earlier notice was recorded.

2. Detained Persons

2.44 For the purposes of the 2004 Act, a 'detained person' is an individual who is a patient in an hospital (other than a short term mental patient) or who is detained in a prison or other place to which the Prison Act 1952 applies.[57]

2.45 Provided they fulfil the eligibility criteria, the 2004 Act enables two individuals to be registered as civil partners of each other at the place at which one

---

[55] ibid, s 18(2).
[56] ibid, s 18(3).
[57] ibid, s 19(2).

of them is detained provided a statement is made by the hospital's managers or the prison's governor (or other officer in charge) confirming that the establishment in question has no objection to its premises being specified in the notice of proposed civil partnership as the place at which the registration will take place.[58]

The standard procedure applies, but with the following modifications:[59]   **2.46**

(a) each notice of proposed civil partnership must be accompanied by the necessary statement from the establishment at which the individual is detained (the receipt of which must be recorded in the register) which must be made not less than 21 days before the day on which the notice is recorded in the register; and

(b) the civil partnership schedule must be signed by the proposed civil partners within three months (instead of 12) of the day on which the notices of proposed civil partnership were recorded in the register; or, if they were not recorded on the same day, within three months of the day on which the earlier notice was recorded.

3. Non-residents

If one of the proposed civil partners resides in Scotland or Northern Ireland or   **2.47** is a member of HM Forces serving outside the UK and the other proposed civil partner resides in England or Wales, the standard registration applies, but with the following modifications:[60]

(a) the non-resident is not required to give a notice of proposed civil partnership;

(b) the civil partnership schedule may only be issued if one of the proposed civil partners produces a certificate of no impediment issued to the non-resident by a registration authority in Scotland or Northern Ireland or, if a proposed civil partner is a member of HM Forces serving abroad, by the commanding officer.

E. THE SPECIAL PROCEDURE

The special procedure applies if one of the proposed civil partners is seriously ill   **2.48** and is not expected to recover. The 2004 Act mirrors the position in relation to prospective spouses under the Marriage (Registrar General's licence) Act 1970 and enables the registration of a civil partnership to occur quickly in these circumstances. The special procedure consists of three stages:

---

[58] ibid, s 19(4) & (6).
[59] ibid, s 19(3).
[60] ibid, s 20(5).

(a) one of the proposed civil partners gives notice of a proposed civil partner-ship to the registration authority in whose area the registration is to take place;

(b) the Registrar General issues a licence;

(c) registration of the civil partnership (by both partners signing the licence) within one month.

1. The Notice of Proposed Civil Partnership

2.49   The first stage of the special procedure requires a notice of proposed civil partnership to be given. Unlike the standard procedure, where both of the proposed civil partners must give a notice, only one of the proposed civil part-ners need give notice of a proposed civil partnership under the special procedure.[61]

2.50   There is no requirement under the special procedure (as there is under the standard procedure) that the notice of proposed civil partnership contain a declaration that each of the proposed civil partners has resided in England or Wales for at least seven days immediately before giving notice.[62]

2.51   The notice of proposed civil partnership under the special procedure must include a declaration signed by the individual giving the notice (in the presence of an authorized person) confirming:

(a) that there is no impediment of kindred or affinity or other lawful hindrance to the formation of the civil partnership;[63]

(b) if one of the proposed civil partners is 16 or 17 (and is not a surviving civil partner), that the consent of each appropriate person has either been obtained or been dispensed with or that the court has given its consent or that no person exists whose consent is required;[64]

(c) if one of the proposed civil partners is subject to immigration control (ie is not a European Economic Area national or has obtained or requires leave to enter or remain in the UK) that the qualifying condition in Sch 23, para 2 is fulfilled.[65]

2.52   The notice must also specify the place at which the registration will take place which must be a place in England or Wales and which must not be religious premises.[66] No religious ceremony is permitted to take place at the time of

---

[61] ibid, s 21(1).
[62] ibid, s 21(3).
[63] ibid, s 21(3).
[64] ibid, Sch 2, para 11.
[65] ibid, Sch 23, para 5.
[66] ibid, s 6(1).

registration.[67] Unlike the standard procedure, the place of registration need not be open to the public.

The individual giving the notice of proposed civil partnership must also pro- **2.53**
duce to the registration authority such evidence as the Registrar General may require to satisfy him:[68]

(a) that there is no lawful impediment to the formation of a civil partnership;

(b) that one of the proposed civil partners is seriously ill and is not expected to recover (for which purposes the certificate of a registered medical practitioner is sufficient) and that the proposed civil partner understands the nature and purport of signing a Registrar General's licence;

(c) that there is sufficient reason why a licence should be granted;

(d) if the consent of an appropriate person is required, that such consent has actually been given.[69]

If the consent of an appropriate person cannot be obtained because he is absent, **2.54**
inaccessible or under a disability:

(a) the Registrar General may dispense with the need for that person's consent, whether or not any other person's consent is also required[70] (this provision contrasts with the standard procedure where the registration authority has no discretion and must dispense with consent if another person's consent is also required); or

(b) the court may, on application, consent on behalf of the appropriate person.

Unlike the standard procedure, the notice of proposed civil partnership under **2.55**
the special procedure is not publicized. The receipt of the notice and the information contained in it is merely recorded in the register.[71]

2. The Registrar General's Licence

The second stage of the special procedure is the issue of the Registrar General's **2.56**
licence. The Registrar General must give his authority for the issue of a Registrar General's licence if he is satisfied that one of the proposed civil partners is seriously ill and is not expected to recover unless:

(a) he is satisfied that there is a lawful impediment to the issue of his licence;[72]

(b) if one of the proposed civil partners is 16 or 17 and the authority to issue a licence has been forbidden by an appropriate person.[73]

---

[67] ibid, s 2(5).
[68] ibid, s 22.
[69] ibid, Sch 2, para 13.
[70] ibid, Sch 2, para 10.
[71] ibid, ss 21(3) & 8(5).
[72] ibid, s 25(3).
[73] ibid, Sch 2, para 14.

2.57　A third party may object to the Registrar General giving his authority for the issue of his licence by giving notice either to the Registrar General or to any registration authority. The notice of objection must be signed and must state the objector's place of residence and the ground of objection.[74]

2.58　The Registrar General is prohibited from giving authority for the issue of his licence until either:[75]

(a) he has investigated the objection and decided that it should not obstruct the issue of his licence (the Registrar General's decision on this issue is final); or[76]

(b) the objection has been withdrawn.

2.59　If the Registrar General declares that the grounds of the objection are frivolous, the objector is liable for the costs of the proceedings before the Registrar General and for damages payable to the proposed civil partner to whom the objection relates.[77]

3. Registration of the Civil Partnership

2.60　The third and final stage of the special procedure is the registration of the civil partnership. Once a Registrar General's licence has been issued, the proposed civil partners must register as civil partners, by signing the licence, within one month from the day on which the notice of proposed civil partnership was given.[78] The Registrar General's licence must be signed by each of the civil partners in the presence of a civil partnership registrar and two witnesses.[79] If the civil partners fail to sign the licence within one month, the notice of proposed civil partnership and the licence are both void.[80]

F. REGISTRATION BY FORMER SPOUSES, ONE OF WHOM HAS CHANGED SEX

2.61　Schedule 3 to the 2004 Act provides a fast-track procedure for former spouses, one of whom has changed sex, to register as civil partners of each other.

2.62　The provisions of the Gender Recognition Act 2004 are beyond the scope of this Guide. In essence, a person aged 18 or over may apply for a gender recognition certificate if:[81]

---

[74] ibid, s 24.
[75] ibid, s 25(6).
[76] ibid, s 25(7).
[77] ibid, s 26(1) & (2).
[78] ibid, s 27(1).
[79] ibid, s 2(1).
[80] ibid, s 27(2).
[81] Gender Recognition Act 2004, s 1.

(a) he or she is living in the other gender ('the acquired gender'); or

(b) he or she has changed gender (to 'the acquired gender') under the law of a foreign jurisdiction.

2.63 An application for a gender recognition certificate is made to a Gender Recognition Panel which must be satisfied that the applicant:[82]

(a) has or has had gender dysphoria;

(b) has lived in the acquired gender for two years prior to the date of the application.

2.64 Unless the applicant is married or already a civil partner, the certificate will be a full certificate. If the applicant is married or already a civil partner, an interim gender recognition certificate will be issued which will be converted to a full certificate upon a nullity order being made in relation to the marriage or civil partnership.[83]

2.65 Where a court:

(a) makes a decree of nullity of a marriage on the grounds that an interim gender recognition certificate has been issued to a spouse; and

(b) issues a full gender recognition certificate under Gender Recognition Act 2004, s 5(1) to that spouse,

the former spouses may register as civil partners of each other without being delayed by the 15 day waiting period.

2.66 Provided each of the former spouses gives a notice of proposed civil partnership within one month of the issue of the full gender recognition certificate and elects to use the fast-track procedure under Sch 3,[84] the standard procedure (and modified procedure if one of the partners is house-bound, detained or non-resident)[85] applies, but with the following modifications:[86]

(a) the notices of proposed civil partnership (or single notice where one of the proposed civil partners is non-resident) are not publicized;

(b) there is no 15 day waiting period.

2.67 As soon as the notices of proposed civil partnership have been given, the registration authority in whose area the registration will take place must, at the request of one or both of the proposed civil partners, issue a civil partnership schedule.[87]

---

[82] ibid, s 2.
[83] ibid, ss 4 & 5. CPA 2004, s 250(4).
[84] CPA 2004, Sch 3, paras 2 & 3.
[85] Resident in Scotland, Northern Ireland or a member of HM Forces serving outside the UK.
[86] CPA 2004, Sch 3, para 4.
[87] ibid, Sch 3, para 4(2).

2.68 The proposed civil partners (including any civil partner who is house-bound, detained or non-resident) must register as civil partners, by signing the civil partnership schedule within one month of the day on which the notices of proposed civil partnership were given; or, if they were not given on the same day, within one month of the day on which the earlier was given.[88]

2.69 If the proposed civil partners do not register as civil partners within the one month period, the notices of proposed civil partnership and the civil partnership schedule are void.

2.70 If one of the proposed civil partners is non-resident (ie resident in Scotland, Northern Ireland or a member of HM Forces serving outside the UK), the civil partnership schedule will only be issued once one of the proposed civil partners has produced a certificate of no impediment issued to the non-resident in Scotland, Northern Ireland or, if a proposed civil partner is a member of HM Forces serving abroad, by the commanding officer.[89]

G. CIVIL PARTNERSHIP AGREEMENTS

2.71 A 'civil partnership agreement' is an agreement:[90]

(a) to register as civil partners in any part of the UK or outside the UK under an Order in Council[91] (registration at a British Consulate or by members of HM Forces serving abroad); or

(b) to enter into an 'overseas relationship'.[92]

2.72 A civil partnership agreement is unenforceable.[93]

2.73 Individuals who enter into civil partnership agreements are, however, granted limited rights under the 2004 Act:

(a) they may claim a share or enhanced share in real or personal property as a result of any improvements made thereto, provided a claim is made within three years of the termination of the agreement (see paras 5.142–5.149 below);

(b) they are treated as 'associated persons' and may make applications for non-molestation orders and (in limited circumstances) for occupation orders as a result of that status provided the application is made within three years of the termination of the agreement (see paras 11.42 and 11.48 below).

---

[88] ibid, Sch 3, paras 4(3) & 7.
[89] ibid, Sch 3, para 7(8).
[90] ibid, s 73(3).
[91] See paras 4.01–4.05 below.
[92] See paras 4.07–4.11 below.
[93] CPA 2004, s 73(1) & (2).

H. THE CREATION OF A CIVIL PARTNERSHIP: A PRACTICAL GUIDE

2.74

Eligibility	• Same sex	s 3
	• Neither party already a civil partner or married	
	• Over 18 (16 or 17 with consent of appropriate persons)	Sch 1
	• Not within the prohibited degrees of relationship	
Standard procedure	• Both proposed civil partners must have resided in England and Wales for at least seven days before giving notice of proposed civil partnership	s 8(1)(b)
	• Both must lodge notices of proposed civil partnership containing all necessary declarations and information	s 8, Sch 2, para 5; Sch 23, para 5
	• 15 day waiting period during which notices are publicized (or shorter period if Registrar General considers there are compelling reasons because of exceptional circumstances)	s 10, s 11, s 12
	• Issue of civil partnership schedule at end of waiting period	s 14, Sch 2, para 8
	• Registration of civil partnership within 12 months of notices of proposed civil partnership being recorded in the register (by signing the civil partnership schedule in the presence of a civil partnership registrar and two witnesses	s 2(1), s 17
Procedure for house-bound persons	• Applies if one of civil partners cannot move or be moved for the following three months because of illness or disability	s 18(2)
	• Standard procedure applies except:	s 18(3)
	(a) statement (made not more than 14 days before notices of proposed civil partnership are recorded) from registered medical practitioner required;	
	(b) civil partnership schedule must be signed within three months of notices of proposed civil partnership being recorded	
Procedure for detained persons	• Applies if one of civil partners is a patient in a hospital or detained in prison	s 19(2)
	• Standard procedure applies except:	s 19(3)
	(a) statement (made not less than 21 days before notices of proposed civil partnership are recorded) from hospital manager or prison governor required confirming no objection to registration at establishment;	
	(b) civil partnership schedule must be signed within three months of notices of proposed civil partnership being recorded	
Procedure for non-residents	• Applies if one of civil partners resides in Scotland, Northern Ireland or is a member of HM Forces serving outside the UK	s 20(2), (3), (4)
	• Standard procedure applies except:	s 20(5)
	(a) non-resident is not required to give a notice of proposed civil partnership;	
	(b) certificate of no impediment must be issued by	

	registration authority in Scotland, Northern Ireland or by commanding officer	
Special procedure	• Applies if one of civil partners is seriously ill and is not expected to recover	s 22(2)
	• Notice of proposed civil partnership required from only one of the civil partners including all necessary declarations and information and any evidence required by the Registrar General	s 21, s 22 Sch 2, para 5 Sch 23, para 5
	• Issue of Registrar General's licence	s 25 Sch 2, para 14
	• Registration of civil partnership by both civil partners signing licence in presence of civil partnership registrar and two witnesses within one month of notice of proposed civil partnership being given	s 27(1) s 2(1)
Fast-track procedure for former spouses in gender recognition cases	• Applies if a full gender recognition certificate has been issued and the marriage has been annulled on the grounds of an interim gender recognition certificate	Sch 3, para 1
	• Both former spouses must give notice of proposed civil partnership within one month of the full gender recognition certificate and elect the fast-track procedure	Sch 3, paras 2 & 3
	• Standard procedure applies except:	Sch 3, paras 3 & 4
	(a) notices of proposed civil partnership not publicized;	
	(b) no waiting period;	
	(c) civil partnership schedule must be signed within one month of the notices of proposed civil partnership being given	Sch 3, para 4(3)
Consent for 16 and 17 year olds	• Consent of 'appropriate person' required unless child is a surviving civil partner	Sch 2 s 4(3)
	• Appropriate person may forbid the issue of a civil partnership schedule or Registrar General's licence	Sch 2, paras 6(2) & 12
	• Court may give consent on behalf of the appropriate person if he refuses consent	Sch 2, paras 4 & 10(5)
	• Under standard procedure, if appropriate person is absent, inaccessible or under a disability:	
	(a) registration authority must dispense with consent if another person's consent is also required	Sch 2, para 3(2)
	(b) if no other person's consent is required, Registrar General may dispense with consent or the court may give consent	Sch 2, para 3(3)
	• Under special procedure, if appropriate person is absent, inaccessible or under a disability:	
	(a) Registrar General may dispense with consent whether or not another person's consent is required or the court may give its consent on behalf of that person	Sch 2, para 10

3

THE TERMINATION OF A CIVIL PARTNERSHIP

A. INTRODUCTION

A civil partnership ends only on death, dissolution or annulment. The 2004 Act **3.01** mirrors, to a large extent, the provisions contained in the Matrimonial Causes Act 1973. Thus a civil partnership may not be dissolved during its first 12 months and may only be dissolved thereafter on the grounds that it has broken down irretrievably.

In the first instance, every dissolution, nullity and presumption of death order **3.02** is a 'conditional order'[1] (akin to Decree Nisi) and may not be made 'final' (akin to Decree Absolute) until the end of a six week period from the making of the conditional order;[2] although the court has the power to shorten the six week period.[3]

---

[1] CPA 2004, s 37(2).

[2] ibid, s 38(1).

[3] ibid, s 38(4).

B. DISSOLUTION ORDERS

1. The Grounds on which a Civil Partnership may be Dissolved: s 44(5)

3.03 As with a marriage, a civil partnership may only be dissolved on the ground that it has broken down irretrievably.[4] For a court to dissolve a civil partnership, it must find not only that the civil partnership has broken down irretrievably but that one of the four facts listed in s 44(5) exists. Once a s 44(5) fact has been proved, a presumption of irretrievable breakdown arises.[5] The four facts are:

(a) **Behaviour s 44(5)(a)**: that the respondent has behaved in such a way that the applicant cannot reasonably be expected to live with the respondent. The requisite behaviour may take many forms ranging from violence to 'dogmatic' behaviour.[6] The particular circumstances, characteristics and personalities of the individual civil partners must be considered.[7]

(b) **Two years' separation s 44(5)(b)**: that the applicant and the respondent have lived apart for a continuous period of at least two years immediately preceding the application *and* that the respondent consents to a dissolution order being made. If the court is later satisfied that the applicant misled the respondent (whether intentionally or unintentionally) about any matter which the respondent took into account in deciding to give his/her consent, it may rescind a conditional dissolution order based solely upon two years' separation.[8]

(c) **Five years' separation s 44(5)(c)**: that the applicant and the respondent have lived apart for a continuous period of at least five years immediately preceding the application. The consent of the respondent to the dissolution order is not required.

(d) **Desertion s 44(5)(d)**: that the respondent has deserted the applicant for a continuous period of at least two years immediately preceding the application. Desertion continues even though the deserting partner was incapable of continuing the necessary intention provided the court would have inferred, from the evidence before it, that the desertion continued had he not been so incapable.[9] The court may count towards the period of desertion any period during which a partner has been excluded from the civil partnership home by an injunction or by an occupation order under the Family Law Act 1996. The concept of desertion is not defined in the Act but has been

---

[4] ibid, s 44(1).
[5] ibid, s 44(4).
[6] *Birch v Birch* [1992] 1 FLR 564, CA.
[7] *O'Neill v O'Neill* [1975] 1 WLR 1118, CA.
[8] CPA 2004, s 48(1).
[9] ibid, s 45(5).

developed, in relation to divorce, by a wealth of case law. There are four key elements to desertion:

(i) cessation of cohabitation;
(ii) an intention by the respondent to cease permanent cohabitation;
(iii) absence of consent by the applicant to the cessation of cohabitation;[10] and
(iv) absence of reasonable cause for the respondent to cease cohabitation.[11]

The four facts set out above are identical to four of the five facts upon which a marriage may be dissolved. Whereas a spouse may rely upon adultery as a fact justifying a divorce, there is no comparable provision in relation to a civil partnership. If a civil partner enters into a relationship with a third party this may, however, constitute behaviour for the purposes of s 44(5)(a). **3.04**

It is not necessary for an applicant to show that the s 44(5) fact has actually caused the irretrievable breakdown of the civil partnership. The respondent's behaviour, for example, may have occurred when the partners had already separated and the partnership had already broken down.[12] **3.05**

All dissolution orders are, in the first instance, conditional orders which may not be made final until the end of a six week period from the making of the conditional order;[13] although the court has power to shorten the six week period.[14] **3.06**

2. Periods of 'Living Together' which are Ignored

The 2004 Act encourages partners to reconcile without jeopardizing the entitlement to a dissolution or separation order. Thus, if the applicant and respondent have lived together in the same household, for a period (or periods) which does not or, which taken together, do not exceed six months: **3.07**

(a) the court must disregard this fact in assessing whether the applicant cannot reasonably be expected to live with the respondent;[15]

(b) the court must disregard this fact in assessing whether a period of two or five years' separation or a period of two years' desertion has been continuous.[16] Such periods of living together may not, however, be counted towards the two or five year period itself.[17]

Section 45(8) of the Act defines 'living together' as living with each other in the same 'household'. Civil partners may, however, continue to live together in **3.08**

---

[10] *Spence v Spence* [1939] 1 All ER 52.
[11] *Dyson v Dyson* [1954] P 198.
[12] *Stevens v Stevens* [1979] 1 WLR 885.
[13] CPA 2004, s 38(1).
[14] ibid, s 38(4).
[15] ibid, s 45(1) & (2).
[16] ibid, s 45(6).
[17] ibid, s 45(7).

the civil partnership home and yet not be considered as living together in the same 'household'. The partners must, however, exist separately in the same home and must not share meals or household chores.[18]

3.09   If a civil partner obtains a separation order[19] based on two years' desertion, then the desertion is deemed to continue even after the separation order for the purposes of obtaining a subsequent dissolution, provided the civil partners have not resumed living together after the separation order.[20]

3. Time-Bar on Applications for Dissolution Orders

3.10   As with divorce, s 41(1) provides an absolute bar to applications for dissolution of civil partnerships before the end of a period of one year from the date on which the civil partnership was formed. The application for a dissolution order may, however, be founded upon events within that one year period.[21]

4. Attempts at Reconciliation

3.11   The court may adjourn the application for a dissolution or separation order at any stage if it considers there to be a 'reasonable possibility of a reconciliation' between the civil partners.[22]

3.12   A solicitor representing an applicant for a dissolution or separation order will be required, as he is required with divorcing couples, to certify whether he has discussed with the applicant the possibility of a reconciliation.[23]

5. Grave Financial or Other Hardship: s 47

3.13   If an application for a dissolution order is based upon five years' separation, s 47 enables a respondent to oppose the grant of a conditional dissolution order on the grounds that:

(a) the dissolution would result in 'grave financial or other hardship' to the civil partner (including the loss of the chance of acquiring any benefit which the respondent might have acquired but for the dissolution); and

(b) in all the circumstances it would be wrong to dissolve the civil partnership.

3.14   The 2004 Act mirrors the provisions contained in the Matrimonial Causes Act 1973, s 5 and provides a defence to a conditional order for dissolution based upon five years' separation.

---

[18] *Mouncer v Mouncer* [1972] 1 All ER 289.
[19] See paras 3.35–3.37 below for separation orders.
[20] CPA 2004, s 46(4).
[21] ibid, s 41(2).
[22] ibid, s 42(3).
[23] ibid, s 42(2).

On an application pursuant to the 2004 Act, s 47, the court must consider all the circumstances, including:[24]   **3.15**

(a) the conduct of the civil partners;

(b) the interests of the civil partners;

(c) the interests of any children or other persons concerned.

The grave financial or other hardship must result from the dissolution of the civil partnership and not merely from the breakdown of the civil partnership.[25]   **3.16**

The court only has the power to refuse to grant a conditional dissolution order on the grounds of grave financial or other hardship if the dissolution order is based solely upon five years' separation.[26]   **3.17**

It is not expected that s 47 will be invoked frequently by respondents. The equivalent provision contained in the Matrimonial Causes Act 1973 is now rarely invoked. Historically, wives relied upon the Matrimonial Causes Act 1973, s 5 in cases where grave financial hardship would result from the loss of a widow's pension. The advent of pension sharing has largely removed this potential hardship for both married couples and civil partners. The defence of grave financial hardship is also unlikely to avail younger civil partners or civil partnerships of short duration.[27]   **3.18**

6. Consideration of the Respondent's Financial Position in Cases of Two and Five Years' Separation: s 48

Where the court has made a conditional dissolution order based solely upon either two or five years' separation, the respondent may apply under s 48 for the court to consider, before the conditional order is made final, his/her financial position after the dissolution of the civil partnership.   **3.19**

The 2004 Act mirrors the Matrimonial Causes Act 1973, s 10(2) and enables a respondent to delay the grant of a final dissolution order based upon two or five years' separation.   **3.20**

The court is precluded from making the conditional dissolution order final unless it is satisfied either:[28]   **3.21**

(a) that the applicant should not be required to make any financial provision for the respondent; or

(b) that the financial provision made by the applicant for the respondent is:

    (i) reasonable and fair; or

    (ii) is the best that can be made in the circumstances.

---

[24] ibid, s 47(3).
[25] *Parker v Parker* [1972] Fam 116.
[26] CPA 2004, s 47(2)(b).
[27] *Mathias v Mathias* [1972] Fam 287, CA.
[28] CPA 2004, s 48(4).

3.22 The equivalent provision contained in the Matrimonial Causes Act 1973 is invoked, in particular, in those cases where the applicant has valuable pension rights which, following dissolution, would be lost to the respondent in the event of the applicant's death prior to the resolution of financial claims.

3.23 If the applicant gives an undertaking that he/she will make such financial provision for the respondent as the court may approve, the court may make the dissolution order final if it considers that there are circumstances which make it desirable for a final order to be made without delay.[29] The undertaking must, however, contain concrete financial proposals; an undertaking to abide by whatever financial order the court may make in the future is insufficient.[30]

3.24 In considering an application under s 48, the court must consider all the circumstances, including:[31]

(a) the age, health, conduct, earning capacity, financial resources and financial obligations of each of the civil partners; and

(b) the financial position of the respondent after the applicant's death in the event that a dissolution order is made.

3.25 The court only has the power to delay a final dissolution order under s 48 if the dissolution order is based solely upon either two or five years' separation.[32]

C. NULLITY ORDERS

3.26 Sections 49 and 50 of the 2004 Act define the circumstances in which a civil partnership is either void or voidable. A void civil partnership is void ab initio and is treated as though it had never existed.[33] In contrast, a nullity order made in relation to a voidable civil partnership annuls the civil partnership only from the date of the final nullity order. The civil partnership is treated as though it had validly existed to the date of the final order.[34]

1. Grounds on which a Civil Partnership is Void: s 49

3.27 The grounds on which a civil partnership is void are set out in s 49. Those grounds relate to breaches (which both partners were aware of at the date of registration) of formal requirements. A civil partnership is void if:

(a) at the date of registration, the partners did not fulfil the eligibility criteria;

---

[29] ibid, s 48(5).

[30] *Grigson v Grigson* [1974] 1 WLR 228, CA.

[31] CPA 2004, s 48(3).

[32] ibid, s 48(2)(b).

[33] Orders for financial relief may still be made even if the civil partnership is void. See *J v S-T (formerly J)* [1997] 1 FLR 402, CA.

[34] CPA 2004, s 37(3).

(b) at the date of registration of the civil partnership:

  (i) both partners knew that due notice of the proposed civil partnership had not been given;

  (ii) both partners knew that the civil partnership document (ie the civil partnership schedule or Registrar General's licence) had not been duly issued;

  (iii) both partners knew that the civil partnership document was void because registration did not take place within the specified period of the notices of proposed civil partnership being recorded (ie 12 months under the standard procedure; one month under the special procedure);[35]

  (iv) both partners knew that the place of registration was not the place specified in the notice(s) of proposed civil partnership and the civil partnership document;

  (v) both partners knew that a civil partnership registrar was not present;

(c) the civil partnership document was void because the partnership involved a child and the issue of a civil partnership schedule had been forbidden under Sch 2, para 6(5).[36]

Whereas the 2004 Act defines the circumstances in which an applicant may be estopped from denying the validity of a voidable civil partnership, there is no such provision in relation to void civil partnerships. At common law, a party to a void marriage may be estopped from denying its validity if there have been previous proceedings between the spouses in which the validity of the marriage has been expressly recognized (eg judicial separation proceedings).[37] In similar circumstances, a civil partner may, by analogy, also be estopped from denying the validity of a void civil partnership. **3.28**

2. Grounds on which a Civil Partnership is Voidable: s 50

The grounds on which a civil partnership is voidable are set out in s 50. A civil partnership is voidable if: **3.29**

(a) Either partner did not validly consent to its formation (whether as a result of duress, mistake, unsoundness of mind or otherwise).

(b) At the time of its formation, either partner, though capable of giving valid consent, was suffering (continuously or intermittently) from a mental disorder which rendered him/her unfit for civil partnership.

(c) At the date of its formation, the respondent was pregnant by some person other than the applicant (a ground only relevant in change of gender cases).

---

[35] See paras 2.39–2.40 & 2.60 above.
[36] See para 2.14 above.
[37] *Woodland v Woodland* [1928] P 169.

The court must not, however, make a nullity order on this ground unless it is satisfied that the applicant was ignorant of this fact at the date of formation of the civil partnership.[38]

(d) After its formation, an interim gender recognition certificate under the Gender Recognition Act 2004[39] has been issued to either partner. A certificate can only be issued on the basis that an individual is either living in the other gender or has changed gender under the law of a foreign jurisdiction.[40] The civil partners would then be living in different genders rather than the same genders. An application for a nullity order on this ground must, however, be made within six months from the date of the interim gender recognition certificate.[41] If the court makes a nullity order on this ground it must, at the same time, grant a full gender recognition certificate.[42]

(e) The respondent is a person whose gender at the time of the formation of the civil partnership has become the acquired gender under the Gender Recognition Act 2004. This ground enables an applicant to apply for a nullity order where the respondent is living in the other gender or has changed gender under the law of a foreign jurisdiction, but has failed to make an application himself/herself for a gender recognition certificate under the Gender Recognition Act 2004. The court must not, however, make a nullity order on this ground unless it is satisfied that the applicant was ignorant of this fact at the date of formation of the civil partnership.[43]

3.30 An applicant may be estopped from denying the validity of a civil partnership which would otherwise be voidable. Thus, s 51 precludes the court from making a nullity order on the grounds that the civil partnership is voidable if the respondent satisfies the court:

(a) that the applicant, with the knowledge that he/she could apply for a nullity order, conducted himself/herself so as to lead the respondent reasonably to believe that he/she would not do so; and

(b) that it would be unjust to the respondent to make the order.

3.31 A time limit within which an application must be made for a nullity order in relation to a voidable civil partnership is imposed by s 51(2). An application must be made within three years of the date of formation of the civil partnership (unless the ground is the issue of an interim gender recognition certificate, in which case the application must be made within six months of the issue of the

---

[38] CPA 2004, s 51(6).
[39] See paras 2.62–2.65 above for a summary of the Gender Recognition Act 2004.
[40] Gender Recognition Act 2004, s 1.
[41] CPA 2004, s 51(5).
[42] Gender Recognition Act 2004, s 5A as inserted by CPA 2004, s 250(4).
[43] CPA 2004, s 51(6).

interim gender recognition certificate). The court may only extend the three year period if:[44]

(a) the applicant suffered from a mental disorder at some time during the three year period; and

(b) it would, in the circumstances of the case, be just to grant leave to the applicant to make an application for a nullity order.

Whereas a marriage is voidable if it has not been consummated or if one of the parties was suffering from a communicable venereal disease at the date of the marriage,[45] there are no comparable provisions within the 2004 Act. **3.32**

All nullity orders are, in the first instance, conditional orders which may not be made final until the end of a six week period from the making of the conditional order;[46] although the court has the power to shorten the six week period.[47] **3.33**

3. Power to Validate a Void Civil Partnership: s 53

The Lord Chancellor has the power by order, under s 53, to validate a civil partnership which would otherwise be void. A draft of the proposed order must be advertised for a period of not less than one month and the Lord Chancellor may direct a local inquiry to be held into the validity of any objections to the proposed order. **3.34**

D. SEPARATION ORDERS

A separation order between civil partners is the equivalent of a judicial separation between spouses. An application for a separation order may be made under s 56 on the ground that any of the four facts exist which are required for a dissolution order under s 44(5) (behaviour, two years' separation, five years' separation or desertion). See paras 3.03–3.09 above. **3.35**

Unlike a dissolution order, the question whether the civil partnership has broken down irretrievably is irrelevant to the grant of a separation order.[48] **3.36**

When the court makes a separation order, it is a final order; there is no conditional stage. **3.37**

---

[44] ibid, s 51(3).
[45] MCA 1973, ss 12(a), (b), (e).
[46] CPA 2004, s 38(1).
[47] ibid, s 38(4).
[48] ibid, s 56(2).

E. PRESUMPTION OF DEATH ORDERS

3.38 The court may make a presumption of death order under s 55 if it is satisfied, at any time, that reasonable grounds exist for supposing that a civil partner is dead.

3.39 The court will presume, unless the contrary is proved, that a civil partner is dead if:

(a) the civil partner has been continually absent from the applicant for a period of seven years or more; and

(b) the applicant has no reason to believe that the civil partner has been alive during that time.

3.40 All presumption of death orders are, in the first instance, conditional orders which may not be made final until the end of a six week period from the making of the conditional order;[49] although the court has the power to shorten the six week period.[50]

F. APPLICATIONS FOR FINAL DISSOLUTION AND NULLITY ORDERS BY RESPONDENTS

3.41 Where an applicant fails to apply for a conditional dissolution or nullity order to be made final, the respondent is entitled to apply for a final order provided three months have elapsed since the date on which the applicant could have made such an application.[51]

3.42 On such an application, the court has a discretion to:[52]

(a) make the order final;

(b) rescind the conditional order;

(c) require further inquiry; or

(d) otherwise deal with the case as it thinks fit.

G. DISSOLUTION, NULLITY AND SEPARATION ORDERS AFFECTING CHILDREN OF THE FAMILY

3.43 Section 63 of the 2004 Act mirrors the Matrimonial Causes Act 1973, s 41. The court is required to consider, in any proceedings for a dissolution, nullity or separation order (but not a presumption of death order):

---

[49] ibid, s 38(1).
[50] ibid, s 38(4).
[51] ibid, s 40(2).
[52] ibid, s 40(3).

(a) whether there are children of the family (defined in s 75(3) as a child of both civil partners or treated by both as a child of their family);

(b) if there are such children whether, in light of arrangements which have been or are proposed to be made for their upbringing and welfare, it should exercise any of its powers under the Children Act 1989 (for example, by making a contact or residence order under s 8 or by making a direction for investigation by the local authority under s 37(1)).

The court may direct that a conditional order of dissolution or nullity 3.44 should not be made final or that a separation order should not be made if it considers:

(a) the circumstances require it or are likely to require it to exercise its powers under the Children Act 1989; and

(b) it is not in a position to exercise those powers without giving further consideration to the case; and

(c) there are 'exceptional circumstances' which make it desirable, in the interests of the child, to give a direction under s 63.

Section 63 applies not only to children of the family under the age of 16 but also 3.45 to children of the family who have reached the age of 16 to whom the court directs that the section should apply.

H. DECLARATIONS IN RELATION TO A CIVIL PARTNERSHIP

A civil partner or a third party, if he/she has a sufficient interest in the applica- 3.46 tion, may apply under s 58 to the High Court or county court for one of five declarations:

(a) a declaration that the civil partnership was valid at its inception;

(b) a declaration that the civil partnership subsisted on a specified date;

(c) a declaration that the civil partnership did not subsist on a specified date;

(d) a declaration that the validity of a dissolution, annulment or separation order obtained outside England and Wales be recognized in England and Wales;

(e) a declaration that the validity of a dissolution, annulment or separation order obtained outside England and Wales not be recognized in England and Wales.

The 2004 Act mirrors the provisions in relation to marriages contained in the 3.47 Family Law Act 1986, ss 55, 58 and 59.

The court is not entitled to make a declaration that the civil partnership was 3.48

void at its inception;[53] the court's jurisdiction is limited, in those circumstances, to making a nullity order on the application of one of the civil partners.

3.49   If the court is satisfied as to the truth of the declaration sought under s 58, it must make the declaration unless it would be 'manifestly contrary to public policy' to do so.[54]

3.50   Rules of court will provide for service of the application for a declaration upon the Attorney-General and upon any person who may be affected by the application. Section 60 enables the Attorney-General to intervene in the proceedings in order to argue any question in relation to the application which the court considers it necessary to have fully argued. Third parties affected by the application may be joined as parties under either s 64(3) or under rules of court pursuant to s 64(1)(c).

I. INTERVENTION OF THE QUEEN'S PROCTOR AND THIRD PARTIES

3.51   Section 39 of the 2004 Act enables the Queen's Proctor to intervene in proceedings for dissolution, nullity or presumption of death orders in relation to civil partnerships in the same manner in which he may intervene in relation to the same proceedings between divorcing couples.

3.52   The court may, of its own motion, direct that the papers be sent to the Queen's Proctor who will, under the instructions of the Attorney-General, then argue any question which the court considers it necessary to be fully argued.[55]

3.53   Alternatively, the Queen's Proctor may apply to intervene or may show cause if he becomes aware of any matter which is material to a decision in the case.[56]

3.54   If a conditional order has been made and the Queen's Proctor shows cause why it should not be made final on the ground that material facts have not been brought to the attention of the court, the court may:[57]

(a) make the order final;

(b) rescind the conditional order;

(c) require further inquiry; or

(d) otherwise deal with the case as it thinks fit.

The same provision applies to third parties who show cause on the same ground.

3.55   Section 63(3) enables the court to permit any person to intervene, on such

---

[53] ibid, s 59(5).
[54] ibid, s 59(1).
[55] ibid, s 39(2).
[56] ibid, s 39(3).
[57] ibid, s 40(1) & (3).

terms as the court considers fit, in proceedings for dissolution, separation and nullity orders and in proceedings for declarations if it considers it to be in the interests of that person to be joined.

J. THE TERMINATION OF A CIVIL PARTNERSHIP: A PRACTICAL GUIDE

3.56

Dissolution order	• Bar on applications within 12 months of registration of civil partnership	s 41(1)
	• Court must find that civil partnership has broken down irretrievably and that one of four facts exists:	s 44(1) s 44(5)
	(1) behaviour;	s 44(5)(a)
	(2) two years' separation and consent of respondent;	s 44(5)(b)
	(3) five years' separation;	s 44(5)(c)
	(4) two years' desertion	s 44(5)(d)
	• Certain periods of 'living together' ignored	s 45(6), (7)
	• Conditional dissolution order in first instance	
	• Respondent has a defence to conditional order in five years' separation cases if grave financial or other hardship will be suffered	s 47
	• Applicant may apply for final order after six weeks from date of conditional order; court has power to shorten this period	s 38(1) s 38(4)
	• Respondent may apply for final order after three months and six weeks from date of conditional order	s 40(2), (3)
	• Respondent may delay final order in cases of two and five years' separation by requiring court to consider financial position after dissolution	s 48
	• Court may delay grant of final order if it considers it necessary to exercise its powers under Children Act 1989	s 63
Nullity order: void civil partnership	• Civil partnership is void if:	s 49
	(a) at registration the eligibility criteria were not fulfilled;	
	(b) at registration both partners knew that:	
	(i) due notice had not been given; or	
	(ii) civil partnership document was not duly issued; or	
	(iii) civil partnership document was void because registration did not occur within requisite period; or	
	(iv) the place of registration was not that specified in the notice; or	
	(v) a civil partnership registrar was not present;	
	(c) one of the civil partners was a child and the issue of a civil partnership schedule had been forbidden by an 'appropriate person'	
	• Lord Chancellor has power to validate a void civil partnership	s 53
	• No time limit within which application for nullity order must be made	
	• Conditional nullity order in first instance	
	• Applicant may apply for final order after six weeks from date of conditional order; court has power to shorten this period	s 38(1) s 38(4)

	• Respondent may apply for final order after three months and six weeks from date of conditional order	s 40(2), (3)
	• Court may delay grant of final order if it considers it necessary to exercise its powers under Children Act 1989	s 63
Nullity order: voidable civil partnership	• Subject to the applicant being estopped, a civil partnership is voidable if:	s 51 s 50

(a) either partner did not validly consent to its formation;

(b) either partner was suffering from a mental disorder at date of registration;

(c) respondent was pregnant by a person other than the applicant at the date of registration and the applicant was unaware of this fact;

(d) an interim gender recognition certificate was issued after registration and the application for a nullity order was made within six months of the issue of the certificate; — s 51(5)

(e) respondent's gender at registration has become the acquired gender and the applicant was unaware of this fact

	• Application for nullity order must be made within three years of registration; court has power to extend this period only if applicant suffered from a mental disorder during the three years	s 51(2) s 51(3)
	• Conditional nullity order in first instance	
	• Applicant may apply for final order after six weeks from date of conditional order; court has power to shorten this period	s 38(1) s 38(4)
	• Respondent may apply for final order after three months and six weeks from date of conditional order	s 40(2), (3)
	• Court may delay grant of final order if it considers it necessary to exercise its powers under Children Act 1989	s 63
Separation order	• Court must find that one of four facts exists:	s 56

(1) behaviour; — s44(5)(a)

(2) two years' separation and consent of respondent; — s44(5)(b)

(3) five years' separation; — s44(5)(c)

(4) two years' desertion — s44(5)(d)

	• Irretrievable breakdown need not be proved	
	• Certain periods of living together are ignored	
	• Court may delay the grant of a separation order if it considers it necessary to exercise any of its powers under the Children Act 1989	
Presumption of death order	• Court must be satisfied that reasonable grounds exist for supposing that the civil partner is dead	s 55
	• Court will presume a civil partner to be dead if:	

(a) he/she was continually absent for seven years;

(b) the applicant has no reason to believe he/she was alive during that period

	• Conditional order in first instance	
	• Applicant may apply for final order after six weeks from date of conditional order; court has power to shorten this period	s 38(1) s 38(4)

4

CIVIL PARTNERSHIPS FORMED OR DISSOLVED ABROAD

A. REGISTRATION OUTISDE THE UK UNDER AN ORDER IN COUNCIL

Section 210 of the 2004 Act enables an Order in Council to be made which will **4.01** enable same sex couples, one of whom is a UK national,[1] to register as civil partners at British Consulates etc in the same manner as opposite sex couples are able to marry at British Consulates etc pursuant to the Foreign Marriage Act 1892.

The ability to register a civil partnership at a British Consulate etc is subject to **4.02** the following conditions:[2]

(a) one of the civil partners must be a UK national;

(b) the civil partners must fulfil the eligibility criteria for registration of a civil partnership in the UK (see paras 2.01–2.02 above);

(c) the country in which the British Consulate etc is situated must not object to the registration of a civil partnership;

(d) sufficient facilities must not exist for the parties to enter into an 'overseas relationship' (ie a relationship akin to a civil partnership in that country).

Section 211 of the 2004 Act enables an Order in Council to be made which will **4.03** enable same sex couples, one of whom is a member of HM Forces serving

---

[1] Defined in CPA 2004, s 245(1).
[2] ibid, s 210(2).

39

abroad (or a child of such member), to be registered abroad as civil partners in the same manner in which opposite sex couples, in the same circumstances, may be married under the Foreign Marriage Act 1892.

4.04 The ability to register a civil partnership under s 211 is subject to the following conditions:[3]

(a) one of the proposed civil partners must either:

  (i) be a member of HM Forces serving abroad or be a child of that person's family who lives with that family; or

  (ii) be employed abroad in such capacity as may be prescribed or be a child of that person's family who lives with that family.

(b) the parties must fulfil the eligibility criteria for registration of a civil partnership in the UK (see paras 2.01–2.02 above);

(c) such other conditions as may be prescribed must be fulfilled.

4.05 The Orders in Council under ss 210 and 211 may provide that the civil partners are to be treated as having registered a civil partnership in the UK for the purposes of establishing whether the courts of the UK have the jurisdiction to entertain an application for a separation, dissolution, nullity etc order in relation to the civil partnership.

B. RECOGNITION OF FOREIGN CIVIL PARTNERSHIPS

4.06 Sections 212 to 218 of the 2004 Act set out the circumstances in which an 'overseas relationship' will be recognized by the court as amounting to a civil partnership. There are two stages to the recognition process:

(a) firstly, the court must be satisfied that the relationship is an 'overseas relationship'; and

(b) secondly, the relationship must fulfil the recognition criteria set out in the 2004 Act.

4.07 There are two types of 'overseas relationship':[4]

(a) a 'specified relationship'; and

(b) a relationship which meets the 'general conditions'.

1. Specified Relationships

4.08 A 'specified relationship' is one which:[5]

---

[3] ibid, s 211(2).
[4] ibid, s 212(1).
[5] ibid, s 213.

(a) is listed in Sch 20 to the 2004 Act. That schedule currently lists 14 types of relationship in different countries (eg a 'civil union' in Vermont, USA and a 'marriage' in the Netherlands, where same sex couples may marry); and

(b) has been registered overseas by two people:

  (i) who are of the same sex under the foreign law and under UK law;[6]

  (ii) neither of whom is already a civil partner or lawfully married.

2. Relationships which Meet the 'General Conditions'

A relationship which is not listed in Sch 20 may nonetheless constitute an 'overseas relationship' if:[7]   **4.09**

(a) the 'general conditions' are satisfied:

  (i) the relationship has exclusivity, ie is one which, under the foreign law, may not be entered into if either of the parties is already a party to a relationship of that kind or is already lawfully married; and

  (ii) there is no time limit on the duration of the relationship under the foreign law; and

  (iii) the effect, under the foreign law, of the parties entering into the relationship is that the parties are either treated as a couple or treated as married; and

(b) the relationship has been registered overseas by two people:

  (i) who are of the same sex under the foreign law or under UK law;[8]

  (ii) neither of whom is already a civil partner or already lawfully married.

3. The Same Sex Requirement

If the parties were not, under UK law, regarded as having the same sex at the date of registration of the overseas relationship (or at the date the 2004 Act came into force, if later than the date of registration), the relationship will not constitute an 'overseas relationship' unless:[9]   **4.10**

(a) the parties were regarded, under the foreign law, as having the same sex at that date as a result of a change of gender of one of the parties; and

(b) a full gender recognition certificate has, after that date, been issued to that person under the Gender Recognition Act 2004 and neither party, in the interim, has entered into a civil partnership or marriage.

---

[6] ibid, ss 216(1) & 212(1)(b).
[7] ibid, s 214.
[8] ibid, ss 216(1) & 212(1)(b).
[9] ibid, s 216.

4.11 If, however, a national of the European Union or of the European Economic Area has been granted legal recognition of a change of gender, there is no need for a full gender recognition certificate to be obtained.[10]

4. Recognition of an 'Overseas Relationship'

4.12 Section 215 of the 2004 Act requires the court to recognize an 'overseas relationship' as the equivalent of a civil partnership if the civil partners:

(a) had the capacity to enter into the relationship under the foreign law;[11] and

(b) fulfilled the criteria for formal validity of the relationship under the foreign law.[12]

4.13 Recognition of an 'overseas relationship' will confer upon the parties to the relationship all the rights and obligations of civil partners under the 2004 Act (eg it will preclude them from entering into a civil partnership or marriage in the UK with third parties and it will enable them to apply for separation or dissolution orders in the UK provided the court has jurisdiction to entertain those proceedings: see Chapter 14).

4.14 If one of the parties was domiciled in the UK at the date of the overseas registration (or at the date the 2004 Act came into force, if later), the overseas relationship will not be recognized as equivalent to a civil partnership unless:[13]

(a) at that date, both parties were over 16; and

(b) the parties were not within the prohibited degrees of relationship in Pt 1 of Sch 1 to the 2004 Act (see para 2.03 above).

4.15 The recognition of such relationships is, however, subject to the overriding public policy exception that an overseas relationship will not be recognized if it would be manifestly contrary to public policy to recognize the capacity, under the foreign law of either or both parties, to enter into the relationship.[14]

C. JURISDICTION TO MAKE NULLITY ORDERS IN RELATION TO CIVIL PARTNERSHIPS FORMED ABROAD

4.16 Section 54 of the 2004 Act addresses the circumstances in which a court in England and Wales may make a nullity order in relation to a civil partnership which has been formed abroad.

---

[10] ibid, s 216(6).
[11] ibid, s 215(1)(a).
[12] ibid, s 215(1)(b).
[13] ibid, s 217.
[14] ibid, s 218.

1. Nullity Orders in Relation to Civil Partnerships Registered in Scotland or Northern Ireland

A civil partnership registered in Scotland or Northern Ireland which is *void* in either of those parts of the UK will be treated as void in England and Wales.[15] **4.17**

A civil partnership registered in Scotland will be treated as *voidable* in England and Wales if an interim gender recognition certificate was issued to either civil partner after the registration of the civil partnership and an application for a nullity order is made in England or Wales within six months of the issue of the certificate.[16] **4.18**

A civil partnership registered in Northern Ireland will be treated as *voidable* in England and Wales if it would have been voidable had it been registered in England and Wales (rather than Northern Ireland)[17] (see para 3.29 above). The restrictions which apply to applications for nullity orders in respect of civil partnerships registered in England and Wales are equally applicable when considering the voidability of civil partnerships registered in Scotland or Northern Ireland (eg estoppel, application to be made within three years of registration etc: see paras 3.30–3.31 above).[18] **4.19**

2. Nullity Orders in Relation to Civil Partnerships Registered Abroad Under an Order in Council

A civil partnership registered abroad under an Order in Council will be treated as *void* in England and Wales if:[19] **4.20**

(a) neither of the civil partners was a UK national; or

(b) the civil partners would not have been eligible to register as civil partners in England and Wales; or

(c) a requirement prescribed by the Order in Council has not been complied with.

A civil partnership registered abroad under an Order in Council will be treated as *voidable* in England and Wales if: **4.21**

(a) Scotland is the appropriate part of the UK prescribed by the Order in Council for the purposes of establishing eligibility to enter into a civil partnership and an interim gender recognition certificate has been issued to one of the civil partners after the registration of the civil partnership. The restrictions which apply to applications for nullity orders in respect of civil

---

[15] ibid, s 54(1)(a) & (2)(a).
[16] ibid, ss 54(1)(b), 54(9) & 51(5).
[17] ibid, s 54(2)(b).
[18] ibid, s 54(9).
[19] ibid, s 54(3) & (4)(a).

partnerships registered in England and Wales are equally applicable (eg estoppel, application to be made within three years of registration etc: see paras 3.30–3.31 above).[20]

(b) England, Wales or Northern Ireland is the appropriate part of the UK prescribed by the Order in Council for the purposes of establishing eligibility to enter into a civil partnership and the civil partnership would have been voidable had it been registered in England and Wales (rather than registered abroad under an Order in Council) (see para 3.29 above). The restrictions which apply to applications for nullity orders in respect of civil partnerships registered in England and Wales are equally applicable (eg estoppel, application to be made within three years of registration etc: see paras 3.30–3.31 above).[21]

3. Nullity Orders in Relation to Apparent or Alleged Overseas Relationships

4.22 An apparent or alleged overseas relationship will be treated as *void* in England and Wales if it is not an 'overseas relationship' for the purposes of s 212 of the 2004 Act (see paras 4.07–4.11 above) or is not recognized as the equivalent of a civil partnership under s 215 of the 2004 Act (see para 4.12 above).[22]

4.23 An 'overseas relationship' will be treated as *voidable* in England and Wales if:[23]

(a) the overseas relationship was voidable in the country in which it was registered. The restrictions which apply to applications for nullity orders in respect of civil partnerships registered in England and Wales are equally applicable (eg estoppel, application to be made within three years of registration etc: see paras 3.30–3.31 above) provided those restrictions accord with the law of the country in which the civil partnership was registered;[24] or

(b) an interim gender recognition certificate was issued to either civil partner after registration of the overseas relationship and the application for a nullity order was made in England or Wales within six months of the date of the certificate;[25] or

(c) if either of the parties was domiciled in England, Wales or Northern Ireland at the date on which the overseas relationship was registered and it would have been voidable had it been registered in England and Wales (rather than overseas) (see para 3.29 above).

---

[20] ibid, s 54(4)(b)(ii) & (9).
[21] ibid, s 54(4)(b)(i) & (9).
[22] ibid, s 54(7).
[23] ibid, s 54(8).
[24] ibid, s 54(9).
[25] ibid, s 54(9).

D. RECOGNITION OF OVERSEAS DISSOLUTION ETC

Sections 234 to 238 of the 2004 Act provide for the circumstances in which the validity of an overseas separation of civil partners or an overseas dissolution or annulment of a civil partnership (ie one which was registered in the UK or was an 'overseas relationship'[26] recognized in the UK) will be recognized in the UK. The provisions mirror those contained in ss 46 and 51 of the Family Law Act 1986 which relate to the recognition of an overseas separation, dissolution or annulment in the case of married couples. **4.24**

Section 235 provides for the mandatory recognition of an overseas separation of civil partners or overseas dissolution or annulment of a civil partnership if certain conditions are satisfied. The section distinguishes between those separations, dissolutions and annulments obtained by means of proceedings and those obtained otherwise than by means of proceedings. **4.25**

Recognition of the overseas separation, dissolution or annulment has important consequences: **4.26**

(a) in the case of dissolution or annulment, it enables the individuals to enter into a civil partnership or marriage with third parties in the UK;

(b) it may enable the individuals to apply in the UK for financial relief under Sch 7 to the 2004 Act (see Chapter 7).

1. Recognition of Overseas Separation etc Obtained by Means of Proceedings

An overseas separation of civil partners or dissolution or annulment of a civil partnership which has been obtained by means of proceedings (defined as 'judicial or other' proceedings)[27] must be recognized in England and Wales if:[28] **4.27**

(a) it is effective under the law of the country in which it was obtained; and

(b) at the date on which the foreign proceedings were commenced (or the date of death of one of the civil partners if annulment was obtained after death)[29] either civil partner:

(i) was habitually resident in that country; or

(ii) was domiciled in that country; or

(iii) was a national of that country.

The court may only refuse to recognize an overseas separation, dissolution or annulment obtained by means of proceedings in the following circumstances: **4.28**

---

[26] See paras 4.07–4.12 above.

[27] CPA 2004, s 237(5). Unless registered with a Sharia Court, a Talaq is not obtained by means of 'judicial or other' proceedings: *El Fadl v El Fadl* [2000] 1 FLR 175.

[28] ibid, s 235(1).

[29] ibid, s 235(3)(a) & (4).

(a) when it was obtained, it was irreconcilable with a previous decision of a UK court as to the subsistence or validity of the civil partnership or with a decision previously given by another court whose decision is recognized in the UK;[30] or

(b) when it was obtained, the UK did not recognize the relationship as a subsisting civil partnership;[31] or

(c) no notice was given to one of the civil partners and reasonable steps should, in all the circumstances, have been taken to give notice;[32] or

(d) one of the civil partners had no opportunity to take part in the proceedings and a reasonable opportunity to do so should, in all the circumstances, have been given;[33] or

(e) recognition would be manifestly contrary to public policy.[34]

2. Recognition of Overseas Separation etc Obtained Otherwise than by Means of Proceedings

4.29 The circumstances in which the court must recognize an overseas separation, dissolution or annulment obtained otherwise than by means of proceedings are more limited than the circumstances in which the court must do so where there have been proceedings.

4.30 An overseas separation of civil partners or dissolution or nullity of a civil partnership obtained otherwise than by means of proceedings must be recognized if:[35]

(a) it is effective under the law of the country in which it was obtained; and

(b) at the date on which the foreign separation, dissolution or annulment occurred (or the date of death of one of the civil partners if annulment was obtained after death):[36]

    (i) both of the civil partners were domiciled in that country; or

    (ii) either of the civil partners was domiciled in that country and the other was domiciled in a country which itself recognized the validity of the separation, dissolution or annulment; and

(c) neither civil partner was habitually resident in the UK for a one year period prior to the date on which the foreign separation, dissolution or annulment occurred (or the date of death of one of the civil partners if annulment was obtained after death).

---

[30] ibid, s 236(1).
[31] ibid, s 236(2).
[32] ibid, s 236(3)(a)(i).
[33] ibid, s 236(3)(a)(ii).
[34] ibid, s 236(3)(c).
[35] ibid, s 235(2).
[36] ibid, s 235(3)(b) & (4).

The court may only refuse to recognize an overseas separation, dissolution or **4.31**
annulment obtained otherwise than by means of proceedings in the following
circumstances:

(a) when it was obtained, it was irreconcilable with a previous decision of a
    UK court as to the subsistence or validity of the civil partnership or with
    a decision previously given by another court whose decision is recognized in
    the UK;[37] or

(b) when it was obtained, the UK did not recognize the relationship as a
    subsisting civil partnership;[38] or

(c) there is no official document certifying that it is effective under the law of the
    country in which it was obtained; or[39]

(d) if a civil partner was domiciled in another country when it was obtained,
    there is no official document certifying that it is effective under the law of
    that other country;[40] or

(e) recognition would be manifestly contrary to public policy.[41]

3. Modifications to the Recognition Criteria

The recognition criteria set out above may be varied by regulations made by the **4.32**
Lord Chancellor under s 237 of the 2004 Act. In particular, such regulations
may:

(a) modify ss 235, 236 and 237(1) (definition of 'domicile') in relation to
    countries which have different systems of law from the UK;

(b) modify ss 235 and 236 in cases where a civil partner is domiciled in a
    country which does not recognize legal relationships between same sex
    couples.

4. Recognition of Separation, Dissolution and Nullity Orders Obtained in a Different Part of the UK

Section 233 of the 2004 Act mirrors ss 44 and 51 of the Family Law Act 1986 **4.33**
and provides that a separation, dissolution or annulment of a civil partnership
obtained in one part of the UK is to be recognized in all parts of the UK unless:

(a) it was obtained at a time when it was irreconcilable with a previous decision
    as to its subsistence or validity made by a court in any other part of the UK

---

[37] ibid, s 236(1).
[38] ibid, s 236(2).
[39] ibid, s 236(3)(b)(i).
[40] ibid, s 236(3)(b)(ii).
[41] ibid, s 236(3)(c).

or made by a court whose decision is recognized in another part of the UK;[42] or

(b) it was obtained at a time when the part of the UK in which recognition is sought did not recognize a subsisting civil partnership.[43]

---

[42] ibid, s 233(3).
[43] ibid, s 233(4).

5

FINANCIAL RELIEF IN THE HIGH COURT AND COUNTY COURT

Prior to the 2004 Act, same sex partners had no financial rights or obligations **5.01** in relation to each other arising from the relationship itself. Their financial claims against each other were limited to:

(a) claims based upon strict proprietary rights arising, for example, by way of express, resulting or constructive trust;

(b) claims pursuant to the Children Act 1989, Sch 1 for the benefit of a child if the respondent partner was the parent (whether natural or by adoption) of the child and the applicant partner was also a parent (whether natural or by adoption) or had a residence order in relation to the child;

(c) claims pursuant to the Child Support Act 1991 for the benefit of a child if the respondent was the parent (whether natural or by adoption) of the child and the other partner had the day to day care of the child.

Schedule 5 to the 2004 Act introduces radical changes for same sex partners **5.02** who choose to register as civil partners. Schedule 5 mirrors the provisions for spouses contained in the Matrimonial Causes Act 1973 ('the MCA 1973') and grants civil partners a full range of financial claims (for both maintenance and capital) against each other for their own benefit and for the benefit of any 'child of the family' (ie a child of both of the civil partners or any child who has been treated by both civil partners as a child of the family).[1]

5.03   The categories of financial relief which are available are:

(a) financial provision orders;

(b) property adjustment orders;

(c) sale of property orders;

(d) pension sharing orders;

(e) financial provision orders in the event of a failure to maintain.

A. BAR ON APPLICATIONS FOR FINANCIAL RELIEF

5.04   A civil partner who wishes to make a claim for financial relief must, however, beware of an important bar which prohibits such relief from being granted by the court. A civil partner who enters into a subsequent civil partnership or marriage is not entitled to issue an application for:[2]

(a) a financial provision order in his/her favour;

(b) a property adjustment order in his/her favour.[3]

Such application may still be made in favour of a child of the family notwithstanding the subsequent civil partnership or marriage.[4]

5.05   An application for a financial provision order or a property adjustment order in favour of a civil partner must therefore be issued *prior* to that partner entering into a subsequent civil partnership or marriage.

5.06   The 2004 Act also amends the MCA 1973, s 28 so as to bar the issue of an application for ancillary relief by a former spouse who has entered into a subsequent civil partnership and to provide for automatic termination of periodical and secured periodical payments if a payee former spouse enters into a subsequent civil partnership.[5]

---

[1] CPA 2004, Sch 5, para 80(2).

[2] ibid, Sch 5, para 48.

[3] para 48 does not expressly bar applications for pension sharing orders; it seems that the draughtsman either considered such an order to be a property adjustment order or that there was an oversight.

[4] The wording of Sch 5, para 48(b) appears to bar applications for a property adjustment order in favour of a child of the family, but the mirror provision in MCA 1973, s 28(3) is widely interpreted to permit such an application.

[5] MCA 1973, s 28 as amended by CPA 2004, Sch 27, para 43.

B. FINANCIAL PROVISION ORDERS

Part 1 of Sch 5 to the 2004 Act mirrors the MCA 1973, s 23 and enables the **5.07** court to make a 'financial provision order' in favour of a civil partner or a child of the family.

A 'financial provision order' is an order:[6] **5.08**

(a) for periodical payments to either civil partner;

(b) for secured periodical payments to either civil partner;

(c) for payment of a lump sum or sums to either civil partner;

(d) for periodical payments to be paid direct to a child of the family or to be paid to such person as may be specified in the order for the benefit of such child;

(e) for secured periodical payments to be paid direct to a child of the family or to be paid to such person as may be specified in the order for the benefit of such child;

(f) for payment of a lump sum to be paid direct to a child of the family or to be paid to such person as may be specified in the order for the benefit of such child.

1. When Applications/Orders for Financial Provision may be Made

The court may only make a 'financial provision order' for the benefit of a civil **5.09** partner if a separation order or a conditional dissolution or conditional nullity order has already been made;[7] although the *application* for a financial provision order may be made immediately after proceedings for separation, dissolution or nullity have been issued.[8]

In the case of dissolution and nullity proceedings, the financial provision **5.10** order is not effective (ie cannot be enforced) until a final dissolution or final nullity order has been made.[9]

In contrast, a lump sum, periodical or secured periodical payments order (but **5.11** not a property adjustment order) for the benefit of a child of the family may be made prior to a separation order, conditional dissolution or conditional nullity being made. A property adjustment order for the benefit of a child of the family cannot be made, however, until a separation order, conditional dissolution order or conditional nullity order has been made[10] and, in the case of dissolution or

---

[6] CPA 2004, Sch 5, para 2.

[7] ibid, Sch 5, para 1(1).

[8] ibid, Sch 5, para 46(2).

[9] ibid, Sch 5, para 4(1).

[10] ibid, Sch 5, para 6.

nullity proceedings, is not effective until a final dissolution or nullity order has been made.

5.12   Schedule 5 to the 2004 Act places a number of restrictions (referable to age and educational status) on the court's ability to make financial provision orders in favour of children of the family:

(a) the court may not make a lump sum order in favour of a child of the family who has reached the age of 18 unless:[11]

  (i) the child is or will be attending an educational establishment or undergoing training for a trade, profession or vocation; or
  (ii) there are 'special circumstances' (eg the child is disabled).[12]

(b) a periodical or secured periodical payments order in favour of a child of the family must expire on the child's 17th birthday unless the child's welfare justifies an extension to a later date.[13] Even if the child's welfare justifies such an extension, the order must expire on the child's 18th birthday unless:[14]

  (i) the child is or will be attending an educational establishment or under-going training for a trade, profession or vocation; or
  (ii) there are 'special circumstances' (eg the child is disabled).

5.13   In proceedings between spouses, the usual form of periodical payments order in favour of a child of the family is: 'until the child attains the age of 17 years or ceases full time secondary education, whichever is the later, or until further order'. Where a child is in or is approaching tertiary education, the order is usually expressed to terminate upon the cessation of tertiary rather than secondary education.

2. Periodical Payments/Secured Periodical Payments Orders

5.14   An order for secured periodical payments requires the payer to provide security to ensure that the periodical payments are actually paid. The security may either be an asset which generates an income from which the periodical payments are discharged or it may be an asset which does not generate an income, in which case the asset would only be sold, on the payee's application, in the event of the payer's default in paying the periodical payments. The payer may not dispose of, charge or otherwise deal with the security during the continuance of the secured periodical payments order.

5.15   An order for secured periodical payments will ordinarily be made where:

(a) the payer is domiciled abroad and the payee therefore has no claim under the

---

[11] ibid, Sch 5, para 49(1)(a) & (5).
[12] *C v F (Disabled Child: Maintenance order)* [1998] 2 FLR 1, CA.
[13] CPA 2004, Sch 5, para 49(3)(a).
[14] ibid, Sch 5, para 49(3)(b) & (5).

Inheritance (Provision for Family and Dependants) Act 1975 in the event of the payer's death;[15] or

(b) there is a real risk of non-payment by the payer.

An order for periodical payments or secured periodical payments may take **5.16** effect from any date beginning with the date on which the application for the periodical or secured periodical payments order was made.[16]

A key difference between periodical payments orders and secured periodical **5.17** payments orders is that whereas a periodical payments order terminates automatically upon the death of either civil partner (or the death of a payee child of the family), an order for secured periodical payments endures beyond the payer's (but not payee's) death.[17]

Periodical payments orders and secured periodical payments orders both ter- **5.18** minate automatically upon the payee civil partner entering into a subsequent civil partnership or marriage.[18] The fact that a payee subsequently cohabits with a third party does not lead to an automatic termination of the order for periodical payments, but may justify an application for a variation of the order by the payer.[19]

Subject to these automatic statutory terminations, the court may order peri- **5.19** odical or secured periodical payments to be paid for such term as it thinks fit. A term order may either be:

(a) an extendable term order: the payee may apply[20] for an extension of the term provided the application is made *before* the expiry of the term.[21] An extension will, however, require exceptional justification;[22]

(b) a non-extendable term order: the court may make a direction under Sch 5, para 47(5) of the 2004 Act (equivalent to a direction under the MCA 1973, s 28(1A)) that the payee is not entitled to apply to extend the term specified in the order. In the absence, however, of such an express direction, the term order is deemed to be extendable.[23]

The court's powers to make periodical and secured periodical payments **5.20** orders in favour of a child of the family pursuant to Sch 5 to the 2004 Act are subject to the restrictions contained in the Child Support Act 1991, s 8[24] if the payer civil partner is the child's parent (whether natural or by adoption) and the

---

[15] *A v A (A Minor: Financial Provision)* [1994] 1 FLR 657.
[16] CPA 2004, Sch 5, paras 47(1) & 49(2).
[17] ibid, Sch 5, paras 47(2)(a), (3)(a) & 49(6).
[18] ibid, Sch 5, para 47(2)(b) & (3)(b).
[19] *Atkinson v Atkinson (No 2)* [1996] 1 FLR 51, CA; *Fleming v Fleming* [2003] EWCA Civ 1841, [2004] 1 FLR 667, CA.
[20] Under CPA 2004, Sch 5, Pt 11.
[21] *Jones v Jones* [2000] 2 FLR 307, CA.
[22] *Fleming v Fleming* [2003] EWCA Civ 1841, [2004] 1 FLR 667, CA.
[23] *Richardson v Richardson* [1994] 1 FLR 286.
[24] As amended by CPA 2004, Sch 24, para 1.

other civil partner is a 'person with care'[25] of the child. In these circumstances, the court may not make a periodical or secured periodical payments order in favour of a child of the family unless:[26]

(a) there is a written agreement between the civil partners for payment of periodical or secured periodical payments for the benefit of the child;[27]

(b) it is a 'top-up' case because the payer civil partner's net income exceeds £2,000 pw;[28]

(c) the order is for the purposes of meeting the expenses of the child's education or training;[29]

(d) the order is for the benefit of a disabled child;[30]

(e) the order is made against the person with care of the child.[31]

5.21 If the court has the power to make a periodical or secured periodical payments order in favour of a child of the family under any of the above exceptions and a child maintenance calculation is already in force in relation to that child, the order may be back-dated to the later of:

(a) six months prior to the application for periodical or secured periodical payments; or

(b) the date on which the maintenance calculation took effect.[32]

5.22 If the court makes a substantive periodical or secured periodical payments order in favour of the civil partner with care, the court may, however, include an element of child maintenance within that order on the basis that the order will be reduced automatically by the quantum of any subsequent child support calculation.[33]

3. Lump Sum Orders

5.23 Although Sch 5, para 2(1)(c) of the 2004 Act refers to payment of 'lump sum or sums', the court only has jurisdiction to make a lump sum order on one occasion; although that single order may require a number of 'sums' to be paid.[34] The court does, however, have the power to adjourn a civil partner's

---

[25] See Child Support Act 1991, s 3(3) for 'person with care'.
[26] ibid, s 8(3).
[27] ibid, s 8(5)(a); Child Maintenance (Written Agreements) Order 1993, SI 1993/620.
[28] ibid, s 8(6).
[29] ibid, s 8(7).
[30] ibid, s 8(8).
[31] ibid, s 8(10).
[32] CPA 2004, Sch 5, para 49(7) & (8). See also para 49(9) for cases where a maintenance calculation has ceased to have effect.
[33] *Dorney-Kingdom v Dorney-Kingdom* [2000] 2 FLR 855, CA.
[34] *de Lasala v de Lasala* [1980] AC 546, HL.

claim for a lump sum order if there is a real possibility of the other civil partner receiving capital from a specific source in the near future.[35]

In contrast to this restriction on lump sum payments to civil partners, the court may make lump sum orders on multiple occasions for the benefit of a child of the family.[36]   **5.24**

The court may order payment of a lump sum to be deferred or to be paid in instalments and may require security for the payment of the instalments (but may not otherwise order security for a lump sum payment).[37]   **5.25**

The court may also order interest to be paid on the deferred lump sum or on the instalments from the date of the order until payment is due at such rate as may be specified in the order.[38] Default in payment of a lump sum or instalment after the due date will attract interest at the prevailing judgment debt rate.[39]   **5.26**

The court has no jurisdiction under Sch 5 to the 2004 Act to make an interim lump sum order pending the resolution of the financial claims between the civil partners.[40]   **5.27**

C. PROPERTY ADJUSTMENT ORDERS

Part 2 of Sch 5 to the 2004 Act mirrors the MCA 1973, s 24 and enables the court to make a property adjustment order in favour of a civil partner or a child of the family.   **5.28**

There are four categories of property adjustment order:[41]   **5.29**

(a) an order for the transfer of property to a civil partner, a child of the family or to any person for the benefit of such a child;

(b) an order for the settlement of property for the benefit of a civil partner and/ or a child of the family;

(c) an order varying, for the benefit of a civil partner and/or a child of the family, any settlement made on the civil partners during the civil partnership or in anticipation of it;

(d) an order extinguishing or reducing the interest of either civil partner under a settlement made on the partners during the civil partnership or in anticipation of it.

The term 'property' is not defined either in the 2004 Act or in the mirror   **5.30**

---

[35] *M-T v M-T (Financial Provision: Lump sum)* [1992] 1 FLR 362.

[36] CPA 2004, Sch 5, para 1(3) & (4).

[37] ibid, Sch 5, para 3(3).

[38] ibid, Sch 5, para 3(5) & (6).

[39] In the High Court: Judgments Act 1838. In the county court, for amounts > £5,000: County Courts (Interest on Judgement Debts) Order 1991, SI 1991/1184.

[40] *Wicks v Wicks* [1998] 1 FLR 470.

[41] CPA 2004, Sch 5, para 7.

provisions contained in the MCA 1973, s 24. As between spouses, property adjustment orders are routinely made in relation to real property, contractual (but not statutory) tenancies,[42] shares, investments, bank accounts, vehicles and other personal property. A property adjustment order may be made against foreign property, although the court will not make such an order if it is unlikely to be enforced abroad.

5.31 A property adjustment order made under one of the four categories of order does not, in theory, prevent a subsequent application for a property adjustment order under a different category (ie in theory a transfer of property order would not prevent a subsequent settlement of property order). In practice, however, a financial order between civil partners will dismiss all future applications for property adjustment orders.[43]

5.32 Unlike financial provision orders where multiple orders may be made in favour of children of the family, multiple property adjustment orders may not be made in favour of children of the family since Pt 2 of Sch 5 to the 2004 Act contains no provision enabling such orders to be made 'from time to time' in favour of children.

5.33 A property adjustment order which amounts to a transfer of property order may not be made to or for the benefit of a child who has attained the age of 18 unless:[44]

(a) the child is or will be attending an educational establishment or undergoing training for a trade, profession or vocation; or

(b) there are 'special circumstances' (eg the child is disabled).[45]

5.34 In contrast, the court has the jurisdiction to make settlement of property and variation of settlement orders for the benefit of children of the family who have reached the age of 18 years, regardless of their educational status or special circumstances. In practice, however, such orders will not be made in favour of children who have attained independence.[46]

5.35 The court has no jurisdiction under Sch 5 to the 2004 Act to make an interim property adjustment order pending the resolution of the financial claims between the civil partners.[47]

---

[42] *Newlon Housing Trust v Alsulaimen* [1999] 1 AC 313, HL. See also Chapter 9 for transfer of tenancies.

[43] *Dinch v Dinch* [1987] 1 WLR 252, HL.

[44] CPA 2004, Sch 5, para 49(1)(b) & (5).

[45] *C v F (Disabled Child: Maintenance order)* [1998] 2 FLR 1, CA.

[46] *A v A (A Minor: Financial Provision)* [1994] 1 FLR 657.

[47] *Wicks v Wicks* [1998] 1 FLR 470.

D. SALE OF PROPERTY ORDERS

Part 3 of Sch 5 to the 2004 Act mirrors s 24A of the MCA 1973 and enables **5.36** the court to make a sale of property order upon making a secured periodical payments order, a lump sum order or a property adjustment order (whether those orders are made in favour of a civil partner or for the benefit of a child of the family).

A sale of property order may either be made in the original order for financial **5.37** relief or it may be made at a later date if, for example, a civil partner fails to pay a lump sum under the original order.[48] A sale of property order is a procedural provision which enables the court to implement or enforce an order for financial relief.[49]

A sale of property order may not be used so as to vary the effect of a property **5.38** adjustment order (eg by bringing forward the date of sale of a property unless that is consistent with the aim of the property adjustment order).[50]

The sale of property order must relate to a property in which (or in the **5.39** proceeds of sale of which) either or both of the civil partners has a beneficial interest in possession or in reversion.[51]

The court has the power to make consequential directions relating to the **5.40** mechanics of the sale of the property (eg that the sale should be to a named individual) and as to the application of the proceeds of sale.[52] It does not, however, have the power, under Pt 3 of Sch 5, to order a civil partner who retains a beneficial interest in the property to give vacant possession.[53]

Third parties who have a beneficial interest in the property or in its proceeds **5.41** of sale have the right to be heard on an application for a sale of the property.[54]

A sale of property order may be a conditional order which only takes effect **5.42** upon the occurrence of a specific event (eg upon a child of the family attaining a certain age).

In financial proceedings between spouses, the court has devised a species of **5.43** order, known as a 'Mesher' or 'Martin' order, which is a combination of a sale of property order, property adjustment order and lump sum order. 'Mesher' and 'Martin' orders may also be made in financial proceedings between civil partners.

A 'Mesher'[55] order is an order by which the trust on which the civil partners **5.44**

---

[48] CPA 2004, Sch 5, para 10(1).
[49] *Omielan v Omielan* [1996] 2 FLR 306, CA.
[50] *Thompson v Thompson* [1985] FLR 863, CA.
[51] CPA 2004, Sch 5, para 11(1).
[52] ibid, Sch 5, para 11(2) & (3).
[53] *Crosthwaite v Crosthwaite* [1989] 2 FLR 86, CA. Such a direction could instead be given under RSC Ord 31, r 1.
[54] CPA 2004, Sch 5, para 14.
[55] *Mesher v Mesher and Hall* [1980] 1 All ER 126, CA.

hold the civil partnership home (or another property) is varied to provide that only one of the civil partners should henceforth be entitled to occupy the property and that the property should not be sold until the children of the family have all attained the age of 18 years (or ceased secondary or tertiary education), whereupon the net proceeds of sale of the property should be divided in specified proportions between the civil partners. As an alternative to the property remaining in the joint names of the civil partners, the court may order the property to be transferred to the occupying civil partner with a charge (which is not to be redeemed until the children of the family have attained the age of 18 years) being registered against the property in favour of the other civil partner.

5.45   A 'Martin'[56] order is similar to a 'Mesher' order save that the order provides for the sale of the property to be postponed or redemption of the charge to be deferred until the occupying civil partner's death, remarriage or cohabitation. In practice, the courts make orders which are a combination of a 'Mesher' and a 'Martin' order.

5.46   A 'Mesher' order is of particular use in those cases where it is in the interests of the children of the family that they remain in the civil partnership home and where the other assets are sufficient to enable the other civil partner to be rehoused.[57] The court may decline to impose a 'Mesher' order and instead order an outright transfer if the occupying civil partner would be unable to rehouse on his/her share of the net proceeds of sale once the children of the family have attained the age of 18.[58]

5.47   A sale of property order is only effective (ie can only be enforced) if a separation order or a final conditional or final nullity order has been made.[59]

5.48   A sale of property order will cease to have effect if the purpose of the sale is to provide a sum to secure periodical payments and the payee civil partner dies or enters into a subsequent civil partnership or marriage.[60]

5.49   Since the primary purpose of a sale of property order is to ensure the enforcement of a lump sum, secured periodical payments or property adjustment order, a sale of property order may be made in favour of a child of the family regardless of the child's age or educational status.

E. PENSION SHARING AND PENSION ATTACHMENT ORDERS

5.50   Part 4 of Sch 5 to the 2004 Act mirrors the MCA 1973, ss 21A and 24B-D and enables the court to make pension sharing orders between civil partners.

5.51   A pension sharing order is an order which transfers a percentage (which may

---

[56] *Martin v Martin* [1978] Fam 12, CA.
[57] *Clutton v Clutton* [1991] 1 All ER 340, CA.
[58] *B v B (Mesher Order)* [2002] EWHC 3106 (Fam), [2003] 2 FLR 285.
[59] CPA 2004, Sch 5, para 12(1).
[60] ibid, Sch 5, para 13.

be up to 100 per cent) of a civil partner's 'shareable rights' under a pension to the other civil partner.[61] The pension sharing order thereby creates a new pension in the transferee civil partner's own right and reduces the value of the original pension by a corresponding amount. The transferee may, depending upon the rules of the scheme, take an internal transfer and become a member of the scheme in his/her own right or take an external transfer.

Part 6 of Sch 5 to the 2004 Act mirrors the MCA 1973, ss 25B-D and enables **5.52** the court to make pension attachment orders between civil partners which provide for the payment to a civil partner of all or part of the other civil partner's pension lump sum or periodic pension when that sum or pension is payable under the terms of the pension scheme. A pension attachment order may also provide for payment to a civil partner of all or part of any lump sum payable under the pension scheme in the event of the member civil partner's death. A pension attachment order is a species of lump sum or periodical payments order.

Pension sharing orders and pension attachment orders differ in the following **5.53** respects:

(a) a pension sharing order may only be made in proceedings for dissolution or nullity, whereas a pension attachment order may be made in proceedings for dissolution, nullity or separation;[62]

(b) a pension sharing order creates a fresh pension for the transferee civil partner, whereas a pension attachment order does not create a fresh pension but is merely a method of implementing a lump sum or periodical payments order;[63]

(c) a pension sharing order is unaffected by the subsequent death of the transferor spouse, whereas:

  (i) a pension attachment order in relation to a pension lump sum, if it has not already been implemented, ceases to have effect upon the death of the member civil partner against whom the order is made (since the member civil partner himself will never receive the pension lump sum which has been attached). The obligation to pay the lump sum endures, but there may be no asset against which it can be enforced. The court may also order that the pension attachment order should cease to have effect in the event of the death, prior to implementation of the order, of the civil partner in whose favour the order has been made;

  (ii) a pension attachment order in relation to a periodic pension ceases to have effect upon the death of either civil partner.

(d) a pension sharing order is unaffected by the subsequent civil partnership or marriage of the transferee civil partner, whereas a pension attachment order

---

[61] The order transfers a percentage of the 'Cash Equivalent Transfer Value' (CETV). See Welfare Reform and Pensions Act 1999, ss 28, 29 as amended by CPA 2004, Sch 27, para 159.

[62] CPA 2004, Sch 5, para 15.

[63] *T v T (Financial Relief: Pensions)* [1998] 1 FLR 1072.

in relation to the periodic pension ceases to have effect upon the subsequent civil partnership or marriage of the civil partner in whose favour the order is made;

(e) a pension sharing order may only be varied *prior* to a final dissolution order or final nullity order being made, whereas a pension attachment order:

    (i) in relation to a pension lump sum or periodic pension may be varied at any time; and

    (ii) in relation to the lump sum payable upon death may be varied at any time prior to the death of either civil partner.[64]

5.54 A plethora of regulations have been made in relation to pension sharing and pension attachment orders between spouses. Some of these regulations will apply to orders between civil partners (eg Pension Sharing (Valuation) Regulations 2000);[65] whereas others will be wholly inapplicable (eg Divorce etc (Pensions) Regulations 2000).[66] A detailed consideration of these regulations is beyond the scope of this Guide. The 2004 Act enables further regulations to be made.

1. Pension Sharing Orders

5.55 The court may make a pension sharing order in favour of a civil partner in respect of virtually any pension except:[67]

(a) the basic state pension (orders may only be made in relation to SERPS or S2P);

(b) a widow's, widower's or dependant's pension;[68]

(c) a pension (including SERPS or S2P) in relation to which a pension sharing order has already been made between the civil partners[69] (a pension sharing order made in a previous civil partnership or marriage does not preclude a subsequent pension sharing order between different civil partners in relation to the same pension);

(d) a pension which is the subject of a pension attachment order (which has not yet been implemented), whether made in relation to the current civil partnership or a previous civil partnership.[70] (The 2004 Act does not preclude a pension sharing order in relation to a pension which has already been the

---

[64] See paras 5.101–5.115 below for variation applications.

[65] SI 2000/1052.

[66] SI 2000/1123.

[67] CPA 2004, Sch 5, para 16. Welfare Reform and Pensions Act 1999, Pt 4, chs 1, 2. The definition of 'pension arrangement' appears to cover foreign occupational and personal pensions.

[68] Pension Sharing (Valuation) Regulations 2000, r 2.

[69] CPA 2004, Sch 5, para 18(1) & (2).

[70] ibid, Sch 5, para 18(3).

subject of a pension attachment order in a previous marriage—this appears to be an oversight);[71]

(e) a pension in relation to which the Pension Protection Fund Board has assumed responsibility.

A pension sharing order may not be made in favour of a child of the family. **5.56**
A pension sharing order does not take effect until:[72] **5.57**

(a) a final dissolution or final nullity order has been made; and

(b) such period as may be prescribed by regulations has expired. (It is expected that, as with the regulations in relation to spouses, such regulations will provide that the order is not to take effect until the time for appealing against the order has expired.)

The pension provider must implement the pension sharing order within four **5.58** months beginning with the later of:[73]

(a) the date on which the pension sharing order takes effect;

(b) the receipt by the pension provider of:
   (i) a copy of the final dissolution or final nullity order; and
   (ii) such information as may be prescribed by regulations (eg full details about the transferor and transferee as required by the Pensions on Divorce etc (Provision of Information) Regulations 2000, r 5).[74]

The pension provider will levy an administrative charge for implementing the **5.59** pension sharing order. The court may direct how those charges should be apportioned between the civil partners.[75] In the absence of such a direction, the transferor civil partner will be liable to pay the administrative charges.[76]

2. Pension Attachment Orders

The court may make a pension attachment order in favour of a civil partner in **5.60** respect of virtually any pension held by the other civil partner except:[77]

(a) the basic state pension *or* SERPS or S2P;[78]

---

[71] Sch 5, para 18(3) only refers to pension attachment orders under Pt 6 of the CPA 2004 and not to orders under the MCA 1973.
[72] CPA 2004, Sch 5, para 19(1) & (2).
[73] Welfare Reform and Pensions Act 1999, s 34 as amended by CPA 2004, Sch 27, para 160.
[74] SI 2000/1048.
[75] CPA 2004, Sch 5, para 17.
[76] Welfare Reform and Pensions Act 1999, s 41(3)(b).
[77] A pension attachment order may be made in relation to a 'pension' arrangement: CPA 2004, Sch 5, paras 29 & 16(4). The definition of 'pension arrangement' appears to cover foreign occupational and personal pensions.
[78] Contrast pension sharing orders which may be made against SERPS and S2P.

    (b) a pension in relation to which a pension sharing order has already been made between the civil partners.[79]

    (c) a pension in relation to which the Pension Protection Fund Board has assumed responsibility.

5.61 A pension attachment order, unlike a pension sharing order, may be made against a civil partner who is in receipt of a widow's, widower's or dependant's pension.

5.62 A pension attachment order may not be made in favour of a child of the family.

5.63 The court may attach up to 100 per cent of each of the following in favour of a civil partner:

    (a) a pension lump sum;

    (b) a periodic pension payment;

    (c) a lump sum payable under the terms of the pension in the event of the death of the civil partner who is a member of the scheme.

The court does not, however, have the power to make a pension attachment order in relation to a widow's, widower's or dependant's pension which is payable in the event of the death of the member civil partner.

5.64 The wording of a pension attachment order must be in the form prescribed by the 2004 Act:[80]

    (a) the court must make a financial provision order (ie a periodical payments, secured periodical payments or lump sum order) in favour of the civil partner;

    (b) the court must direct the pension trustees or managers to make a payment to that civil partner (if, at any time, payment of pension benefits becomes due under the pension scheme to the civil partner who is a scheme member) in satisfaction of the member civil partner's liability under the financial provision order;

    (c) the financial provision order must express the amount of the payment to be made by the pension trustees or managers as a percentage of the pension benefit which becomes due to the member civil partner.

5.65 In relation to a lump sum payable in the event of a member civil partner's death, the court may:[81]

    (a) if the pension trustees or managers have a discretion to determine to whom the sum should be paid, direct the trustees or managers to pay (up to 100 per cent of) the sum to the other civil partner;

---

[79] CPA 2004, Sch 5, para 25(8).
[80] ibid, Sch 5, para 25(2) & (3).
[81] ibid, Sch 5, para 26(3) & (4).

(b) if the member civil partner has the right to nominate the individual to whom the sum should be paid, direct the member civil partner to nominate the other civil partner to receive (up to 100 per cent of) the lump sum.

The court also has the power to order the member spouse to exercise any right he/she may have to commute part of the pension in order to receive a lump sum.[82] The court is not, however, entitled to direct the member to retire or to take pension benefits under a pension scheme on a particular date.[83] **5.66**

Part 7 of Sch 5 to the 2004 Act makes provision for property attachment orders in relation to pensions for which the Pension Protection Fund Board has assumed responsibility pursuant to the Pensions Act 2004. **5.67**

F. MAINTENANCE PENDING OUTCOME ORDERS

Part 8 of Sch 5 to the 2004 Act mirrors the MCA 1973, s 22 (maintenance pending suit) and enables the court to make a maintenance order in favour of a civil partner in proceedings for separation, dissolution or nullity prior to any separation or conditional dissolution or conditional nullity order being made. **5.68**

The order for maintenance pending outcome may be back-dated to the date on which the proceedings for separation, dissolution or nullity were commenced (even if the application for a maintenance pending outcome order was made at a later date). The maintenance pending outcome order ceases to have effect upon a separation order or a final dissolution or final nullity order being made. **5.69**

There are no detailed criteria in the 2004 Act which govern the exercise of the court's discretion to make a maintenance pending outcome order. The court is entitled to make such order as it 'thinks reasonable'. **5.70**

In financial proceedings between spouses, the court has interpreted the term 'maintenance' in the identical provisions of the MCA 1973, s 22 to extend to orders requiring one party to make a periodic contribution to the other party's ongoing legal costs of the financial proceedings.[84] **5.71**

G. MATTERS TO WHICH THE COURT MUST HAVE REGARD

Part 5 of Sch 5 to the 2004 Act mirrors the MCA 1973, ss 25 and 25A and lists the matters to which the court must have regard in exercising its discretion to make orders for financial relief (ie lump sum, periodical payments, secured periodical payments, property adjustment and pension sharing orders). **5.72**

Since the factors to which the court must have regard in claims between civil **5.73**

---

[82] ibid, Sch 5, para 25(5).
[83] *T v T (Financial Relief: Pensions)* [1998] 1 FLR 1072.
[84] *A v A (Maintenance Pending Suit) (No 2)* [2001] 1 FLR 377.

partners are identical to those to which it must have regard in claims between spouses, the wealth of case law which has developed in relation to financial claims under the MCA 1973 will be of equal applicability to civil partners.

5.74 The 2004 Act distinguishes between the matters which must be taken into account in making orders in favour of civil partners and those which must be taken into account in making orders in favour of children of the family.

1. First Consideration: Welfare of the Children of the Family

5.75 Whenever the court makes an order for financial relief, whether in favour of a civil partner or a child of the family, its first consideration must be the welfare, whilst a minor, of any child of the family who has not attained the age of 18 years.[85]

5.76 In giving their welfare first consideration, the court will ordinarily seek to ensure that the housing needs of any children of the family are adequately met during their minority.[86]

5.77 Their welfare should not, however, be elevated to a paramount or overriding consideration.[87]

2. Orders in Favour of Civil Partners: Relevant Matters

5.78 In exercising its discretion to make an order for financial relief in favour of a civil partner, the court must have regard to all the circumstances of the case and must have particular regard to:[88]

(a) The income, earning capacity, property and other financial resources which each civil partner has or is likely to have in the foreseeable future, including any increase in earning capacity which it would be reasonable to expect a civil partner to take steps to acquire.

- The court must have regard to any pension benefits, including pension protection fund compensation, which either civil partner has or is likely to have, whether they will be received in the foreseeable future or not.[89]
- 'Financial resources' has been given a wide interpretation and includes, for example, potential receipts under a discretionary trust,[90] financial support from the wider family,[91] an ability to borrow[92] and an award of damages.[93]

---

[85] CPA 2004, Sch 5, para 20.
[86] *M v B (Ancillary Proceedings: Lump Sum)* [1998] 1 FLR 53, CA.
[87] *Suter v Suter* [1987] 3 WLR 9, CA.
[88] CPA 2004, Sch 5, para 21(2).
[89] ibid, Sch 5, paras 24(1) & 30(1).
[90] *J v J (C Intervening)* [1989] 1 FLR 453, CA.
[91] *Thomas v Thomas* [1995] 2 FLR 668, CA.
[92] *Newton v Newton* [1990] 1 FLR 33, CA.
[93] *Wagstaff v Wagstaff* [1992] 1 FLR 333, CA.

- 'Foreseeable future' has been interpreted to mean a period of up to ten or more years.[94]

(b) The financial needs, obligations and responsibilities which each civil partner has or is likely to have in the foreseeable future.

(c) The standard of living enjoyed by the civil partners prior to the breakdown of the civil partnership.

(d) The age of each civil partner and the duration of the civil partnership.

- By analogy with cases involving spouses, the court is entitled to have regard to the duration of the relationship *prior* to the registration of the civil partnership if that relationship demonstrated a degree of commitment akin to civil partnership.[95]

(e) Any physical or mental disability of either civil partner.

(f) The contributions which either civil partner has made or is likely to make in the foreseeable future to the welfare of the family, including any contribution by looking after the home or caring for the family.

(g) The conduct of either civil partner if it would be inequitable to disregard such conduct.

- It is necessary to distinguish between litigation conduct (eg non-disclosure of assets in the proceedings) which sounds in costs[96] and other conduct which affects the quantum of the award. The type of conduct which has affected awards between spouses is usually extreme, eg violence and sexual assault on a spouse[97] and deception by a transsexual about her gender.[98]
- If a civil partner has freely, with competent legal advice, entered into an agreement compromising his/her claims for financial relief, an attempt to resile from the agreement will be conduct to which the court must have regard.[99]

(h) In the case of proceedings for dissolution or nullity, the value of any benefit which either civil partner will lose the chance of acquiring as a result of the dissolution or nullity.

- The court must have regard to any pension benefits, including pension protection fund compensation, which will be lost.[100]

---

[94] See *MT v MT (Financial Provision: Lump Sum)* [1992] 1 FLR 362 for a review of the authorities.

[95] *Kokosinski v Kokosinski* [1980] 1 All ER 1106, CA; *GW v RW (Financial Provision: Departure from Equality)* [2003] 1 FLR 108.

[96] *Young v Young* [1998] 2 FLR 1131, CA.

[97] *H v H (Financial Provision: Conduct)* [1994] 2 FLR 801.

[98] *J v S-T (Formerly J) (Transsexual: Ancillary Relief)* [1997] 1 FLR 402, CA.

[99] *Edgar v Edgar* (1981) 2 FLR 19, CA.

[100] CPA 2004, Sch 5, paras 24(2) & 30(2).

5.79 In *White v White*,[101] the House of Lords emphasized that the contribution of a home-maker was of equal value to the contribution of a bread-winner and that there should be no discrimination between a husband and wife and their respective roles. This led, at least in a long marriage,[102] to a 'yardstick of equality' against which the division of the assets ought to be tested. It is expected that the court will apply *White v White*, and the cases which have followed it, to financial claims between civil partners.

3. Orders in Favour of Children of the Family: Relevant Factors

5.80 In exercising its discretion to make an order for financial relief in favour of a child of the family, the court must have regard to all the circumstances of the case and must have particular regard to:[103]

(a) the financial needs of the child;

(b) the income, earning capacity (if any), property and other financial resources of the child;

(c) any physical or mental disability of the child;

(d) the way in which the child was being, or was expected to be, educated or trained;

(e) the income, earning capacity, property and other financial resources which each civil partner has or is likely to have in the foreseeable future, including any increase in earning capacity which it would be reasonable to expect a civil partner to take steps to acquire;

(f) the financial needs, obligations and responsibilities which each civil partner has or is likely to have in the foreseeable future;

(g) the standard of living enjoyed by the family prior to the breakdown of the civil partnership;

(h) any physical or mental disability of either civil partner.

5.81 If the civil partner against whom the order for financial relief is made is not a parent (whether natural or by adoption) of the child, the court must additionally have regard to the following factors:[104]

(a) whether that civil partner has assumed any responsibility for the child's maintenance;

(b) if so, the extent of any such assumption of responsibility and the duration for which such responsibility was discharged;

---

[101] [2001] 1 AC 596.

[102] See *GW v RW (Financial Provision: Departure from Equality)* [2003] 1 FLR 108 and *Foster v Foster* [2003] EWCA Civ 565, [2003] 2 FLR 299, CA for shorter relationships.

[103] CPA 2004, Sch 5, para 22(2).

[104] ibid, Sch 5, para 22(3).

(c) whether, in assuming and discharging that responsibility, the civil partner knew that the child was not his child (only of relevance if one civil partner has changed gender);

(d) the liability of any other person to maintain the child.

4. Clean Break

Paragraph 23 of Sch 5 mirrors the MCA 1973, s 25A in requiring the court to consider, whenever it makes an order for financial provision, whether a clean break should be imposed between the civil partners. A clean break order is an order which terminates all financial obligations between the civil partners. **5.82**

The duty to consider whether to impose a clean break arises only in dissolution and nullity proceedings; it does not arise in separation proceedings. **5.83**

The court's duty is to consider whether it would be appropriate to exercise its powers to order financial relief in such a way that the financial obligations of each civil partner towards the other will be terminated as soon after the making of the dissolution or nullity order as the court considers just and reasonable.[105] **5.84**

Whenever the court makes an order for periodical or secured periodical payments, the duty to consider a clean break includes a duty to consider whether it would be appropriate to require the payments to be made or secured only for such term as would be sufficient to enable the payee to adjust without undue financial hardship to the termination of the payee's financial dependence on the payer.[106] See para 5.19 above in relation to term orders. **5.85**

H. FAILURE TO MAINTAIN

Where there are no proceedings for separation, dissolution or nullity of the civil partnership, but a civil partner has failed to provide reasonable maintenance for the other civil partner or has failed to provide a proper contribution to the reasonable maintenance of a child of the family, an application may nonetheless be made in the High Court or county court for a financial provision order, ie:[107] **5.86**

(a) for periodical payments to the civil partner;

(b) for secured periodical payments to the civil partner;

(c) for payment of a lump sum or sums to the civil partner;

(d) for periodical payments to be paid direct to a child of the family or to be paid to such person as may be specified in the order for the benefit of such child;

---

[105] ibid, Sch 5, para 23(2).
[106] ibid, Sch 5, para 23(3).
[107] ibid, Sch 5, para 41.

(e) for secured periodical payments to be paid direct to a child of the family or to be paid to such person as may be specified in the order for the benefit of such child;

(f) for payment of a lump sum to be paid direct to a child of the family or to be paid to such person as may be specified in the order for the benefit of such child.

5.87 Part 9 of Sch 5 to the 2004 Act mirrors the 'neglect to maintain' provisions contained in the MCA 1973, s 27. In practice, it is rare for such applications to be made since a neglect to maintain often signals the breakdown of a relationship and triggers proceedings for dissolution or separation.

5.88 In a failure to maintain case, a civil partner has a choice whether to apply to the High Court or county court under Pt 9 of Sch 5 to the 2004 Act or to the magistrates' court under Pt 1 of Sch 6 to the 2004 Act. See paras 6.04–6.21 below for applications to the magistrates' court and paras 6.64–6.65 below for a consideration of the differences between applications to the High Court or county court and to the magistrates' court.

5.89 The court may order a lump sum to cover any liabilities or expenses which have been incurred in maintaining a civil partner or child of the family even if they were incurred prior to the application under Pt 9.[108]

5.90 The court may also order a lump sum to be paid in instalments and for security to be provided for the instalments.[109] The court does not, however, have the power to order security for payment of a single lump sum.

5.91 If a civil partner or child of the family is in immediate need of financial assistance, the court may make such order for interim periodical payments to the civil partner for his/her own benefit or for the benefit of the child (but not direct to the child) as it 'thinks reasonable'.[110] The court does not, however, have jurisdiction to make an order for an interim lump sum.

5.92 The court has no jurisdiction to make a property adjustment, pension sharing or pension attachment order in a failure to maintain case.

1. When an Application or Order may be Made in Failure to Maintain Cases

5.93 An application for financial provision in the event of a failure to maintain may only be made if:[111]

(a) the applicant or respondent civil partner was domiciled in England or Wales on the date of the application; or

(b) the applicant civil partner was habitually resident in England or Wales for one year prior to the date of the application; or

---

[108] ibid, Sch 5, para 42(1).
[109] ibid, Sch 5, para 42(2).
[110] ibid, Sch 5, paras 39(3) & 40.
[111] ibid, Sch 5, para 39(2).

(c) the respondent civil partner was habitually resident in England or Wales on the date of the application.

The same restrictions upon making orders in favour of children of the family **5.94** (referable to age and educational status) apply in relation to failure to maintain cases as they do in relation to financial provision orders in the event of separation, dissolution or nullity.[112] (See para 5.12 above for those restrictions.) The court's powers to make orders for periodical payments and secured periodical payments are also subject to the restrictions imposed by the Child Support Act 1991, s 8. (See para 5.20 above.)

A periodical payments order made under Pt 9 in favour of a civil partner **5.95** ceases to have effect if:[113]

(a) either civil partner dies; or

(b) the recipient civil partner enters into a subsequent civil partnership or marriage (the dissolution or nullity of the original civil partnership does not otherwise affect the validity of the failure order under Pt 9).

A secured periodical payments order made under Pt 9 in favour of a civil **5.96** partner ceases to have effect if:[114]

(a) the payee civil partner dies; or

(b) the civil partnership is subsequently dissolved or annulled and the recipient civil partner enters into a subsequent civil partnership or marriage.

2. Orders in Favour of Civil Partners: Relevant Factors

In exercising its discretion to make an order for financial provision in favour **5.97** of a civil partner in a failure to maintain case, the court must have regard to all the circumstances of the case and must have particular regard to the same factors (contained in Sch 5, para 21(2)) which are relevant in making orders for financial provision in favour of civil partners in proceedings for separation, dissolution or nullity.[115] (See para 5.78 above for those factors.) The only modifications to those factors, in failure to maintain cases, are:

(a) the standard of living which the court must take into account is the standard enjoyed prior to the failure to provide reasonable maintenance;[116] and

(b) since there are no dissolution or nullity proceedings, the court is not required to have regard to any benefits which would be lost upon dissolution or nullity.

---

[112] ibid, Sch 5, para 45.
[113] ibid, Sch 5, para 47(2) & (6).
[114] ibid, Sch 5, para 47(3) & (6).
[115] ibid, Sch 5, para 43(1) & (2).
[116] ibid, Sch 5, para 43(4).

5.98 Unlike financial provision in the case of separation, dissolution or nullity, however, the welfare of any child of the family who has not attained the age of 18 is *not* the court's first consideration unless an order in favour of that child is sought.[117]

3. Orders in Favour of Children of the Family: Relevant Considerations

5.99 In exercising its discretion to make an order for financial provision in favour of a child of the family in a failure to maintain case, the court must have regard to all the circumstances of the case and must have particular regard to the same factors which are relevant in making orders for financial provision in favour of children in proceedings for separation, dissolution or nullity.[118] (See para 5.80 above for those factors.) The only modification to those factors, in failure to maintain cases, is that the standard of living which the court must take into account is the standard enjoyed prior to the failure to provide reasonable maintenance.[119]

5.100 In making an order in favour of a child who has not attained the age of 18, the court must give first consideration to the child's welfare whilst a minor.[120]

I. VARIATION AND DISCHARGE OF FINANCIAL RELIEF ORDERS

5.101 Part 11 of Sch 5 to the 2004 Act mirrors the MCA 1973, s 31 and enables the court to vary orders for financial relief. The court has wide ranging powers to vary orders for periodical payments and secured periodical payments, whereas its powers to vary capital orders are more limited.

5.102 The court may vary any of the following orders:[121]

(a) a periodical or secured periodical payments order (including an attachment order in relation to a periodic pension) made in favour of a civil partner or child of the family in separation, dissolution, nullity or failure to maintain proceedings;[122]

(b) an order for maintenance pending outcome made in separation, dissolution or nullity proceedings;

(c) an interim periodical payments order made in failure to maintain proceedings;

---

[117] ibid, Sch 5, para 43(3).
[118] ibid, Sch 5, para 44.
[119] ibid, Sch 5, para 44(4).
[120] ibid, Sch 5, para 43(3).
[121] ibid, Sch 5, para 50.
[122] Such an order made in favour of a child in failure to maintain proceedings may be varied on the application by that child if he has reached the age of 16: Sch 5, para 55.

(d) a lump sum by instalments order made in favour of a civil partner or child of the family in separation, dissolution, nullity or failure to maintain proceedings (the court may vary the number, timing and quantum of individual instalments; but may not vary the total quantum payable);

(e) a deferred lump sum order which includes a pension attachment order in relation to a pension lump sum or lump sum payable upon death made in separation, dissolution or nullity proceedings. A pension attachment order in relation to the lump sum payable upon death cannot, however, be varied or discharged after the death of either civil partner;[123]

(f) a settlement of property order or a variation of settlement order (but not a transfer of property order) made in favour of a civil partner or child of the family in separation (but not in dissolution or nullity) proceedings. The court may only vary or discharge the order, however, if the separation order is subsequently rescinded or replaced by a dissolution order;[124]

(g) a sale of property order made in favour of a civil partner or child of the family;

(h) a pension sharing order which has not yet taken effect and which was made before a dissolution or nullity order was made final.[125]

There is no jurisdiction at all to vary an immediate lump sum or a transfer of property order. **5.103**

Subject to the prohibition in Sch 5, para 47(5) on extending non-extendable term orders for periodical or secured periodical payments, the court may:[126] **5.104**

(a) vary or discharge any of the above orders;

(b) suspend temporarily any provision of such order;

(c) revive the operation of any provision of such order which has been suspended.

The court also has the power to remit any arrears which may have arisen under a periodical payments, secured periodical payments, maintenance pending outcome or interim periodical payments order.[127] See paras 5.125–5.127 below in relation to enforcement of arrears which are more than 12 months old. **5.105**

If the court varies an order for periodical or secured periodical payments it may defer the date of implementation of the variation or discharge[128] or it may, if there are special circumstances, back-date the variation to the date of the original order itself.[129] **5.106**

---

[123] CPA 2004, Sch 5, para 50(2).
[124] ibid, Sch 5, para 56.
[125] ibid, Sch 5, para 57.
[126] ibid, Sch 5, para 51(1).
[127] ibid, Sch 5, para 52.
[128] ibid, Sch 5, para 61.
[129] *S v S* [1987] 1 WLR 382, CA.

5.107   If a child support maintenance calculation has been made after the original order, the court has the ability, in limited circumstances, to back-date the variation of a periodical or secured periodical payments order in favour of a civil partner or a child to a date which pre-dates the application for variation (see Sch 5, para 62).

1. Capitalization of Periodical Payments or Secured Periodical Payments

5.108   In relation to periodical and secured periodical payments orders made in dissolution (but not in separation or nullity) proceedings, the court has additional powers to capitalize the payments (ie to order a capital payment in lieu of ongoing periodical or secured periodical payments) if, but only if, either:[130]

(a) the periodical or secured periodical payments order is discharged by the court; or

(b) a term (whether extendable or non-extendable) is imposed by the court upon the duration of the periodical or secured periodical payments order.

5.109   The capital orders which the court may make in such circumstances are:[131]

(a) A lump sum order (whether or not the original order contained a lump sum order). The court may order the lump sum to be paid in instalments, in which case it may also order security for the instalments and order interest to be paid from the date of the order until payment is due.[132]

(b) One or more property adjustment orders (whether or not the original order contained a property adjustment order). On a variation or discharge application, the court is not, however, entitled to make more than one type of property adjustment order (ie it may make a transfer of property order *and* a settlement of property order; but it may not make two transfer of property orders).[133]

(c) A pension sharing order in relation to one or more pensions (whether or not a pension sharing order was made in the original order). On a variation or discharge application, the court may not, however, make a pension sharing order in relation to a pension which has already been the subject of a pension sharing order in this civil partnership or which is subject to a pension attachment order (which has not yet been implemented) in this or in another civil partnership.[134]

5.110   In exercising its powers to capitalize periodical or secured periodical

---

[130] CPA 2004, Sch 5, para 53(1).
[131] ibid, Sch 5, para 53(2).
[132] ibid, Sch 5, para 54(1) & (2).
[133] ibid, Sch 5, para 54(3).
[134] ibid, Sch 5, para 54(5).

payments, the court's function is not to reopen capital claims; but to substitute compensation (by reference to Duxbury tables) for the periodical payments.[135]

Unless made by way of capitalization under Sch 5, para 53, the court has no **5.111** jurisdiction to make a property adjustment or pension sharing order on an application to vary periodical or secured periodical payments.[136] Similarly the court may not make a lump sum order in favour of a civil partner on an application to vary; although it may make a lump sum order in favour of a child of the family.[137]

2. Variation or Discharge of Secured Periodical Payments Order on Death of Payer

Since orders for secured periodical payments endure beyond the death of the **5.112** payer, Sch 5, para 60 enables an application for variation or discharge of the order (or of any order for the sale of property for the purposes of securing payment) to be made either by the payee or by the deceased payer's personal representatives.

The application for variation or discharge must, however, be made within six **5.113** months of the date on which representation was first taken out in relation to the estate.[138] The court has no power to extend the six month period. The court has the power to direct that the application for variation or discharge be deemed to have been accompanied by an application under the Inheritance (Provision for Family and Dependants) Act 1975.[139]

3. Matters to which the Court must have Regard

In exercising its discretion to vary, discharge, suspend or revive an order, the **5.114** court must:[140]

(a) give first consideration to the welfare, whilst a minor, of any child of the family who has not attained the age of 18;

(b) have regard to all the circumstances of the case including any change in the matters to which the court was required to have regard in making the original order (see paras 5.78 and 5.80 above for those matters);

(c) in dissolution and nullity (but not separation) proceedings, consider whether there should be a clean break and whether a term should be imposed on a periodical or secured periodical payments order for such period as will be

---

[135] *Pearce v Pearce* [2003] EWCA Civ 1052, [2003] 2 FLR 1144, CA.
[136] CPA 2004, Sch 5, para 58(2).
[137] ibid, Sch 5, para 58(3).
[138] ibid, Sch 5, para 60(3).
[139] Inheritance (Provision for Family and Dependants) Act 1975, s 18A as inserted by CPA 2004, Sch 4, para 25. See also IPFDA 1975, s 16 as amended by CPA 2004, Sch 4, para 23.
[140] CPA 2004, Sch 5, para 59(1) & (2).

sufficient to enable the payee civil partner to adjust, without undue financial hardship, to the termination of those payments.[141]

5.115 A change of circumstances is not, however, a precondition of a successful variation application. On the contrary, the court is required to consider the matter de novo.[142]

J. CONSENT ORDERS AND MAINTENANCE AGREEMENTS

1. Consent Orders

5.116 Civil partners may agree the terms of an order for financial relief (or any variation or discharge of such an order) without the need for a contested hearing. The decision as to the nature of the financial relief which should be ordered is, however, a matter for the court and not for the civil partners, notwithstanding their agreement. The court is not a 'rubber stamp'; it must scrutinize the draft order and consider all the matters to which the 2004 Act directs it to have regard.[143] The court is entitled to refuse to make the order upon which the civil partners have agreed.[144]

2. Maintenance Agreements

5.117 The civil partners may enter into a 'maintenance agreement', whether or not there are proceedings for separation, dissolution or nullity. A 'maintenance agreement' is a written agreement which is either:[145]

(a) made during the subsistence of the civil partnership or after its dissolution or nullity which governs the civil partners' rights and liabilities (in relation to each other and any child, whether or not a child of the family), whilst living separately, in respect of:
  (i) the making or securing of payments; or
  (ii) the disposition or use of any property;
(b) a separation agreement (which may simply govern living arrangements) which is silent as to financial arrangements and where there is no other written agreement containing financial arrangements.

5.118 A maintenance agreement cannot oust the jurisdiction of the court to make orders for financial relief and any provision in a maintenance agreement which

---

[141] ibid, Sch 5, para 59(3) & (4).
[142] *Flavell v Flavell* [1997] 1 FLR 353, CA.
[143] *Kelley v Corston* [1998] 1 FLR 986, CA.
[144] CPA 2004, Sch 5, para 66.
[145] ibid, Sch 5, para 67.

purports to do so is void (although this will not affect the validity of the remainder of the agreement).[146]

Although a maintenance agreement emanates from the civil partners them- **5.119** selves and is reached without any court involvement, the High Court and county court[147] have the jurisdiction to vary the maintenance agreement if there has been a change of circumstances or if the court considers that proper financial arrangements have not been made for a child of the family. The court's jurisdiction arises if:[148]

(a) the maintenance agreement subsists;

(b) each of the civil partners is domiciled or resident in England or Wales;

(c) the court is satisfied either:

  (i) due to a change in circumstances (including a change foreseen at the date of the agreement), the agreement should be altered so as to add financial arrangements or make different financial arrangements; or

  (ii) that the agreement does not contain proper financial arrangements in relation to any child of the family.

The court also has the jurisdiction to vary a maintenance agreement which **5.120** provides for continuing payments after the payer's death if:[149]

(a) the deceased payer civil partner dies whilst domiciled in England or Wales; and

(b) the application is made by the payee civil partner or the personal representatives of the deceased within six months of the date on which representation was taken out in relation to the estate.

The court has wide ranging powers to vary, revoke or insert financial **5.121** arrangements (defined as arrangements for making or securing payments or for the disposition or use of any property)[150] into the maintenance agreement as it considers 'just'. The only specific criteria to which the court is directed to have regard relate solely to those cases where the payer civil partner is not the parent (whether natural or by adoption) of a child of the family, ie:[151]

(a) whether that civil partner has assumed any responsibility for the child's maintenance;

(b) if so, the extent of any such assumption of responsibility and the duration for which such responsibility was discharged;

---

[146] ibid, Sch 5, para 68.

[147] See paras 6.59–6.63 below for the jurisdiction of the magistrates' court.

[148] CPA 2004, Sch 5, para 69(1) & (2).

[149] ibid, Sch 5, para 73. See also Inheritance (Provision for Family and Dependants) Act 1975, ss 17 & 18.

[150] ibid, Sch 5, para 67(2).

[151] ibid, Sch 5, para 69(4).

(c) whether, in assuming and discharging that responsibility, the civil partner knew that the child was not his child (only of relevance in gender recognition cases);

(d) the liability of any other person to maintain the child.

5.122 In varying any periodical or secured periodical payments in the maintenance agreement in favour of a civil partner or child of the family, the court is subject to the same restrictions which would apply if the court made an order under Sch 5, Pt 1 (ie age/educational status of child; death/subsequent civil partnership/marriage of civil partner: see paras 5.12, 5.17 and 5.18 above).[152]

5.123 The court's power to vary a maintenance agreement is also subject to the restrictions imposed by the Child Support Act 1991, s 9 in a case in which the Child Support Agency would otherwise have jurisdiction. The restrictions are:

(a) the court must not insert a provision for periodical or secured periodical payments for the benefit of a child if the maintenance agreement did not originally contain such provision;

(b) the court must not increase the quantum of any periodical or secured periodical payments payable under the maintenance agreement for the benefit of a child (unless the maintenance agreement was made before 5 April 1993 and the civil partner with care is not on benefits; in which case, the court has power to increase the quantum).

5.124 A civil partner who has entered into a maintenance agreement is not precluded (provided there are or have been proceedings for separation, dissolution or nullity) from issuing an application for financial relief (ie financial provision, property adjustment and, in dissolution and nullity proceedings, pension sharing). The existence of the agreement will, however, be an important factor for the court to take into account in exercising its discretion.[153]

K. ARREARS AND REPAYMENTS

1. Arrears

5.125 Paragraph 63 of Sch 5 to the 2004 Act mirrors the MCA 1973, s 32 and requires the leave of the court to be obtained before arrears of periodical payments, secured periodical payments, maintenance pending outcome or interim periodical payments which are more than 12 months old may be enforced.

5.126 On an application for such leave, the court may:[154]

(a) refuse leave;

---

[152] ibid, Sch 5, para 71.
[153] *Edgar v Edgar* (1981) 2 FLR 19, CA.
[154] CPA 2004, Sch 4, para 63(3).

(b) grant leave on such conditions as it considers fit (eg defer payment of arrears or order payment in instalments);

(c) remit all or part of the arrears.

In practice, the court will not enforce arrears over 12 months old unless there are special circumstances.[155] **5.127**

2. Repayments

Paragraph 64 of Sch 5 to the 2004 Act mirrors the MCA 1973, ss 33 and 38 and enables the court to order the repayment by the payee of a periodical payments, secured periodical payments, maintenance pending outcome or interim periodical payments order if it considers there has been an overpayment. **5.128**

If there has been a change in the payer's or payee's circumstances or the payee has died and the court considers that, as a result, there has been an overpayment, it may order the payee to repay to the payer (or to the payer's personal representatives) such part of the overpayment as it thinks fit. The order may provide for the repayment to be paid in instalments. **5.129**

If a payee has entered into a subsequent civil partnership or marriage, but the payer has continued to make periodical or secured periodical payments in the mistaken belief that the order still subsisted, the court may order the payee to repay to the payer (or to the payer's personal representatives) the whole of the overpayment or, if the repayment of the whole would be unjust, to order repayment of only part of the overpayment or dismiss the application. The order may provide for the repayment to be paid in instalments. **5.130**

The 2004 Act requires the application for repayment to be made to the county court unless there are proceedings in the High Court for leave to enforce or for enforcement of arrears, or (in the case of overpayment following a change of circumstances only) there are proceedings in the High Court for the variation or discharge of the order.[156] **5.131**

The 2004 Act also amends the MCA 1973, s 38 to permit orders for repayment of periodical payments which have been paid after a payee former spouse has entered into a subsequent civil partnership.[157] **5.132**

L. FREEZING AND AVOIDANCE OF DISPOSITION ORDERS

Paragraph 74 of Sch 5 to the 2004 Act mirrors the MCA 1973, s 37 and enables the court to freeze assets and set aside dispositions so as to ensure that **5.133**

---

[155] *C v S (Maintenance Order: Enforcement)* [1997] 1 FLR 298.

[156] CPA 2004, Sch 5, paras 64(7) & 65(6).

[157] MCA 1973, s 38 as amended by CPA 2004, Sch 27, para 45.

its orders or claims before it are not defeated. The court has the power to protect the assets if there are proceedings for any of the following orders:[158]

(a) financial provision;

(b) property adjustment;

(c) pension sharing;

(d) maintenance pending outcome;

(e) financial provision in failure to maintain cases;

(f) variation or discharge of any order (other than variation of secured periodical payments following the death of the payer);

(g) variation of a maintenance agreement during the lives of both civil partners.

1. Freezing Orders

5.134 If the court considers that a civil partner is, with the intention of defeating the other civil partner's claim for financial relief (whether by preventing or reducing the relief or impeding its enforcement)[159] about to make a disposition or transfer out of the jurisdiction or otherwise deal with any property, it may make such order as it thinks fit restraining that civil partner from disposing of or otherwise dealing with the property.

5.135 A presumption arises that a civil partner intends to defeat a claim if the disposition or dealing would have the consequence of defeating the claim.[160]

5.136 The court's powers should not, however, be exercised so as to freeze the entirety of a civil partner's assets; the injunction should be limited to protecting the extent of the other civil partner's claims.[161]

5.137 The court's powers under para 74 are in addition to its powers to grant freezing injunctions under its inherent jurisdiction.[162]

2. Avoidance of Disposition Orders

5.138 The court may set aside a disposition if it considers that:[163]

(a) a civil partner has made a 'reviewable disposition' (whether before or after an order for financial relief has been made); and

(b) if the disposition is set aside, financial relief or different financial relief would be granted to the other civil partner.

---

[158] CPA 2004, Sch 5, para 74(1).
[159] ibid, Sch 5, para 75.
[160] ibid, Sch 5, para 75(4).
[161] *Ghoth v Ghoth* [1992] 2 FLR 300, CA.
[162] Supreme Court Act 1981, s 31 (applicable in the county court by virtue of County Courts Act 1984, s 38).
[163] CPA 2004, Sch 5, para 74(3).

A disposition is 'reviewable' unless:[164] 5.139

(a) it was made for valuable consideration; and

(b) the disponee acted in good faith and without notice of the intention to defeat the claim.

A presumption arises that a civil partner intended to defeat a claim if:[165] 5.140

(a) the disposition took place less than three years before the date of the application for an avoidance of disposition order; and

(b) the disposition had the consequence of defeating the claim.

The court does not have the power under the 2004 Act to set aside a 5.141
disposition contained in a will or codicil.[166]

M. IMPROVEMENTS TO PROPERTY AND PROPERTY DISPUTES

1. Improvements to Property

Section 65 of the 2004 Act mirrors the Matrimonial Proceedings and Property 5.142
Act 1970, ss 30, 37 and 39 and enables a civil partner to acquire a share or an
enlarged share of the beneficial interest in real or personal property as a result of
improvements which he/she has carried out.

If a civil partner makes a 'substantial' contribution in money or money's 5.143
worth to the improvement of real or personal property in which (or in the
proceeds of sale of which) either or both of the civil partners has a beneficial
interest, the contributing civil partner acquires such share or enlarged share in
the property:[167]

(a) as may have been agreed between the civil partners; or

(b) if there was no agreement, as seems 'just' to the court.

The court may make such order as it thinks fit in relation to the property, 5.144
including an order for sale.[168]

If the real or personal property no longer exists, the court may order the non- 5.145
contributing civil partner to pay such sum to the contributing civil partner as it
considers appropriate.[169]

---

[164] ibid, Sch 5, para 75(3).
[165] ibid, Sch 5, para 75(4).
[166] ibid, Sch 5, para 75(2). The disposition may be set aside, after death, under Inheritance (Provision for Family and Dependants) Act 1975, s 10.
[167] CPA 2004, s 65(2).
[168] ibid, s 66.
[169] ibid, s 67.

5.146   An application under s 65 or s 66 must be made within three years of any dissolution or annulment of the civil partnership.[170]

5.147   Section 65 applies whether or not there are proceedings for separation, dissolution or nullity.

5.148   The real advantage of s 65 can be seen in enforcement proceedings brought by third parties against the interest of one of the civil partners in the civil partnership home. In those circumstances, the other civil partner may rely upon s 65 in order to assert or enlarge a beneficial interest. Unlike the position at common law, s 65 effectively gives rise to a presumption of common intention that any improvements carried out would result in the contributing civil partner acquiring a share or enlarged share of the home.

5.149   Sections 65 to 67 of the 2004 Act also apply to same sex couples who have not entered into a civil partnership but who have entered into a civil partnership agreement (see para 2.71 above). The application must, however, be brought within three years of the termination of the agreement.[171]

---

[170] ibid, s 68.
[171] ibid, s 74.

6

FINANCIAL RELIEF IN THE MAGISTRATES' COURT

Schedule 6 to the 2004 Act mirrors the Domestic Proceedings and Magis- **6.01**
trates' Courts Act 1978 ('the DPMCA 1978') and enables the magistrates' court
to make orders for periodical payments and lump sums in favour of civil
partners and children of the family. The powers of the magistrates' court are
much more limited than the powers of the High Court and county court.[1] The
magistrates' court may only make orders for financial relief in the following
circumstances:

(a) where a civil partner has failed to provide reasonable maintenance, has
    behaved in such a way that the other civil partner cannot reasonably be
    expected to live with him/her or has deserted the other civil partner: a 'Part 1
    order';

(b) where the civil partners have agreed on an order for financial provision: a
    'Part 2 order';

(c) where the civil partners are separated: a 'Part 3' order.

---

[1] See Chapter 5 for financial relief in the High Court and county court.

6.02 Different considerations apply in relation to each of the above orders.

6.03 A magistrates' court only has the jurisdiction to hear an application under Sch 6 to the 2004 Act if either civil partner ordinarily resides in its local justice area on the date on which the application is issued.[2]

A. ORDERS IN FAILURE TO MAINTAIN/BEHAVIOUR/ DESERTION CASES: PART 1 ORDERS

6.04 A magistrates' court may make an order under Pt 1 of Sch 6 if it satisfied that:[3]

(a) a civil partner has failed to provide reasonable maintenance for the other civil partner or has failed to provide a proper contribution towards the reasonable maintenance of a 'child of the family' (ie a child of both civil partners or any other child who has been treated by them as a child of their family);[4] or

(b) a civil partner has behaved in such a way that the other civil partner cannot reasonably be expected to live with him/her;[5] or

(c) a civil partner has deserted the other civil partner.[6] (There is no minimum period for which the desertion must have lasted before an application may be made.)

1. The Orders which the Court may Make

6.05 If the magistrates' court is satisfied that one of the above situations applies, it may make any of the following orders:[7]

(a) a periodical payments order for a civil partner;

(b) a lump sum order for a civil partner (maximum £1,000);[8]

(c) a periodical payments order payable to a civil partner for the benefit of a child of the family or payable direct to such a child;

(d) a lump sum order (maximum £1,000)[9] payable to a civil partner for the benefit of a child of the family or payable direct to such child.

6.06 A magistrates' court has no jurisdiction to make orders for secured periodical payments, property adjustment, pension sharing or pension attachment.

---

[2] CPA 2004, Sch 6, para 47.
[3] ibid, Sch 6, para 1(1).
[4] ibid, Sch 6, para 48.
[5] For the interpretation of 'behaviour' see para 3.03 above.
[6] For the interpretation of 'desertion' see para 3.03 above.
[7] CPA 2004, Sch 6, para 2(1).
[8] ibid, Sch 6, para 2(2).
[9] ibid, Sch 6, para 2(2).

A lump sum order may relate to expenses incurred before the date of the **6.07** application[10] and may provide for payment in instalments.[11]

A periodical payments order may include a 'means of payment' order (eg for **6.08** payment through the court, for attachment of earnings, payment by standing order etc)[12] or provide for payment to a third party on behalf of the payee.[13]

A periodical payments order in favour of a civil partner:[14] **6.09**

(a) may be back-dated to the date of the application;

(b) ceases to have effect upon the death of either civil partner;

(c) is unaffected by the subsequent dissolution or nullity of the civil partnership, but ceases automatically upon the payee entering into a subsequent civil partnership or marriage.

A periodical payments order in favour of a child of the family may also be **6.10** back-dated to the date of the application and automatically ceases to have effect upon the death of the payer civil partner.[15]

The same restrictions (referable to age and educational status) which apply to **6.11** orders in favour of children of the family in the High Court and county court apply equally in the magistrates' court[16] (see para 5.12 above). The powers of the magistrates' court are also subject to the restrictions imposed by the Child Support Act 1991, s 8 (see para 5.20 above).

Where a child support maintenance calculation is in force, an order for period- **6.12** ical payments in favour of a child of the family may be back-dated to a date which pre-dates the application under Pt 1 (see Sch 6, para 27(7) & (8)).

An order for periodical payments (or interim periodical payments) in proceed- **6.13** ings under Pt 1 of Sch 6 (whether payable to a civil partner or payable to a civil partner for the benefit of a child of the family) ceases to have effect if the civil partners resume living together for a continuous period in excess of six months after the order has taken effect.[17]

In contrast, an order for periodical payments (or interim periodical payments) **6.14** in proceedings under Pt 1 of Sch 6 payable direct to a child of the family (rather than to a civil partner for the benefit of such child) is unaffected by the resumption of cohabitation of the civil partners unless the court directs otherwise.[18]

The 2004 Act also amends the DPMCA 1978, s 4 to provide for automatic **6.15**

---

[10] ibid, Sch 6, para 3.
[11] Magistrates' Courts Act 1980, s 75.
[12] ibid, s 59.
[13] DPMCA 1978, s 32(2) as applied to civil partnerships by virtue of CPA 2004, Sch 6, para 43.
[14] CPA 2004, Sch 6, para 26.
[15] ibid, Sch 6, para 27(2) & (6).
[16] ibid, Sch 6, para 27.
[17] ibid, Sch 6, para 29(1) & (2).
[18] ibid, Sch 6, para 29(3) & (4).

termination of orders for financial provision upon a payee former spouse entering into a subsequent civil partnership.[19]

2. Matters to which the Court must have Regard

6.16   Prior to making a final order or dismissing the application under Pt 1 of Sch 6, the court must consider whether it needs to exercise any of its powers under the Children Act 1989 (eg by making contact, residence orders etc) in relation to any child of the family who is under the age of 18 years.[20]

6.17   In exercising its discretion to make a lump sum or periodical payments order under Pt 1 of Sch 6 (whether for a civil partner or for a child of the family), the court's first consideration must be the welfare, whilst a minor, of any child of the family who has not attained the age of 18.[21]

3. Orders in Favour of Civil Partners: Relevant Factors

6.18   In making a lump sum or periodical payments order in favour of a civil partner, the factors to which the magistrates' court is directed to have regard mirror those to which the High Court and county court must have regard under Sch 5, para 21(1) (see para 5.78 above for a detailed consideration of those factors), save that the magistrates' court is not required to have regard to pension benefits. The factors to which the magistrates' court must have regard are:[22]

(a) the income, earning capacity, property and other financial resources which each civil partner has or is likely to have in the foreseeable future, including any increase in earning capacity which it would be reasonable to expect a civil partner to take steps to acquire;

(b) the financial needs, obligations and responsibilities which each civil partner has or is likely to have in the foreseeable future;

(c) the standard of living enjoyed by the civil partners prior to the conduct complained of (upon which jurisdiction under Pt 1 is founded);

(d) the age of each civil partner and the duration of the civil partnership;

(e) any physical or mental disability of either civil partner;

(f) the contributions which either civil partner has made or is likely to make in the foreseeable future to the welfare of the family, including any contribution by looking after the home or caring for the family;

(g) the conduct of either civil partner if it would be inequitable to disregard such conduct.

---

[19] ibid, Sch 27, para 57.
[20] ibid, Sch 6, para 45.
[21] ibid, Sch 6, para 4.
[22] ibid, Sch 6, para 5(2).

4. Orders in Favour of Children of the Family: Relevant Factors

In making a lump sum or periodical payments order in favour of a child of **6.19** the family, the factors to which the magistrates' court is directed to have regard mirror those to which the High Court and county court must have regard under Sch 5, para 22, save that the magistrates' court is not required to have regard to any physical or mental disability of the payer civil partner. The factors to which the magistrates' court must have regard are:[23]

(a) the financial needs of the child;

(b) the income, earning capacity (if any), property and other financial resources of the child;

(c) any physical or mental disability of the child;

(d) the standard of living enjoyed by the family prior to the conduct complained of (upon which jurisdiction under Pt 1 is founded);

(e) the way in which the child was being, or was expected to be, educated or trained;

(f) the income, earning capacity, property and other financial resources which each civil partner has or is likely to have in the foreseeable future, including any increase in earning capacity which it would be reasonable to expect a civil partner to take steps to acquire;

(g) the financial needs, obligations and responsibilities which each civil partner has or is likely to have in the foreseeable future.

If the civil partner against whom the order for financial relief is made is not a **6.20** parent (whether natural or by adoption) of the child, the court must additionally have regard to the following factors:[24]

(a) whether that civil partner has assumed any responsibility for the child's maintenance;

(b) if so, the extent of any such assumption of responsibility and the duration for which such responsibility was discharged;

(c) whether, in assuming and discharging that responsibility, the civil partner knew that the child was not his child (only of relevance in change of gender cases);

(d) the liability of any other person to maintain the child.

The magistrates' court may transfer the application to the High Court if it **6.21** considers that the application could be dealt with more 'conveniently' in that court.[25]

---

[23] ibid, Sch 6, para 6.
[24] ibid, Sch 6, para 6(3).
[25] ibid, Sch 6, para 8.

B. ORDERS FOR AGREED FINANCIAL PROVISION: PART 2 ORDERS

6.22 The magistrates' court may make an order under Pt 2 of Sch 6 if it is satisfied:[26]

(a) that the civil partners have agreed upon the financial provision to be made for a civil partner or child of the family; and

(b) it would not be contrary to the interests of justice to make an order in the terms agreed; and

(c) that any agreed financial provision for a child of the family constitutes a proper contribution towards the financial needs of that child.[27]

6.23 If the magistrates' court is satisfied that the above conditions are fulfilled it may convert the agreement into an order.

6.24 The financial provision upon which the civil partners have agreed must be limited to periodical payments and lump sum orders for the benefit of a civil partner or child of the family if the magistrates' court is to make an order in the same terms.[28] There is no limit, however, to the quantum of the lump sum upon which the civil partners may agree and which the court may convert into an order.

1. Matters to which the Court must have Regard

6.25 Prior to making a final order or dismissing the application under Pt 2, the court must consider whether it needs to exercise any of its powers under the Children Act 1989 (eg by making contact, residence orders etc) in relation to any child of the family who is under the age of 18 years.[29]

6.26 The same restrictions on the commencement and duration of periodical payments in favour of civil partners (death, subsequent civil partnership/marriage) and on the duration of periodical payments in favour of a child (age, educational status) which apply to an application under Pt 1 of Sch 6 apply equally to an application under Pt 2 (see paras 6.09–6.11 above).[30]

6.27 If the magistrates' court declines to convert the agreement into an order on the grounds that it would not be in the interests of justice to do so or that it does not make proper provision for the financial needs of a child of the family, it may make a different order which does satisfy those criteria provided both civil partners consent to such a different order being made.[31]

---

[26] ibid, Sch 6, para 9.
[27] ibid, Sch 6, para 12.
[28] ibid, Sch 6, para 10.
[29] ibid, Sch 6, para 45.
[30] ibid, Sch 6, para 28.
[31] ibid, Sch 6, para 13.

If the civil partners do not agree on a different order, a civil partner may still make an application under Pt 1 of Sch 6 provided that the conditions under that part are fulfilled (ie that there has been a failure to maintain, behaviour or desertion).[32] **6.28**

C. ORDERS WHERE THE CIVIL PARTNERS ARE LIVING SEPARATELY: PART 3 ORDERS

The magistrates' court may make an order under Pt 3 of Sch 6 if it is satisfied that:[33] **6.29**

(a) the civil partners have been living apart, by agreement, for a continuous period exceeding three months; and

(b) one of the civil partners has been making periodical payments to the other for the other's benefit or for the benefit of a child of the family.

If it is satisfied that the above conditions have been fulfilled, it may make an order for periodical payments to be paid to a civil partner, to a civil partner for the benefit of a child of the family or direct to such a child. **6.30**

1. Matters to which the Court must have Regard

Prior to making a final order or dismissing the application under Pt 3, the court must consider whether it needs to exercise any of its powers under the Children Act 1989 (eg by making contact, residence orders etc) in relation to any child of the family who is under the age of 18 years.[34] **6.31**

In making an order under Pt 3, the magistrates' court's first consideration must be the welfare, whilst a minor, of any child of the family who has not attained the age of 18 and it must have regard to all the same factors which are relevant in making orders under Pt 1 (income, earning capacity etc. See paras 6.18–6.20 above).[35] **6.32**

2. Restrictions on the Quantum of Periodical Payments

The quantum of periodical payments which the magistrates' court may order under Pt 3 is, however, limited to a maximum amount referable to the periodical payments actually paid in the three months prior to the application.[36] **6.33**

Although the periodical payments actually paid prior to the application set **6.34**

---

[32] ibid, Sch 6, para 14.
[33] ibid, Sch 6, para 15.
[34] ibid, Sch 6, para 45.
[35] ibid, Sch 6, para 19.
[36] ibid, Sch 6, para 17(a).

the maximum limit, the court is free to make an order for a *lesser* amount than that paid in the three months prior to the application if:[37]

(a) the court considers that it would have made an order for a lesser sum had there been a contested application under Pt 1 of Sch 6 (failure to maintain etc); or

(b) if the child of the family is not the child of the payer, the court considers that it would not have made an order in favour of such a child had there been a contested application under Pt 1 of Sch 6.

6.35   The same restrictions on the commencement and duration of periodical payments in favour of civil partners (death, subsequent civil partnership/marriage) and on the duration of periodical payments in favour of a child (age, educational status) which apply to an application under Pt 1 of Sch 6 apply equally to an application under Pt 3 (see paras 6.09–6.11 above).[38]

6.36   An order for periodical payments (or interim periodical payments) made in proceedings under Pt 3 (whether to a civil partner, to a civil partner for the benefit of a child of the family or direct to such child) ceases to have effect if the civil partners resume cohabitation.[39]

6.37   A periodical payments order may include a 'means of payment' order (eg for payment through the court, for attachment of earnings, payment by standing order etc)[40] or provide for payment to a third party on behalf of the payee.[41]

6.38   If the magistrates' court considers that the periodical payments actually paid in the three months prior to the application were insufficient in that:

(a) they did not provide reasonable maintenance for the civil partner; or

(b) they did not provide for a proper contribution to be made towards the reasonable maintenance of a child of the family

the court may treat the application as having been made under Pt 1 (failure to maintain etc) and make an order under that part instead.[42]

D. INTERIM ORDERS

6.39   The magistrates' court has the power in proceedings under Pts 1, 2 and 3 of Sch 6 (and upon transfer of an application to the High Court) to make an order for interim periodical payments (but not interim lump sum) to a civil partner, to

---

[37] ibid, Sch 6, para 17(b) & (c).
[38] ibid, Sch 6, paras 26 & 27.
[39] ibid, Sch 6, para 29(5).
[40] Magistrates' Courts Act 1980, s 59.
[41] DPMCA 1978, s 32(2) as applied to civil partnerships by virtue of CPA 2004, Sch 6, para 43.
[42] CPA 2004, Sch 6, para 18.

a civil partner for the benefit of a child of the family who is under the age of 18 or direct to such a child.[43]

The powers of the magistrates' court are, however, extremely limited: **6.40**

(a) only one interim order may be made;[44]

(b) the duration of an interim order is limited to three months which may be extended only for a further three months (ie maximum duration six months).[45]

Subject to the above restrictions, the magistrates' court may make such **6.41** interim order as it 'thinks reasonable'[46] and may back-date the interim order to the date of the application under Pts 1, 2 or 3. Where a child maintenance calculation is already in force in relation to a child, the order may be back-dated to the later of:

(a) six months prior to the application for periodical or secured periodical payments; or

(b) the date on which the maintenance calculation took effect.[47]

E. VARIATION OF ORDERS

The magistrates' court has the power to vary any order for periodical pay- **6.42** ments (or interim periodical payments) made under Pts 1, 2 or 3. The court may:[48]

(a) vary or revoke the order;

(b) suspend temporarily any provision of the order;

(c) revive any provision which has been suspended.

The court may not, however, extend the duration of an interim periodical **6.43** payments order beyond six months or extend the duration of a periodical payments order beyond the statutorily imposed limits.

There is no power to vary a lump sum order, save that if a lump sum order **6.44** provided for payment by instalments, the court may vary the number, timing and quantum of the instalments.[49]

---

[43] ibid, Sch 6, paras 20(1), (2), 21.

[44] ibid, Sch 6, para 20(4).

[45] ibid, Sch 6, para 24.

[46] ibid, Sch 6, para 21(1).

[47] ibid, Sch 6, para 27(7) & (8). See also para 27(9) for cases where a maintenance calculation has ceased to have effect.

[48] ibid, Sch 6, para 30(1) & (2). See also para 36 for variation of 'means of payment orders'.

[49] ibid, Sch 6, para 41.

1. Orders which the Court may Make

6.45 On an application to vary, discharge, suspend or revive a periodical payments order, the court has the jurisdiction to order a lump sum payment (to a civil partner, to a civil partner for the benefit of a child of the family or direct to such child: maximum £1,000 per person) even though the original order itself contained a lump sum order.[50]

6.46 The order for variation, discharge etc may be back-dated to the date of the application for such variation, discharge etc;[51] or, in special circumstances, where a child support maintenance calculation has subsequently been made to a date which pre-dates such application.[52]

6.47 If the court is satisfied that payment under the original order has not been made it may, upon varying the order, make a 'means of payment' order.[53]

2. Matters to which the Court must have Regard

6.48 In exercising its powers to vary, discharge, suspend or revive an order, the magistrates' court must:[54]

(a) give effect, so far as it is just to do so, to any agreement between the civil partners;

(b) (in the absence of such an agreement or if the court decides not to give effect to such an agreement) have regard to all the circumstances of the case and give first consideration to the welfare, whilst a minor, of any child of the family who has not attained the age of 18;

(c) have regard to any change in the matters to which it was required to have regard when making its original order.

6.49 It is not, however, a precondition of a successful variation application that there has actually been a change of circumstances. On the contrary, the magistrates' court is required to consider the matter de novo.[55]

6.50 A child who has reached the age of 16 may make an application to vary a periodical payments order (but not an interim order) under Pts 1, 2 or 3 which was payable direct to him/her or to a civil partner for his/her benefit.[56]

---

[50] ibid, Sch 6, para 31.
[51] ibid, Sch 6, para 32.
[52] ibid, Sch 6, para 33.
[53] ibid, Sch 6, paras 35 & 37.
[54] ibid, Sch 6, para 34.
[55] *Riley v Riley* [1988] 1 FLR 273.
[56] CPA 2004, Sch 6, para 39.

F. ENFORCEMENT, ARREARS AND REPAYMENTS

1. Enforcement

The 2004 Act amends the Attachment of Earnings Act 1971[57] and the   **6.51**
Administration of Justice Act 1970[58] so that 'maintenance order' is redefined to
include an order for periodical or other payments made between civil partners
under Sch 6 to the 2004 Act. Accordingly, orders under Sch 6 to the 2004 Act
may be enforced in the magistrates' court by:

(a) an attachment of earnings order;

(b) a means of payment order;[59]

(c) distress;[60]

(d) committal to prison.[61]

2. Arrears

As a matter of practice, arrears of periodical payments will not be enforced in   **6.52**
the magistrates' court if they are more than 12 months old.[62]

   A maintenance order made in the magistrates' court may be registered and   **6.53**
enforced in the High Court.[63] Arrears of periodical payments pursuant to orders
under Pts 1, 2 or 3 of Sch 6 which are more than 12 months old may not be
enforced through the High Court or county court without the leave of that
court.

   The High Court or county court may:[64]   **6.54**

(a) refuse leave;

(b) grant leave subject to such conditions as it considers proper (eg deferred
payment/payment by instalments);

(c) remit all or part of the arrears.

3. Repayments

The magistrates' court has no jurisdiction to order the repayment of period-   **6.55**
ical payments in the event that the payee civil partner has entered into a

---

[57] Sch 1 amended by CPA 2004, Sch 27, para 35.
[58] Sch 2 amended by CPA 2004, Sch 27, para 34.
[59] Magistrates' Courts Act 1980, ss 59 & 59B.
[60] ibid, s 76.
[61] ibid, s 93.
[62] *Bernstein v O'Neill* [1989] 2 FLR 1.
[63] Maintenance Orders Act 1958, s 1.
[64] DPMCA 1978, s 32(4) & (5) applied to civil partnerships by CPA 2004, Sch 6, para 43.

subsequent civil partnership or marriage and the payer has continued to make payments in the mistaken belief that the order under Pts 1, 2 or 3 subsisted. In such circumstances, an application for repayment must be made to the county court or, if there are proceedings for enforcement in the High Court or county court, within the existing enforcement proceedings.[65]

6.56   The High Court or county court may order the payee to repay to the payer (or to the payer's personal representatives) the whole of the overpayment or, if the repayment of the whole would be unjust, to order repayment of only part of the overpayment or dismiss the application. The order may provide for the repayment to be paid in instalments.[66]

6.57   No court has jurisdiction to order repayment of any overpayment under a magistrates' court order under Pts 1, 2 or 3 of Sch 6 resulting from any other change of circumstances.[67]

6.58   The 2004 Act also amends the DPMCA 1978, s 35 to permit orders for repayment of periodical payments which have been paid after a payee former spouse has entered into a subsequent civil partnership.[68]

G. VARIATION OF MAINTENANCE AGREEMENTS

6.59   A magistrates' court has the power, under Pt 13 of Sch 5 to the 2004 Act[69] to vary a maintenance agreement (see para 5.117 above for the meaning of 'maintenance agreement') during the lives of the civil partners if:[70]

(a) the maintenance agreement subsists; and

(b) both of the civil partners are resident in England or Wales; and

(c) either civil partner resides in the court's local justice area; and

(d) the court is satisfied either:
    (i) that due to a change in circumstances (including a change foreseen at the date of the agreement), the agreement should be altered so as to add financial arrangements or make different financial arrangements; or
    (ii) that the agreement does not contain proper financial arrangements in relation to any child of the family.[71]

6.60   The same restrictions upon the duration of periodical payments in favour of a civil partner (death, subsequent civil partnership/marriage) and in favour of

---

[65] CPA 2004, Sch 6, para 44.

[66] ibid, Sch 6, para 44(4) & (6).

[67] In contrast to the jurisdiction in relation to High Court and county court orders. See para 5.129 above..

[68] CPA 2004, Sch 27, para 58.

[69] para 69.

[70] CPA 2004, Sch 5, paras 69(1) & 70(1).

[71] ibid, Sch 5, para 69(2) & (3).

children (age, educational status) which apply in the High Court and county court apply equally to variations of maintenance agreements in the magistrates' court (see paras 5.12, 5.17 and 5.18 above).

1. Orders which the Court may Make

The powers of the magistrates' court to vary a maintenance agreement are, however, extremely limited. The only orders which the magistrates' court has the jurisdiction to make are:[72] **6.61**

(a) if the agreement contains no provision for periodical payments, an order inserting such a provision in favour of a civil partner or child of the family; and

(b) if the agreement does contain provision for periodical payments, an order increasing, reducing or terminating those payments.

The power to vary a maintenance agreement which provides for periodical payments to be made for the benefit of a child of the family is subject to the restrictions imposed by the Child Support Act 1991, s 9 (see para 5.123 above). **6.62**

Unlike the High Court or county court, the magistrates' court has no power to vary provisions in a maintenance agreement relating to secured periodical payments or the disposition or use of any property or to vary a maintenance agreement after the death of either civil partner. **6.63**

H. FAILURE TO MAINTAIN: MAGISTRATES' COURT AND HIGH COURT/COUNTY COURT COMPARED

In the event of a failure to maintain, a civil partner has a choice whether to proceed in the magistrates' court under Pt 1 of Sch 6 to the 2004 Act or in the High Court/county court under Pt 9 of Sch 5 to the 2004 Act. **6.64**

There are, however, important differences between the remedies available in the magistrates' court and those available in the High Court/county court: **6.65**

(a) the magistrates' court has no power to order secured periodical payments,[73] whereas the High Court/county court does have such power;[74]

(b) the lump sum which a magistrates' court may make is limited to £1,000,[75] whereas there is no limit in the High Court/county court;

(c) the magistrates' court may order interim periodical payments to be paid

---

[72] ibid, Sch 5, para 70(2).
[73] ibid, Sch 6, para 2.
[74] ibid, Sch 5, para 41(1)(b) & (e).
[75] ibid, Sch 6, para 2(2).

direct to a child of the family,[76] whereas the High Court/county court has no power to order direct payment;[77]

(d) the maximum duration of an interim periodical payments order in the magistrates' court is six months,[78] whereas there is no maximum duration in the High Court/county court.

---

[76] ibid, Sch 6, para 21.
[77] ibid, Sch 5, para 40.
[78] ibid, Sch 6, para 24.

7

FINANCIAL RELIEF FOLLOWING AN OVERSEAS DISSOLUTION, ANNULMENT OR SEPARATION

Schedule 7 to the 2004 Act mirrors ss 12 to 24 of the Matrimonial and Family **7.01** Proceedings Act 1984 ('the MFPA 1984') and enables the courts of England and Wales to make orders for financial relief if a civil partnership has been dissolved or annulled or the civil partners have been legally separated abroad by means of overseas judicial (or other) proceedings which are recognized in England and Wales (see paras 4.24–4.31 above for the recognition criteria). The court may entertain an application under Sch 7 even if a financial order has already been made abroad.

The courts in England and Wales have no jurisdiction to make orders for **7.02** financial relief if an overseas separation, dissolution or annulment has been obtained otherwise than by means of proceedings.

An application under Sch 7 may be made in the High Court[1] or, if designated **7.03** by regulations under the MFPA 1984, s 36A(8),[2] to a civil partnership proceedings county court.

---

[1] CPA 2004, Sch 7, para 19.
[2] Inserted by ibid, Sch 27, para 92.

A. BAR TO APPLICATIONS FOR FINANCIAL RELIEF

7.04 An application under Sch 7 to the 2004 Act may be made by either of the civil partners. Paragraph 3 of Sch 7, however, contains an absolute bar on a civil partner making such an application if he/she has entered into a subsequent civil partnership or marriage *prior* to the issue of the application.

B. JURISDICTION OF THE COURTS IN ENGLAND AND WALES TO MAKE ORDERS FOR FINANCIAL RELIEF

7.05 A court in England and Wales has jurisdiction to entertain an application for financial relief following an overseas separation, dissolution or annulment in three situations:[3]

(a) Domicile in England or Wales—if either of the civil partners was:
   (i) domiciled in England or Wales on the date on which the application for leave to pursue a claim under Sch 7 was issued; or
   (ii) was domiciled in England or Wales on the date on which the legal separation, dissolution or annulment took effect overseas.

(b) Habitual residence in England or Wales—if either of the civil partners:
   (i) was habitually resident in England or Wales for the one year period prior to the date on which the application for leave to pursue a claim under Sch 7 was issued; or
   (ii) was habitually resident in England or Wales for the one year period prior to the date on which the legal separation, dissolution or annulment took effect overseas.

(c) Presence of civil partnership home in England or Wales—if, at the date on which the application for leave to pursue a claim under Sch 7 was issued, either or both of the civil partners had a beneficial interest in possession (a beneficial interest in reversion is insufficient) in a dwelling-house situated in England or Wales which has, at some time, been the civil partnership home.

7.06 An application for financial relief under Sch 7 is a two-stage process:

(a) Firstly, there is a filter stage in which the applicant civil partner must obtain the leave of the court to pursue an application under Sch 7. Such leave will only be granted if the court considers that there is a 'substantial ground' for making the application under Sch 7.[4] If the sole purpose of the application is to secure enforcement of a foreign order, the application for leave is likely

---

[3] ibid, Sch 7, para 7.
[4] ibid, Sch 7, para 4.

to fail unless the enforcement remedies of the foreign court (and of the courts of England and Wales) have either been exhausted or are manifestly inadequate.[5] It is anticipated that, by analogy with case law in relation to spouses, applications by civil partners under Sch 7 to the 2004 Act will only be successful if adequate financial provision has plainly not been made by the foreign court or if all enforcement remedies have been exhausted.

(b) Secondly, if leave is granted, there is a substantive stage at which the court must consider whether England and Wales is the appropriate forum and whether it would be appropriate for a court in England and Wales to make the type of order for financial relief for which the civil partner has applied.[6]

In considering the question of forum, the court must have regard to the following factors:[7]   **7.07**

(a) the connection which the civil partners have with England and Wales;

(b) the connection which the civil partners have with the country in which the legal separation, dissolution or annulment was obtained;

(c) the connection which the civil partners have with any other country;

(d) any financial benefit which the applicant civil partner or child of the family has received or is likely to receive as a result of the legal separation, dissolution or annulment under the law of any country outside England and Wales or as a result of any agreement;

(e) the extent to which any financial order made in any other country in favour of a civil partner or child of the family has been or is likely to be complied with;

(f) any right which the applicant civil partner has, or has had, to apply for a financial order in any other country and the reasons for any failure to apply for such relief;

(g) the availability in England and Wales of any property against which orders could be made under Sch 7;

(h) the extent to which any order under Sch 7 is likely to be enforceable;

(i) the length of time which has elapsed since the date of legal separation, dissolution or annulment.

If the court is not satisfied that England and Wales is the appropriate forum, it must dismiss the application under Sch 7.   **7.08**

---

[5] *Jordan v Jordan* [1999] 2 FLR 1069, CA.
[6] CPA 2004, Sch 7, para 8.
[7] ibid, Sch 7, para 8(3).

C. FINANCIAL ORDERS WHICH THE COURT MAY MAKE

7.09 The type of financial order which the court may make depends upon the ground upon which the court has jurisdiction under Sch 7.

1. Orders Where Jurisdiction is Based Upon Domicile or Habitual Residence in England or Wales

7.10 If the court has jurisdiction on the grounds of a civil partner's domicile or habitual residence, it may make the following orders:[8]

(a) if the civil partnership was dissolved or annulled abroad, an order for financial provision (periodical payments, secured periodical payments, lump sum), property adjustment or pension sharing in favour of a civil partner or an order for financial provision or property adjustment in favour of a child of the family or payable to any person for the benefit of such a child;

(b) if the civil partners were legally separated abroad, an order for financial provision or property adjustment in favour of a civil partner, in favour of a child of the family or payable to any person on behalf of such a child;

(c) a sale of property order if the court makes (or has previously made) a secured periodical payments, lump sum or property adjustment order;

(d) a transfer of the tenancy under Sch 7 to the Family Law Act 1996 (as amended by the 2004 Act—see paras 9.03–9.17 below) of a dwelling-house in England or Wales which is or was the civil partnership home and which either or both of the civil partners are entitled to occupy.[9]

2. Orders Where Jurisdiction is Based Upon Civil Partnership Home in England or Wales

7.11 If, however, the sole ground upon which the court has accepted jurisdiction is the presence, in England or Wales, of a civil partnership home, the orders which the court may make are more limited:[10]

(a) a lump sum to a civil partner, to a child of the family or to any person for the benefit of such a child. The maximum quantum of such a lump sum (or sums) is the quantum of the payer civil partner's interest in the net proceeds of sale of the civil partnership home in England or Wales;[11]

(b) a transfer of a civil partner's interest in the civil partnership home in

---

[8] ibid, Sch 7, para 9.
[9] ibid, Sch 7, para 13.
[10] ibid, Sch 7, para 11.
[11] ibid, Sch 7, para 11(3)–(5).

England or Wales to the other civil partner, to a child of the family or to any person for the benefit of such a child;

(c) a settlement of a civil partner's interest in the civil partnership home in England or Wales for the benefit of the other civil partner and/or any child of the family;

(d) a variation, for the benefit of a civil partner and/or any child of the family, of any settlement of the civil partnership home in England or Wales made on the civil partners during the civil partnership or in anticipation of it;

(e) an order extinguishing or reducing the interest of a civil partner under a settlement of the civil partnership home in England or Wales made on the civil partners during the civil partnership or in anticipation of it;

(f) an order for sale of the interest of one of the civil partners in the civil partnership home in England or Wales (including an order for sale where a third party also has a beneficial interest in the home);[12]

(g) a transfer of the tenancy under Sch 7 to the Family Law Act 1996 (as amended by the 2004 Act—see paras 9.03–9.17 below) of a dwelling-house in England or Wales which is or was the civil partnership home and which either or both of the civil partners are entitled to occupy.[13]

3. General Provisions in Relation to Orders for Financial Relief

A number of the provisions of Sch 5 to the 2004 Act (financial relief following **7.12** dissolution etc in England and Wales) are applied to orders for financial relief made under Sch 7 after an overseas dissolution, annulment or legal separation. Specific reference should be made to para 14 of Sch 7 and to the particular provisions in Sch 5 (see Chapter 5). In essence:

(a) a lump sum order may relate to expenses incurred pre-application, may provide for payment in instalments and may provide for security for such instalments;

(b) a third party who has a beneficial interest in a property is entitled to make representations before an order for sale of that property is made;

(c) the same restrictions apply on making a pension sharing order which is already the subject of a pension sharing order between the civil partners or is subject to a pension attachment order which has not yet been implemented;

(d) the court may make pension attachment orders unless the sole ground of jurisdiction is the presence of a civil partnership home in England and Wales, in which case there is no power to make a pension attachment order;

---

[12] ibid, Sch 7, para 11(6)(a).
[13] ibid, Sch 7, para 13.

(e) the same restrictions apply in relation to the commencement and duration of orders for periodical and secured periodical payments in favour of a civil partner (see paras 5.17–5.18 above);

(f) the same restrictions apply in relation to the making and duration of orders for periodical payments, secured periodical payments, lump sum and property adjustment orders in favour of a child of the family (see para 5.12 above);

(g) the court may subsequently vary any order which it makes under Sch 7 in the same way it may vary orders under Sch 5 (see paras 5.101–5.115 above), save that it may not vary a property adjustment order;

(h) the same provisions apply to the enforcement of arrears over 12 months old and to repayments of periodical or secured periodical payments in the event of a change of circumstances or in the event of the payee forming a subsequent civil partnership or marriage (see paras 5.125–5.132 above).

4. Interim Orders

7.13 The court may make an interim order for maintenance to a civil partner or to a child of the family if:[14]

(a) leave to pursue a claim under Sch 7 has been granted; and

(b) the court considers that it has jurisdiction on the grounds either of a civil partner's domicile or a civil partner's habitual residence (there is no jurisdiction to make an interim maintenance order if the sole ground of jurisdiction is the presence of a civil partnership home in England or Wales);[15] and

(c) a civil partner or a child of the family is in need of immediate financial assistance.

7.14 The court may make such order as it 'thinks reasonable' and may back-date the interim maintenance order to the date on which leave to pursue a claim under Sch 7 was granted.[16]

5. Consent Orders

7.15 If the civil partners compromise the claim under Sch 7, they may invite the court to make a consent order in the terms agreed.[17] As with an application for financial relief under Sch 5 (financial relief following dissolution etc in England and Wales), the court has a duty to scrutinize the terms of the draft order (see para 5.116 above).

---

[14] ibid, Sch 7, para 5.
[15] ibid, Sch 7, para 5(4).
[16] ibid, Sch 7, para 5(3).
[17] ibid, Sch 7, para 12.

D. MATTERS TO WHICH THE COURT MUST HAVE REGARD

In exercising its powers to make an order for financial relief under Sch 7, the **7.16** court must have regard to all the circumstances of the case and must give first consideration to the welfare, whilst a minor, of any child of the family who has not attained the age of 18.[18]

1. Orders in Favour of Civil Partners: Relevant Factors

In exercising its powers to make an order for financial relief under Sch 7 in **7.17** favour of a civil partner, the court must:[19]

(a) have regard to the same factors to which it is required to have regard when making an order in favour of a civil partner under Sch 5 (financial relief after dissolution etc in England and Wales) (see para 5.78 above); and

(b) consider whether to impose a clean break (see paras 5.82–5.85 above); and

(c) if an overseas order has been made requiring payments to be made or property to be transferred, consider the extent to which that order has been or is likely to be complied with.[20]

2. Orders in Favour of Children of the Family: Relevant Factors

In exercising its powers to make an order for financial relief under Sch 7 in **7.18** favour of a child of the family, the court must:[21]

(a) have regard to the same factors to which it is required to have regard when making an order in favour of a child of the family under Sch 5 (financial relief after dissolution etc in England and Wales) (see paras 5.80 and 5.81 above); and

(b) if an overseas order has been made requiring payments to be made or property to be transferred, consider the extent to which that order has been or is likely to be complied with.[22]

---

[18] ibid, Sch 7, para 10(2).
[19] ibid, Sch 7, para 10(3).
[20] ibid, Sch 7, para 10(8).
[21] ibid, Sch 7, para 10(6) & (7).
[22] ibid, Sch 7, para 10(8).

E. ORDERS RESTRAINING AND SETTING
ASIDE DISPOSITIONS

7.19 Paragraph 15 of Sch 7 to the 2004 Act enables the court to make freezing orders and to set aside dispositions if a civil partner has an intention to defeat the other's claim for financial relief under Sch 7.

7.20 The provisions are identical to those which apply in relation to applications under Sch 5 (financial relief after dissolution etc in England and Wales) (see paras 5.133–5.141 above). The only difference is that, if the sole basis of the court's jurisdiction under Sch 7 is the presence of a civil partnership home in England or Wales, the court's powers are limited to making freezing and setting aside orders in relation to that civil partnership home.[23]

7.21 Paragraph 17 of Sch 7 makes special provision for those cases in which a civil partner intends to apply for financial relief under Sch 7 on the grounds of his/her habitual residence in England and Wales for one year; but has not yet been habitually resident in England and Wales for the full year. In such circumstances, the civil partner may apply for a freezing order if the other civil partner is about to make any disposition or transfer out of the jurisdiction or otherwise deal with any property with the intention of defeating the future claim.

---

[23] ibid, Sch 7, para 15(5).

8

WILLS, ADMINISTRATION OF ESTATES AND FAMILY PROVISION

A. REVOCATION OF WILLS UPON FORMATION OF A CIVIL PARTNERSHIP

Schedule 4 to the 2004 Act amends the Wills Act 1837 to ensure that the effect of the formation of a civil partnership upon the wills of civil partners mirrors the effect of a marriage upon spouses' wills.   **8.01**

Thus, upon formation of a civil partnership, the will of a civil partner (and the dispositions therein) are automatically revoked unless it appears from the will:[1]   **8.02**

(a) that the testator was, at the date of the will, intending to form a civil partnership with a particular individual; and

(b) that the testator intended that the will (or a particular disposition therein) should not be revoked by the formation of the civil partnership.

The formation of a civil partnership does not, however, revoke a disposition in exercise of a power of appointment unless the property would, in default of appointment, have passed to the personal representatives.[2]   **8.03**

---

[1] Wills Act 1837, s 18B as inserted by CPA 2004, Sch 4, paras 1 & 2.
[2] Wills Act 1837, s 18B(2) as inserted by CPA 2004, Sch 4, para 2.

B. EFFECT OF DISSOLUTION AND ANNULMENT ORDERS UPON WILLS

8.04 Schedule 4 to the 2004 Act amends the Wills Act 1837 to ensure that the effect of the dissolution or annulment of a civil partnership upon the wills of civil partners mirrors the effect of the dissolution or annulment of a marriage upon spouses' wills.

8.05 The dissolution or annulment of a civil partnership (whether by an order in England or Wales or by an overseas order which is recognized in England and Wales) has the following effects upon the will of a civil partner:[3]

(a) any provision in the will which appoints the testator's former civil partner as an executor or trustee or which confers a power of appointment upon the former civil partner will be ineffective unless it appears from the will that the testator intended the appointment/power to endure beyond the dissolution or annulment;

(b) any bequest by the testator to the former civil partner takes effect as though the former civil partner were dead unless it appears from the will that the testator intended otherwise.

C. INTESTACY

8.06 Schedule 4 to the 2004 Act makes various amendments to the Administration of Estates Act 1925 to ensure that civil partners receive the same treatment as spouses under the rules of intestacy.

8.07 Thus, for UK domiciled civil partners who die intestate (or partially intestate)[4] leaving a surviving civil partner:

(a) If the deceased civil partner had no issue,[5] no siblings[6] and no surviving parents, the surviving civil partner will receive the entirety of the estate.

(b) If the deceased civil partner had issue, the surviving civil partner will receive:
   (i)   a fixed sum of £125,000 plus interest;[7]
   (ii) the deceased's personal chattels;
   (iii) a life interest in 50 per cent of the residue (which may be capitalized).[8]

---

[3] Wills Act 1837, s 18C as inserted by CPA 2004, Sch 4, paras 1 & 2.

[4] The rules apply to any property not disposed of by a will: Administration of Estates Act 1925, s 49(1).

[5] Children, grandchildren, great-grandchildren etc (whether adopted or otherwise) including children en ventre sa mere at the date of death.

[6] Brothers and sisters of the whole blood.

[7] Interest at 6% pa from date of death: Intestate Succession (Interest and Capitalization) Order 1977 (Amendment) Order 1983, SI 1983/1374.

[8] Administration of Estates Act 1925, s 47A as amended by CPA 2004, Sch 4, para 7.

The deceased's issue will receive the other 50 per cent of the residue and the remainder in the life interest of the surviving civil partner. The share of a deceased child passes to his/her issue.

(c) If the deceased civil partner had no issue but had surviving parent(s), the surviving civil partner will receive:

(i) a fixed sum of £200,000 plus interest;
(ii) the deceased's personal chattels;
(iii) 50 per cent of the residue.

The deceased's surviving parent(s) will receive the other 50 per cent of the residue.

(d) If the deceased civil partner had no issue, no surviving parent(s) but had siblings, the surviving civil partner will receive:

(i) a fixed sum of £200,000 plus interest;
(ii) the deceased's personal chattels;
(iii) 50 per cent of the residue.

The deceased's siblings will receive the other 50 per cent of the residue. The share of a deceased sibling passes to his/her issue.

8.08 A surviving civil partner must survive the deceased by 28 days in order to receive under the above rules.[9]

8.09 Under the lex situs, the same rules apply to immovable property in England and Wales owned by non-UK domiciled civil partners who die intestate.

8.10 The rules of intestacy do not apply to a civil partnership home (or to the home of a cohabiting same sex couple) which is held on a joint tenancy since the legal (and beneficial) title will automatically pass to the surviving civil partner (or surviving same sex partner) under the right of survivorship.

8.11 If a civil partnership home was owned solely by the deceased civil partner, the surviving civil partner has the right (provided he/she was resident in the home at the date of death) to require the personal representatives to appropriate that home for the survivor in satisfaction of his/her absolute interest in the estate[10] (with the survivor paying a balancing sum to the personal representatives, if necessary).[11]

8.12 If a separation order has been made in relation to the civil partnership and the separation is continuing at the date of death, the surviving civil partner is not entitled to receive any part of the estate under the rules of intestacy; the estate devolves as though the surviving civil partner were also dead.[12]

8.13 As with cohabiting opposite sex couples, cohabiting same sex couples who have not registered as civil partners are not recognized under the rules of intestacy.

---

[9] Administration of Estates Act 1925, s 46(2A) as amended by CPA 2004, Sch 4, para 7.
[10] Intestates Act 1952, s 5, Sch 2 as amended by CPA 2004, Sch 4, para 13.
[11] *Re Phelps* [1980] Ch 275.
[12] CPA 2004, s 57.

D. APPLICATIONS FOR FAMILY PROVISION

1. Categories of Applicant

8.14 The Inheritance (Provision for Family and Dependants) Act 1975 ('the IPFDA 1975') enables certain categories of applicant to make applications for financial provision against a deceased's estate if the deceased's will (or the rules of intestacy) did not make reasonable financial provision for the applicant.

8.15 The court only has jurisdiction to entertain a claim under the IPFDA 1975 if the deceased was domiciled in England or Wales at the date of death.[13]

8.16 Prior to the 2004 Act, the ability of a same sex partner to make a claim against a deceased partner's estate under the IPFDA 1975 was very limited. In order to mount a claim, a same sex partner had to demonstrate that the deceased partner wholly or partly maintained him/her by making a substantial contribution towards his/her reasonable needs immediately prior to the deceased's death.[14]

8.17 Schedule 4 to the 2004 Act makes various amendments to the IPFDA 1975 which will enable:

(a) civil partners to make claims under the IPFDA 1975 on the same basis as married couples;[15]

(b) former civil partners who have not entered into a subsequent civil partnership or marriage to make claims under the IPFDA 1975 on the same basis as former spouses who have not entered into a subsequent civil partnership or marriage;[16]

(c) same sex partners who have not registered as civil partners to make claims under the IPFDA 1975 on the same basis as unmarried opposite sex couples (ie if the same sex partners have lived together in the same household as if they were civil partners for a two year period prior to the deceased's death);[17]

(d) any person who is not a child of the deceased civil partner, but who was, at any time, treated as a child of the civil partnership (ie a minor or adult child), to make claims under the IPFDA 1975 on the same basis as persons who have been treated as children of the family of married couples.[18]

8.18 The IPFDA 1975 draws an important distinction between claims made by civil partners and claims made by former civil partners (see para 8.21 below). A former civil partner who has not entered into a subsequent civil partnership or

---

[13] IPFDA 1975, s 1(1).
[14] ibid, s 1(1)(e) & (3).
[15] ibid, s 1(1)(a) as amended by CPA 2004, Sch 4, para 15(2).
[16] ibid, s 1(1)(b) as amended by CPA 2004, Sch 4, para 15(2).
[17] ibid, s 1(1B) as inserted by CPA 2004, Sch 4, para 15(5).
[18] ibid, s 1(1)(d) as amended by CPA 2004, Sch 4, para 15(4).

marriage may nevertheless be treated as an existing civil partner rather than a former civil partner for the purposes of the IPFDA 1975 if:[19]

(a) the separation order, final dissolution or final nullity order was made within 12 months of the deceased's death; and

(b) an application for financial relief under the 2004 Act had not been made by the surviving civil partner, or such an application had been made but had not been determined by the date of the deceased's death; and

(c) the court considers it just to treat the civil partnership as continuing.

2. 'Reasonable Financial Provision'

An application against the deceased's estate may be made on only one ground: **8.19** that the deceased's will or, if there was no will, the rules of intestacy did not make reasonable financial provision for the applicant.

The court must therefore consider: **8.20**

(a) whether reasonable financial provision has been made for the applicant (if the court concludes that reasonable financial provision has been made, it has no jurisdiction to interfere with the deceased's will or with the rules of intestacy);

(b) if reasonable financial provision has not been made, the financial provision which ought now to be made for the applicant.

The term 'reasonable financial provision' bears a different meaning in relation to **8.21** civil partners than it does in relation to former civil partners, civil partners who are separated under a separation order, unregistered same sex partners and children of the civil partnership:

(a) in relation to civil partners, 'reasonable financial provision' means such provision as it would be reasonable for a civil partner to receive by way of *capital and maintenance*;[20]

(b) in relation to former civil partners, former civil partners who are separated under a separation order, unregistered same sex partners and children of the civil partnership, 'reasonable financial provision' means such provision as it would be reasonable for the applicant to receive solely for his/her *maintenance*.[21]

The court's ability to treat former civil partners as subsisting civil partners **8.22** pursuant to the IPFDA 1975, s 14A and thereby consider whether reasonable

---

[19] ibid, s 14A as inserted by CPA 2004, Sch 4, para 20.
[20] ibid, s 1(2)(aa) as inserted by CPA 2004, Sch 4, para 15(6).
[21] ibid, s 1(2)(b).

capital provision (and not merely maintenance provision) has been made is therefore important and should not be overlooked. (See para 8.18 above.)

8.23   If former civil partners have compromised their financial claims against each other prior to the deceased's death, it will be rare for the court to conclude that 'reasonable financial provision' has not been made (unless the compromise provided for continuing dependency, eg a joint lives periodical payments order).[22]

3. 'Reasonable Financial Provision' for Civil Partners, Former Civil Partners and Same Sex Partners

8.24   In deciding whether reasonable financial provision has been made by the deceased for a civil partner, former civil partner or same sex partner, and, if it has not been made, in deciding what order to make, the court is required to have regard to the following criteria:[23]

(a) the financial resources and financial needs which the applicant has or is likely to have in the foreseeable future;

- The standard of living enjoyed by the applicant during the civil partnership/relationship and the extent to which the deceased contributed to that standard will be a relevant factor in determining the applicant's 'financial needs'.[24]

(b) the financial resources and financial needs which any other competing applicant has or is likely to have in the foreseeable future;

(c) the financial resources and financial needs which any beneficiary of the estate has or is likely to have in the foreseeable future;

(d) any obligations and responsibilities which the deceased had towards the applicant or competing applicant or towards any beneficiary of the estate;

- 'Obligations' includes moral obligations and is not limited to purely legal obligations.[25]

(e) the size and nature of the net estate;

- 'Net estate' is defined in IPFDA 1975, ss 8 and 25(1).
- Foreign property may be taken into account in deciding whether reasonable financial provision has been made for the applicant, but the court may not have any power to make an order affecting the foreign property.[26]
- The court has a broad discretion to treat any property (real or personal) which was held on a joint tenancy prior to the deceased's death and which

---

[22] *Fullard (Dec'd), Re, Fullard v King* [1982] Fam 42, CA.
[23] IPFDA 1975, s 3(1), (2) & (2A) as amended by CPA 2004, Sch 4, paras 17 & 18.
[24] *Harrington v Gill* [1983] 4 FLR 265, CA.
[25] *Espinosa v Bourke* [1999] 1 FLR 747, CA.
[26] *Bheekhun v Williams* [1999] 2 FLR 229, CA.

would otherwise pass under the right of survivorship outside the estate, to be treated as forming part of the deceased's estate. The application must, however, be made within a six month period (which cannot be extended) of the date on which representation was taken out in relation to the estate.[27]

(f) any physical or mental disability of the applicant or competing applicant or of any beneficiary of the estate;

(g) any other matter, including the conduct of the applicant or any other person;

- The testator's express reasons for rejecting an applicant may be a relevant consideration.[28]

(h) the age of the applicant and the duration of the civil partnership or the length of time during which the applicant and deceased lived together as though they were civil partners;

(i) the contribution made by the applicant to the welfare of the family of the deceased, including any contribution in looking after the home or caring for the family.

The above factors must be considered as at the date of the hearing of the application.[29] **8.25**

In relation to claims by civil partners,[30] the court must additionally have regard to the financial relief which would have been made for the applicant under the 2004 Act if the civil partnership had been terminated by a final dissolution order instead of the deceased's death.[31] **8.26**

4. 'Reasonable Financial Provision' for Children of the Civil Partnership

In deciding whether 'reasonable financial provision' has been made for a minor or adult child of the civil partnership, and, if it has not been made, in deciding what order to make, the court is required to have regard to the following criteria:[32] **8.27**

(a) the criteria listed at (a) to (g) in para 8.24 above;

(b) the manner in which the applicant was being or expected to be educated or trained;

(c) whether the deceased civil partner had assumed any responsibility for the applicant's maintenance, the extent and basis of any such assumption of responsibility and the period for which it had been assumed;

---

[27] IPFDA 1975, s 9.

[28] *Re Coventry* [1980] Ch 461, CA.

[29] IPFDA 1975, s 3(5).

[30] Excluding civil partners separated under a separation order at the date of the deceased's death.

[31] IPFDA 1975, s 3(2) as amended by CPA 2004, Sch 4, para 17(5). See Chapter 5 for financial orders in the event of dissolution.

[32] IPFDA 1975, s 3(3).

(d) whether the deceased civil partner was aware that the child was not his own child (a factor which could only be relevant in change of gender cases);

(e) the liability of any other person to maintain the applicant.

5. Orders which the Court may Make

8.28 If the court decides that 'reasonable financial provision' has not been made, it may make any of the following orders against the estate:[33]

(a) a periodical payments order for such term as may be specified;
- The order may provide for a property or lump sum to be set aside for the purposes of generating an income to satisfy the periodical payments order.[34]
- A periodical payments order may subsequently be varied, discharged, suspended or revived. The court has the power, on such an application, to order the payment of a lump sum or order the transfer of the property which wholly or partly generates the periodical payments (ie an order for capitalization of the periodical payments).[35]
- The court also has the power to extend a term order for periodical payments even after the term has expired provided the application for an extension is made within six months of the term ending.[36]

(b) a lump sum order;
- The court may order the lump sum to be paid in instalments which may later be varied as to quantum, timing and number.[37]

(c) a transfer of property order;

(d) a settlement of property order;

(e) an order for property to be acquired and either transferred to or settled upon the applicant;

(f) an order for the variation of any settlement made on the civil partners during the civil partnership or in anticipation of it;

(g) an order varying, discharging or reviving any order for secured periodical payments made during a deceased civil partner's lifetime under the 2004 Act, Sch 5;[38]

(h) an order varying or revoking any maintenance agreement entered into

---

[33] ibid, s 2(1) as amended by CPA 2004, Sch 4, para 16.
[34] ibid, s 2(3).
[35] ibid, s 6(2)(b), (c) & (6).
[36] ibid, s 6(3).
[37] ibid, s 7.
[38] ibid, s 16 as amended by CPA 2004, Sch 4, para 23.

during a deceased civil partner's lifetime which provided for continuation of payments after death.[39]

The court has the power to order interim lump sums or interim periodical payments where the applicant is in immediate need of financial assistance. Such interim provision may (or may not) be treated as payment on account of any final entitlement under the IPFDA 1975.[40]   **8.29**

The court has wide-ranging powers to set aside any disposition made by the deceased within six years of death and to set aside any contract to leave property by will which was made with the intention of defeating the applicant's claims under the IPFDA 1975.[41]   **8.30**

6. Time Limit on Applications under the IPFDA 1975

It is important to note that an application under the IPFDA 1975 must be made within six months from the date on which the representation in relation to the deceased's estate was taken out.[42]   **8.31**

The court has a discretion to extend this time limit. The IPFDA 1975 gives no guidance as to the circumstances in which the court's discretion should be exercised. In general terms, the court will consider all of the circumstances and will consider whether it is in the interests of justice to allow an extension of time. A check-list of relevant factors has been judicially formulated:[43]   **8.32**

(a) the circumstances in which and how promptly the applicant has sought leave after the time limit has expired, the reasons for the delay and the promptitude of any letter before action or other warning to the proposed defendants;

(b) whether negotiations have been commenced within the time limit;

(c) whether or not the estate has been distributed and whether beneficiaries have changed their position in reliance upon the distribution;

(d) whether the applicant has a negligence claim against his/her solicitors.

The burden is on the applicant to show a 'substantial case' for extending the time limit. Applicants should not assume that the discretion will be exercised readily.

---

[39] ibid, s 17 as amended by CPA 2004, Sch 4, para 24. A maintenance agreement need not be in writing but must be an agreement governing rights and liabilities towards each other (and to any child of the civil partnership) whilst separated (whether by virtue of an order or not).

[40] ibid, s 5.

[41] ibid, ss 10–13.

[42] ibid, s 4.

[43] *Re Salmon (Dec'd); Coard v National Westminster Bank* [1981] Ch 167.

7. Barring Applications under the IPFDA 1975

8.33   The court has the power, if it considers it just to do so, to prevent a former civil partner from making a claim against the estate of the other former partner by making an order pursuant to the IPFDA 1975, s 15ZA.[44]

8.34   Such an order may be made upon the making of a conditional dissolution, conditional nullity order or conditional presumption of death order; but is not effective until such an order is made final.

8.35   Such an order may also be made upon the making of a separation order, but is not effective to bar a surviving civil partner's claims under the IPFDA 1975 if the civil partners have resumed living together at the date of the deceased's death.[45]

8.36   The court has similar powers to bar applications under the IPFDA 1975 upon making orders for financial provision, property adjustment and pension sharing following an overseas dissolution, nullity or separation order in relation to the civil partnership.[46]

8.37   It is expected that orders pursuant to the IPFDA 1975, s 15ZA will be routinely made in financial orders containing clean breaks[47] between civil partners in the same way in which they are routinely made under the IPFDA 1975, s 15 in ancillary relief orders containing clean breaks between spouses.

E. LIFE ASSURANCE POLICIES

8.38   Section 70 of the 2004 Act mirrors the Married Women's Property Act 1882, s 11. Thus, the proceeds of a policy of assurance effected on the life of a male (but not female) civil partner and expressed to be for the benefit of his civil partner and/or his children belong to his civil partner and/or his children.

8.39   The policy is, however, capable of being varied pursuant to para 7(1)(c) of Sch 5 to the 2004 Act (property adjustment order) and care should be taken to include such a variation in any order for financial relief if the male civil partner wishes to retain the proceeds of the policy.

8.40   Civil partners are presumed to have unlimited insurable interests in each other's lives under the Life Assurance Act 1774, s 1.[48]

---

[44] Inserted by CPA 2004, Sch 4, para 21.
[45] IPFDA 1975, s 15ZA(5) as inserted by CPA 2004, Sch 4, para 21.
[46] ibid, s 15B as inserted by CPA 2004, Sch 4, para 22.
[47] See Chapter 5 for financial orders and clean breaks.
[48] CPA 2004, s 253.

F. FATAL ACCIDENT CLAIMS

1. Categories of Dependant

Prior to the 2004 Act, a same sex partner had no right to compensation under **8.41** the Fatal Accidents Act 1976 ('the FAA 1976') following the death of the other partner if caused by the wrongful act, neglect or default of a third party.

Section 83 of the 2004 Act makes various amendments to the FAA 1976 to **8.42** ensure that civil partners are treated in the same way as spouses and that same sex couples who do not register as civil partners are treated in the same way as cohabiting opposite sex couples.

Those amendments will enable damages to be paid to the following new **8.43** categories of dependant:

(a) civil partners or former civil partners (whether the civil partnership has been dissolved or annulled);[49]

(b) same sex partners who have not registered as civil partners provided:
  (i) the survivor was living with the deceased in the same household at the date of death; and
  (ii) had been living with the deceased in the same household, as if they were civil partners, for at least two years prior to death.[50]

(c) any person who was not a child of the deceased; but who was, at any time, treated as a child of the civil partnership (ie a minor or adult child).[51]

The claim will ordinarily be made on behalf of the above dependants by the **8.44** executors or administrators of the deceased,[52] but may be brought by the dependants themselves in certain circumstances. An application under the FAA 1976 must be brought within three years of the date of death or within three years of the 'date of knowledge' of the dependant.[53] The court has the power to extend this time limit.[54]

Damages payable under the FAA 1976 fall into three categories: **8.45**

(a) Damages for bereavement. A civil partner, like a spouse, will be entitled to claim damages for bereavement (currently £10,000).[55] Cohabiting same sex partners and children of the family have no claim for damages for bereavement.

---

[49] FAA 1976, s 1(3)(aa) & (4A) as inserted by CPA 2004, s 83(2) & (5).
[50] FAA 1976, s 1(3)(b) as amended by CPA 2004, s 83(3).
[51] FAA 1976, s 1(3)(fa) as inserted by CPA 2004, s 83(4).
[52] FAA 1976, s 2.
[53] Limitation Act 1980, s 12.
[54] ibid, s 33.
[55] FAA 1976, s 1A(2) as amended by CPA 2004, s 83(7). Damages for Bereavement (Variation of Sum) (England and Wales) Order 2002, SI 2002/644.

(b) Damages caused to the dependant as a result of the death.[56] In assessing the damages payable to a same sex partner (rather than civil partner), the court must take into account the fact that the survivor had no enforceable right to financial support by the deceased.[57]

(c) Funeral expenses, if paid by the dependant.[58]

---

[56] FAA 1976, s 3.
[57] ibid, s 3(4) as amended by CPA 2004, s 83(8).
[58] ibid, s 3(5).

9

HOUSING AND TENANCIES

A. SUCCESSION TO TENANCIES

Schedule 8 to the 2004 Act makes amendments to a wide variety of statutes **9.01** relating to housing and tenancies to ensure that there is equality of treatment between spouses and civil partners and between unmarried opposite sex couples and unregistered same sex partners. The amendments also ensure equality of treatment for the children of such individuals. The amendments relate to a variety of matters such as the grounds for possession, succession to tenancies and right to buy schemes.

A detailed consideration of these amendments is beyond the scope of this **9.02** Guide. Some of the key changes which are made by the 2004 Act are:

(a) **Leasehold Reform Act 1967**: a civil partner will be entitled to succeed to a long leasehold upon the death of the other civil partner in the same way as a surviving spouse is entitled to succeed;[1]

(b) **Rent (Agriculture) Act 1976**: a surviving civil partner will be entitled to succeed to protected and statutory tenancies of agricultural land in the same way as a surviving spouse. An unregistered same sex partner will also be entitled to succeed to a statutory tenancy of agricultural land in the same way as an unmarried opposite sex partner;[2]

(c) **Rent Act 1977**: a surviving civil partner or unregistered same sex partner will be entitled to succeed to a statutory tenancy in the same way as a surviving spouse or unmarried opposite sex partner;[3]

(d) **Housing Act 1985**: a surviving civil partner will be entitled to succeed to a

---

[1] CPA 2004, Sch 8, para 6.
[2] ibid, Sch 8, paras 9 & 10.
[3] ibid, Sch 8, para 13.

secure tenancy in the same way as a surviving spouse. An unregistered same sex partner will also be entitled to succeed to a secure tenancy (in the same way as an unmarried opposite sex partner) provided he/she lived with the deceased as if they were civil partners for 12 months prior to the deceased's death.[4]

Civil partners will also be treated in the same way as spouses for the purposes of the 'right to buy' and 'rent to mortgage' schemes.[5]

(e) **Agricultural Holdings Act 1986**: a civil partner will be eligible to apply, in the same way as a spouse, for a new tenancy on the death or retirement of the other civil partner provided the applicant civil partner derived his/her livelihood from agricultural work on the holding for five out of the seven years prior to the death or retirement;[6]

(f) **Housing Act 1988**: a surviving civil partner or unregistered same sex partner will be entitled to succeed to an assured tenancy in the same way as a surviving spouse or unmarried opposite sex partner;[7]

(g) **Housing Act 1996**: a surviving civil partner will be entitled to succeed to an introductory tenancy in the same way as a surviving spouse. A surviving unregistered same sex partner will also be entitled to succeed (in the same way as an unmarried opposite sex partner) to an introductory tenancy provided he/she resided in the property for the 12 months prior to the deceased's death.

A surviving civil partner or unregistered same sex partner will be entitled to succeed (in the same way as a spouse or unmarried opposite sex partner) to a demoted tenancy provided he/she resided in the property for 12 months prior to the deceased's death and the property was his/her principal home at the date of death.

B. TRANSFER OF TENANCIES

9.03 The 2004 Act makes various amendments to Sch 7 to the Family Law Act 1996 ('the FLA 1996') which will enable civil partners (but not former civil partners) to apply for the transfer of the tenancy of the civil partnership home if that tenancy is:

(a) a protected or statutory tenancy under the Rent Act 1977;

(b) a statutory tenancy under the Rent (Agriculture) Act 1976;

(c) a secure tenancy under the Housing Act 1985, s 79;

---

[4] ibid, Sch 8, para 20.
[5] ibid, Sch 8, para 28.
[6] ibid, Sch 8, paras 37 & 38.
[7] ibid, Sch 8, para 41.

(d) an assured tenancy or assured agricultural occupancy under the Housing Act 1988, Pt I; or

(e) an introductory tenancy under the Housing Act 1996, Pt V, Ch 1.

1. Transfer of Tenancies to Civil Partners

The tenancy must relate to a dwelling-house[8] which is or was the civil partner- **9.04** ship home.[9] It is not sufficient that the dwelling-house was merely intended to be the civil partnership home.

The jurisdiction to transfer a tenancy of the civil partnership home arises **9.05** whether the tenancy is held by one of the civil partners or jointly by both civil partners. The court does not, however, have the jurisdiction to order the transfer of a tenancy which is held jointly by a civil partner and a third party.[10]

The court may transfer a tenancy to a civil partner at any time when it has the **9.06** power to make a property adjustment order in relation to the civil partnership (ie after a separation order or a conditional dissolution or conditional nullity order has been made).[11]

In the case of dissolution or nullity proceedings, the order for transfer of a **9.07** tenancy cannot take effect until a final dissolution or final nullity order has been made.[12]

The court has no jurisdiction to order the transfer of a tenancy of the civil **9.08** partnership home if *either* of the civil partners (and not merely the applicant) has entered into a subsequent civil partnership or has married.[13]

In deciding whether to transfer a tenancy of the civil partnership home, the **9.09** court must have regard to all the circumstances including:[14]

(a) the circumstances in which the tenancy was granted to either or both of the civil partners or the circumstances in which either or both of them became tenant under the tenancy (eg by succession);

(b) the housing needs and housing resources of each of the civil partners and of any relevant child;

(c) the financial resources of each of the civil partners;

(d) the likely effect of any transfer, or of any decision not to transfer the tenancy, upon the health, safety or well-being of the civil partners and of any relevant child;

---

[8] The definition excludes a caravan or houseboat: FLA 1996, s 63(4).
[9] ibid 1996, Sch 7, para 4(aa) as amended by CPA 2004, Sch 9, para 16(7).
[10] *Gay v Sheeran* [1999] 2 FLR 519.
[11] FLA 1996, Sch 7, para 2(2) as amended by CPA 2004, Sch 9, para 16(4). See Chapter 5 for property adjustment orders.
[12] ibid, Sch 7, para 12 as amended by CPA 2004, Sch 9, para 16(17).
[13] ibid, Sch 7, para 13 as amended by CPA 2004, Sch 9, para 16(18).
[14] ibid, Sch 7, para 5 as amended by CPA 2004, Sch 9, para 16(6).

(e) the suitability of the civil partners as tenants.

9.10 'Relevant child' is given a wide definition[15] and extends to any child who is living with or might reasonably be expected to live with either civil partner and any other child whose interests the court considers relevant.

9.11 An application for a transfer of tenancy must be served on the landlord of the civil partnership home who is entitled to be heard on the application.[16]

9.12 Upon a transfer of tenancy order being made, the transferor civil partner steps into the shoes of the transferee civil partner. Thus:

(a) the transferee is subject to all the same covenants, obligations, liabilities and encumbrances as the transferor was subject;[17]

(b) if the transferor was a successor under the Rent (Agriculture) Act 1976, the Housing Act 1985, Pt IV, the Housing Act 1996, s 132 or the Housing Act 1988, s 17, the transferee is also deemed to be a successor;[18]

(c) if the tenancy was a statutory tenancy under the Rent Act 1977, the rights of third parties to succeed to the transferred tenancy or to retain possession of the property upon the transferee's death will depend upon whether previous third parties (or the transferor) have already exercised those rights prior to transfer.[19]

9.13 Upon transferring a tenancy of the civil partnership home, the court may order the transferee civil partner to pay compensation to the transferor civil partner.[20] In deciding whether to make a compensation order, the court must have regard to all the circumstances including:[21]

(a) the financial loss that would otherwise be suffered by the transferor civil partner as a result of the order;

(b) the financial needs and financial resources of the civil partners;

(c) the financial obligations which the civil partners have, or are likely to have in the foreseeable future, including financial obligations to each other and to any relevant child.

9.14 The court may order the compensation payment to be deferred or paid in instalments if it considers that immediate payment would cause financial hardship to the transferee which is greater than any financial hardship to the transferor if the payment is made in instalments or deferred.[22]

9.15 In addition, the court may order that both civil partners should be jointly and

---

[15] ibid, s 62(2).
[16] ibid, Sch 7, para 14; Family Proceedings Rules 1991, SI 1991/1247, r 3.8(12).
[17] ibid, Sch 7, para 7(1) & (2) as amended by CPA 2004, Sch 9, para 16(8).
[18] ibid, Sch 7, paras 7(3), (3A), (4) and 9 as amended by CPA 2004, Sch 9, para 16(9) & (14).
[19] ibid, Sch 7, para (8) as amended by CPA 2004, Sch 9, para 16(12) & (13).
[20] ibid, Sch 7, para 10 as amended by CPA 2004, Sch 9, para 16(4).
[21] ibid, Sch 7, para 10(4).
[22] ibid, Sch 7, para 10(5).

severally liable to discharge or perform any obligations in respect of the civil partnership home (whether arising as a result of the tenancy or otherwise) which are due to be discharged or performed by only one of the civil partners prior to the date on which the transfer of tenancy order takes effect or which should already have been discharged or performed prior to the order having been made.[23]

The court may also order either civil partner to indemnify the other (either **9.16** wholly or partly) against any payment made or expenses incurred in discharging or performing liabilities or obligations which have already arisen prior to the order for transfer or which will arise prior to the order taking effect.

A contractual tenancy (but not a statutory tenancy) is 'property' which may **9.17** be transferred by a property adjustment order pursuant to Sch 5, para 7(1)(a). The court therefore has dual powers to order the transfer of a contractual tenancy of the civil partnership home under the FLA 1996, Sch 7 and under the 2004 Act Sch 5, para 7. There are, however, important differences between the respective powers:

(a) Statutory tenancies are not 'property' and cannot be transferred by way of property adjustment orders;[24] an application for transfer must be made under the FLA 1996.

(b) Only the tenancy of a dwelling-house which is or was the civil partnership home may be transferred under the FLA 1996, whereas the contractual tenancy of any property may be transferred by way of a property adjustment order.

(c) A transfer of tenancy by way of a property adjustment order requires the civil partners to execute an assignment, whereas a transfer pursuant to the FLA 1996 is effected by the order itself without the need for any assignment. If a contractual tenancy contains a covenant against assignment the application should therefore be made under the FLA 1996.[25]

(d) The factors which the court must consider in ordering a transfer of tenancy by way of property adjustment differ from the more limited factors which it must consider in ordering a transfer under the FLA 1996.

2. Transfer of Tenancies to Unregistered Same Sex Partners

Although the 2004 Act redefines 'cohabitants' to include unregistered same sex **9.18** partners who are living together as if they were civil partners,[26] it does not

---

[23] ibid, Sch 7, para 11 as amended by CPA 2004, Sch 9, para 16(15) & (16).

[24] *Newlon Housing Trust v Alsulaimen* [1999] 1 AC 313, HL.

[25] A covenant against assignment in a secured tenancy is not breached by a property adjustment order (Housing Act 1985, s 91(3)(b)(iv) as amended by CPA 2004, Sch 8, para 24) nor is a covenant against assignment in an introductory tenancy (Housing Act 1996, s 134 as amended by CPA 2004, Sch 8, para 54).

[26] FLA 1996, s 62(1) as amended by CPA 2004, Sch 9, para 13(2).

appear that such partners are able to apply for transfers of tenancies under Sch 7 to the FLA 1996 in the same way that opposite sex cohabitees may apply.

9.19 Pursuant to the FLA 1996, Sch 7, para 3(2), the court may only make a transfer of tenancy order if 'the cohabitants cease to live together as husband and wife'. The 2004 Act neglects to amend the reference to 'husband and wife'. This appears to be an oversight. If, however, the courts adopt a purposive interpretation of para 3(2) as they are required to do by the Human Rights Act 1998, s 3,[27] unregistered same sex partners ought to be able to apply for transfers of tenancies in the same way as unmarried opposite sex couples.

---

[27] *Ghaidan v Godin-Mendoza* [2004] UKHL 30, [2004] 2 FLR 600, HL.

10

CHILDREN OF CIVIL PARTNERS

A. PARENTAL RESPONSIBILITY

A civil partner is able to gain parental responsibility for a child either through   **10.01**
agreement or by order of the court. The 2004 Act grants the same rights to a
civil partner in this respect as are granted to a step-parent who marries a parent.[1]

In determining an application for parental responsibility, the child's welfare is   **10.02**
the paramount consideration. The court will also consider the degree of commitment the applicant has shown to the child, the degree of attachment between
the applicant and the child and the reasons why the applicant is applying.[2]

B. GUARDIANSHIP

Sections 5 and 6 of the Children Act 1989 deal with the appointment of a   **10.03**
guardian by a parent of a child with parental responsibility. Where the
appointed guardian is the spouse of the parent with parental responsibility, the
appointment is automatically revoked, unless the document giving effect to
the appointment states to the contrary, by dissolution or annulment of the
marriage. The 2004 Act amends the Children Act 1989, s 6 to provide that
where the appointed guardian is the civil partner of the parent with parental
responsibility, the appointment will also be automatically revoked, unless the

---

[1] Children Act 1989, s 4A(1) as amended by CPA 2004, s 75(2).
[2] *Re H (Parental Responsibility)* [1998] 1 FLR 855, CA.

appointment document states to the contrary, on the dissolution or annulment of the civil partnership.[3]

C. RESIDENCE AND CONTACT ORDERS

10.04   A civil partner is entitled, without permission of the court and whether or not the civil partnership is subsisting, to apply for a contact or residence order in respect of a child of the family.[4]

10.05   The definition of 'child of the family', which appears in the Children Act 1989, s 105(1), is widened by the 2004 Act to include a child who has been treated by both of the parties to a civil partnership as a child of the family.[5]

10.06   As the text of the Children Act 1989, s 105 suggests, the test of 'child of the family' is an objective one based on all the evidence.[6]

D. FINANCIAL PROVISION FOR CHILDREN

10.07   For the purposes of financial claims for a child pursuant to Sch 1 to the Children Act 1989, the 2004 Act extends the meaning of 'parent' to include any civil partner (whether or not the civil partnership is subsisting) in relation to whom the child concerned is a child of the family.[7]

10.08   Hence, one civil partner or former civil partner may apply to the High Court or county court for the following orders in relation to a child of the family:[8]

(a) a periodical payments order (including an interim order)[9] or a secured periodical payments order payable direct to the child or to the civil partner for the benefit of the child;

(b) a lump sum order (which may be payable in instalments)[10] payable direct to the child or the civil partner for the benefit of the child. The lump sum may cover expenses which have already been incurred;[11]

(c) a settlement to be made for the benefit of the child of such property to which either civil partner is entitled (in possession or reversion);

(d) a transfer to the child or to the civil partner for the benefit of the child of

---

[3] Children Act 1989, s 6(3B) as amended by CPA 2004, s 76.
[4] ibid, s 10(5)(aa) as inserted by CPA 2004, s 77.
[5] CPA 2004, s 75(3).
[6] D v D (Child of the Family) (1981) 2 FLR 93, CA.
[7] Children Act 1989, Sch 1, para 16(2) as amended by CPA 2004, s 78(4).
[8] ibid, Sch 1, para 1.
[9] ibid, Sch 1, para 9.
[10] ibid, Sch 1, para 5(5).
[11] ibid, Sch 1, para 5(1).

such property to which either civil partner is entitled (in possession or reversion).

The magistrates' court is restricted to making orders for periodical payments and lump sums (limited to £1,000).[12]   **10.09**

The factors to be taken into account in determining an application by a civil partner for financial relief for a child of the family under the Children Act 1989 are:[13]   **10.10**

(a) the income, earning capacity, property and other financial resources which the civil partners and any parent of the child have or are likely to have in the foreseeable future;

(b) the financial needs, obligations and responsibilities which the civil partners and any parent of the child have or are likely to have in the foreseeable future;

(c) the financial needs of the child;

(d) the income, earning capacity (if any), property and other financial resources of the child;

(e) any physical or mental disability of the child;

(f) the manner in which the child was being, or was expected to be, educated or trained.

If the respondent is not the mother or father of the child, the court must additionally consider:[14]   **10.11**

(a) whether the respondent had assumed responsibility for the maintenance of the child and, if so, the extent of such responsibility and the duration of time for which it has been assumed;

(b) whether the respondent assumed responsibility in the knowledge that the child was not his (of relevance in change of gender cases);

(c) the liability of any other person to maintain the child.

A number of restrictions are imposed upon the duration of periodical and secured periodical payments orders in favour of children of the family. Such orders must expire on the child's 17th birthday unless the court thinks it 'right in the circumstances' to specify a later date.[15] Even if the court considers that the order should be extended, the order must expire on the child's 18th birthday unless:[16]   **10.12**

---

[12] ibid, Sch 1, paras 1(b) & 5(2).
[13] ibid, Sch 1, para 4(1).
[14] ibid, Sch 1, para 4(3).
[15] ibid, Sch 1, para 3(1)(a).
[16] ibid, Sch 1, para 3(1)(b) & (2).

(a) the child is or will be attending an educational establishment or undergoing training for a trade, profession or vocation; or

(b) there are special circumstances (eg the child is disabled).[17]

10.13 A periodical or secured periodical payments order ceases to have effect if the civil partners live together for a period in excess of six months.[18]

10.14 The court's ability to make periodical and secured periodical payments orders is subject to the restrictions imposed by the Child Support Act 1991, s 8. (See para 5.20 above.)[19]

10.15 Lump sum, transfer of property and settlement of property orders may only be made in favour of a child who is under the age of 18.[20]

10.16 The court may only make one transfer of property or settlement of property order in favour of any individual child of the family. The court may, however, make multiple orders for periodical payments, secured periodical payments and lump sums.[21]

10.17 Property settled on a child will generally speaking be for his/her minority only, including his/her period of tertiary education or training. In exceptional cases, such as long term disability, a civil partner may be required to buy a home for a child for life. Smaller lump sums may be ordered by the court to provide for necessaries such as vehicles and setting up the home.[22]

10.18 The court has power to vary orders for periodical and secured periodical payments[23] and to vary an instalment lump sum order (insofar as the variation relates to the number of instalments, the amount of any instalment or the date on which any instalment is payable).[24]

10.19 The 2004 Act therefore places same sex couples who enter into a civil partnership in the same position as married couples. In both cases, the applicant in respect of a child of the family need not be a parent (whether by birth or adoption), a guardian or have a residence order in respect of the child.

10.20 Unmarried heterosexual couples or same sex couples who do not enter into a civil partnership may only make a financial claim for the benefit of the child if the potential payer is a parent of the child and the applicant is a parent or guardian or has a residence order in respect of the child.

10.21 A child over 18 who is or will be in tertiary education or training and who was treated as a child of the family by the civil partners may, provided the civil partners are no longer living together, make his/her own application for period-

---

[17] *C v F (Disabled child: Maintenance order)* [1998] 2 FLR 1, CA.

[18] Children Act 1989, Sch 1, para 3(4).

[19] See also ibid, Sch 1, para 3(5)–(8) for cases where a maintenance calculation is in force or where it ceases to have effect.

[20] ibid, s 105(1) defines 'child' as a person under the age of 18.

[21] ibid, Sch 1, para 16(3) & (5)(b).

[22] *Re P (Child: Financial Provision)* [2003] EWCA Civ 837, [2003] 2 FLR 865.

[23] Children Act 1989, Sch 1, paras 6 & 6A.

[24] ibid, Sch 1, para 5(6).

ical payments and/or a lump sum. However, he/she may only make an application against his/her natural or adoptive parent and not against the non-parental civil partner who treated him as a child of the family. Furthermore, no such application may be made by the child if, before he/she reached the age of 16, a periodical payments order was in force in respect of him/her and that periodical payments order was made under Pts 1 or 9 of Sch 5 to the 2004 Act (periodical payments order on dissolution etc or failure to maintain made in High Court or county court) or Sch 6 to the 2004 Act (orders in the magistrates' court upon a failure to maintain etc). In these circumstances, the child's remedy is to apply in the proceedings in which that order was made to extend that order.

E. ADOPTION

The 2004 Act expressly permits civil partners to apply for adoption orders.[25] The **10.22** impact of the amendments made by the 2004 Act is, however, somewhat limited in view of the fact that same sex couples could, in any event, apply for adoption under the Adoption and Children Act 2002, s 50.

A detailed discussion of the Adoption and Children Act 2002 is beyond **10.23** the remit of this Guide. Some of the amendments made to the Adoption and Children Act 2002 by the 2004 Act are as follows:

(a) a placement order, which precedes an adoption order, comes to an end when the placed child enters into a civil partnership;[26]

(b) an adoption order cannot be made in respect of a person who is or has been a civil partner;[27]

(c) an adoption order may be made on the application of one civil partner alone if the court is satisfied that the applicant's civil partner cannot be found or the civil partners have separated and the separation is likely to be permanent, or the other civil partner is by reason of physical or mental ill-health, incapable of making an application for an adoption order;[28]

(d) the definition of 'relative' in the Adoption and Children Act 2002 is widened to include those related by way of civil partnership to the child to be adopted or an adopted person. This has the effect, for example, of allowing a person who wants to make contact with an adopted person to register such a wish on the Adoption Contact Register provided such a person would be related to the adopted person by civil partnership but for the adoption.[29]

---

[25] CPA 2004, s 79.
[26] ibid, s 79(2).
[27] ibid, s 79(3).
[28] ibid, s 79(4) & (5).
[29] ibid, s 79(9).

11

CIVIL PARTNERSHIP HOMES AND DOMESTIC VIOLENCE

A. RIGHTS TO OCCUPY THE CIVIL PARTNERSHIP HOME

The Family Law Act 1996 ('the FLA 1996') distinguishes between: **11.01**

(a) persons who are entitled to occupy a home by virtue of:

   (i) a beneficial estate or interest in the home;

   (ii) a contract in relation to the home (eg a tenancy agreement);

   (iii) any enactment granting that person the right to remain in occupation (eg succession under the Rent Act 1977);

(b) persons who are not so entitled.

In this chapter, the same distinction is drawn between 'entitled' partners and 'non-entitled' partners.

Prior to the 2004 Act, cohabiting same sex partners (like cohabiting opposite **11.02** sex partners) only had rights of occupation of the partnership home if they were 'entitled' partners. The relationship per se did not give rise to any rights of occupation. In contrast, 'non-entitled' spouses did enjoy rights of occupation (known as 'matrimonial home rights') in relation to the matrimonial home pursuant to the FLA 1996, s 30.

In pursuance of the aim of the 2004 Act to grant the same rights to civil **11.03** partners as are enjoyed by married couples, Sch 9 to the 2004 Act makes various amendments to the FLA 1996. As a result of those amendments 'non-entitled' civil partners are granted, by virtue of the relationship itself, rights of occupation of the civil partnership home.

11.04 The rights of occupation enjoyed both by civil partners and by spouses are described as 'home rights'.[1] These rights are:[2]

(a) if in occupation, a right not to be evicted or excluded from the civil partnership home or any part of it by the other civil partner except with the permission of the court;

(b) if not in occupation, a right with the permission of the court to enter into and occupy the civil partnership home.

11.05 The rights of occupation apply only to a 'dwelling-house'[3] which is or was intended to be the civil partnership home.[4]

11.06 The 'home rights' subsist for so long as:[5]

(a) The civil partnership itself subsists. The 'home rights' may, however, be extended beyond the dissolution of the civil partnership or beyond the death of the civil partner who has an interest in or contract in relation to the civil partnership home. An application to extend the 'home rights' must be made prior to the dissolution or death. The court will grant an extension if it is just and reasonable in all the circumstances for the rights to be extended.[6] There is no limit to the period for which the 'home rights' may be extended.

(b) The other civil partner is entitled to occupy the civil partnership home by virtue of a beneficial estate or interest or contract or any enactment granting the right to occupy. By virtue of the FLA 1996, s 30(5),[7] the payment of rent or mortgage by the 'non-entitled' civil partner is treated as having been made by the other, 'entitled' civil partner. Accordingly, if a civil partner who is, for example, a statutory tenant leaves the civil partnership home, the tenancy is treated as continuing provided:

(i) the civil partnership subsists; and

(ii) the civil partner who has no tenancy continues to pay rent.

11.07 A civil partner may prevent the unilateral termination of a tenancy of the civil partnership home (whether in joint names or in the other civil partner's sole name) by obtaining an injunction prohibiting termination which may then be served upon the landlord.[8]

11.08 By virtue of the FLA 1996, s 31[9] the 'non-entitled' civil partner's 'home rights' are a charge on the other, 'entitled' civil partner's estate or interest in the

---

[1] FLA 1996, s 30 as amended by CPA 2004, Sch 9, para 1.
[2] ibid, s 30(2) as amended.
[3] Which includes a caravan or houseboat: FLA 1996, s 63(1).
[4] ibid, s 30(7) as amended by CPA 2004, Sch 9, para 1(8).
[5] ibid, s 30(8) as amended by CPA 2004, Sch 9, para 1(9).
[6] ibid, s 33(8) & (5) as amended by CPA 2004, Sch 9, para 4(6).
[7] As amended by CPA 2004, Sch 9, para 1(6).
[8] *Bater v Greenwich LBC* [1999] 2 FLR 993, CA.
[9] As amended by CPA 2004, Sch 9, para 2.

civil partnership home. The charge must, however, be registered in order to give protection against purchasers and mortgagees.[10]

B. OCCUPATION ORDERS

There are two categories of occupation order:

11.09

(a) a declaratory occupation order which declares the extent of a civil partner's rights to occupy the civil partnership home; and

(b) a regulatory occupation order which regulates (by suspending or restricting rights of occupation) the physical occupation of the civil partnership home or part of it by either of the civil partners.

Prior to amendments to the FLA 1996, the court's powers to regulate the occupation of a home occupied by same sex partners was extremely limited. For the purposes of the FLA 1996, same sex partners were treated merely as 'associated persons' (ie persons who were living or had lived in the same household otherwise than by reason of one of them being the other's employee, tenant, lodger or boarder).[11] As a consequence, only an 'entitled' same sex partner could apply for an occupation order; the other, 'non-entitled' partner (unlike a spouse or opposite sex partner) was unable to apply for an occupation order.

11.10

The ability of same sex partners to apply for occupation orders was brought into line with the ability of opposite sex (but unmarried) partners by the Domestic Violence, Crimes and Victims Act 2004, s 3. The Civil Partnership Act 2004 brings the position of same sex partners who choose to register as civil partners into line with the position of married couples. Consequently, the Civil Partnership Act 2004 Act redefines 'cohabitants' for the purposes of the FLA 1996 to expressly exclude civil partners who are now granted more extensive rights. 'Cohabitants' are now redefined by the 2004 Act as 'two persons who are neither married to each other nor civil partners of each other but are living together as husband and wife or as if they were civil partners'.[12]

11.11

1. Occupation Order where Applicant has Estate or Interest etc or 'Home Rights': Family Law Act 1996, s 33

The FLA 1996, s 33 applies to civil partners if:[13]

11.12

(a) the civil partnership subsists, or if no civil partnership was registered but

---

[10] By way of an agreed notice under the Land Registration Act 2002, Sch 11 (formerly a Class F land charge).

[11] FLA 1996, s 62(3).

[12] ibid, s 62(1) as amended by CPA 2004, Sch 9, para 13(2).

[13] ibid, s 33(1) as amended by CPA 2004, Sch 9, para 4.

there was an agreement[14] to enter into a civil partnership and the application is brought within three years of the agreement being terminated; and

(b) the dwelling-house is or was intended to be the civil partnership home; and

(c) the applicant civil partner is entitled to occupy the civil partnership home by virtue of a beneficial estate or interest or contract or by virtue of any enactment or as a result of 'home rights'.

11.13 The court may make any one of the following orders if an application is made under the FLA 1996, s 33:[15]

(a) an order enforcing the applicant's entitlement to remain in occupation as against the respondent civil partner;

(b) an order requiring the respondent civil partner to permit the applicant to enter and remain in the civil partnership home or part of it;

(c) an order regulating the occupation of the civil partnership home by either or both civil partners;

(d) if the respondent civil partner is entitled to occupy the civil partnership home by virtue of a beneficial estate or interest or contract, an order prohibiting, suspending or restricting the exercise by him/her of his/her right to occupy the civil partnership home;

(e) if the respondent civil partner has 'home rights', an order restricting or terminating those rights;

(f) an order requiring the respondent civil partner to leave the civil partnership home or part of it;

(g) an order excluding the respondent civil partner from a defined area in which the civil partnership home is included (eg excluding the respondent from a 100m radius of the home).

11.14 The court has a *duty* under the FLA 1996, s 33(7) to make one of the above orders if it appears that the applicant civil partner or any relevant child is likely to suffer significant harm attributable to the conduct of the respondent civil partner if the order is not made unless it appears to the court that:

(a) the respondent civil partner or any relevant child is likely to suffer significant harm if the order is made; and

(b) the harm likely to be suffered by the respondent civil partner or child is as great as, or greater than, the harm attributable to the conduct of the respondent civil partner which is likely to be suffered by the applicant civil partner or child if the order is not made.

---

[14] ibid, s 33(2A) as inserted by CPA 2004, Sch 9, para 4(3). There must be written evidence of the agreement or evidence of a gift or ceremony marking the agreement: FLA 1996, s 44(3) as inserted by CPA 2004, Sch 9, para 10.

[15] FLA 1996, s 33(3).

This is known as the 'balance of harm test'.

In considering whether any harm likely to be suffered is attributable to the **11.15** conduct of the respondent civil partner, it is the effect of the conduct upon the applicant civil partner and any relevant child rather than the intention of the respondent which is important.[16]

The definition of 'harm' differs for children and for adults. For a person who **11.16** has reached the age of 18 years, 'harm' means 'ill treatment or the impairment of health'. In relation to a person under the age of 18 years, 'harm' means 'ill-treatment or the impairment of health or development'.[17] The term 'significant' is not defined in the FLA 1996 but has been judicially interpreted as 'considerable or noteworthy or important'.[18]

If the court considers that the balance of harm test is not satisfied and that it **11.17** is not under a duty to make an order, it is required to consider whether, in the exercise of its discretion, it should make one of the above orders. In considering whether to exercise its discretion it must have regard to all the circumstances including:[19]

(a) the housing needs and housing resources of each of the civil partners and of any relevant child;

(b) the financial resources of each of the civil partners;

(c) the likely effect of any order, or of a decision not to make an order, on the health, safety or well-being of the civil partners and of any relevant child; and

(d) the conduct of the civil partners in relation to each other and otherwise.

It is well established, however, that occupation orders are draconian orders **11.18** which should only be made in 'exceptional circumstances'.[20] The court may, upon making one of the above orders, also declare that the applicant civil partner has 'home rights' or is entitled to occupy the civil partnership home by virtue of an interest or contract.[21]

A 'relevant child' is given a wide definition[22] and extends to any child who is **11.19** living with or might reasonably be expected to live with either civil partner and any other child whose interests the court considers relevant.

There is no maximum duration for an occupation order under the FLA 1996, **11.20** s 33.[23] Ordinarily, the occupation order will endure until the resolution of financial claims between the civil partners.

---

[16] *G v G (Occupation order: Conduct)* [2000] 2 FLR 36, CA.
[17] FLA 1996, s 63(1). 'Ill-treatment', 'health' and 'development' are further defined by that section.
[18] *Chalmers v Johns* [1999] 1 FLR 392, CA.
[19] FLA 1996, s 33(6).
[20] *Chalmers v Johns* [1999] 1 FLR 392, CA; *G v G (Occupation order: Conduct)* [2000] 2 FLR 36, CA.
[21] FLA 1996, s 33(4) as amended by CPA 2004, Sch 9, para 4(5).
[22] ibid, s 62(2).
[23] ibid, s 33(10).

11.21   The occupation order ceases automatically upon the death of either civil partner unless an order extending a civil partner's 'home rights' beyond the death of the other civil partner has been made under the FLA 1996, s 33(5).[24]

11.22   It is expected that the majority of occupation orders made in favour of civil partners will be made pursuant to the FLA 1996, s 33 since, prior to dissolution of the civil partnership, all civil partners will have 'home rights' in relation to the civil partnership home.

2. Former Civil Partner with no Existing Right to Occupy the Partnership Home: Family Law Act 1996, s 35

11.23   The FLA 1996, s 35 applies to civil partners if:[25]

(a) the civil partnership no longer subsists;

(b) the applicant former civil partner has no interest in or tenancy of the former civil partnership home;

(c) the respondent civil partner has a right to occupy the former civil partnership home by virtue of an estate or interest or contract or enactment granting rights of occupation;

(d) the dwelling-house is or was intended to be the civil partnership home.

11.24   If the court decides to make a declaratory occupation order under the FLA 1996, s 35, the order must contain certain mandatory provisions:

(a) if the applicant civil partner is in occupation of the civil partnership home:[26]

    (i) an order giving the applicant civil partner a right not to be evicted or excluded from the civil partnership home or any part of it by the respondent civil partner for such period as may be specified in the order;

    (ii) an order prohibiting the respondent civil partner from evicting or excluding the applicant civil partner during that period;

(b) if the applicant civil partner is not in occupation of the civil partnership home:[27]

    (i) an order giving the applicant civil partner the right to enter into and occupy the civil partnership home for the period specified in the order;

    (ii) an order requiring the respondent civil partner to permit the exercise of that right.

11.25   In deciding whether to make a declaratory occupation order, the court must have regard to all the circumstances including:[28]

---

[24] ibid, s 33(9).
[25] ibid, s 35(1) as amended by CPA 2004, Sch 9, para 6.
[26] ibid, s 35(3).
[27] ibid, s 35(4).
[28] ibid, s 35(6) as amended by CPA 2004, Sch 9, para 6(5) & (6).

(a) the housing needs and housing resources of each of the civil partners and of any relevant child (see para 11.19 above for the definition of 'relevant child');

(b) the financial resources of each of the civil partners;

(c) the likely effect of any order, or of any decision not to make an order under s 35(3) or (4) (see above) on the health, safety and well-being of the civil partners and of any relevant child;

(d) the conduct of the civil partners in relation to each other and otherwise;

(e) the length of time that has elapsed since the civil partners ceased to live together;

(f) the length of time that has elapsed since the civil partnership was dissolved or annulled;

(g) the existence of any pending proceedings between the civil partners:
   (i) for a property adjustment order under the Civil Partnership Act 2004, Sch 5, Pt 5;
   (ii) for an order for financial relief under the Children Act 1989, Sch 1, para 1(2)(d) to (e);
   (iii) relating to the legal or beneficial ownership of the civil partnership home.

11.26 The court may also make any one of the following regulatory occupation orders if an application is made under the FLA 1996, s 35:[29]

(a) an order regulating the occupation of the civil partnership home by either or both of the civil partners;

(b) an order prohibiting, suspending or restricting the exercise by the respondent civil partner of his/her right to occupy the civil partnership home;

(c) an order requiring the respondent civil partner to leave the civil partnership home or part of it;

(d) an order excluding the respondent civil partner from a defined area in which the civil partnership home is included.

11.27 The court has a *duty*[30] to make a regulatory occupation order if it considers the 'balance of harm test' to be satisfied. (See para 11.14 above for the 'balance of harm test'.)

11.28 If the court considers that the balance of harm test is not satisfied and that it is not under a duty to make an order, it is required to consider whether, in the exercise of its discretion, it should make one of the above regulatory orders. In considering whether to exercise its discretion it must have regard to all the circumstances including:[31]

---

[29] ibid, s 35(5).
[30] ibid, s 35(8).
[31] ibid, s 35(7).

(a) the housing needs and housing resources of each of the civil partners and of any relevant child (see para 11.19 above for the definition of 'relevant child');

(b) the financial resources of each of the civil partners;

(c) the likely effect of any order, or of any decision not to make an order, on the health, safety and well-being of the civil partners and of any relevant child;

(d) the conduct of the civil partners in relation to each other and otherwise;

(e) the length of time that has elapsed since the civil partners ceased to live together.

11.29 These criteria mirror the criteria for making declaratory occupation orders, save that factors (f) and (g) are omitted (see para 11.25 above).

11.30 A declaratory or regulatory occupation order pursuant to the FLA 1996, s 35 ends automatically upon the death of either civil partner and is limited in duration to six months; but may be extended on multiple occasions for up to six months on each occasion.[32]

11.31 It is therefore important for those civil partners who do not have an interest in or tenancy of the civil partnership home to consider applying for occupation orders and for an extension of their 'home rights' *prior* to the dissolution of the civil partnership. This will enable the 'non-entitled' civil partner to obtain an occupation order under the FLA 1996, s 33 which lasts, for example, until the resolution of financial claims and which will avoid the six month time limit imposed in relation to orders under the FLA 1996, s 35.

3. Neither Civil Partner or Former Civil Partner Entitled to Occupy the Civil Partnership Home: Family Law Act 1996, s 37

11.32 The FLA 1996, s 37 applies to civil partners if:[33]

(a) the civil partners or former civil partners occupy a dwelling-house which is or was the civil partnership home;

(b) neither of them is entitled to remain in occupation because neither of them has an estate or interest or contract and neither is entitled to occupy by virtue of any enactment.

11.33 The circumstances in which neither civil partner has a right to occupy the civil partnership home will be rare, eg where a licence to occupy has been terminated. Either civil partner may apply to the court for an order:[34]

(a) requiring the respondent civil partner to permit the applicant civil partner to enter and remain in the civil partnership home or part of it;

---

[32] ibid, s 35(9) & (10) as amended by CPA 2004, Sch 9, para 6(7).
[33] ibid, s 37(1A) as inserted by CPA 2004, Sch 9, para 8.
[34] ibid, s 37(3).

(b) regulating the occupation of the civil partnership home by either or both of the civil partners;

(c) requiring the respondent civil partner to leave the civil partnership home or part of it;

(d) excluding the respondent civil partner from a defined area in which the civil partnership home is included.

11.34 The criteria for making such orders mirror the criteria under the FLA 1996, s 33 where one of the civil partners does have a right to occupy the civil partnership home.[35] Thus, the court must first consider whether it is under a duty to make an occupation order (s 33(7): para 11.14 above); and, if it is not under a duty, whether it should, in the exercise of its discretion, make an order (s 33(6): para 11.17 above).

11.35 An order pursuant to the FLA 1996, s 37 is limited in duration to six months but may be extended on multiple occasions for up to six months on each occasion.[36]

4. Same Sex Partners who have not Registered as Civil Partners

11.36 A same sex partner who has not entered into a civil partnership but who has a right to occupy the civil partnership home by virtue of an estate or interest or contract or enactment (ie an 'entitled' partner) will be able to apply for an occupation order pursuant to the FLA 1996, s 33 since the same sex partners will be 'associated persons'. The same applies to a same sex partner who has entered into a civil partnership agreement and who is an 'entitled partner', provided the application under s 33 is made within three years of the date of termination of the agreement.[37]

11.37 An unregistered same sex partner or former partner who has no right to occupy the civil partnership home (ie a 'non-entitled' partner) will only be able to apply, as a 'cohabitant', for an occupation order under the more restrictive provisions of the FLA 1996, ss 36 and 38. The key differences between applications for occupation orders by civil partners and applications by unregistered same sex partners or former partners are:[38]

(a) the court has no duty to make an occupation order in favour of an unregistered same sex partner or former partner if it finds the 'balance of harm' test to be satisfied (see para 11.14 above), whereas it does have a duty to make an occupation order in favour of a civil partner or former civil partner in the same circumstances;[39]

---

[35] ibid, s 37(4).

[36] ibid, s 37(5).

[37] ibid, s 33(2A) as inserted by CPA 2004, Sch 9, para 4(3).

[38] The factors to which the court must have regard are contained in FLA 1996, s 36(6),(7) & (8).

[39] ibid, s 36(8).

(b) the duration of an occupation order in favour of a non-entitled, unregistered same sex partner or former partner is limited to six months with an ability to extend the duration for only one further six month period;[40] whereas no time limit applies to orders in favour of non-entitled civil partners and a time limit of six months applies to orders in favour of non-entitled former civil partners which can be extended on multiple occasions for up to six months on each occasion.

11.38 Section 38 of the FLA 1996 applies where:

(a) the unregistered same sex partners or former partners occupy a dwelling-house which is or was the partnership home; and

(b) neither of the unregistered same sex partners or former partners is entitled to remain in occupation.

11.39 The court may make the same occupation orders regulating the occupation of the partnership home in such circumstances as it may make in relation to civil partners under s 37 of the FLA 1996 (see para 11.33 above).

11.40 In considering whether to make an order under the FLA 1996, s 38, the court must have regard to all the circumstances, including:[41]

(a) the housing needs and housing resources of each of the partners and of any relevant child;

(b) the financial resources of each of the partners;

(c) the likely effect of any order, or of a decision not to make an order, upon the health, safety or well-being of the partners and of any relevant child;

(d) the conduct of the partners in relation to each other and otherwise;

(e) whether the applicant or any relevant child is likely to suffer significant harm attributable to the conduct of the respondent if an order is not made;

(f) whether the harm likely to be suffered by the respondent or any relevant child if an order is made is as great as or greater than the harm attributable to the conduct of the respondent which is likely to be suffered by the applicant or relevant child if the order is not made.

5. Ancillary Orders

11.41 Upon making an occupation order under the FLA 1996, ss 33, 35 or 36 (but not ss 37 or 38), the court may make a number of ancillary orders:[42]

(a) an order requiring either partner to pay for the rent, mortgage or other outgoings for the partnership home or to repair and maintain the home;

---

[40] ibid, s 36(10).
[41] ibid, s 38(4) & (5).
[42] ibid, s 40.

(b) an order requiring the partner occupying the partnership home to make periodical payments to the other partner if the other partner would (but for the occupation order) be entitled to occupy the partnership home by virtue of an estate or interest or contract or enactment;

(c) an order granting to either partner the possession or use of the furniture or contents of the partnership home;

(d) an order requiring either partner to take reasonable care of the furniture or contents of the partnership home;

(e) an order requiring either partner to take reasonable steps to keep the partnership home and any furniture or contents secure.

In deciding whether to make an ancillary order, the court must have regard to all the circumstances including:[43]   **11.42**

(a) the financial needs and financial resources of the partners;

(b) the financial obligations which they have or are likely to have in the foreseeable future, including any financial obligations to each other and to any relevant child.

The ancillary order ends when the occupation order to which it relates ends.[44]   **11.43**

It appears, however, that ancillary orders pursuant to the FLA 1996, s 40 are unenforceable since such orders are not included in the list of enforceable maintenance orders in the Administration of Justice Act 1970, Sch 8 or the Attachment of Earnings Act 1971, Sch 1. This lacuna has been described as rendering the provisions of s 40 a 'dead letter'.[45] As an alternative, a civil partner (but not an unregistered same sex partner) could apply for interim periodical payments or a maintenance pending outcome order pursuant to paras 2 or 38 of Sch 5 to the 2004 Act.   **11.44**

C. NON-MOLESTATION ORDERS

A non-molestation order is an order prohibiting one person from molesting another person with whom he is 'associated'[46] or from molesting a relevant child. There is no statutory definition of 'molesting', but the term encompasses any form of violence, threatening violence, pestering and harassing.[47] The FLA 1996 is not, however, intended to protect an individual's privacy.[48]   **11.45**

---

[43] ibid, s 40(2).
[44] ibid, s 40(3).
[45] *Nwogbe v Nwogbe* [2000] 2 FLR 744.
[46] FLA 1996, s 62(3).
[47] *Vaughan v Vaughan* [1973] 1 WLR 1159, CA.
[48] *C v C (Non-molestation order: Jurisdiction)* [1998] 1 FLR 554.

11.46   The following 'associated persons' may apply for non-molestation orders:

(a) civil partners and former civil partners;[49]

(b) unregistered same sex partners or former partners;[50]

(c) same sex couples who have not registered as civil partners but who have entered into a civil partnership agreement[51] provided the application is made within three years of the termination of the agreement.[52]

11.47   In deciding whether to grant a non-molestation order, the court must have regard to all the circumstances including the need to secure the health, safety and well-being of the applicant partner and of any relevant child.[53]

11.48   There is no maximum duration for a non-molestation order pursuant to the FLA 1996.[54]

11.49   The ability of same sex partners and civil partners to apply for an injunction in tort (whether to prevent the statutory tort of harassment under the Protection from Harassment Act 1997 or to prevent the common law tort of assault and battery) is unaffected by the 2004 Act.

D. EX PARTE ORDERS, POWERS OF ARREST AND UNDERTAKINGS

11.50   The ability of the court to make ex parte orders, attach powers of arrest and accept undertakings in applications concerning civil partners and unregistered same sex partners pursuant to the FLA 1996 is unaffected by the 2004 Act.

11.51   Thus, the court may make an ex parte non-molestation order or occupation order against a civil partner or unregistered same sex partner pursuant to the FLA 1996, s 45. It is, however, rare for an occupation order to be made ex parte.[55]

11.52   The court is required, pursuant to the FLA 1996, s 47, to attach a power of arrest to any non-molestation or occupation order if it appears that the respondent civil partner or unregistered same sex partner has used or threatened violence against the applicant or a relevant child unless the court is satisfied that the applicant or relevant child will be adequately protected without a power of arrest. Ordinarily, the power of arrest will endure for the duration of the

---

[49] FLA 1996, s 62(3)(aa) as amended by CPA 2004, Sch 9, para 13(3).

[50] ibid, s 62(1) as amended by CPA 2004, Sch 9, para 13(2).

[51] There must be written evidence of the agreement or evidence of a gift or ceremony marking the agreement: ibid, s 44(3) as inserted by CPA 2004, Sch 9, para 10.

[52] ibid, s 42(4ZA) as inserted by CPA 2004, Sch 9, para 9 and ibid, s 62(3)(eza) as amended by CPA 2004, Sch 9, para 13(4).

[53] ibid, s 42(5).

[54] ibid, s 42(7).

[55] *G v G (Ouster: Ex parte application)* [1990] 1 FLR 395, CA.

non-molestation or occupation order itself, but may be attached for a shorter period.[56]

Pursuant to the FLA 1996, s 46, the court may, in lieu of making a non-molestation or occupation order, accept an undertaking from the respondent civil partner or unregistered same sex partner provided the court would not otherwise have been required to attach a power of arrest if it had made an order instead of accepting an undertaking. **11.53**

---

[56] *Re B-J (Power of Arrest)* [2000] 2 FLR 443, CA.

12

CHILD SUPPORT, SOCIAL SECURITY AND TAXATION

Schedule 24 to the 2004 Act makes various amendments to the child support, **12.01** social security and tax credits legislation so that:

(a) civil partners are treated in the same way as married couples;

(b) same sex couples who do not register as civil partners but who live together as if they were civil partners are treated in the same way as opposite sex, unmarried couples who live together as husband and wife.

A. CHILD SUPPORT

1. Definition of 'Child Maintenance Order'

Civil partners and unregistered same sex couples may make applications to the **12.02** Child Support Agency if:[1]

(a) the respondent is a parent (whether natural or by adoption) of the child,[2] but the child does not live in the same household as that parent (the 'non-resident' parent);

(b) the other usually provides day to day care of the child and has his/her home with that child.

Section 8 of the Child Support Act 1991 limits the ability of the court to **12.03** make 'maintenance orders' for children if the Child Support Agency has the

---

[1] Child Support Act 1991, s 3.
[2] 'Child' is defined in ibid, s 55. A person is not a 'child' if he/she is or has been a civil partner: ibid, s 55(2) as amended by CPA 2004, Sch 24, para 3.

jurisdiction to make a maintenance calculation (see para 5.20 above). Paragraph 1 of Sch 24 to the 2004 Act extends the definition of 'maintenance order' so as to include orders made in financial proceedings between civil partners under the 2004 Act.

2. Amendments to the Old Child Support Regime

12.04   Under the old child support regime (ie maintenance assessments made before 3 March 2003), the income of the non-resident parent is treated as including the income of any adult of the opposite sex living together in the same household with that parent (whether they are married or not). Paragraph 4 of Sch 24 to the 2004 Act enables regulations to be made which will treat the income of a same sex adult living in the same household as the non-resident parent (whether civil partners or living together as civil partners) to be treated in the same way.

3. Amendments to the New Child Support Regime

12.05   Under the new child support regime (ie maintenance calculations made after 3 March 2003), a flat rate of £5 per week is payable by the non-resident parent if that parent's opposite sex partner (whether married or living together as husband and wife) is in receipt of prescribed benefits. Paragraph 6 of Sch 24 to the 2004 Act applies the flat rate to those cases where the non-resident parent's same sex partner (whether registered as civil partners or living together as civil partners) is in receipt of prescribed benefits.

B. SOCIAL SECURITY BENEFITS

12.06   Prior to the 2004 Act, same sex couples were treated as two separate persons for the purposes of claims for social security benefits.

12.07   Schedule 24 to the 2004 Act makes amendments to the Social Security Contributions and Benefits Act 1992 ('the SSCBA 1992'), the Social Security Administration Act 1992, the State Pension Credit Act 2002 and the Tax Credits Act 2002 so that same sex partners (whether registered as civil partners or not) will, in future, be treated as a single family unit for the purposes of income-related benefits. Civil partners and unregistered same sex partners who were previously entitled to income-related benefits may therefore find that they are no longer entitled to such benefits.

12.08   A detailed analysis of the circumstances in which social security benefits are payable is beyond the scope of this Guide. The key changes which are made by Sch 24 are:

(a) Bereavement payment:

- a surviving civil partner (like a surviving spouse) will be entitled to claim a bereavement payment provided the survivor was not living with a third party (as if they were civil partners or as if they were husband and wife) at the date of death.[3]

(b) Widowed parents' allowance and bereavement allowance:

- a surviving civil partner (like a surviving spouse) who is not of pensionable age will be entitled to claim a widowed parent's allowance or, where there are no dependent children, a bereavement allowance. The allowances will be lost if the survivor forms a subsequent civil partnership or marriage or if the survivor cohabits with another person as if they were civil partners or as if they were husband and wife;[4]
- the entitlement of a woman who currently receives a widowed mother's allowance (replaced by a widowed parent's allowance for deaths after April 2001) or a widow's allowance (replaced by a bereavement allowance for deaths after April 2001) will be lost if she subsequently enters into a civil partnership or lives with another woman as if they were civil partners.[5]

(c) Income support, council tax benefit and housing benefit:

- civil partners and unregistered same sex partners will, in future, be treated as a single family unit in the same way that married couples and cohabiting opposite sex couples are treated as a single unit for the purposes of claims for income support, council tax benefit and housing benefit. Thus, only one of the civil partners (or only one of the members of an unregistered same sex couple) will be able to claim income support, council tax benefit and housing benefit and the other's financial resources will, in future, be taken into account in assessing entitlement to the benefits.[6]

(d) Mortgage interest payments (included in income support or jobseeker's allowance):

- civil partners and unregistered same sex couples will, in future, receive mortgage interest payments on the same basis as married couples and cohabiting opposite sex couples currently receive such payments.[7]

(e) Jobseeker's allowance:

- civil partners and unregistered same sex couples will, in future, be treated as a single family unit in the same way that married couples and cohabiting opposite sex couples are treated as a single unit for the purposes of claims for jobseeker's allowance. The circumstances in which married and

---

[3] SSCBA 1992, s 36 as amended by CPA 2004, Sch 24, para 16.
[4] ibid, ss 39A, 39B & 39C as amended by CPA 2004, Sch 24, paras 20–22.
[5] ibid, ss 37 & 38 as amended by CPA 2004, Sch 24, paras 18 & 19.
[6] ibid, ss 124, 126, 127, 132 & 137 as amended by CPA 2004, Sch 24, paras 42–46.
[7] Social Security Administration Act 1992, s 15A as amended by CPA 2004, Sch 24, para 57.

opposite sex couples are currently required to make a joint claim for jobseeker's allowance will be extended to civil partners and unregistered same sex couples.[8]

(f) State pension credit:

- civil partners and unregistered same sex couples will, in future, be treated as a single family unit for the purposes of claims for state pension credit. Thus, for example, a claimant will not be entitled to state pension credit, if his/her civil partner or same sex partner is currently receiving it.[9]

(g) Child tax credit and working tax credit:

- civil partners and unregistered same sex partners will, in future, be treated as a single family unit for the purposes of claims for child tax credit and working tax credit. Claims for such credits must be made jointly by the same sex couple or by the civil partners (unless they are separated under a court order or separated in circumstances in which the separation is likely to be permanent).[10]

(h) Recovery of payments made by the Secretary of State:

- the Secretary of State will be entitled to recover payments of income support and jobseeker's allowance from a civil partner who is liable to maintain the recipient.[11]

12.09 The phrase 'living together as if they were civil partners' is not defined in any of the amendments made by the 2004 Act. It is intended, however, that the body of Social Security Commissioners' case law which exists in relation to cohabitation between opposite sex couples will apply to same sex couples. To this end, the amendments made by the 2004 Act provide that two people of the same sex are to be regarded as living together as if they were civil partners if, but only if, they would be regarded as living together as husband and wife if they were two people of the opposite sex.[12]

C. TAXATION

12.10 Married couples enjoy a number of concessions in relation to taxation which are not enjoyed either by cohabiting opposite sex or same sex partners. By way of example:

---

[8] Jobseekers Act 1995 as amended by CPA 2004, Sch 24, paras 118–124.

[9] State Pension Credit Act 2002 as amended by CPA 2004, Sch 24, paras 140–143.

[10] Tax Credits Act 2002 as amended by CPA 2004, Sch 24, paras 144–147.

[11] Social Security Administration Act 1992, ss 105 & 107 and Jobseekers Act 1995, s 23 as amended by CPA 2004, Sch 24, paras 62, 63 & 122.

[12] eg, SSCBA 1992, s 137(1A) as inserted by CPA 2004, Sch 24, para 46. See Department for Work and Pensions, *A Guide to Income Support*, IS20 April 2004 for guidance as to what constitutes cohabitation.

(a) transfers of property between spouses are exempt from capital gains tax provided the spouses have been living together during the tax year in which the asset was transferred;[13]

(b) a transfer of a former matrimonial home which has been the principal private residence may be exempt from capital gains tax (even if transferred more than 36 months after separation) if the property has been the other spouse's only or main residence and the transferor has not elected any other residence as his/her principal private residence;[14]

(c) transfers of property made in connection with the dissolution or annulment of a marriage or the judicial separation of spouses is exempt from stamp duty land tax;[15]

(d) transfers of property between spouses during a marriage and, ordinarily, also after dissolution or annulment are exempt from inheritance tax provided both spouses were domiciled in the UK.[16]

The 2004 Act does not alter the tax regime for civil partners. **12.11**

The government's intention is that, for tax purposes, civil partners should be **12.12** treated in the same way as spouses. It is intended that the necessary changes will be introduced in the 2005 Finance Bill.[17] The changes will not benefit unregistered same sex couples.

---

[13] Taxation of Chargeable Gains Act 1992, s 58.

[14] Inland Revenue Concession D6. Transfers within 36 months of separation are potentially exempt under ibid, ss 222 & 223.

[15] Finance Act 2003, s 49, Sch 3.

[16] Inheritance Tax Act 1984, ss 18 & 10.

[17] Baroness Hollis, *Hansard*, HL vol 663, col 424 (1 July 2004).

13

PENSIONS

A. STATE RETIREMENT PENSION

A detailed analysis of the state retirement pension is beyond the scope of this **13.01** Guide. This chapter addresses only the key changes which will affect the entitlement of civil partners to the state retirement pension.

The state retirement pension falls into two categories: **13.02**

(a) 'Category A': a flat rate basic pension;

(b) 'Category B': a flat rate basic pension ('Category A') plus an earnings related component known as SERPS (or S2P).[1]

The intention of the 2004 Act is that civil partners should, in general, be treated **13.03** as widowers (rather than widows) for the purposes of calculating entitlement to Category A and Category B pensions.

1. Category A Pensions

Where a civil partnership has ended, whether as a result of death or dissolution, **13.04** the surviving or former civil partner (like a spouse) may be entitled to rely upon the deceased's contributions in order to qualify for a Category A pension, provided the claimant has not entered into a subsequent civil partnership or marriage.[2]

A civil partner may be able to claim, but only from 6 April 2010, an increase in **13.05** the rate of a Category A pension if the other civil partner resides with him/her and is a dependant.[3] (In this respect a female civil partner is treated less

---

[1] S2P replaced SERPS from 6 April 2002.
[2] SSCBA 1992, s 48 as amended by CPA 2004, Sch 24, para 24.
[3] ibid, s 83A as amended by CPA 2004, Sch 24, para 36.

favourably than a married woman who has a current entitlement under the Social Security Contributions and Benefits Act 1992 ('the SSCBA 1992') to claim an adult dependant's increase).

2. Category B Pension

13.06 Where a civil partnership subsists and both civil partners have attained state retirement age, a civil partner may be entitled to rely upon the other civil partner's contributions in order to qualify for a Category B pension. Female civil partners will qualify from 6 April 2010 and male partners will qualify from 6 April 2015.[4] (In this respect a female civil partner is treated less favourably than a married woman who has a current entitlement under the SSCBA 1992 to make a claim based upon her husband's contributions.)

13.07 Where a civil partner dies, the surviving civil partner, if he/she has attained state retirement age at the date of the other's death, may be entitled to rely upon the deceased's contributions in order to qualify for a Category B pension:

(a) if the deceased died before 6 April 2010 and the deceased had reached state retirement age by the date of death[5] (in this respect a female civil partner is treated less favourably than a widow who has a current entitlement under the SSCBA 1992 to make a claim whatever her late husband's age at the date of death);

(b) if the deceased died after 6 April 2010, the survivor will be entitled to make a claim regardless of the age of the deceased at the date of death.[6]

13.08 Where a civil partner dies and the survivor has not attained state retirement age at the date of death, a bereavement payment,[7] a bereavement allowance[8] or widowed parent's allowance[9] may be payable to the survivor provided he/she has not entered into a subsequent civil partnership or marriage.

B. OCCUPATIONAL AND PERSONAL PENSION SCHEMES

1. Occupational Pension Schemes

13.09 Occupational pension schemes (ie schemes operated by an employer) which are 'final salary'/'defined benefit' schemes ordinarily provide for the payment of spouses' and dependants' pensions upon the death of the member in service or in retirement. Occupational pension schemes which are 'money purchase'/

---

[4] ibid, s 48A(2A) as inserted by CPA 2004, Sch 24, para 25.
[5] ibid, s 51(1A) as inserted by CPA 2004, Sch 24, para 28.
[6] ibid, s 48B(1A) as inserted by CPA 2004, Sch 24, para 26.
[7] ibid, s 36 as amended by CPA 2004, Sch 24, para 16.
[8] ibid, s 39B as amended by CPA 2004, Sch 24, para 21.
[9] ibid, s 39A as amended by CPA 2004, Sch 24, para 20.

'defined contribution' do not routinely provide for the payment of spouses' and dependants' pensions. If the scheme, whether 'final salary' or 'money purchase' is 'contracted-out' of SERPS/S2P, it is required to provide, from the National Insurance contribution rebate, a pension for a surviving widow (on rights accrued since 1978) and for a surviving widower (on rights accrued since 1988). Thus, the survivor of a same sex couple has a limited claim to survivor benefits only if the scheme provides dependants' pensions and he/she could show financial dependence upon the deceased at the date of death. The 2004 Act does not change this position either for civil partners or for unregistered same sex couples.

Section 255 of the 2004 Act, however, allows a Minister of the Crown to make **13.10** amendments to legislation relating to pensions for the purpose of 'provision with respect to pensions, allowances or gratuities for the surviving civil partners or dependants of civil partners'. Section 255(4)(b) of the 2004 Act provides that the amendments may be retrospective and may take into account rights which have accrued or service which has occurred before the 2004 Act was passed.

The explanatory notes to the 2004 Act state that the power under s 255 will be **13.11** used to require contracted-out defined benefit pension schemes to take account of periods of pensionable service from April 1988 and to require contracted-out defined contribution pension schemes to provide survivor benefits from the protected rights accrued from April 1988. The intention is therefore to treat surviving civil partners as widowers (rather than widows) for the purposes of entitlement to survivor benefits under contracted-out schemes.

Entitlement to survivors' pensions (by both civil partners and unregistered **13.12** same sex couples) in relation to occupational pension schemes which are not contracted-out will continue to depend upon the scheme rules since the 2004 Act contains no general prohibition against discrimination on the grounds of sexual orientation. It is, however, the government's policy that public sector pension schemes should provide survivor pensions for civil partners on the same basis as they are currently provided for spouses and that the availability of survivors' pensions to cohabiting opposite sex couples and to unregistered same sex couples should be determined by the scheme members.[10]

In keeping with this policy, Schs 25 and 26 to the 2004 Act amend various **13.13** statutes which expressly refer to the payment of widows' and dependants' pensions in certain public sector and armed forces pension schemes.

Thus, an amendment is made, for example, to the Fire Services Act 1947 to **13.14** enable the Secretary of State to provide, by order, for civil partners to be treated in the same manner as spouses in relation to the payment of survivors' benefits.

A number of the key public sector pensions are not referred to in the 2004 Act **13.15** because the statutes which enabled those schemes to be established do not,

[10] DTI Consultation document, June 2003, 'Civil Partnership: A framework for the legal recognition of same-sex couples'.

unlike the Fire Services Act 1947, expressly refer to the payment of survivors' benefits. The Police Pensions Act 1976, for example, is silent as to the payment of survivors' benefits. The detailed police pension scheme is regulated by the Police Pensions Regulations 1987[11] which, together with many other regulations governing public sector schemes, will require amendment in order to avoid future discrimination against civil partners.

13.16   The ability to make pension sharing and pension attachment orders in favour of civil partners is addressed at paras 5.55–5.59 above.

2. Personal Pension Schemes

13.17   Ordinarily, personal pension schemes do not provide for payment of either spouses' or dependants' pensions and the opportunity for discrimination against civil partners and same sex couples does not, therefore, arise. If, however, a personal pension scheme is contracted-out of SERPS/S2P, it is required to provide a pension for a surviving spouse. It is intended that this obligation will be amended, pursuant to s 255 of the 2004 Act, so as to require the personal pension scheme to provide a pension to a surviving civil partner (see paras 13.10–13.11 above).

13.18   The ability to make pension sharing and pension attachment orders in favour of civil partners is addressed at paras 5.55–5.59 above.

---

[11] SI 1987/257.

14

JURISDICTION

A. JURISDICTION OF THE COURTS IN RELATION TO DISSOLUTION, SEPARATION, NULLITY, PRESUMPTION OF DEATH AND DECLARATIONS AS TO VALIDITY

Sections 220 to 224 of the 2004 Act define the jurisdiction of the courts in England and Wales to make dissolution, separation, nullity and presumption of death orders and to grant declarations as to validity. **14.01**

It is intended that the Lord Chancellor will make regulations pursuant to s 219 of the 2004 Act for the purposes of applying Council Regulation (EC) No 2201/2003 ('Brussels IIA') to civil partnerships. Brussels IIA provides that the courts of England and Wales will have jurisdiction to entertain applications for dissolution, separation and nullity orders in relation to civil partnerships if:[1] **14.02**

(a) the civil partners are habitually resident in England or Wales; or

(b) the civil partners were last habitually resident in England or Wales, insofar as one of them still resides there; or

(c) the respondent civil partner is habitually resident in England or Wales; or

(d) the applicant civil partner is habitually resident in England and Wales if he/she resided there for at least six months immediately before the application was made and is domiciled in England or Wales;

(e) both civil partners are domiciled in England or Wales.

If the court of a Member State is already seised of proceedings relating to dissolution, legal separation or annulment of the civil partnership, the courts of **14.03**

---

[1] Council Regulation (EC) No 2201/2003 [2003] OJ L338/1, Art 3.

England and Wales must stay any proceedings, if issued later, in relation to dissolution, legal separation or annulment until the jurisdiction of the court of the other Member State has been established.[2]

1. Jurisdiction to Make Dissolution and Separation Orders

14.04 The courts in England and Wales have jurisdiction to entertain applications for dissolution and separation orders in relation to civil partnerships if:[3]

(a) the court has jurisdiction under Brussels IIA; or

(b) if no court has, or is recognized as having, jurisdiction under Brussels IIA and either civil partner is domiciled in England or Wales on the date when proceedings are begun; or

(c) all of the following conditions are met:
   (i) the registration of the civil partnership occurred in England or Wales;
   (ii) no court has, or is recognized as having, jurisdiction under Brussels IIA;
   (iii) it appears to the court to be in the interests of justice to assume jurisdiction; or

(d) if the application is for a dissolution order, the court has already assumed jurisdiction in pending proceedings for a separation order;[4]

(e) if the application is for a separation order, the court has already assumed jurisdiction in pending proceedings for a dissolution order.[5]

2. Jurisdiction to Make Nullity Orders

14.05 The courts in England and Wales have jurisdiction to make nullity orders in relation to civil partnerships if:[6]

(a) the court has jurisdiction under Brussels IIA; or

(b) no court has, or is recognized as having, jurisdiction under Brussels IIA and either civil partner:
   (i) is domiciled in England or Wales on the date when proceedings are begun; or
   (ii) died before that date and was either domiciled in England or Wales at the date of death or had been habitually resident in England or Wales for one year ending with the date of death; or

---

[2] ibid, Art 19.
[3] CPA 2004, s 221(1).
[4] ibid, s 221(3).
[5] ibid, s 221(3).
[6] ibid, s 221(2).

(c) all of the following conditions are met:

    (i) the registration of the civil partnership occurred in England or Wales;

    (ii) no court has, or is recognized as having, jurisdiction under Brussels IIA;

    (iii) it appears to the court to be in the interests of justice to assume jurisdiction; or

(d) the court has already assumed jurisdiction in pending proceedings for a dissolution or separation order.[7]

3. Jurisdiction to Make Presumption of Death Orders

The courts of England and Wales have jurisdiction to make presumption of death orders if:[8]   **14.06**

(a) the applicant is domiciled in England or Wales when the application is made; or

(b) the applicant was habitually resident in England or Wales for one year prior to the application; or

(c) the registration of the civil partnership occurred in England or Wales and it appears to the court to be in the interests of justice to assume jurisdiction.

4. Jurisdiction to Make Declarations as to Validity

The courts of England and Wales have jurisdiction to make declarations as to the validity of a civil partnership under s 58 of the 2004 Act if:[9]   **14.07**

(a) either of the civil partners:

    (i) was domiciled in England or Wales at the date of the application; or

    (ii) had been habitually resident in England or Wales for one year prior to the date of the application; or

    (iii) died before the application was made but was either domiciled in England or Wales at the date of death or had been habitually resident in England or Wales for one year prior to the date of death; or

(b) the registration of the civil partnership occurred in England or Wales and it appears to the court to be in the interests of justice to assume jurisdiction.

5. Jurisdiction to Make Orders in Failure to Maintain Cases

For the jurisdiction of the courts of England and Wales in relation to applications arising from a failure to maintain see para 6.03 above (magistrates' court) and para 5.93 above (High Court/county court).   **14.08**

---

[7] ibid, s 221(3).
[8] ibid, s 222.
[9] ibid, s 224.

6. Jurisdiction to Make Financial Orders Following Overseas Dissolution etc

14.09   For the jurisdiction of the courts of England and Wales to make orders for financial relief following an overseas separation, dissolution or annulment see para 7.05 above.

7. Domicile

14.10   'Domicile' is not defined in the 2004 Act. There are three types of domicile: domicile of origin, domicile of dependence and domicile of choice.

14.11   Domicile of origin is acquired at birth. A child will have the domicile of his/her father (if his/her parents are married) or of his/her mother (if his/her parents are unmarried).[10]

14.12   A child's domicile of origin changes if his/her father's domicile changes (if his/her parents are married) or if his/her mother's domicile changes (if his/her parents are unmarried).[11] This is known as the child's domicile of dependence.

14.13   Upon attaining the age of 16, a child will therefore have either a domicile of origin or a domicile of dependence. From age 16, that domicile may be changed by the child acquiring a domicile of choice. In order to acquire a domicile of choice there must be a combination of both residence in and an intention of permanently or indefinitely residing in a different jurisdiction.[12]

8. Habitual Residence

14.14   Habitual residence is not defined in the 2004 Act. The concept denotes the place in which an individual is ordinarily resident. Continual presence in a certain place is not, however, required in order for an individual to be habitually resident there. It is possible for individuals to be habitually resident in more than one place at any given time.[13]

9. Obligatory and Discretionary Stays of Proceedings for Dissolution, Separation, Nullity and Declarations as to Validity

14.15   Section 224 of the 2004 Act enables rules of court to be made for the purposes of introducing provisions, in non-Brussels IIA cases, comparable to those contained in the Domicile and Matrimonial Proceedings Act 1973, Sch 1 which relate to married couples. In essence, once introduced, the rules will provide for:

(a) obligatory stays: of proceedings in England and Wales for dissolution of a

---

[10] Dicey & Morris, *The Conflict of Laws* (13th edn, London: Sweet & Maxwell) Vol 1, ch 6.

[11] Domicile and Matrimonial Proceedings Act 1973, s 4.

[12] *Winans v A-G* [1904] AC 287, *Ramsay v Liverpool Infirmary* [1930] AC 588, *IRC v Bullock* [1976] 1 WLR 1178.

[13] *Ikimi v Ikimi* [2001] 2 FLR 1288.

civil partnership if proceedings for dissolution or nullity are continuing in Scotland, Northern Ireland, Jersey, Guernsey or the Isle of Man;

(b) discretionary stays: of proceedings in England and Wales for dissolution, separation or nullity orders or for declarations as to the validity of the civil partnership if:

   (i) any proceedings in respect of the civil partnership, or capable of affecting its validity or subsistence, are continuing in any other jurisdiction; and

   (ii) the balance of fairness (including convenience) is such that it is appropriate for the proceedings in the other jurisdiction to be disposed of before any further steps are taken in England or Wales.

10. 'Hemain' Injunctions

Where the court concludes that England and Wales is the proper forum, it may make an 'Hemain' injunction[14] restraining a civil partner from pursuing proceedings in a foreign jurisdiction if such pursuit would be vexatious or oppressive. **14.16**

B. ALLOCATION TO THE HIGH COURT AND COUNTY COURT

Civil partnership causes and matters, declarations in relation to civil partnerships and applications for the consent to the formation of a civil partnership by a minor are 'family business' and are assigned, in the High Court, to the Family Division.[15] **14.17**

The Lord Chancellor will designate certain county courts as 'Civil Partnership Proceedings County Courts' which will have jurisdiction, as designated courts of trial, to hear civil partnership causes (ie proceedings for dissolution, annulment and separation). All civil partnership causes *must* be commenced in a Civil Partnership Proceedings County Court, although they may later be transferred to the High Court.[16] **14.18**

A county court which has been designated as a Civil Partnership Proceedings County Court has the following jurisdiction:[17] **14.19**

(a) to exercise powers under the Children Act 1989 where it considers it necessary to do so in connection with any cause pending before it;

(b) to hear applications for financial relief under Sch 5 to the 2004 Act;

---

[14] *Hemain v Hemain* [1988] 2 FLR 388, CA.
[15] Supreme Court Act 1981, Sch 1 as amended by CPA 2004, Sch 27, para 70.
[16] Matrimonial and Family Proceedings Act 1984, s 36A as inserted by CPA 2004, Sch 27, para 92.
[17] ibid, s 36B as inserted by CPA 2004, Sch 27, para 92.

(c) subject to designation by the Lord Chancellor, to hear applications for financial relief following an overseas dissolution etc under Sch 7 to the 2004 Act. In the absence of such designation, applications must be made to the Family Division of the High Court.

14.20 Any county court (whether a Civil Partnership Proceedings County Court or not) has the jurisdiction to hear the following matters:

(a) applications in relation to arrears and repayments under Pt 12 of Sch 5 to the 2004 Act (see para 5.131 above for the allocation of such applications to the High Court/county court); and

(b) applications to vary maintenance agreements after the death of one of the civil partners under para 73 of Sch 5 to the 2004 Act.

14.21 Subject to any rules which may be made to the contrary, the Principal Registry of the Family Division has the jurisdiction to hear civil partnership causes and ancillary proceedings.[18]

---

[18] ibid, s 42 as amended by CPA 2004, Sch 27, para 96.

APPENDIX 1

Civil Partnership Act 2004

Please note that the copy of the Act contained in this Guide omits any sections and schedules which refer to Scottish or Northern Irish Law, as follows: ss 85–209, 225–232, 248, 252, Schs 10–19, 22, Pts 3 and 4 of Sch 23, Pts 2, 5, 6, 9, 10, 12 and 15 of Sch 24, Schs 28 and 29.

CONTENTS

157

159

CHAPTER 3
PROPERTY AND FINANCIAL ARRANGEMENTS

CHAPTER 4
CIVIL PARTNERSHIP AGREEMENTS

CHAPTER 5
CHILDREN

CHAPTER 6
MISCELLANEOUS

. . .

. . .

PART 1
INTRODUCTION

1. Civil Partnership

(1) A civil partnership is a relationship between two people of the same sex ('civil partners')—

    (a) which is formed when they register as civil partners of each other—

        (i) in England or Wales (under Part 2),

        (ii) in Scotland (under Part 3),

        (iii) in Northern Ireland (under Part 4), or

        (iv) outside the United Kingdom under an Order in Council made under Chapter 1 of Part 5 (registration at British consulates etc. or by armed forces personnel), or

    (b) which they are treated under Chapter 2 of Part 5 as having formed (at the time determined under that Chapter) by virtue of having registered an overseas relationship.

(2) Subsection (1) is subject to the provisions of this Act under or by virtue of which a civil partnership is void.

(3) A civil partnership ends only on death, dissolution or annulment.

(4) The references in subsection (3) to dissolution and annulment are to dissolution and annulment having effect under or recognised in accordance with this Act.

(5) References in this Act to an overseas relationship are to be read in accordance with Chapter 2 of Part 5.

PART 2
CIVIL PARTNERSHIP: ENGLAND AND WALES

CHAPTER 1
REGISTRATION

Formation, Eligibility and Parental Etc. Consent

2. Formation of Civil Partnership by Registration

(1) For the purposes of section 1, two people are to be regarded as having registered as civil partners of each other once each of them has signed the civil partnership document—

    (a) at the invitation of, and in the presence of, a civil partnership registrar, and

    (b) in the presence of each other and two witnesses.

(2) Subsection (1) applies regardless of whether subsections (3) and (4) are complied with.

(3) After the civil partnership document has been signed under subsection (1), it must also be signed, in the presence of the civil partners and each other, by—

    (a) each of the two witnesses, and

    (b) the civil partnership registrar.

(4) After the witnesses and the civil partnership registrar have signed the civil partnership document, the relevant registration authority must ensure that—

    (a) the fact that the two people have registered as civil partners of each other, and

(b) any other information prescribed by regulations,

is recorded in the register as soon as is practicable.

(5) No religious service is to be used while the civil partnership registrar is officiating at the signing of a civil partnership document.

(6) 'The civil partnership document' has the meaning given by section 7(1).

(7) 'The relevant registration authority' means the registration authority in whose area the registration takes place.

3. Eligibility

(1) Two people are not eligible to register as civil partners of each other if—

(a) they are not of the same sex,

(b) either of them is already a civil partner or lawfully married,

(c) either of them is under 16, or

(d) they are within prohibited degrees of relationship.

(2) Part 1 of Schedule 1 contains provisions for determining when two people are within prohibited degrees of relationship.

4. Parental etc. Consent where Proposed Civil Partner Under 18

(1) The consent of the appropriate persons is required before a child and another person may register as civil partners of each other.

(2) Part 1 of Schedule 2 contains provisions for determining who are the appropriate persons for the purposes of this section.

(3) The requirement of consent under subsection (1) does not apply if the child is a surviving civil partner.

(4) Nothing in this section affects any need to obtain the consent of the High Court before a ward of court and another person may register as civil partners of each other.

(5) In this Part 'child', except where used to express a relationship, means a person who is under 18.

Registration Procedure: General

5. Types of Pre-registration Procedure

(1) Two people may register as civil partners of each other under—

(a) the standard procedure;

(b) the procedure for house-bound persons;

(c) the procedure for detained persons;

(d) the special procedure (which is for cases where a person is seriously ill and not expected to recover).

(2) The procedures referred to in subsection (1)(a) to (c) are subject to—

(a) section 20 (modified procedures for certain non-residents);

(b) Schedule 3 (former spouses one of whom has changed sex).

(3) The procedures referred to in subsection (1) (including the procedures as modified by section 20 and Schedule 3) are subject to—

(a) Part 2 of Schedule 1 (provisions applicable in connection with prohibited degrees of relationship), and

(b) Parts 2 and 3 of Schedule 2 (provisions applicable where proposed civil partner is under 18).

(4) This section is also subject to section 249 and Schedule 23 (immigration control and formation of civil partnerships).

6. Place of Registration

(1) The place at which two people may register as civil partners of each other—
   (a) must be in England or Wales,
   (b) must not be in religious premises, and
   (c) must be specified in the notices, or notice, of proposed civil partnership required by this Chapter.

(2) 'Religious premises' means premises which—
   (a) are used solely or mainly for religious purposes, or
   (b) have been so used and have not subsequently been used solely or mainly for other purposes.

(3) In the case of registration under the standard procedure (including that procedure modified as mentioned in section 5), the place—
   (a) must be one which is open to any person wishing to attend the registration, and
   (b) before being specified in a notice of proposed civil partnership, must be agreed with the registration authority in whose area that place is located.

(4) If the place specified in a notice is not so agreed, the notice is void.

(5) A registration authority may provide a place in its area for the registration of civil partnerships.

7. The Civil Partnership Document

(1) In this Part 'the civil partnership document' means—
   (a) in relation to the special procedure, a Registrar General's licence, and
   (b) in relation to any other procedure, a civil partnership schedule.

(2) Before two people are entitled to register as civil partners of each other—
   (a) the civil partnership document must be delivered to the civil partnership registrar, and
   (b) the civil partnership registrar may then ask them for any information required (under section 2(4)) to be recorded in the register.

The Standard Procedure

8. Notice of Proposed Civil Partnership and Declaration

(1) For two people to register as civil partners of each other under the standard procedure, each of them must—
   (a) give a notice of proposed civil partnership to a registration authority, and
   (b) have resided in England or Wales for at least 7 days immediately before giving the notice.

(2) A notice of proposed civil partnership must contain such information as may be prescribed by regulations.

(3) A notice of proposed civil partnership must also include the necessary declaration, made and signed by the person giving the notice—
   (a) at the time when the notice is given, and
   (b) in the presence of an authorised person;
and the authorised person must attest the declaration by adding his name, description and place of residence.

(4) The necessary declaration is a solemn declaration in writing—
   (a) that the proposed civil partner believes that there is no impediment of kindred or affinity or other lawful hindrance to the formation of the civil partnership;

167

(b) that each of the proposed civil partners has had a usual place of residence in England or Wales for at least 7 days immediately before giving the notice.

(5) Where a notice of proposed civil partnership is given to a registration authority in accordance with this section, the registration authority must ensure that the following information is recorded in the register as soon as possible—

(a) the fact that the notice has been given and the information in it;

(b) the fact that the authorised person has attested the declaration.

(6) 'Authorised person' means an employee or officer or other person provided by a registration authority who is authorised by that authority to attest notices of proposed civil partnership.

(7) For the purposes of this Chapter, a notice of proposed civil partnership is recorded when subsection (5) is complied with.

9. Power to Require Evidence of Name etc.

(1) The registration authority to which a notice of proposed civil partnership is given may require the person giving the notice to provide it with specified evidence—

(a) relating to that person, or

(b) if the registration authority considers that the circumstances are exceptional, relating not only to that person but also to that person's proposed civil partner.

(2) Such a requirement may be imposed at any time before the registration authority issues the civil partnership schedule under section 14.

(3) 'Specified evidence', in relation to a person, means such evidence as may be specified in guidance issued by the Registrar General—

(a) of the person's name and surname,

(b) of the person's age,

(c) as to whether the person has previously formed a civil partnership or a marriage and, if so, as to the ending of the civil partnership or marriage,

(d) of the person's nationality, and

(e) as to the person's residence in England or Wales during the period of 7 days preceding the giving of a notice of proposed civil partnership by that person.

10. Proposed Civil Partnership to be Publicised

(1) Where a notice of proposed civil partnership has been given to a registration authority, the relevant information must be publicised during the waiting period—

(a) by that registration authority,

(b) by any registration authority in whose area the person giving the notice has resided during the period of 7 days preceding the giving of the notice,

(c) by any registration authority in whose area the proposed civil partner of the person giving the notice has resided during the period of 7 days preceding the giving of that notice,

(d) by the registration authority in whose area the place specified in the notice as the place of proposed registration is located, and

(e) by the Registrar General.

(2) 'The relevant information' means—

(a) the name of the person giving the notice,

(b) the name of that person's proposed civil partner, and

(c) such other information as may be prescribed by regulations.

11. Meaning of 'the Waiting Period'

In this Chapter 'the waiting period', in relation to a notice of proposed civil partnership, means the period—

(a) beginning the day after the notice is recorded, and

(b) subject to section 12, ending at the end of the period of 15 days beginning with that day.

12. Power to Shorten the Waiting Period

(1) If the Registrar General, on an application being made to him, is satisfied that there are compelling reasons because of the exceptional circumstances of the case for shortening the period of 15 days mentioned in section 11(b), he may shorten it to such period as he considers appropriate.

(2) Regulations may make provision with respect to the making, and granting, of applications under subsection (1).

(3) Regulations under subsection (2) may provide for—

    (a) the power conferred by subsection (1) to be exercised by a registration authority on behalf of the Registrar General in such classes of case as are prescribed by the regulations;

    (b) the making of an appeal to the Registrar General against a decision taken by a registration authority in accordance with regulations made by virtue of paragraph (a).

13. Objection to Proposed Civil Partnership

(1) Any person may object to the issue of a civil partnership schedule under section 14 by giving any registration authority notice of his objection.

(2) A notice of objection must—

    (a) state the objector's place of residence and the ground of objection, and

    (b) be signed by or on behalf of the objector.

(3) If a notice of objection is given to a registration authority, it must ensure that the fact that it has been given and the information in it are recorded in the register as soon as possible.

14. Issue of Civil Partnership Schedule

(1) As soon as the waiting period in relation to each notice of proposed civil partnership has expired, the registration authority in whose area it is proposed that the registration take place is under a duty, at the request of one or both of the proposed civil partners, to issue a document to be known as a 'civil partnership schedule'.

(2) Regulations may make provision as to the contents of a civil partnership schedule.

(3) The duty in subsection (1) does not apply if the registration authority is not satisfied that there is no lawful impediment to the formation of the civil partnership.

(4) If an objection to the issue of the civil partnership schedule has been recorded in the register, no civil partnership schedule is to be issued until—

    (a) the relevant registration authority has investigated the objection and is satisfied that the objection ought not to obstruct the issue of the civil partnership schedule, or

    (b) the objection has been withdrawn by the person who made it.

(5) 'The relevant registration authority' means the authority which first records that a notice of proposed civil partnership has been given by one of the proposed civil partners.

15. Appeal Against Refusal to Issue Civil Partnership Schedule

(1) If the registration authority refuses to issue a civil partnership schedule—
    (a) because an objection to its issue has been made under section 13, or
    (b) in reliance on section 14(3),
either of the proposed civil partners may appeal to the Registrar General.

(2) On an appeal under this section the Registrar General must either confirm the refusal or direct that a civil partnership schedule be issued.

16. Frivolous Objections and Representations: Liability for Costs etc.

(1) Subsection (3) applies if—
    (a) a person objects to the issue of a civil partnership schedule, but
    (b) the Registrar General declares that the grounds on which the objection is made are frivolous and ought not to obstruct the issue of the civil partnership schedule.

(2) Subsection (3) also applies if—
    (a) in reliance on section 14(3), the registration authority refuses to issue a civil partnership schedule as a result of a representation made to it, and
    (b) on an appeal under section 15 against the refusal, the Registrar General declares that the representation is frivolous and ought not to obstruct the issue of the civil partnership schedule.

(3) The person who made the objection or representation is liable for—
    (a) the costs of the proceedings before the Registrar General, and
    (b) damages recoverable by the proposed civil partner to whom the objection or representation relates.

(4) For the purpose of enabling any person to recover any such costs and damages, a copy of a declaration of the Registrar General purporting to be sealed with the seal of the General Register Office is evidence that the Registrar General has made the declaration.

17. Period During which Registration may Take Place

(1) The proposed civil partners may not register as civil partners of each other on the production of the civil partnership schedule until the waiting period in relation to each notice of proposed civil partnership has expired.

(2) Subject to subsection (1), under the standard procedure, they may register as civil partners by signing the civil partnership schedule at any time during the applicable period.

(3) If they do not register as civil partners by signing the civil partnership schedule before the end of the applicable period—
    (a) the notices of proposed civil partnership and the civil partnership schedule are void, and
    (b) no civil partnership registrar may officiate at the signing of the civil partnership schedule by them.

(4) The applicable period, in relation to two people registering as civil partners of each other, is the period of 12 months beginning with—

(a) the day on which the notices of proposed civil partnership are recorded, or

(b) if the notices are not recorded on the same day, the earlier of those days.

The Procedures for House-Bound and Detained Persons

18. House-Bound Persons

(1) This section applies if two people wish to register as civil partners of each other at the place where one of them is house-bound.

(2) A person is house-bound at any place if, in relation to that person, a statement is made by a registered medical practitioner that, in his opinion—

(a) because of illness or disability, that person ought not to move or be moved from the place where he is at the time when the statement is made, and

(b) it is likely to be the case for at least the following 3 months that because of the illness or disability that person ought not to move or be moved from that place.

(3) The procedure under which the two people concerned may register as civil partners of each other is the same as the standard procedure, except that—

(a) each notice of proposed civil partnership must be accompanied by a statement under subsection (2) ('a medical statement'), which must have been made not more than 14 days before the day on which the notice is recorded,

(b) the fact that the registration authority to whom the notice is given has received the medical statement must be recorded in the register, and

(c) the applicable period (for the purposes of section 17) is the period of 3 months beginning with—

(i) the day on which the notices of proposed civil partnership are recorded, or

(ii) if the notices are not recorded on the same day, the earlier of those days.

(4) A medical statement must contain such information and must be made in such manner as may be prescribed by regulations.

(5) A medical statement may not be made in relation to a person who is detained as described in section 19(2).

(6) For the purposes of this Chapter, a person in relation to whom a medical statement is made is to be treated, if he would not otherwise be so treated, as resident and usually resident at the place where he is for the time being.

19. Detained Persons

(1) This section applies if two people wish to register as civil partners of each other at the place where one of them is detained.

(2) 'Detained' means detained—

(a) as a patient in a hospital (but otherwise than by virtue of section 2, 4, 5, 35, 36 or 136 of the Mental Health Act 1983 (c. 20) (short term detentions)), or

(b) in a prison or other place to which the Prison Act 1952 (c. 52) applies.

(3) The procedure under which the two people concerned may register as civil partners of each other is the same as the standard procedure, except that—

(a) each notice of proposed civil partnership must be accompanied by a supporting statement, which must have been made not more than 21 days before the day on which the notice is recorded,

(b) the fact that the registration authority to whom the notice is given has received the supporting statement must be recorded in the register, and

    (c) the applicable period (for the purposes of section 17) is the period of 3 months beginning with—

        (i) the day on which the notices of proposed civil partnership are recorded, or

        (ii) if the notices are not recorded on the same day, the earlier of those days.

(4) A supporting statement, in relation to a detained person, is a statement made by the responsible authority which—

    (a) identifies the establishment where the person is detained, and

    (b) states that the responsible authority has no objection to that establishment being specified in a notice of proposed civil partnership as the place at which the person is to register as a civil partner.

(5) A supporting statement must contain such information and must be made in such manner as may be prescribed by regulations.

(6) 'The responsible authority' means—

    (a) if the person is detained in a hospital, the hospital's managers;

    (b) if the person is detained in a prison or other place to which the 1952 Act applies, the governor or other officer for the time being in charge of that prison or other place.

(7) 'Patient' and 'hospital' have the same meaning as in Part 2 of the 1983 Act and 'managers', in relation to a hospital, has the same meaning as in section 145(1) of the 1983 Act.

(8) For the purposes of this Chapter, a detained person is to be treated, if he would not otherwise be so treated, as resident and usually resident at the place where he is for the time being.

Modified Procedures for Certain Non-Residents

20. Modified Procedures for Certain Non-Residents

(1) Subsection (5) applies in the following three cases.

(2) The first is where—

    (a) two people wish to register as civil partners of each other in England and Wales, and

    (b) one of them ('A') resides in Scotland and the other ('B') resides in England or Wales.

(3) The second is where—

    (a) two people wish to register as civil partners of each other in England and Wales, and

    (b) one of them ('A') resides in Northern Ireland and the other ('B') resides in England or Wales.

(4) The third is where—

    (a) two people wish to register as civil partners of each other in England and Wales, and

    (b) one of them ('A') is a member of Her Majesty's forces who is serving outside the United Kingdom and the other ('B') resides in England or Wales.

(5) For the purposes of the standard procedure, the procedure for house-bound persons and the procedure for detained persons—

    (a) A is not required to give a notice of proposed civil partnership under this Chapter;

    (b) B may give a notice of proposed civil partnership and make the necessary declaration without regard to the requirement that would otherwise apply that A must reside in England or Wales;

    (c) the waiting period is calculated by reference to the day on which B's notice is recorded;

    (d) the civil partnership schedule is not to be issued by a registration authority unless A or B produces to that registration authority a certificate of no impediment issued to A under the relevant provision;

    (e) the applicable period is calculated by reference to the day on which B's notice is recorded and, where the standard procedure is used in the first and second cases, is the period of 3 months beginning with that day;

    (f) section 31 applies as if in subsections (1)(a) and (2)(c) for 'each notice' there were substituted 'B's notice'.

(6) 'The relevant provision' means—

    (a) if A resides in Scotland, section 97;

    (b) if A resides in Northern Ireland, section 150;

    (c) if A is a member of Her Majesty's forces who is serving outside the United Kingdom, section 239.

(7) 'Her Majesty's forces' has the same meaning as in the Army Act 1955 (3 & 4 Eliz. 2 c. 18).

The Special Procedure

21. Notice of Proposed Civil Partnership

(1) For two people to register as civil partners of each other under the special procedure, one of them must—

    (a) give a notice of proposed civil partnership to the registration authority for the area in which it is proposed that the registration take place, and

    (b) comply with any requirement made under section 22.

(2) The notice must contain such information as may be prescribed by regulations.

(3) Subsections (3) to (6) of section 8 (necessary declaration etc.), apart from paragraph (b) of subsection (4), apply for the purposes of this section as they apply for the purposes of that section.

22. Evidence to be Produced

(1) The person giving a notice of proposed civil partnership to a registration authority under the special procedure must produce to the authority such evidence as the Registrar General may require to satisfy him—

    (a) that there is no lawful impediment to the formation of the civil partnership,

    (b) that the conditions in subsection (2) are met, and

    (c) that there is sufficient reason why a licence should be granted.

(2) The conditions are that one of the proposed civil partners—

    (a) is seriously ill and not expected to recover, and

    (b) understands the nature and purport of signing a Registrar General's licence.

(3) The certificate of a registered medical practitioner is sufficient evidence of any or all of the matters referred to in subsection (2).

23. Application to be Reported to Registrar General

On receiving a notice of proposed civil partnership under section 21 and any evidence under section 22, the registration authority must—

(a) inform the Registrar General, and

(b) comply with any directions the Registrar General may give for verifying the evidence given.

24. Objection to Issue of Registrar General's Licence

(1) Any person may object to the Registrar General giving authority for the issue of his licence by giving the Registrar General or any registration authority notice of his objection.

(2) A notice of objection must—

    (a) state the objector's place of residence and the ground of objection, and

    (b) be signed by or on behalf of the objector.

(3) If a notice of objection is given to a registration authority, it must ensure that the fact that it has been given and the information in it are recorded in the register as soon as possible.

25. Issue of Registrar General's Licence

(1) This section applies where a notice of proposed civil partnership is given to a registration authority under section 21.

(2) The registration authority may issue a Registrar General's licence if, and only if, given authority to do so by the Registrar General.

(3) The Registrar General—

    (a) may not give his authority unless he is satisfied that one of the proposed civil partners is seriously ill and not expected to recover, but

    (b) if so satisfied, must give his authority unless a lawful impediment to the issue of his licence has been shown to his satisfaction to exist.

(4) A licence under this section must state that it is issued on the authority of the Registrar General.

(5) Regulations may (subject to subsection (4)) make provision as to the contents of a licence under this section.

(6) If an objection has been made to the Registrar General giving authority for the issue of his licence, he is not to give that authority until—

    (a) he has investigated the objection and decided whether it ought to obstruct the issue of his licence, or

    (b) the objection has been withdrawn by the person who made it.

(7) Any decision of the Registrar General under subsection (6)(a) is final.

26. Frivolous Objections: Liability for Costs

(1) This section applies if—

    (a) a person objects to the Registrar General giving authority for the issue of his licence, but

    (b) the Registrar General declares that the grounds on which the objection is made are frivolous and ought not to obstruct the issue of his licence.

(2) The person who made the objection is liable for—

    (a) the costs of the proceedings before the Registrar General, and

    (b) damages recoverable by the proposed civil partner to whom the objection relates.

(3) For the purpose of enabling any person to recover any such costs and damages, a copy of a declaration of the Registrar General purporting to be sealed with the seal of the General Register Office is evidence that the Registrar General has made the declaration.

27. Period During which Registration may Take Place

(1) If a Registrar General's licence has been issued under section 25, the proposed civil partners may register as civil partners by signing it at any time within 1 month from the day on which the notice of proposed civil partnership was given.

(2) If they do not register as civil partners by signing the licence within the 1 month period—

   (a) the notice of proposed civil partnership and the licence are void, and

   (b) no civil partnership registrar may officiate at the signing of the licence by them.

Supplementary

28. Registration Authorities

In this Chapter 'registration authority' means—

(a) in relation to England, a county council, the council of any district comprised in an area for which there is no county council, a London borough council, the Common Council of the City of London or the Council of the Isles of Scilly;

(b) in relation to Wales, a county council or a county borough council.

29. Civil Partnership Registrars

(1) A civil partnership registrar is an individual who is designated by a registration authority as a civil partnership registrar for its area.

(2) It is the duty of each registration authority to ensure that there is a sufficient number of civil partnership registrars for its area to carry out in that area the functions of civil partnership registrars.

(3) Each registration authority must inform the Registrar General as soon as is practicable—

   (a) of any designation it has made of a person as a civil partnership registrar, and

   (b) of the ending of any such designation.

(4) The Registrar General must make available to the public a list—

   (a) of civil partnership registrars, and

   (b) of the registration authorities for which they are designated to act.

30. The Registrar General and the Register

(1) In this Chapter 'the Registrar General' means the Registrar General for England and Wales.

(2) The Registrar General must provide a system for keeping any records that relate to civil partnerships and are required by this Chapter to be made.

(3) The system may, in particular, enable those records to be kept together with other records kept by the Registrar General.

(4) In this Chapter 'the register' means the system for keeping records provided under subsection (2).

31. Offences Relating to Civil Partnership Schedule

(1) A person commits an offence if he issues a civil partnership schedule knowing that he does so—

   (a) before the waiting period in relation to each notice of proposed civil partnership has expired,

   (b) after the end of the applicable period, or

    (c) at a time when its issue has been forbidden under Schedule 2 by a person entitled to forbid its issue.

(2) A person commits an offence if, in his actual or purported capacity as a civil partnership registrar, he officiates at the signing of a civil partnership schedule by proposed civil partners knowing that he does so—

    (a) at a place other than the place specified in the notices of proposed civil partnership and the civil partnership schedule,

    (b) in the absence of a civil partnership registrar,

    (c) before the waiting period in relation to each notice of proposed civil partnership has expired, or

    (d) even though the civil partnership is void under section 49(b) or (c).

(3) A person guilty of an offence under subsection (1) or (2) is liable on conviction on indictment to imprisonment for a term not exceeding 5 years or to a fine (or both).

(4) A prosecution under this section may not be commenced more than 3 years after the commission of the offence.

32. Offences Relating to Registrar General's Licence

(1) A person commits an offence if—

    (a) he gives information by way of evidence in response to a requirement under section 22(1), knowing that the information is false;

    (b) he gives a certificate as provided for by section 22(3), knowing that the certificate is false.

(2) A person commits an offence if, in his actual or purported capacity as a civil partnership registrar, he officiates at the signing of a Registrar General's licence by proposed civil partners knowing that he does so—

    (a) at a place other than the place specified in the licence,

    (b) in the absence of a civil partnership registrar,

    (c) after the end of 1 month from the day on which the notice of proposed civil partnership was given, or

    (d) even though the civil partnership is void under section 49(b) or (c).

(3) A person guilty of an offence under subsection (1) or (2) is liable—

    (a) on conviction on indictment, to imprisonment not exceeding 3 years or to a fine (or both);

    (b) on summary conviction, to a fine not exceeding the statutory maximum.

(4) A prosecution under this section may not be commenced more than 3 years after the commission of the offence.

33. Offences Relating to the Recording of Civil Partnerships

(1) A civil partnership registrar commits an offence if he refuses or fails to comply with the provisions of this Chapter or of any regulations made under section 36.

(2) A civil partnership registrar guilty of an offence under subsection (1) is liable—

    (a) on conviction on indictment, to imprisonment for a term not exceeding 2 years or to a fine (or both);

    (b) on summary conviction, to a fine not exceeding the statutory maximum;

and on conviction shall cease to be a civil partnership registrar.

(3) A person commits an offence if—

    (a) under arrangements made by a registration authority for the purposes of section

2(4), he is under a duty to record information required to be recorded under section 2(4), but

(b) he refuses or without reasonable cause omits to do so.

(4) A person guilty of an offence under subsection (3) is liable on summary conviction to a fine not exceeding level 3 on the standard scale.

(5) A person commits an offence if he records in the register information relating to the formation of a civil partnership by the signing of a civil partnership schedule, knowing that the civil partnership is void under section 49(b) or (c).

(6) A person guilty of an offence under subsection (5) is liable on conviction on indictment, to imprisonment for a term not exceeding 5 years or to a fine (or both).

(7) A person commits an offence if he records in the register information relating to the formation of a civil partnership by the signing of a Registrar General's licence, knowing that the civil partnership is void under section 49(b) or (c).

(8) A person guilty of an offence under subsection (7) is liable—

(a) on conviction on indictment, to imprisonment for a term not exceeding 3 years or to a fine (or both);

(b) on summary conviction, to a fine not exceeding the statutory maximum.

(9) A prosecution under subsection (5) or (7) may not be commenced more than 3 years after the commission of the offence.

34. Fees

(1) The Chancellor of the Exchequer may by order provide for fees, of such amounts as may be specified in the order, to be payable to such persons as may be prescribed by the order in respect of—

(a) the giving of a notice of proposed civil partnership and the attestation of the necessary declaration;

(b) the making of an application under section 12(1) (application to reduce waiting period);

(c) the issue of a Registrar General's licence;

(d) the attendance of the civil partnership registrar when two people sign the civil partnership document;

(e) such other services provided in connection with civil partnerships either by registration authorities or by or on behalf of the Registrar General as may be prescribed by the order.

(2) The Registrar General may remit the fee for the issue of his licence in whole or in part in any case where it appears to him that the payment of the fee would cause hardship to the proposed civil partners.

35. Power to Assimilate Provisions Relating to Civil Registration

(1) The Chancellor of the Exchequer may by order make—

(a) such amendments of this Act as appear to him appropriate for the purpose of assimilating any provision connected with the formation or recording of civil partnerships in England and Wales to any provision made (whether or not under an order under section 1 of the Regulatory Reform Act 2001 (c. 6)) in relation to civil marriage in England and Wales, and

(b) such amendments of other enactments and of subordinate legislation as appear to him appropriate in consequence of any amendments made under paragraph (a).

(2) 'Civil marriage' means marriage solemnised otherwise than according to the rites of the Church of England or any other religious usages.

(3) 'Amendment' includes repeal or revocation.

(4) 'Subordinate legislation' has the same meaning as in the Interpretation Act 1978 (c. 30).

36. Regulations and Orders

(1) Regulations may make provision supplementing the provisions of this Chapter.

(2) Regulations may in particular make provision—

  (a) relating to the use of Welsh in documents and records relating to civil partnerships;

  (b) with respect to the retention of documents relating to civil partnerships;

  (c) prescribing the duties of civil partnership registrars;

  (d) prescribing the duties of persons in whose presence any declaration is made for the purposes of this Chapter;

  (e) for the issue by the Registrar General of guidance supplementing any provision made by the regulations.

  (f) for the issue by registration authorities or the Registrar General of certified copies of entries in the register and for such copies to be received in evidence.

(3) In this Chapter 'regulations' means regulations made by the Registrar General with the approval of the Chancellor of the Exchequer.

(4) Any power to make regulations or an order under this Chapter is exercisable by statutory instrument.

(5) A statutory instrument containing an order under section 34 is subject to annulment in pursuance of a resolution of either House of Parliament.

(6) No order may be made under section 35 unless a draft of the statutory instrument containing the order has been laid before, and approved by a resolution of, each House of Parliament.

CHAPTER 2
DISSOLUTION, NULLITY AND OTHER PROCEEDINGS

Introduction

37. Powers to Make Orders and Effect of Orders

(1) The court may, in accordance with this Chapter—

  (a) make an order (a 'dissolution order') which dissolves a civil partnership on the ground that it has broken down irretrievably;

  (b) make an order (a 'nullity order') which annuls a civil partnership which is void or voidable;

  (c) make an order (a 'presumption of death order') which dissolves a civil partnership on the ground that one of the civil partners is presumed to be dead;

  (d) make an order (a 'separation order') which provides for the separation of the civil partners.

(2) Every dissolution, nullity or presumption of death order—

  (a) is, in the first instance, a conditional order, and

  (b) may not be made final before the end of the prescribed period (see section 38);

  and any reference in this Chapter to a conditional order is to be read accordingly.

178

(3) A nullity order made where a civil partnership is voidable annuls the civil partnership only as respects any time after the order has been made final, and the civil partnership is to be treated (despite the order) as if it had existed up to that time.

(4) In this Chapter, other than in sections 58 to 61, 'the court' means—

    (a) the High Court, or

    (b) if a county court has jurisdiction by virtue of Part 5 of the Matrimonial and Family Proceedings Act 1984 (c. 42), a county court.

(5) This Chapter is subject to sections 219 to 224 (jurisdiction of the court).

38. The Period Before Conditional Orders may be Made Final

(1) Subject to subsections (2) to (4), the prescribed period for the purposes of section 37(2)(b) is—

    (a) 6 weeks from the making of the conditional order, or

    (b) if the 6 week period would end on a day on which the office or registry of the court dealing with the case is closed, the period of 6 weeks extended to the end of the first day on which the office or registry is next open.

(2) The Lord Chancellor may by order amend this section so as to substitute a different definition of the prescribed period for the purposes of section 37(2)(b).

(3) But the Lord Chancellor may not under subsection (2) provide for a period longer than 6 months to be the prescribed period.

(4) In a particular case the court dealing with the case may by order shorten the prescribed period.

(5) The power to make an order under subsection (2) is exercisable by statutory instrument.

(6) An instrument containing such an order is subject to annulment in pursuance of a resolution of either House of Parliament.

39. Intervention of the Queen's Proctor

(1) This section applies if an application has been made for a dissolution, nullity or presumption of death order.

(2) The court may, if it thinks fit, direct that all necessary papers in the matter are to be sent to the Queen's Proctor who must under the directions of the Attorney General instruct counsel to argue before the court any question in relation to the matter which the court considers it necessary or expedient to have fully argued.

(3) If any person at any time—

    (a) during the progress of the proceedings, or

    (b) before the conditional order is made final,

gives information to the Queen's Proctor on any matter material to the due decision of the case, the Queen's Proctor may take such steps as the Attorney General considers necessary or expedient.

(4) If the Queen's Proctor intervenes or shows cause against the making of the conditional order in any proceedings relating to its making, the court may make such order as may be just as to—

    (a) the payment by other parties to the proceedings of the costs incurred by him in doing so, or

    (b) the payment by the Queen's Proctor of any costs incurred by any of those parties because of his doing so.

(5) The Queen's Proctor is entitled to charge as part of the expenses of his office—

(a) the costs of any proceedings under subsection (2);

(b) if his reasonable costs of intervening or showing cause as mentioned in subsection (4) are not fully satisfied by an order under subsection (4)(a), the amount of the difference;

(c) if the Treasury so directs, any costs which he pays to any parties under an order made under subsection (4)(b).

40. Proceedings Before Order has been Made Final

(1) This section applies if—

    (a) a conditional order has been made, and

    (b) the Queen's Proctor, or any person who has not been a party to proceedings in which the order was made, shows cause why the order should not be made final on the ground that material facts have not been brought before the court.

(2) This section also applies if—

    (a) a conditional order has been made,

    (b) 3 months have elapsed since the earliest date on which an application could have been made for the order to be made final,

    (c) no such application has been made by the civil partner who applied for the conditional order, and

    (d) the other civil partner makes an application to the court under this subsection.

(3) The court may—

    (a) make the order final,

    (b) rescind the order,

    (c) require further inquiry, or

    (d) otherwise deal with the case as it thinks fit.

(4) Subsection (3)(a)—

    (a) applies despite section 37(2) (period before conditional orders may be made final), but

    (b) is subject to section 48(4) (protection for respondent in separation cases) and section 63 (restrictions on making of orders affecting children).

41. Time Bar on Applications for Dissolution Orders

(1) No application for a dissolution order may be made to the court before the end of the period of 1 year from the date of the formation of the civil partnership.

(2) Nothing in this section prevents the making of an application based on matters which occurred before the end of the 1 year period.

42. Attempts at Reconciliation of Civil Partners

(1) This section applies in relation to cases where an application is made for a dissolution or separation order.

(2) Rules of court must make provision for requiring the solicitor acting for the applicant to certify whether he has—

    (a) discussed with the applicant the possibility of a reconciliation with the other civil partner, and

    (b) given the applicant the names and addresses of persons qualified to help effect a reconciliation between civil partners who have become estranged.

(3) If at any stage of proceedings for the order it appears to the court that there is a reasonable possibility of a reconciliation between the civil partners, the court may

adjourn the proceedings for such period as it thinks fit to enable attempts to be made to effect a reconciliation between them.

(4) The power to adjourn under subsection (3) is additional to any other power of adjournment.

43. Consideration by the Court of Certain Agreements or Arrangements

(1) This section applies in relation to cases where—
    (a) proceedings for a dissolution or separation order are contemplated or have begun, and
    (b) an agreement or arrangement is made or proposed to be made between the civil partners which relates to, arises out of, or is connected with, the proceedings.

(2) Rules of court may make provision for enabling—
    (a) the civil partners, or either of them, to refer the agreement or arrangement to the court, and
    (b) the court—
        (i) to express an opinion, if it thinks it desirable to do so, as to the reasonableness of the agreement or arrangement, and
        (ii) to give such directions, if any, in the matter as it thinks fit.

Dissolution of Civil Partnership

44. Dissolution of Civil Partnership which has Broken Down Irretrievably

(1) Subject to section 41, an application for a dissolution order may be made to the court by either civil partner on the ground that the civil partnership has broken down irretrievably.

(2) On an application for a dissolution order the court must inquire, so far as it reasonably can, into—
    (a) the facts alleged by the applicant, and
    (b) any facts alleged by the respondent.

(3) The court hearing an application for a dissolution order must not hold that the civil partnership has broken down irretrievably unless the applicant satisfies the court of one or more of the facts described in subsection (5)(a), (b), (c) or (d).

(4) But if the court is satisfied of any of those facts, it must make a dissolution order unless it is satisfied on all the evidence that the civil partnership has not broken down irretrievably.

(5) The facts referred to in subsections (3) and (4) are—
    (a) that the respondent has behaved in such a way that the applicant cannot reasonably be expected to live with the respondent;
    (b) that—
        (i) the applicant and the respondent have lived apart for a continuous period of at least 2 years immediately preceding the making of the application ('2 years' separation'), and
        (ii) the respondent consents to a dissolution order being made;
    (c) that the applicant and the respondent have lived apart for a continuous period of at least 5 years immediately preceding the making of the application ('5 years' separation');

(d) that the respondent has deserted the applicant for a continuous period of at least 2 years immediately preceding the making of the application.

45. Supplemental Provisions as to Facts Raising Presumption of Breakdown

(1) Subsection (2) applies if—
   (a) in any proceedings for a dissolution order the applicant alleges, in reliance on section 44(5)(a), that the respondent has behaved in such a way that the applicant cannot reasonably be expected to live with the respondent, but
   (b) after the date of the occurrence of the final incident relied on by the applicant and held by the court to support his allegation, the applicant and the respondent have lived together for a period (or periods) which does not, or which taken together do not, exceed 6 months.

(2) The fact that the applicant and respondent have lived together as mentioned in subsection (1)(b) must be disregarded in determining, for the purposes of section 44(5)(a), whether the applicant cannot reasonably be expected to live with the respondent.

(3) Subsection (4) applies in relation to cases where the applicant alleges, in reliance on section 44(5)(b), that the respondent consents to a dissolution order being made.

(4) Rules of court must make provision for the purpose of ensuring that the respondent has been given such information as will enable him to understand—
   (a) the consequences to him of consenting to the making of the order, and
   (b) the steps which he must take to indicate his consent.

(5) For the purposes of section 44(5)(d) the court may treat a period of desertion as having continued at a time when the deserting civil partner was incapable of continuing the necessary intention, if the evidence before the court is such that, had he not been so incapable, the court would have inferred that the desertion continued at that time.

(6) In considering for the purposes of section 44(5) whether the period for which the civil partners have lived apart or the period for which the respondent has deserted the applicant has been continuous, no account is to be taken of—
   (a) any one period not exceeding 6 months, or
   (b) any two or more periods not exceeding 6 months in all,
   during which the civil partners resumed living with each other.

(7) But no period during which the civil partners have lived with each other counts as part of the period during which the civil partners have lived apart or as part of the period of desertion.

(8) For the purposes of section 44(5)(b) and (c) and this section civil partners are to be treated as living apart unless they are living with each other in the same household, and references in this section to civil partners living with each other are to be read as references to their living with each other in the same household.

46. Dissolution Order not Precluded by Previous Separation Order etc.

(1) Subsections (2) and (3) apply if any of the following orders has been made in relation to a civil partnership—
   (a) a separation order;
   (b) an order under Schedule 6 (financial relief in magistrates' courts etc.);
   (c) an order under section 33 of the Family Law Act 1996 (c. 27) (occupation orders);

(d) an order under section 37 of the 1996 Act (orders where neither civil partner entitled to occupy the home).

(2) Nothing prevents—
   (a) either civil partner from applying for a dissolution order, or
   (b) the court from making a dissolution order,

on the same facts, or substantially the same facts, as those proved in support of the making of the order referred to in subsection (1).

(3) On the application for the dissolution order, the court—
   (a) may treat the order referred to in subsection (1) as sufficient proof of any desertion or other fact by reference to which it was made, but
   (b) must not make the dissolution order without receiving evidence from the applicant.

(4) If—
   (a) the application for the dissolution order follows a separation order or any order requiring the civil partners to live apart,
   (b) there was a period of desertion immediately preceding the institution of the proceedings for the separation order, and
   (c) the civil partners have not resumed living together and the separation order has been continuously in force since it was made,

the period of desertion is to be treated for the purposes of the application for the dissolution order as if it had immediately preceded the making of the application.

(5) For the purposes of section 44(5)(d) the court may treat as a period during which the respondent has deserted the applicant any period during which there is in force—
   (a) an injunction granted by the High Court or a county court which excludes the respondent from the civil partnership home, or
   (b) an order under section 33 or 37 of the 1996 Act which prohibits the respondent from occupying a dwelling-house in which the applicant and the respondent have, or at any time have had, a civil partnership home.

47. Refusal of Dissolution in 5 Year Separation Cases on Ground of Grave Hardship

(1) The respondent to an application for a dissolution order in which the applicant alleges 5 years' separation may oppose the making of an order on the ground that—
   (a) the dissolution of the civil partnership will result in grave financial or other hardship to him, and
   (b) it would in all the circumstances be wrong to dissolve the civil partnership.

(2) Subsection (3) applies if—
   (a) the making of a dissolution order is opposed under this section,
   (b) the court finds that the applicant is entitled to rely in support of his application on the fact of 5 years' separation and makes no such finding as to any other fact mentioned in section 44(5), and
   (c) apart from this section, the court would make a dissolution order.

(3) The court must—
   (a) consider all the circumstances, including the conduct of the civil partners and the interests of the civil partners and of any children or other persons concerned, and
   (b) if it is of the opinion that the ground mentioned in subsection (1) is made out, dismiss the application for the dissolution order.

(4) 'Hardship' includes the loss of the chance of acquiring any benefit which the respondent might acquire if the civil partnership were not dissolved.

48. Proceedings Before Order Made Final: Protection for Respondent in Separation Cases

(1) The court may, on an application made by the respondent, rescind a conditional dissolution order if—

   (a) it made the order on the basis of a finding that the applicant was entitled to rely on the fact of 2 years' separation coupled with the respondent's consent to a dissolution order being made,

   (b) it made no such finding as to any other fact mentioned in section 44(5), and

   (c) it is satisfied that the applicant misled the respondent (whether intentionally or unintentionally) about any matter which the respondent took into account in deciding to give his consent.

(2) Subsections (3) to (5) apply if—

   (a) the respondent to an application for a dissolution order in which the applicant alleged—

      (i) 2 years' separation coupled with the respondent's consent to a dissolution order being made, or

      (ii) 5 years' separation,

   has applied to the court for consideration under subsection (3) of his financial position after the dissolution of the civil partnership, and

   (b) the court—

      (i) has made a conditional dissolution order on the basis of a finding that the applicant was entitled to rely in support of his application on the fact of 2 years' or 5 years' separation, and

      (ii) has made no such finding as to any other fact mentioned in section 44(5).

(3) The court hearing an application by the respondent under subsection (2) must consider all the circumstances, including—

   (a) the age, health, conduct, earning capacity, financial resources and financial obligations of each of the parties, and

   (b) the financial position of the respondent as, having regard to the dissolution, it is likely to be after the death of the applicant should the applicant die first.

(4) Subject to subsection (5), the court must not make the order final unless it is satisfied that—

   (a) the applicant should not be required to make any financial provision for the respondent, or

   (b) the financial provision made by the applicant for the respondent is—

      (i) reasonable and fair, or

      (ii) the best that can be made in the circumstances.

(5) The court may if it thinks fit make the order final if—

   (a) it appears that there are circumstances making it desirable that the order should be made final without delay, and

   (b) it has obtained a satisfactory undertaking from the applicant that he will make such financial provision for the respondent as it may approve.

Nullity

49. Grounds on which Civil Partnership is Void

Where two people register as civil partners of each other in England and Wales, the civil partnership is void if—

(a) at the time when they do so, they are not eligible to register as civil partners of each other under Chapter 1 (see section 3),

(b) at the time when they do so they both know—
- (i) that due notice of proposed civil partnership has not been given,
- (ii) that the civil partnership document has not been duly issued,
- (iii) that the civil partnership document is void under section 17(3) or 27(2) (registration after end of time allowed for registering),
- (iv) that the place of registration is a place other than that specified in the notices (or notice) of proposed civil partnership and the civil partnership document, or
- (v) that a civil partnership registrar is not present, or

(c) the civil partnership document is void under paragraph 6(5) of Schedule 2 (civil partnership between child and another person forbidden).

50. Grounds on which Civil Partnership is Voidable

(1) Where two people register as civil partners of each other in England and Wales, the civil partnership is voidable if—
- (a) either of them did not validly consent to its formation (whether as a result of duress, mistake, unsoundness of mind or otherwise);
- (b) at the time of its formation either of them, though capable of giving a valid consent, was suffering (whether continuously or intermittently) from mental disorder of such a kind or to such an extent as to be unfitted for civil partnership;
- (c) at the time of its formation, the respondent was pregnant by some person other than the applicant;
- (d) an interim gender recognition certificate under the Gender Recognition Act 2004 (c. 7) has, after the time of its formation, been issued to either civil partner;
- (e) the respondent is a person whose gender at the time of its formation had become the acquired gender under the 2004 Act.

(2) In this section and section 51 'mental disorder' has the same meaning as in the Mental Health Act 1983 (c. 20).

51. Bars to Relief where Civil Partnership is Voidable

(1) The court must not make a nullity order on the ground that a civil partnership is voidable if the respondent satisfies the court—
- (a) that the applicant, with knowledge that it was open to him to obtain a nullity order, conducted himself in relation to the respondent in such a way as to lead the respondent reasonably to believe that he would not seek to do so, and
- (b) that it would be unjust to the respondent to make the order.

(2) Without prejudice to subsection (1), the court must not make a nullity order by virtue of section 50(1)(a), (b), (c) or (e) unless—
- (a) it is satisfied that proceedings were instituted within 3 years from the date of the formation of the civil partnership, or
- (b) leave for the institution of proceedings after the end of that 3 year period has been granted under subsection (3).

(3) A judge of the court may, on an application made to him, grant leave for the institution of proceedings if he—

    (a) is satisfied that the applicant has at some time during the 3 year period suffered from mental disorder, and

    (b) considers that in all the circumstances of the case it would be just to grant leave for the institution of proceedings.

(4) An application for leave under subsection (3) may be made after the end of the 3 year period.

(5) Without prejudice to subsection (1), the court must not make a nullity order by virtue of section 50(1)(d) unless it is satisfied that proceedings were instituted within the period of 6 months from the date of issue of the interim gender recognition certificate.

(6) Without prejudice to subsections (1) and (2), the court must not make a nullity order by virtue of section 50(1)(c) or (e) unless it is satisfied that the applicant was at the time of the formation of the civil partnership ignorant of the facts alleged.

52. Proof of Certain Matters not Necessary to Validity of Civil Partnership

(1) Where two people have registered as civil partners of each other in England and Wales, it is not necessary in support of the civil partnership to give any proof—

    (a) that any person whose consent to the civil partnership was required by section 4 (parental etc. consent) had given his consent, or

    (b) that the civil partnership registrar was designated as such by the registration authority in whose area the registration took place;

and no evidence is to be given to prove the contrary in any proceedings touching the validity of the civil partnership.

(2) Subsection (1)(a) is subject to section 49(c) (civil partnership void if forbidden).

53. Power to Validate Civil Partnership

(1) Where two people have registered as civil partners of each other in England and Wales, the Lord Chancellor may by order validate the civil partnership if it appears to him that it is or may be void under section 49(b).

(2) An order under subsection (1) may include provisions for relieving a person from any liability under section 31(2), 32(2) or 33(5) or (7).

(3) The draft of an order under subsection (1) must be advertised, in such manner as the Lord Chancellor thinks fit, not less than one month before the order is made.

(4) The Lord Chancellor must—

    (a) consider all objections to the order sent to him in writing during that month, and

    (b) if it appears to him necessary, direct a local inquiry into the validity of any such objections.

(5) An order under subsection (1) is subject to special parliamentary procedure.

54. Validity of Civil Partnerships Registered Outside England and Wales

(1) Where two people register as civil partners of each other in Scotland, the civil partnership is—

    (a) void, if it would be void in Scotland under section 123, and

    (b) voidable, if the circumstances fall within section 50(1)(d).

(2) Where two people register as civil partners of each other in Northern Ireland, the civil partnership is—

    (a) void, if it would be void in Northern Ireland under section 173, and

(b) voidable, if the circumstances fall within any paragraph of section 50(1).

(3) Subsection (4) applies where two people register as civil partners of each other under an Order in Council under—

    (a) section 210 (registration at British consulates etc.), or

    (b) section 211 (registration by armed forces personnel),

('the relevant section').

(4) The civil partnership is—

    (a) void, if—

        (i) the condition in subsection (2)(a) or (b) of the relevant section is not met, or

        (ii) a requirement prescribed for the purposes of this paragraph by an Order in Council under the relevant section is not complied with, and

    (b) voidable, if—

        (i) the appropriate part of the United Kingdom is England and Wales or Northern Ireland and the circumstances fall within any paragraph of section 50(1), or

        (ii) the appropriate part of the United Kingdom is Scotland and the circumstances fall within section 50(1)(d).

(5) The appropriate part of the United Kingdom is the part by reference to which the condition in subsection (2)(b) of the relevant section is met.

(6) Subsections (7) and (8) apply where two people have registered an apparent or alleged overseas relationship.

(7) The civil partnership is void if—

    (a) the relationship is not an overseas relationship, or

    (b) (even though the relationship is an overseas relationship) the parties are not treated under Chapter 2 of Part 5 as having formed a civil partnership.

(8) The civil partnership is voidable if—

    (a) the overseas relationship is voidable under the relevant law,

    (b) the circumstances fall within section 50(1)(d), or

    (c) where either of the parties was domiciled in England and Wales or Northern Ireland at the time when the overseas relationship was registered, the circumstances fall within section 50(1)(a), (b), (c) or (e).

(9) Section 51 applies for the purposes of—

    (a) subsections (1)(b), (2)(b) and (4)(b),

    (b) subsection (8)(a), in so far as applicable in accordance with the relevant law, and

    (c) subsection (8)(b) and (c).

(10) In subsections (8)(a) and (9)(b) 'the relevant law' means the law of the country or territory where the overseas relationship was registered (including its rules of private international law).

(11) For the purposes of subsections (8) and (9)(b) and (c), references in sections 50 and 51 to the formation of the civil partnership are to be read as references to the registration of the overseas relationship.

Presumption of Death Orders

55. Presumption of Death Orders

(1) The court may, on an application made by a civil partner, make a presumption of death order if it is satisfied that reasonable grounds exist for supposing that the other civil partner is dead.

(2) In any proceedings under this section the fact that—
- (a) for a period of 7 years or more the other civil partner has been continually absent from the applicant, and
- (b) the applicant has no reason to believe that the other civil partner has been living within that time,

is evidence that the other civil partner is dead until the contrary is proved.

Separation Orders

56. Separation Orders

(1) An application for a separation order may be made to the court by either civil partner on the ground that any such fact as is mentioned in section 44(5)(a), (b), (c) or (d) exists.

(2) On an application for a separation order the court must inquire, so far as it reasonably can, into—
- (a) the facts alleged by the applicant, and
- (b) any facts alleged by the respondent,

but whether the civil partnership has broken down irretrievably is irrelevant.

(3) If the court is satisfied on the evidence of any such fact as is mentioned in section 44(5)(a), (b), (c) or (d) it must, subject to section 63, make a separation order.

(4) Section 45 (supplemental provisions as to facts raising presumption of breakdown) applies for the purposes of an application for a separation order alleging any such fact as it applies in relation to an application for a dissolution order alleging that fact.

57. Effect of Separation Order

If either civil partner dies intestate as respects all or any of his or her real or personal property while—
(a) a separation order is in force, and
(b) the separation is continuing,
the property as respects which he or she died intestate devolves as if the other civil partner had then been dead.

Declarations

58. Declarations

(1) Any person may apply to the High Court or a county court for one or more of the following declarations in relation to a civil partnership specified in the application—
- (a) a declaration that the civil partnership was at its inception a valid civil partnership;
- (b) a declaration that the civil partnership subsisted on a date specified in the application;
- (c) a declaration that the civil partnership did not subsist on a date so specified;
- (d) a declaration that the validity of a dissolution, annulment or legal separation obtained outside England and Wales in respect of the civil partnership is entitled to recognition in England and Wales;
- (e) a declaration that the validity of a dissolution, annulment or legal separation so obtained in respect of the civil partnership is not entitled to recognition in England and Wales.

(2) Where an application under subsection (1) is made to a court by a person other than a civil partner in the civil partnership to which the application relates, the court must refuse to hear the application if it considers that the applicant does not have a sufficient interest in the determination of that application.

59. General Provisions as to Making and Effect of Declarations

(1) Where on an application for a declaration under section 58 the truth of the proposition to be declared is proved to the satisfaction of the court, the court must make the declaration unless to do so would be manifestly contrary to public policy.

(2) Any declaration under section 58 binds Her Majesty and all other persons.

(3) The court, on the dismissal of an application for a declaration under section 58, may not make any declaration for which an application has not been made.

(4) No declaration which may be applied for under section 58 may be made otherwise than under section 58 by any court.

(5) No declaration may be made by any court, whether under section 58 or otherwise, that a civil partnership was at its inception void.

(6) Nothing in this section affects the powers of any court to make a nullity order in respect of a civil partnership.

60. The Attorney General and Proceedings for Declarations

(1) On an application for a declaration under section 58 the court may at any stage of the proceedings, of its own motion or on the application of any party to the proceedings, direct that all necessary papers in the matter be sent to the Attorney-General.

(2) The Attorney General, whether or not he is sent papers in relation to an application for a declaration under section 58, may—
    (a) intervene in the proceedings on that application in such manner as he thinks necessary or expedient, and
    (b) argue before the court dealing with the application any question in relation to the application which the court considers it necessary to have fully argued.

(3) Where any costs are incurred by the Attorney General in connection with any application for a declaration under section 58, the court may make such order as it considers just as to the payment of those costs by parties to the proceedings.

61. Supplementary Provisions as to Declarations

(1) Any declaration made under section 58, and any application for such a declaration, must be in the form prescribed by rules of court.

(2) Rules of court may make provision—
    (a) as to the information required to be given by any applicant for a declaration under section 58;
    (b) requiring notice of an application under section 58 to be served on the Attorney General and on persons who may be affected by any declaration applied for.

(3) No proceedings under section 58 affect any final judgment or order already pronounced or made by any court of competent jurisdiction.

(4) The court hearing an application under section 58 may direct that the whole or any part of the proceedings must be heard in private.

(5) An application for a direction under subsection (4) must be heard in private unless the court otherwise directs.

General Provisions

62. Relief for Respondent in Dissolution Proceedings

(1) If in any proceedings for a dissolution order the respondent alleges and proves any such fact as is mentioned in section 44(5)(a), (b), (c) or (d) the court may give to the respondent the relief to which he would have been entitled if he had made an application seeking that relief.

(2) When applying subsection (1), treat—
   (a) the respondent as the applicant, and
   (b) the applicant as the respondent,
   for the purposes of section 44(5).

63. Restrictions on Making of Orders Affecting Children

(1) In any proceedings for a dissolution, nullity or separation order, the court must consider—
   (a) whether there are any children of the family to whom this section applies, and
   (b) if there are any such children, whether (in the light of the arrangements which have been, or are proposed to be, made for their upbringing and welfare) it should exercise any of its powers under the Children Act 1989 (c. 41) with respect to any of them.

(2) If, in the case of any child to whom this section applies, it appears to the court that—
   (a) the circumstances of the case require it, or are likely to require it, to exercise any of its powers under the 1989 Act with respect to any such child,
   (b) it is not in a position to exercise the power or (as the case may be) those powers without giving further consideration to the case, and
   (c) there are exceptional circumstances which make it desirable in the interests of the child that the court should give a direction under this section,
   it may direct that the order is not to be made final, or (in the case of a separation order) is not to be made, until the court orders otherwise.

(3) This section applies to—
   (a) any child of the family who has not reached 16 at the date when the court considers the case in accordance with the requirements of this section, and
   (b) any child of the family who has reached 16 at that date and in relation to whom the court directs that this section shall apply.

64. Parties to Proceedings Under this Chapter

(1) Rules of court may make provision with respect to—
   (a) the joinder as parties to proceedings under sections 37 to 56 of persons involved in allegations of improper conduct made in those proceedings,
   (b) the dismissal from such proceedings of any parties so joined, and
   (c) the persons who are to be parties to proceedings on an application under section 58.

(2) Rules of court made under this section may make different provision for different cases.

(3) In every case in which the court considers, in the interest of a person not already a party to the proceedings, that the person should be made a party, the court may if it thinks fit allow the person to intervene upon such terms, if any, as the court thinks just.

CHAPTER 3
PROPERTY AND FINANCIAL ARRANGEMENTS

65. Contribution by Civil Partner to Property Improvement

(1) This section applies if—
    (a) a civil partner contributes in money or money's worth to the improvement of real or personal property in which or in the proceeds of sale of which either or both of the civil partners has or have a beneficial interest, and
    (b) the contribution is of a substantial nature.
(2) The contributing partner is to be treated as having acquired by virtue of the contribution a share or an enlarged share (as the case may be) in the beneficial interest of such an extent—
    (a) as may have been then agreed, or
    (b) in default of such agreement, as may seem in all the circumstances just to any court before which the question of the existence or extent of the beneficial interest of either of the civil partners arises (whether in proceedings between them or in any other proceedings).
(3) Subsection (2) is subject to any agreement (express or implied) between the civil partners to the contrary.

66. Disputes between Civil Partners about Property

(1) In any question between the civil partners in a civil partnership as to title to or possession of property, either civil partner may apply to—
    (a) the High Court, or
    (b) such county court as may be prescribed by rules of court.
(2) On such an application, the court may make such order with respect to the property as it thinks fit (including an order for the sale of the property).
(3) Rules of court made for the purposes of this section may confer jurisdiction on county courts whatever the situation or value of the property in dispute.

67. Applications Under Section 66 where Property not in Possession etc.

(1) The right of a civil partner ('A') to make an application under section 66 includes the right to make such an application where A claims that the other civil partner ('B') has had in his possession or under his control—
    (a) money to which, or to a share of which, A was beneficially entitled, or
    (b) property (other than money) to which, or to an interest in which, A was beneficially entitled,
and that either the money or other property has ceased to be in B's possession or under B's control or that A does not know whether it is still in B's possession or under B's control.
(2) For the purposes of subsection (1)(a) it does not matter whether A is beneficially entitled to the money or share—
    (a) because it represents the proceeds of property to which, or to an interest in which, A was beneficially entitled, or
    (b) for any other reason.
(3) Subsections (4) and (5) apply if, on such an application being made, the court is satisfied that B—

(a) has had in his possession or under his control money or other property as mentioned in subsection (1)(a) or (b), and

(b) has not made to A, in respect of that money or other property, such payment or disposition as would have been appropriate in the circumstances.

(4) The power of the court to make orders under section 66 includes power to order B to pay to A—

(a) in a case falling within subsection (1)(a), such sum in respect of the money to which the application relates, or A's share of it, as the court considers appropriate, or

(b) in a case falling within subsection (1)(b), such sum in respect of the value of the property to which the application relates, or A's interest in it, as the court considers appropriate.

(5) If it appears to the court that there is any property which—

(a) represents the whole or part of the money or property, and

(b) is property in respect of which an order could (apart from this section) have been made under section 66,

the court may (either instead of or as well as making an order in accordance with subsection (4)) make any order which it could (apart from this section) have made under section 66.

(6) Any power of the court which is exercisable on an application under section 66 is exercisable in relation to an application made under that section as extended by this section.

68. Applications Under Section 66 by Former Civil Partners

(1) This section applies where a civil partnership has been dissolved or annulled.

(2) Subject to subsection (3), an application may be made under section 66 (including that section as extended by section 67) by either former civil partner despite the dissolution or annulment (and references in those sections to a civil partner are to be read accordingly).

(3) The application must be made within the period of 3 years beginning with the date of the dissolution or annulment.

69. Actions in Tort between Civil Partners

(1) This section applies if an action in tort is brought by one civil partner against the other during the subsistence of the civil partnership.

(2) The court may stay the proceedings if it appears—

(a) that no substantial benefit would accrue to either civil partner from the continuation of the proceedings, or

(b) that the question or questions in issue could more conveniently be disposed of on an application under section 66.

(3) Without prejudice to subsection (2)(b), the court may in such an action—

(a) exercise any power which could be exercised on an application under section 66, or

(b) give such directions as it thinks fit for the disposal under that section of any question arising in the proceedings.

70. Assurance Policy by Civil Partner for Benefit of Other Civil Partner etc.

Section 11 of the Married Women's Property Act 1882 (c. 75) (money payable under policy of assurance not to form part of the estate of the insured) applies in relation to a policy of assurance—

(a) effected by a civil partner on his own life, and

(b) expressed to be for the benefit of his civil partner, or of his children, or of his civil partner and children, or any of them,

as it applies in relation to a policy of assurance effected by a husband and expressed to be for the benefit of his wife, or of his children, or of his wife and children, or of any of them.

71. Wills, Administration of Estates and Family Provision

Schedule 4 amends enactments relating to wills, administration of estates and family provision so that they apply in relation to civil partnerships as they apply in relation to marriage.

72. Financial Relief for Civil Partners and Children of Family

(1) Schedule 5 makes provision for financial relief in connection with civil partnerships that corresponds to provision made for financial relief in connection with marriages by Part 2 of the Matrimonial Causes Act 1973 (c. 18).

(2) Any rule of law under which any provision of Part 2 of the 1973 Act is interpreted as applying to dissolution of a marriage on the ground of presumed death is to be treated as applying (with any necessary modifications) in relation to the corresponding provision of Schedule 5.

(3) Schedule 6 makes provision for financial relief in connection with civil partnerships that corresponds to provision made for financial relief in connection with marriages by the Domestic Proceedings and Magistrates' Courts Act 1978 (c. 22).

(4) Schedule 7 makes provision for financial relief in England and Wales after a civil partnership has been dissolved or annulled, or civil partners have been legally separated, in a country outside the British Islands.

CHAPTER 4
CIVIL PARTNERSHIP AGREEMENTS

73. Civil Partnership Agreements Unenforceable

(1) A civil partnership agreement does not under the law of England and Wales have effect as a contract giving rise to legal rights.

(2) No action lies in England and Wales for breach of a civil partnership agreement, whatever the law applicable to the agreement.

(3) In this section and section 74 'civil partnership agreement' means an agreement between two people—

    (a) to register as civil partners of each other—

        (i) in England and Wales (under this Part),

        (ii) in Scotland (under Part 3),

        (iii) in Northern Ireland (under Part 4), or

        (iv) outside the United Kingdom under an Order in Council made under Chapter 1 of Part 5 (registration at British consulates etc. or by armed forces personnel), or

    (b) to enter into an overseas relationship.

(4) This section applies in relation to civil partnership agreements whether entered into before or after this section comes into force, but does not affect any action commenced before it comes into force.

74. Property where Civil Partnership Agreement is Terminated

(1) This section applies if a civil partnership agreement is terminated.

(2) Section 65 (contributions by civil partner to property improvement) applies, in relation to any property in which either or both of the parties to the agreement had a beneficial interest while the agreement was in force, as it applies in relation to property in which a civil partner has a beneficial interest.

(3) Sections 66 and 67 (disputes between civil partners about property) apply to any dispute between or claim by one of the parties in relation to property in which either or both had a beneficial interest while the agreement was in force, as if the parties were civil partners of each other.

(4) An application made under section 66 or 67 by virtue of subsection (3) must be made within 3 years of the termination of the agreement.

(5) A party to a civil partnership agreement who makes a gift of property to the other party on the condition (express or implied) that it is to be returned if the agreement is terminated is not prevented from recovering the property merely because of his having terminated the agreement.

CHAPTER 5
CHILDREN

75. Parental Responsibility, Children of the Family and Relatives

(1) Amend the Children Act 1989 (c. 41) ('the 1989 Act') as follows.

(2) In section 4A(1) (acquisition of parental responsibility by step-parent) after 'is married to' insert ', or a civil partner of,'.

(3) In section 105(1) (interpretation), for the definition of 'child of the family' (in relation to the parties to a marriage) substitute—

'child of the family', in relation to parties to a marriage, or to two people who are civil partners of each other, means—
(a) a child of both of them, and
(b) any other child, other than a child placed with them as foster parents by a local authority or voluntary organisation, who has been treated by both of them as a child of their family.'

(4) In the definition of 'relative' in section 105(1), for 'by affinity)' substitute 'by marriage or civil partnership)'.

76. Guardianship

In section 6 of the 1989 Act (guardians: revocation and disclaimer) after subsection (3A) insert—

'(3B) An appointment under section 5(3) or (4) (including one made in an unrevoked will or codicil) is revoked if the person appointed is the civil partner of the person who made the appointment and either—

(a) an order of a court of civil jurisdiction in England and Wales dissolves or annuls the civil partnership, or

(b) the civil partnership is dissolved or annulled and the dissolution or annulment is entitled to recognition in England and Wales by virtue of Chapter 3 of Part 5 of the Civil Partnership Act 2004,

unless a contrary intention appears by the appointment.'

77. Entitlement to Apply for Residence or Contact Order

In section 10(5) of the 1989 Act (persons entitled to apply for residence or contact order) after paragraph (a) insert—

'(aa) any civil partner in a civil partnership (whether or not subsisting) in relation to whom the child is a child of the family;'.

78. Financial Provision for Children

(1) Amend Schedule 1 to the 1989 Act (financial provision for children) as follows.

(2) In paragraph 2(6) (meaning of 'periodical payments order') after paragraph (d) insert—

'(e) Part 1 or 9 of Schedule 5 to the Civil Partnership Act 2004 (financial relief in the High Court or a county court etc.);
(f) Schedule 6 to the 2004 Act (financial relief in the magistrates' courts etc.),'.

(3) In paragraph 15(2) (person with whom a child lives or is to live) after 'husband or wife' insert 'or civil partner'.

(4) For paragraph 16(2) (extended meaning of 'parent') substitute—

'(2) In this Schedule, except paragraphs 2 and 15, "parent" includes—
    (a) any party to a marriage (whether or not subsisting) in relation to whom the child concerned is a child of the family, and
    (b) any civil partner in a civil partnership (whether or not subsisting) in relation to whom the child concerned is a child of the family;

and for this purpose any reference to either parent or both parents shall be read as a reference to any parent of his and to all of his parents.'

79. Adoption

(1) Amend the Adoption and Children Act 2002 (c. 38) as follows.

(2) In section 21 (placement orders), in subsection (4)(c), after 'child marries' insert ', forms a civil partnership'.

(3) In section 47 (conditions for making adoption orders), after subsection (8) insert—

'(8A) An adoption order may not be made in relation to a person who is or has been a civil partner.'

(4) In section 51 (adoption by one person), in subsection (1), after 'is not married' insert 'or a civil partner'.

(5) After section 51(3) insert—

'(3A) An adoption order may be made on the application of one person who has attained the age of 21 years and is a civil partner if the court is satisfied that—
    (a) the person's civil partner cannot be found,
    (b) the civil partners have separated and are living apart, and the separation is likely to be permanent, or

     (c) the person's civil partner is by reason of ill-health, whether physical or mental, incapable of making an application for an adoption order.'

(6) In section 64 (other provision to be made by regulations), in subsection (5) for 'or marriage' substitute ', marriage or civil partnership'.

(7) In section 74(1) (enactments for whose purposes section 67 does not apply), for paragraph (a) substitute—

    '(a) section 1 of and Schedule 1 to the Marriage Act 1949 or Schedule 1 to the Civil Partnership Act 2004 (prohibited degrees of kindred and affinity),'.

(8) In section 79 (connections between the register and birth records), in subsection (7)—
    (a) in paragraph (b), after 'intends to be married' insert 'or form a civil partnership', and
    (b) for 'the person whom the applicant intends to marry' substitute 'the intended spouse or civil partner'.

(9) In section 81 (Adoption Contact Register: supplementary), in subsection (2) for 'or marriage' substitute ', marriage or civil partnership'.

(10) In section 98 (pre-commencement adoptions: information), in subsection (7), in the definition of 'relative' for 'or marriage' substitute ', marriage or civil partnership'.

(11) In section 144 (interpretation), in the definition of 'relative' in subsection (1), after 'by marriage' insert 'or civil partnership'.

(12) In section 144(4) (meaning of 'couple'), after paragraph (a) insert—

    '(aa) two people who are civil partners of each other, or'.

CHAPTER 6
MISCELLANEOUS

80. False Statements etc. with Reference to Civil Partnerships

(1) A person commits an offence if—
    (a) for the purpose of procuring the formation of a civil partnership, or a document mentioned in subsection (2), he—
      (i) makes or signs a declaration required under this Part or Part 5, or
      (ii) gives a notice or certificate so required,
    knowing that the declaration, notice or certificate is false,
    (b) for the purpose of a record being made in any register relating to civil partnerships, he—
      (i) makes a statement as to any information which is required to be registered under this Part or Part 5, or
      (ii) causes such a statement to be made,
    knowing that the statement is false,
    (c) he forbids the issue of a document mentioned in subsection (2)(a) or (b) by representing himself to be a person whose consent to a civil partnership between a child and another person is required under this Part or Part 5, knowing the representation to be false, or
    (d) with respect to a declaration made under paragraph 5(1) of Schedule 1 he makes

a statement mentioned in paragraph 6 of that Schedule which he knows to be false in a material particular.

(2) The documents are—

    (a) a civil partnership schedule or a Registrar General's licence under Chapter 1;

    (b) a document required by an Order in Council under section 210 or 211 as an authority for two people to register as civil partners of each other;

    (c) a certificate of no impediment under section 240.

(3) A person guilty of an offence under subsection (1) is liable—

    (a) on conviction on indictment, to imprisonment for a term not exceeding 7 years or to a fine (or both);

    (b) on summary conviction, to a fine not exceeding the statutory maximum.

(4) The Perjury Act 1911 (c. 6) has effect as if this section were contained in it.

81. Housing and Tenancies

Schedule 8 amends certain enactments relating to housing and tenancies.

82. Family Homes and Domestic Violence

Schedule 9 amends Part 4 of the Family Law Act 1996 (c. 27) and related enactments so that they apply in relation to civil partnerships as they apply in relation to marriages.

83. Fatal Accidents Claims

(1) Amend the Fatal Accidents Act 1976 (c. 30) as follows.

(2) In section 1(3) (meaning of 'dependant' for purposes of right of action for wrongful act causing death), after paragraph (a) insert—

'(aa) the civil partner or former civil partner of the deceased;'.

(3) In paragraph (b)(iii) of section 1(3), after 'wife' insert 'or civil partner'.

(4) After paragraph (f) of section 1(3) insert—

'(fa) any person (not being a child of the deceased) who, in the case of any civil partnership in which the deceased was at any time a civil partner, was treated by the deceased as a child of the family in relation to that civil partnership;'.

(5) After section 1(4) insert—

'(4A) The reference to the former civil partner of the deceased in subsection (3)(aa) above includes a reference to a person whose civil partnership with the deceased has been annulled as well as a person whose civil partnership with the deceased has been dissolved.'

(6) In section 1(5)(a), for 'by affinity' substitute 'by marriage or civil partnership'.

(7) In section 1A(2) (persons for whose benefit claim for bereavement damages may be made)—

    (a) in paragraph (a), after 'wife or husband' insert 'or civil partner', and

    (b) in paragraph (b), after 'was never married' insert 'or a civil partner'.

(8) In section 3 (assessment of damages), in subsection (4), after 'wife' insert 'or civil partner'.

84. Evidence

(1) Any enactment or rule of law relating to the giving of evidence by a spouse applies in relation to a civil partner as it applies in relation to the spouse.

(2) Subsection (1) is subject to any specific amendment made by or under this Act which relates to the giving of evidence by a civil partner.

(3) For the avoidance of doubt, in any such amendment, references to a person's civil partner do not include a former civil partner.

(4) References in subsections (1) and (2) to giving evidence are to giving evidence in any way (whether by supplying information, making discovery, producing documents or otherwise).

(5) Any rule of law—

    (a) which is preserved by section 7(3) of the Civil Evidence Act 1995 (c. 38) or section 118(1) of the Criminal Justice Act 2003 (c. 44), and

    (b) under which in any proceedings evidence of reputation or family tradition is admissible for the purpose of proving or disproving the existence of a marriage,

is to be treated as applying in an equivalent way for the purpose of proving or disproving the existence of a civil partnership.

. . .

PART 5
CIVIL PARTNERSHIP FORMED OR DISSOLVED ABROAD ETC.

CHAPTER 1
REGISTRATION OUTSIDE UK UNDER ORDER IN COUNCIL

210. Registration at British Consulates etc.

(1) Her Majesty may by Order in Council make provision for two people to register as civil partners of each other—

    (a) in prescribed countries or territories outside the United Kingdom, and

    (b) in the presence of a prescribed officer of Her Majesty's Diplomatic Service,

in cases where the officer is satisfied that the conditions in subsection (2) are met.

(2) The conditions are that—

    (a) at least one of the proposed civil partners is a United Kingdom national,

    (b) the proposed civil partners would have been eligible to register as civil partners of each other in such part of the United Kingdom as is determined in accordance with the Order,

    (c) the authorities of the country or territory in which it is proposed that they register as civil partners will not object to the registration, and

    (d) insufficient facilities exist for them to enter into an overseas relationship under the law of that country or territory.

(3) An officer is not required to allow two people to register as civil partners of each other if in his opinion the formation of a civil partnership between them would be inconsistent with international law or the comity of nations.

(4) An Order in Council under this section may make provision for appeals against a refusal, in reliance on subsection (3), to allow two people to register as civil partners of each other.

(5) An Order in Council under this section may provide that two people who register as civil partners of each other under such an Order are to be treated for the purposes of sections 221(1)(c)(i) and (2)(c)(i), 222(c), 224(b), 225(1)(c)(i) and (3)(c)(i), 229(1)(c)(i) and (2)(c)(i), 230(c) and 232(b) and section 1(3)(c)(i) of the Presumption of Death

(Scotland) Act 1977 (c. 27) as if they had done so in the part of the United Kingdom determined as mentioned in subsection (2)(b).

211. Registration by Armed Forces Personnel

(1) Her Majesty may by Order in Council make provision for two people to register as civil partners of each other—
   (a) in prescribed countries or territories outside the United Kingdom, and
   (b) in the presence of an officer appointed by virtue of the Registration of Births, Deaths and Marriages (Special Provisions) Act 1957 (c. 58),
   in cases where the officer is satisfied that the conditions in subsection (2) are met.
(2) The conditions are that—
   (a) at least one of the proposed civil partners—
      (i) is a member of a part of Her Majesty's forces serving in the country or territory,
      (ii) is employed in the country or territory in such other capacity as may be prescribed, or
      (iii) is a child of a person falling within sub-paragraph (i) or (ii) and has his home with that person in that country or territory,
   (b) the proposed civil partners would have been eligible to register as civil partners of each other in such part of the United Kingdom as is determined in accordance with the Order, and
   (c) such other requirements as may be prescribed are complied with.
(3) In determining for the purposes of subsection (2) whether one person is the child of another, a person who is or was treated by another as a child of the family in relation to—
   (a) a marriage to which the other is or was a party, or
   (b) a civil partnership in which the other is or was a civil partner,
   is to be regarded as the other's child.
(4) An Order in Council under this section may provide that two people who register as civil partners of each other under such an Order are to be treated for the purposes of section 221(1)(c)(i) and (2)(c)(i), 222(c), 224(b), 225(1)(c)(i) and (3)(c)(i), 229(1)(c)(i) and (2)(c)(i), 230(c) and 232(b) and section 1(3)(c)(i) of the Presumption of Death (Scotland) Act 1977 (c. 27) as if they had done so in the part of the United Kingdom determined in accordance with subsection (2)(b).
(5) Any references in this section—
   (a) to a country or territory outside the United Kingdom,
   (b) to forces serving in such a country or territory, and
   (c) to persons employed in such a country or territory,
   include references to ships which are for the time being in the waters of a country or territory outside the United Kingdom, to forces serving in any such ship and to persons employed in any such ship.

CHAPTER 2
OVERSEAS RELATIONSHIPS TREATED AS CIVIL PARTNERSHIPS

212. Meaning of 'Overseas Relationship'

(1) For the purposes of this Act an overseas relationship is a relationship which—

    (a) is either a specified relationship or a relationship which meets the general conditions, and

    (b) is registered (whether before or after the passing of this Act) with a responsible authority in a country or territory outside the United Kingdom, by two people—

        (i) who under the relevant law are of the same sex at the time when they do so, and

        (ii) neither of whom is already a civil partner or lawfully married.

(2) In this Chapter, 'the relevant law' means the law of the country or territory where the relationship is registered (including its rules of private international law).

213. Specified Relationships

(1) A specified relationship is a relationship which is specified for the purposes of section 212 by Schedule 20.

(2) The Secretary of State may by order amend Schedule 20 by—

    (a) adding a relationship,

    (b) amending the description of a relationship, or

    (c) omitting a relationship.

(3) No order may be made under this section without the consent of the Scottish Ministers and the Department of Finance and Personnel.

(4) The power to make an order under this section is exercisable by statutory instrument.

(5) An order which contains any provision (whether alone or with other provisions) amending Schedule 20 by—

    (a) amending the description of a relationship, or

    (b) omitting a relationship,

may not be made unless a draft of the statutory instrument containing the order is laid before, and approved by a resolution of, each House of Parliament.

(6) A statutory instrument containing any other order under this section is subject to annulment in pursuance of a resolution of either House of Parliament.

214. The General Conditions

The general conditions are that, under the relevant law—

(a) the relationship may not be entered into if either of the parties is already a party to a relationship of that kind or lawfully married,

(b) the relationship is of indeterminate duration, and

(c) the effect of entering into it is that the parties are—

    (i)   treated as a couple either generally or for specified purposes, or

    (ii)   treated as married.

215. Overseas Relationships Treated as Civil Partnerships: the General Rule

(1) Two people are to be treated as having formed a civil partnership as a result of having registered an overseas relationship if, under the relevant law, they—

    (a) had capacity to enter into the relationship, and

    (b) met all requirements necessary to ensure the formal validity of the relationship.

(2) Subject to subsection (3), the time when they are to be treated as having formed the civil partnership is the time when the overseas relationship is registered (under the relevant law) as having been entered into.

(3) If the overseas relationship is registered (under the relevant law) as having been entered into before this section comes into force, the time when they are to be treated as having formed a civil partnership is the time when this section comes into force.

(4) But if—
(a) before this section comes into force, a dissolution or annulment of the overseas relationship was obtained outside the United Kingdom, and
(b) the dissolution or annulment would be recognised under Chapter 3 if the overseas relationship had been treated as a civil partnership at the time of the dissolution or annulment,
subsection (3) does not apply and subsections (1) and (2) have effect subject to subsection (5).

(5) The overseas relationship is not to be treated as having been a civil partnership for the purposes of any provisions except—
(a) Schedules 7, 11 and 17 (financial relief in United Kingdom after dissolution or annulment obtained outside the United Kingdom);
(b) such provisions as are specified (with or without modifications) in an order under section 259;
(c) Chapter 3 (so far as necessary for the purposes of paragraphs (a) and (b)).

(6) This section is subject to sections 216, 217 and 218.

216. The Same-Sex Requirement

(1) Two people are not to be treated as having formed a civil partnership as a result of having registered an overseas relationship if, at the critical time, they were not of the same sex under UK law.

(2) But if a full gender recognition certificate is issued under the 2004 Act to a person who has registered an overseas relationship which is within subsection (4), after the issue of the certificate the relationship is no longer prevented from being treated as a civil partnership on the ground that, at the critical time, the parties were not of the same sex.

(3) However, subsection (2) does not apply to an overseas relationship which is within subsection (4) if either of the parties has formed a subsequent civil partnership or lawful marriage.

(4) An overseas relationship is within this subsection if (and only if), at the time mentioned in section 215(2)—
(a) one of the parties ('A') was regarded under the relevant law as having changed gender (but was not regarded under United Kingdom law as having done so), and
(b) the other party was (under United Kingdom law) of the gender to which A had changed under the relevant law.

(5) In this section—
'the critical time' means the time determined in accordance with section 215(2) or (as the case may be) (3);
'the 2004 Act' means the Gender Recognition Act 2004 (c. 7);
'United Kingdom law' means any enactment or rule of law applying in England and Wales, Scotland and Northern Ireland.

(6) Nothing in this section prevents the exercise of any enforceable Community right.

217. Person Domiciled in a Part of the United Kingdom

(1) Subsection (2) applies if an overseas relationship has been registered by a person who was at the time mentioned in section 215(2) domiciled in England and Wales.

(2) The two people concerned are not to be treated as having formed a civil partnership if, at the time mentioned in section 215(2)—

(a) either of them was under 16, or

(b) they would have been within prohibited degrees of relationship under Part 1 of Schedule 1 if they had been registering as civil partners of each other in England and Wales.

(3) Subsection (4) applies if an overseas relationship has been registered by a person who at the time mentioned in section 215(2) was domiciled in Scotland.

(4) The two people concerned are not to be treated as having formed a civil partnership if, at the time mentioned in section 215(2), they were not eligible by virtue of paragraph (b), (c) or (e) of section 86(1) to register in Scotland as civil partners of each other.

(5) Subsection (6) applies if an overseas relationship has been registered by a person who at the time mentioned in section 215(2) was domiciled in Northern Ireland.

(6) The two people concerned are not to be treated as having formed a civil partnership if, at the time mentioned in section 215(2)—

(a) either of them was under 16, or

(b) they would have been within prohibited degrees of relationship under Schedule 12 if they had been registering as civil partners of each other in Northern Ireland.

218. The Public Policy Exception

Two people are not to be treated as having formed a civil partnership as a result of having entered into an overseas relationship if it would be manifestly contrary to public policy to recognize the capacity, under the relevant law, of one or both of them to enter into the relationship.

CHAPTER 3
DISSOLUTION ETC.: JURISDICTION AND RECOGNITION

Introduction

219. Power to Make Provision Corresponding to EC Regulation 2201/2003

(1) The Lord Chancellor may by regulations make provision—

(a) as to the jurisdiction of courts in England and Wales or Northern Ireland in proceedings for the dissolution or annulment of a civil partnership or for legal separation of the civil partners in cases where a civil partner—

(i) is or has been habitually resident in a member State,

(ii) is a national of a member State, or

(iii) is domiciled in a part of the United Kingdom or the Republic of Ireland, and

(b) as to the recognition in England and Wales or Northern Ireland of any judgment of a court of another member State which orders the dissolution or annulment of a civil partnership or the legal separation of the civil partners.

(2) The Scottish Ministers may by regulations make provision—

(a) as to the jurisdiction of courts in Scotland in proceedings for the dissolution or annulment of a civil partnership or for legal separation of the civil partners in such cases as are mentioned in subsection (1)(a), and

(b) as to the recognition in Scotland of any such judgment as is mentioned in subsection (1)(b).

(3) The regulations may in particular make provision corresponding to that made by Council Regulation (EC) No 2201/2003 of 27th November 2003 in relation to jurisdiction and the recognition and enforcement of judgments in matrimonial matters.

(4) The regulations may provide that for the purposes of this Part and the regulations 'member State' means—

(a) all member States with the exception of such member States as are specified in the regulations, or

(b) such member States as are specified in the regulations.

(5) The regulations may make provision under subsections (1)(b) and (2)(b) which applies even if the date of the dissolution, annulment or legal separation is earlier than the date on which this section comes into force.

(6) Regulations under subsection (1) are to be made by statutory instrument and may only be made if a draft has been laid before and approved by resolution of each House of Parliament.

(7) Regulations under subsection (2) are to be made by statutory instrument and may only be made if a draft has been laid before and approved by resolution of the Scottish Parliament.

(8) In this Part 'section 219 regulations' means regulations made under this section.

Jurisdiction of Courts in England and Wales

220. Meaning of 'the Court'

In sections 221 to 224 'the court' means—

(a) the High Court, or

(b) if a county court has jurisdiction by virtue of Part 5 of the Matrimonial and Family Proceedings Act 1984 (c. 42), a county court.

221. Proceedings for Dissolution, Separation or Nullity Order

(1) The court has jurisdiction to entertain proceedings for a dissolution order or a separation order if (and only if)—

(a) the court has jurisdiction under section 219 regulations,

(b) no court has, or is recognised as having, jurisdiction under section 219 regulations and either civil partner is domiciled in England and Wales on the date when the proceedings are begun, or

(c) the following conditions are met—

(i) the two people concerned registered as civil partners of each other in England or Wales,

(ii) no court has, or is recognised as having, jurisdiction under section 219 regulations, and

(iii) it appears to the court to be in the interests of justice to assume jurisdiction in the case.

(2) The court has jurisdiction to entertain proceedings for a nullity order if (and only if)—

(a) the court has jurisdiction under section 219 regulations,

(b) no court has, or is recognised as having, jurisdiction under section 219 regulations and either civil partner—

      (i) is domiciled in England and Wales on the date when the proceedings are begun, or

      (ii) died before that date and either was at death domiciled in England and Wales or had been habitually resident in England and Wales throughout the period of 1 year ending with the date of death, or

  (c) the following conditions are met—

      (i) the two people concerned registered as civil partners of each other in England or Wales,

      (ii) no court has, or is recognised as having, jurisdiction under section 219 regulations, and

      (iii) it appears to the court to be in the interests of justice to assume jurisdiction in the case.

(3) At any time when proceedings are pending in respect of which the court has jurisdiction by virtue of subsection (1) or (2) (or this subsection), the court also has jurisdiction to entertain other proceedings, in respect of the same civil partnership, for a dissolution, separation or nullity order, even though that jurisdiction would not be exercisable under subsection (1) or (2).

222. Proceedings for Presumption of Death Order

The court has jurisdiction to entertain proceedings for a presumption of death order if (and only if)—

(a) the applicant is domiciled in England and Wales on the date when the proceedings are begun,

(b) the applicant was habitually resident in England and Wales throughout the period of 1 year ending with that date, or

(c) the two people concerned registered as civil partners of each other in England and Wales and it appears to the court to be in the interests of justice to assume jurisdiction in the case.

223. Proceedings for Dissolution, Nullity or Separation Order: Supplementary

(1) Rules of court may make provision in relation to civil partnerships corresponding to the provision made in relation to marriages by Schedule 1 to the Domicile and Matrimonial Proceedings Act 1973 (c. 45).

(2) The rules may in particular make provision—

  (a) for the provision of information by applicants and respondents in proceedings for dissolution, nullity or separation orders where proceedings relating to the same civil partnership are continuing in another jurisdiction, and

  (b) for proceedings before the court to be stayed by the court where there are concurrent proceedings elsewhere in respect of the same civil partnership.

224. Applications for Declarations as to Validity etc.

The court has jurisdiction to entertain an application under section 58 if (and only if)—

(a) either of the civil partners in the civil partnership to which the application relates—

      (i) is domiciled in England and Wales on the date of the application,

      (ii) has been habitually resident in England and Wales throughout the period of 1 year ending with that date, or

      (iii) died before that date and either was at death domiciled in England and Wales or had been habitually resident in England and Wales throughout the period of 1 year ending with the date of death, or

(b) the two people concerned registered as civil partners of each other in England and Wales and it appears to the court to be in the interests of justice to assume jurisdiction in the case.

. . .

Recognition of Dissolution, Annulment and Separation

233. Effect of Dissolution, Annulment or Separation Obtained in the United Kingdom

(1) No dissolution or annulment of a civil partnership obtained in one part of the United Kingdom is effective in any part of the United Kingdom unless obtained from a court of civil jurisdiction.

(2) Subject to subsections (3) and (4), the validity of a dissolution or annulment of a civil partnership or a legal separation of civil partners which has been obtained from a court of civil jurisdiction in one part of the United Kingdom is to be recognised throughout the United Kingdom.

(3) Recognition of the validity of a dissolution, annulment or legal separation obtained from a court of civil jurisdiction in one part of the United Kingdom may be refused in any other part if the dissolution, annulment or separation was obtained at a time when it was irreconcilable with a decision determining the question of the subsistence or validity of the civil partnership—

(a) previously given by a court of civil jurisdiction in the other part, or

(b) previously given by a court elsewhere and recognised or entitled to be recognised in the other part.

(4) Recognition of the validity of a dissolution or legal separation obtained from a court of civil jurisdiction in one part of the United Kingdom may be refused in any other part if the dissolution or separation was obtained at a time when, according to the law of the other part, there was no subsisting civil partnership.

234. Recognition in the United Kingdom of Overseas Dissolution, Annulment or Separation

(1) Subject to subsection (2), the validity of an overseas dissolution, annulment or legal separation is to be recognised in the United Kingdom if, and only if, it is entitled to recognition by virtue of sections 235 to 237.

(2) This section and sections 235 to 237 do not apply to an overseas dissolution, annulment or legal separation as regards which provision as to recognition is made by section 219 regulations.

(3) For the purposes of subsections (1) and (2) and sections 235 to 237, an overseas dissolution, annulment or legal separation is a dissolution or annulment of a civil partnership or a legal separation of civil partners which has been obtained outside the United Kingdom (whether before or after this section comes into force).

235. Grounds for Recognition

(1) The validity of an overseas dissolution, annulment or legal separation obtained by means of proceedings is to be recognised if—

(a) the dissolution, annulment or legal separation is effective under the law of the country in which it was obtained, and

(b) at the relevant date either civil partner—

(i) was habitually resident in the country in which the dissolution, annulment or legal separation was obtained,

      (ii) was domiciled in that country, or

      (iii) was a national of that country.

(2) The validity of an overseas dissolution, annulment or legal separation obtained otherwise than by means of proceedings is to be recognised if—

  (a) the dissolution, annulment or legal separation is effective under the law of the country in which it was obtained,

  (b) at the relevant date—

    (i) each civil partner was domiciled in that country, or

    (ii) either civil partner was domiciled in that country and the other was domiciled in a country under whose law the dissolution, annulment or legal separation is recognised as valid, and

  (c) neither civil partner was habitually resident in the United Kingdom throughout the period of 1 year immediately preceding that date.

(3) In this section 'the relevant date' means—

  (a) in the case of an overseas dissolution, annulment or legal separation obtained by means of proceedings, the date of the commencement of the proceedings;

  (b) in the case of an overseas dissolution, annulment or legal separation obtained otherwise than by means of proceedings, the date on which it was obtained.

(4) Where in the case of an overseas annulment the relevant date fell after the death of either civil partner, any reference in subsection (1) or (2) to that date is to be read in relation to that civil partner as a reference to the date of death.

236. Refusal of Recognition

(1) Recognition of the validity of an overseas dissolution, annulment or legal separation may be refused in any part of the United Kingdom if the dissolution, annulment or separation was obtained at a time when it was irreconcilable with a decision determining the question of the subsistence or validity of the civil partnership—

  (a) previously given by a court of civil jurisdiction in that part of the United Kingdom, or

  (b) previously given by a court elsewhere and recognised or entitled to be recognised in that part of the United Kingdom.

(2) Recognition of the validity of an overseas dissolution or legal separation may be refused in any part of the United Kingdom if the dissolution or separation was obtained at a time when, according to the law of that part of the United Kingdom, there was no subsisting civil partnership.

(3) Recognition of the validity of an overseas dissolution, annulment or legal separation may be refused if—

  (a) in the case of a dissolution, annulment or legal separation obtained by means of proceedings, it was obtained—

    (i) without such steps having been taken for giving notice of the proceedings to a civil partner as, having regard to the nature of the proceedings and all the circumstances, should reasonably have been taken, or

    (ii) without a civil partner having been given (for any reason other than lack of notice) such opportunity to take part in the proceedings as, having regard to those matters, he should reasonably have been given, or

  (b) in the case of a dissolution, annulment or legal separation obtained otherwise than by means of proceedings—

      (i) there is no official document certifying that the dissolution, annulment or legal separation is effective under the law of the country in which it was obtained, or

      (ii) where either civil partner was domiciled in another country at the relevant date, there is no official document certifying that the dissolution, annulment or legal separation is recognised as valid under the law of that other country, or

  (c) in either case, recognition of the dissolution, annulment or legal separation would be manifestly contrary to public policy.

(4) In this section—

'official', in relation to a document certifying that a dissolution, annulment or legal separation is effective, or is recognised as valid, under the law of any country, means issued by a person or body appointed or recognised for the purpose under that law;

'the relevant date' has the same meaning as in section 235.

237. Supplementary Provisions Relating to Recognition of Dissolution etc.

(1) For the purposes of sections 235 and 236, a civil partner is to be treated as domiciled in a country if he was domiciled in that country—

  (a) according to the law of that country in family matters, or

  (b) according to the law of the part of the United Kingdom in which the question of recognition arises.

(2) The Lord Chancellor or the Scottish Ministers may by regulations make provision—

  (a) applying sections 235 and 236 and subsection (1) with modifications in relation to any country whose territories have different systems of law in force in matters of dissolution, annulment or legal separation;

  (b) applying sections 235 and 236 with modifications in relation to—

      (i) an overseas dissolution, annulment or legal separation in the case of an overseas relationship (or an apparent or alleged overseas relationship);

      (ii) any case where a civil partner is domiciled in a country or territory whose law does not recognise legal relationships between two people of the same sex;

  (c) with respect to recognition of the validity of an overseas dissolution, annulment or legal separation in cases where there are cross-proceedings;

  (d) with respect to cases where a legal separation is converted under the law of the country or territory in which it is obtained into a dissolution which is effective under the law of that country or territory;

  (e) with respect to proof of findings of fact made in proceedings in any country or territory outside the United Kingdom.

(3) The power to make regulations under subsection (2) is exercisable by statutory instrument.

(4) A statutory instrument containing such regulations—

  (a) if made by the Lord Chancellor, is subject to annulment in pursuance of a resolution of either House of Parliament;

  (b) if made by the Scottish Ministers, is subject to annulment in pursuance of a resolution of the Scottish Parliament.

(5) In this section (except subsection (4)) and sections 233 to 236 and 238—

'annulment' includes any order annulling a civil partnership, however expressed;

'part of the United Kingdom' means England and Wales, Scotland or Northern Ireland;

'proceedings' means judicial or other proceedings.

(6) Nothing in this Chapter is to be read as requiring the recognition of any finding of fault made in proceedings for dissolution, annulment or legal separation or of any maintenance, custody or other ancillary order made in any such proceedings.

238. Non-recognition Elsewhere of Dissolution or Annulment

(1) This section applies where, in any part of the UK—
  (a) a dissolution or annulment of a civil partnership has been granted by a court of civil jurisdiction, or
  (b) the validity of a dissolution or annulment of a civil partnership is recognised by virtue of this Chapter.

(2) The fact that the dissolution or annulment would not be recognised outside the United Kingdom does not—
  (a) preclude either party from forming a subsequent civil partnership or marriage in that part of the United Kingdom, or
  (b) cause the subsequent civil partnership or marriage of either party (wherever it takes place) to be treated as invalid in that part.

CHAPTER 4
MISCELLANEOUS AND SUPPLEMENTARY

239. Commanding Officers' Certificates for Part 2 Purposes

(1) Her Majesty may by Order in Council make provision in relation to cases where—
  (a) two people wish to register as civil partners of each other in England and Wales (under Chapter 1 of Part 2), and
  (b) one of them ('A') is a member of Her Majesty's forces serving outside the United Kingdom and the other is resident in England and Wales,
  for the issue by A's commanding officer to A of a certificate of no impediment.

(2) The Order may provide for the issue of the certificate to be subject to the giving of such notice and the making of such declarations as may be prescribed.

(3) A certificate of no impediment is a certificate that no legal impediment to the formation of the civil partnership has been shown to the commanding officer issuing the certificate to exist.

(4) 'Commanding officer'—
  (a) in relation to a person subject to military law, means the officer who would be that person's commanding officer for the purposes of section 82 of the Army Act 1955 (3 & 4 Eliz. 2 c. 18) if he were charged with an offence;
  (b) in relation to a person subject to air-force law, means the officer who would be that person's commanding officer for the purposes of section 82 of the Air Force Act 1955 (3 & 4 Eliz. 2 c. 19) if he were charged with an offence;
  (c) in relation to a person subject to the Naval Discipline Act 1957 (c. 53), means the officer in command of the ship or naval establishment to which he belongs.

240. Certificates of No Impediment to Overseas Relationships

(1) Her Majesty may by Order in Council make provision for the issue of certificates of no impediment to—

(a) United Kingdom nationals, and

(b) such other persons falling within subsection (2) as may be prescribed,

who wish to enter into overseas relationships in prescribed countries or territories outside the United Kingdom with persons who are not United Kingdom nationals and who do not fall within subsection (2).

(2) A person falls within this subsection if under any enactment for the time being in force in any country mentioned in Schedule 3 to the British Nationality Act 1981 (c. 61) (Commonwealth countries) that person is a citizen of that country.

(3) A certificate of no impediment is a certificate that, after proper notices have been given, no legal impediment to the recipient entering into the overseas relationship has been shown to the person issuing the certificate to exist.

241. Transmission of Certificates of Registration of Overseas Relationships

(1) Her Majesty may by Order in Council provide—

(a) for the transmission to the Registrar General, by such persons or in such manner as may be prescribed, of certificates of the registration of overseas relationships entered into by United Kingdom nationals in prescribed countries or territories outside the United Kingdom,

(b) for the issue by the Registrar General of a certified copy of such a certificate received by him, and

(c) for such certified copies to be received in evidence.

(2) 'The Registrar General' means—

(a) in relation to England and Wales, the Registrar General for England and Wales,

(b) in relation to Scotland, the Registrar General of Births, Deaths and Marriages for Scotland, and

(c) in relation to Northern Ireland, the Registrar General for Northern Ireland.

242. Power to Make Provision Relating to Certain Commonwealth Forces

(1) This section applies if it appears to Her Majesty that any law in force in Canada, the Commonwealth of Australia or New Zealand (or in a territory of either of the former two countries) makes, in relation to forces raised there, provision similar to that made by section 211 (registration by armed forces personnel).

(2) Her Majesty may by Order in Council make provision for securing that the law in question has effect as part of the law of the United Kingdom.

243. Fees

(1) The power to make an order under section 34(1) (fees) includes power to make an order prescribing fees in respect of anything which, by virtue of an Order in Council under this Part, is required to be done by registration authorities in England and Wales or by or on behalf of the Registrar General for England and Wales.

(2) Regulations made by the Registrar General of Births, Deaths and Marriages for Scotland may prescribe fees in respect of anything which, by virtue of an Order in Council under this Part, is required to be done by him or on his behalf.

(3) Subsections (3) and (4) of section 126 apply to regulations made under subsection (2) as they apply to regulations under Part 3.

(4) The power to make an order under section 157(1) includes power to make an order prescribing fees in respect of anything which, by virtue of an Order in Council

under this Part, is required to be done by or on behalf of the Registrar General for Northern Ireland.

244. Orders in Council: Supplementary

(1) An Order in Council under section 210, 211, 239, 240, 241 or 242 may make—
    (a) different provision for different cases, and
    (b) such supplementary, incidental, consequential, transitional, transitory or saving provision as appears to Her Majesty to be appropriate.

(2) The provision that may be made by virtue of subsection (1)(b) includes in particular provision corresponding to or applying with modifications any provision made by or under—
    (a) this Act, or
    (b) any Act relating to marriage outside the United Kingdom.

(3) A statutory instrument containing an Order in Council under section 210, 211, 239, 240, 241 or 242 is subject to annulment in pursuance of a resolution of either House of Parliament.

(4) Subsection (3) applies whether or not the Order also contains other provisions made by Order in Council under—
the Foreign Marriage Act 1892 (c. 23),
section 3 of the Foreign Marriage Act 1947 (c. 33), or
section 39 of the Marriage Act 1949 (c. 76).

(5) In sections 210, 211, 239, 240 and 241 'prescribed' means prescribed by an Order in Council under the section in question.

245. Interpretation

(1) In this Part 'United Kingdom national' means a person who is—
    (a) a British citizen, a British overseas territories citizen, a British Overseas citizen or a British National (Overseas),
    (b) a British subject under the British Nationality Act 1981 (c. 61), or
    (c) a British protected person, within the meaning of that Act.

(2) In this Part 'Her Majesty's forces' has the same meaning as in the Army Act 1955 (3 & 4 Eliz. 2 c. 18).

PART 6
RELATIONSHIPS ARISING THROUGH CIVIL PARTNERSHIP

246. Interpretation of Statutory References to Stepchildren etc.

(1) In any provision to which this section applies, references to a stepchild or step-parent of a person (here, 'A'), and cognate expressions, are to be read as follows—
A's stepchild includes a person who is the child of A's civil partner (but is not A's child);
A's step-parent includes a person who is the civil partner of A's parent (but is not A's parent);
A's stepdaughter includes a person who is the daughter of A's civil partner (but is not A's daughter);
A's stepson includes a person who is the son of A's civil partner (but is not A's son);
A's stepfather includes a person who is the civil partner of A's father (but is not A's parent);

A's stepmother includes a person who is the civil partner of A's mother (but is not A's parent);

A's stepbrother includes a person who is the son of the civil partner of A's parent (but is not the son of either of A's parents);

A's stepsister includes a person who is the daughter of the civil partner of A's parent (but is not the daughter of either of A's parents).

(2) For the purposes of any provision to which this section applies—

'brother-in-law' includes civil partner's brother,

'daughter-in-law' includes daughter's civil partner,

'father-in-law' includes civil partner's father,

'mother-in-law' includes civil partner's mother,

'parent-in-law' includes civil partner's parent,

'sister-in-law' includes civil partner's sister, and

'son-in-law' includes son's civil partner.

247. Provisions to which Section 246 Applies: Acts of Parliament etc.

(1) Section 246 applies to—

    (a) any provision listed in Schedule 21 (references to stepchildren, in-laws etc. in existing Acts),

    (b) except in so far as otherwise provided, any provision made by a future Act, and

    (c) except in so far as otherwise provided, any provision made by future subordinate legislation.

(2) A Minister of the Crown may by order—

    (a) amend Schedule 21 by adding to it any provision of an existing Act;

    (b) provide for section 246 to apply to prescribed provisions of existing subordinate legislation.

(3) The power conferred by subsection (2) is also exercisable—

    (a) by the Scottish Ministers, in relation to a relevant Scottish provision;

    (b) by a Northern Ireland department, in relation to a provision which deals with a transferred matter;

    (c) by the National Assembly for Wales, if the order is made by virtue of subsection (2)(b) and deals with matters with respect to which functions are exercisable by the Assembly.

(4) Subject to subsection (5), the power to make an order under subsection (2) is exercisable by statutory instrument.

(5) Any power of a Northern Ireland department to make an order under subsection (2) is exercisable by statutory rule for the purposes of the Statutory Rules (Northern Ireland) Order 1979 (S.I. 1979/1573 (N.I. 12)).

(6) A statutory instrument containing an order under subsection (2) made by a Minister of the Crown is subject to annulment in pursuance of a resolution of either House of Parliament.

(7) A statutory instrument containing an order under subsection (2) made by the Scottish Ministers is subject to annulment in pursuance of a resolution of the Scottish Parliament.

(8) A statutory rule containing an order under subsection (2) made by a Northern Ireland department is subject to negative resolution (within the meaning of section 41(6) of the Interpretation Act (Northern Ireland) 1954 (c. 33 (N.I.))).

(9) In this section—

'Act' includes an Act of the Scottish Parliament;

'existing Act' means an Act passed on or before the last day of the Session in which this Act is passed;

'existing subordinate legislation' means subordinate legislation made before the day on which this section comes into force;

'future Act' means an Act passed after the last day of the Session in which this Act is passed;

'future subordinate legislation' means subordinate legislation made on or after the day on which this section comes into force;

'Minister of the Crown' has the same meaning as in the Ministers of the Crown Act 1975 (c. 26);

'prescribed' means prescribed by the order;

'relevant Scottish provision' means a provision that would be within the legislative competence of the Scottish Parliament if it were included in an Act of that Parliament;

'subordinate legislation' has the same meaning as in the Interpretation Act 1978 (c. 30) except that it includes an instrument made under an Act of the Scottish Parliament;

'transferred matter' has the meaning given by section 4(1) of the Northern Ireland Act 1998 (c. 47) and 'deals with' in relation to a transferred matter is to be construed in accordance with section 98(2) and (3) of the 1998 Act.

. . .

PART 7
MISCELLANEOUS

249. Immigration Control and Formation of Civil Partnerships

Schedule 23 contains provisions relating to the formation of civil partnerships in the United Kingdom by persons subject to immigration control.

250. Gender Recognition where Applicant a Civil Partner

(1) Amend the Gender Recognition Act 2004 (c. 7) as follows.

(2) In—

    (a) section 3 (evidence), in subsection (6)(a), and

    (b) section 4 (successful applications), in subsections (2) and (3),

after 'is married' insert 'or a civil partner'.

(3) In section 5 (subsequent issue of full certificates)—

    (a) in subsection (2), after 'is again married' insert 'or is a civil partner',

    (b) in subsection (6)(a), for 'is not married' substitute 'is neither married nor a civil partner', and

    (c) for the heading substitute 'Issue of full certificates where applicant has been married'.

(4) After section 5 insert—

'5A Issue of full certificates where applicant has been a civil partner

    (1) A court which—

   (a) makes final a nullity order made on the ground that an interim gender recognition certificate has been issued to a civil partner, or

   (b) (in Scotland) grants a decree of dissolution on that ground,

must, on doing so, issue a full gender recognition certificate to that civil partner and send a copy to the Secretary of State.

(2) If an interim gender recognition certificate has been issued to a person and either—

   (a) the person's civil partnership is dissolved or annulled (otherwise than on the ground mentioned in subsection (1)) in proceedings instituted during the period of six months beginning with the day on which it was issued, or

   (b) the person's civil partner dies within that period,

the person may make an application for a full gender recognition certificate at any time within the period specified in subsection (3) (unless the person is again a civil partner or is married).

(3) That period is the period of six months beginning with the day on which the civil partnership is dissolved or annulled or the death occurs.

(4) An application under subsection (2) must include evidence of the dissolution or annulment of the civil partnership and the date on which proceedings for it were instituted, or of the death of the civil partner and the date on which it occurred.

(5) An application under subsection (2) is to be determined by a Gender Recognition Panel.

(6) The Panel—

   (a) must grant the application if satisfied that the applicant is neither a civil partner nor married, and

   (b) otherwise must reject it.

(7) If the Panel grants the application it must issue a full gender recognition certificate to the applicant.'

(5) In—

   (a) section 7 (applications: supplementary), in subsection (1),

   (b) section 8 (appeals etc.), in subsections (1) and (5), and

   (c) section 22 (prohibition on disclosure of information), in subsection (2)(a),

after '5(2)' insert ', 5A(2)'.

(6) In section 21 (foreign gender change and marriage), in subsection (4), after 'entered into a later (valid) marriage' insert 'or civil partnership'.

(7) In section 25 (interpretation), in the definition of 'full gender recognition certificate' and 'interim gender recognition certificate', for 'or 5' substitute ', 5 or 5A'.

(8) In Schedule 1 (Gender Recognition Panels), in paragraph 5, after '5(2)' insert ', 5A(2)'.

(9) In Schedule 3 (registration), in paragraphs 9(1), 19(1) and 29(1), for 'or 5(2)' substitute ', 5(2) or 5A(2)'.

251. Discrimination Against Civil Partners in Employment Field

(1) Amend the Sex Discrimination Act 1975 (c. 65) as follows.

(2) For section 3 (discrimination against married persons in employment field) substitute—

'3 Discrimination Against Married Persons and Civil Partners in Employment Field

(1) In any circumstances relevant for the purposes of any provision of Part 2, a person discriminates against a person ('A') who fulfils the condition in subsection (2) if—

   (a) on the ground of the fulfilment of the condition, he treats A less favourably than he treats or would treat a person who does not fulfil the condition, or

   (b) he applies to A a provision, criterion or practice which he applies or would apply equally to a person who does not fulfil the condition, but—

        (i)   which puts or would put persons fulfilling the condition at a particular disadvantage when compared with persons not fulfilling the condition, and

        (ii)   which puts A at that disadvantage, and

        (iii)   which he cannot show to be a proportionate means of achieving a legitimate aim.

(2)   The condition is that the person is—

    (a)   married, or

    (b)   a civil partner.

(3)   For the purposes of subsection (1), a provision of Part 2 framed with reference to discrimination against women is to be treated as applying equally to the treatment of men, and for that purpose has effect with such modifications as are requisite.'

(3)   In section 5 (interpretation), for subsection (3) substitute—

'(3) Each of the following comparisons, that is—

    (a)   a comparison of the cases of persons of different sex under section 1(1) or (2),

    (b)   a comparison of the cases of persons required for the purposes of section 2A, and

    (c)   a comparison of the cases of persons who do and who do not fulfil the condition in section 3(2),

must be such that the relevant circumstances in the one case are the same, or not materially different, in the other.';

and omit section 1(4).

(4)   In section 7 (exception where sex is a genuine occupational qualification), in subsection (2)(h) for 'by a married couple' substitute'—

        (i)   by a married couple,

        (ii)   by a couple who are civil partners of each other, or

        (iii)   by a married couple or a couple who are civil partners of each other'.

(5)   In section 65 (remedies on complaint under section 63), in subsection (1B) for 'or marital status as the case may be' substitute 'or (as the case may be) fulfilment of the condition in section 3(2)'.

. . .

253. Civil Partners to have Unlimited Insurable Interest in Each Other

(1)   Where two people are civil partners, each of them is to be presumed for the purposes of section 1 of the Life Assurance Act 1774 (c. 48) to have an interest in the life of the other.

(2)   For the purposes of section 3 of the 1774 Act, there is no limit on the amount of value of the interest.

254. Social Security, Child Support and Tax Credits

(1)   Schedule 24 contains amendments relating to social security, child support and tax credits.

(2)   Subsection (3) applies in relation to any provision of any Act, Northern Ireland legislation or subordinate legislation which—

    (a)   relates to social security, child support or tax credits, and

    (b)   contains references (however expressed) to persons who are living or have lived together as husband and wife.

(3)   The power under section 259 to make orders amending enactments, Northern Ireland legislation and subordinate legislation is to be treated as including power to amend the provision to refer to persons who are living or have lived together as if they were civil partners.

(4) Subject to subsection (5), section 175(3), (5) and (6) of the Social Security Contributions and Benefits Act 1992 (c. 4) applies to the exercise of the power under section 259 in relation to social security, child support or tax credits as it applies to any power under that Act to make an order (there being disregarded for the purposes of this subsection the exceptions in section 175(3) and (5) of that Act).

(5) Section 171(3), (5) and (6) of the Social Security Contributions and Benefits (Northern Ireland) Act 1992 (c. 7) applies to the exercise by a Northern Ireland department of the power under section 259 in relation to social security and child support as it applies to any power under that Act to make an order (there being disregarded for the purposes of this subsection the exceptions in section 171(3) and (5) of that Act).

(6) The reference in subsection (2) to an Act or Northern Ireland legislation relating to social security is to be read as including a reference to—
(a) the Pneumoconiosis etc. (Workers' Compensation) Act 1979 (c. 41), and
(b) the Pneumoconiosis, etc., (Workers' Compensation) (Northern Ireland) Order 1979 (S.I. 1979/925 (N.I. 9));
and the references in subsections (4) and (5) to social security are to be construed accordingly.

255. Power to Amend Enactments Relating to Pensions

(1) A Minister of the Crown may by order make such amendments, repeals or revocations in any enactment, Northern Ireland legislation, subordinate legislation or Church legislation relating to pensions, allowances or gratuities as he considers appropriate for the purpose of, or in connection with, making provision with respect to pensions, allowances or gratuities for the surviving civil partners or dependants of deceased civil partners.

(2) The power conferred by subsection (1) is also exercisable—
(a) by the Scottish Ministers, if the provision making the amendment, repeal or revocation is a relevant Scottish provision;
(b) by a Northern Ireland department, if the provision making the amendment, repeal or revocation deals with a transferred matter.

(3) In the case of judicial pensions, allowances or gratuities, the power conferred by subsection (1) is exercisable—
(a) in relation to any judicial office whose jurisdiction is exercised exclusively in relation to Scotland, by the Secretary of State, or
(b) subject to paragraph (a), by the Lord Chancellor.

(4) The provision which may be made by virtue of subsection (1)—
(a) may be the same as, or different to, the provision made with respect to widows, widowers or the dependants of persons who are not civil partners, and
(b) may be made with a view to ensuring that pensions, allowances or gratuities take account of rights which accrued, service which occurred or any other circumstances which existed before the passing of this Act.

(5) The power conferred by subsection (1) is not restricted by any provision of this Act.

(6) Before the appropriate person makes an order under subsection (1) he must consult such persons as he considers appropriate.

(7) Subsection (6) does not apply—
(a) to an order in the case of which the appropriate person considers that consultation is inexpedient because of urgency, or

(b) to an order made before the end of the period of 6 months beginning with the coming into force of this section.

(8) Subject to subsection (9), the power to make an order under subsection (1) is exercisable by statutory instrument.

(9) Any power of a Northern Ireland department to make an order under this section is exercisable by statutory rule for the purposes of the Statutory Rules (Northern Ireland) Order 1979 (S.I. 1979/1573 (N.I. 12)).

(10) An order under subsection (1) may not be made—

(a) by a Minister of the Crown, unless a draft of the statutory instrument containing the order has been laid before, and approved by a resolution of, each House of Parliament;

(b) by the Scottish Ministers, unless a draft of the statutory instrument containing the order has been laid before, and approved by a resolution of, the Scottish Parliament;

(c) by a Northern Ireland department, unless a draft of the statutory rule containing the order has been laid before, and approved by a resolution of, the Northern Ireland Assembly.

(11) In this section—

'the appropriate person', in relation to an order under this section, means the person making the order;

'Church legislation' means—

(a) any Measure of the Church Assembly or of the General Synod of the Church of England, or

(b) any order, regulation or other instrument made under or by virtue of such a Measure;

'enactment' includes an enactment comprised in an Act of the Scottish Parliament;

'Minister of the Crown' has the same meaning as in the Ministers of the Crown Act 1975 (c. 26);

'relevant Scottish provision' means a provision that would be within the legislative competence of the Scottish Parliament if it were included in an Act of that Parliament;

'subordinate legislation' has the same meaning as in the Interpretation Act 1978 (c. 30) except that it includes any instrument made under an Act of the Scottish Parliament and any instrument within the meaning of section 1(c) of the Interpretation Act (Northern Ireland) 1954 (1954 c. 33 (N.I.));

'transferred matter' has the meaning given by section 4(1) of the Northern Ireland Act 1998 (c. 47) and 'deals with' in relation to a transferred matter is to be construed in accordance with section 98(2) and (3) of the 1998 Act.

256. Amendment of Certain Enactments Relating to Pensions

Schedule 25 amends certain enactments relating to pensions.

257. Amendment of Certain Enactments Relating to the Armed Forces

Schedule 26 amends certain enactments relating to the armed forces.

PART 8
SUPPLEMENTARY

258. Regulations and Orders

(1) This section applies to any power conferred by this Act to make regulations or an order (except a power of a court to make an order).

(2) The power may be exercised so as to make different provision for different cases and different purposes.

(3) The power includes power to make any supplementary, incidental, consequential, transitional, transitory or saving provision which the person making the regulations or order considers expedient.

259. Power to Make Further Provision in Connection with Civil Partnership

(1) A Minister of the Crown may by order make such further provision (including supplementary, incidental, consequential, transitory, transitional or saving provision) as he considers appropriate—

    (a) for the general purposes, or any particular purpose, of this Act,

    (b) in consequence of any provision made by or under this Act, or

    (c) for giving full effect to this Act or any provision of it.

(2) The power conferred by subsection (1) is also exercisable—

    (a) by the Scottish Ministers, in relation to a relevant Scottish provision;

    (b) by a Northern Ireland department, in relation to a provision which deals with a transferred matter;

    (c) by the National Assembly for Wales, in relation to a provision which is made otherwise than by virtue of subsection (3) and deals with matters with respect to which functions are exercisable by the Assembly.

(3) An order under subsection (1) may—

    (a) amend or repeal any enactment contained in an Act passed on or before the last day of the Session in which this Act is passed, including an enactment conferring power to make subordinate legislation where the power is limited by reference to persons who are or have been parties to a marriage;

    (b) amend, repeal or (as the case may be) revoke any provision contained in Northern Ireland legislation passed or made on or before the last day of the Session in which this Act is passed, including a provision conferring power to make subordinate legislation where the power is limited by reference to persons who are or have been parties to a marriage;

    (c) amend, repeal or (as the case may be) revoke any Church legislation.

(4) An order under subsection (1) may—

    (a) provide for any provision of this Act which comes into force before another such provision has come into force to have effect, until that other provision has come into force, with such modifications as are specified in the order;

    (b) amend or revoke any subordinate legislation.

(5) The power to make an order under subsection (1) is not restricted by any other provision of this Act.

(6) Subject to subsection (7), the power to make an order under subsection (1) is exercisable by statutory instrument.

(7) Any power of a Northern Ireland department to make an order under this section is

exercisable by statutory rule for the purposes of the Statutory Rules (Northern Ireland) Order 1979 (S.I. 1979/1573 (N.I. 12)).

(8) An order under subsection (1) which contains any provision (whether alone or with other provisions) made by virtue of subsection (3) may not be made—

    (a) by a Minister of the Crown, unless a draft of the statutory instrument containing the order has been laid before, and approved by a resolution of, each House of Parliament;

    (b) by the Scottish Ministers, unless a draft of the statutory instrument containing the order has been laid before, and approved by a resolution of, the Scottish Parliament;

    (c) by a Northern Ireland department, unless a draft of the statutory rule containing the order has been laid before, and approved by a resolution of, the Northern Ireland Assembly.

(9) A statutory instrument containing an order under subsection (1) to which subsection (8) does not apply—

    (a) if made by a Minister of the Crown, is subject to annulment in pursuance of a resolution of either House of Parliament;

    (b) if made by the Scottish Ministers, is subject to annulment in pursuance of a resolution of the Scottish Parliament.

(10) A statutory rule made by a Northern Ireland department and containing an order to which subsection (8) does not apply is subject to negative resolution (within the meaning of section 41(6) of the Interpretation Act (Northern Ireland) 1954 (c. 33 (N.I.))).

(11) In this section—

    'Act' includes an Act of the Scottish Parliament;

    'Church legislation' has the same meaning as in section 255;

    'Minister of the Crown' has the same meaning as in the Ministers of the Crown Act 1975 (c. 26);

    'relevant Scottish provision' means a provision that would be within the legislative competence of the Scottish Parliament if it were included in an Act of that Parliament;

    'subordinate legislation' has the same meaning as in the Interpretation Act 1978 (c. 30) except that it includes any instrument made under an Act of the Scottish Parliament and any instrument within the meaning of section 1(c) of the Interpretation Act (Northern Ireland) 1954 (c. 33 (N.I.));

    'transferred matter' has the meaning given by section 4(1) of the Northern Ireland Act 1998 (c. 47) and 'deals with' in relation to a transferred matter is to be construed in accordance with section 98(2) and (3) of the 1998 Act.

260. Community Obligations and Civil Partners

(1) Subsection (2) applies where any person, by Order in Council or regulations under section 2(2) of the European Communities Act 1972 (c. 68) (general implementation of Treaties)—

    (a) is making provision for the purpose of implementing, or for a purpose concerning, a Community obligation of the United Kingdom which relates to persons who are or have been parties to a marriage, or

    (b) has made such provision and it has not been revoked.

(2) The appropriate person may by Order in Council or (as the case may be) by regulations make provision in relation to persons who are or have been civil partners in a civil partnership that is the same or similar to the provision referred to in subsection (1).

(3) 'Marriage' and 'civil partnership' include a void marriage and a void civil partnership respectively.

(4) 'The appropriate person' means—
   (a) if subsection (1)(a) applies, the person making the provision referred to there;
   (b) if subsection (1)(b) applies, any person who would have power to make the provision referred to there if it were being made at the time of the exercise of the power under subsection (2).

(5) The following provisions apply in relation to the power conferred by subsection (2) to make an Order in Council or regulations as they apply in relation to the power conferred by section 2(2) of the 1972 Act to make an Order in Council or regulations—
   (a) paragraph 2 of Schedule 2 to the 1972 Act (procedure etc. in relation to making of Orders in Council and regulations: general);
   (b) paragraph 15(3)(c) of Schedule 8 to the Scotland Act 1998 (c. 46) (modifications of paragraph 2 in relation to Scottish Ministers and to Orders in Council made on the recommendation of the First Minister);
   (c) paragraph 3 of Schedule 2 to the 1972 Act (modifications of paragraph 2 in relation to Northern Ireland departments etc.) and the Statutory Rules (Northern Ireland) Order 1979 (S.I. 1979/1573 (N.I. 12)) (treating the power conferred by subsection (2) as conferred by an Act passed before 1st January 1974 for the purposes of the application of that Order);
   (d) section 29(3) of the Government of Wales Act 1998 (c. 38) (modifications of paragraph 2 in relation to the National Assembly for Wales).

261. Minor and Consequential Amendments, Repeals and Revocations

(1) Schedule 27 contains minor and consequential amendments.

(2) Schedule 28 contains consequential amendments of enactments relating to Scotland.

(3) Schedule 29 contains minor and consequential amendments relating to Northern Ireland.

(4) Schedule 30 contains repeals and revocations.

262. Extent

(1) Part 2 (civil partnership: England and Wales), excluding section 35 but including Schedules 1 to 9, extends to England and Wales only.

(2) Part 3 (civil partnership: Scotland), including Schedules 10 and 11, extends to Scotland only.

(3) Part 4 (civil partnership: Northern Ireland), including Schedules 12 to 19, extends to Northern Ireland only.

(4) In Part 5 (civil partnerships formed or dissolved abroad etc.)—
   (a) sections 220 to 224 extend to England and Wales only;
   (b) sections 225 to 227 extend to Scotland only;
   (c) sections 228 to 232 extend to Northern Ireland only.

(5) In Part 6—
   (a) any amendment made by virtue of section 247(1)(a) and Schedule 21 has the same extent as the provision subject to the amendment;

(b) section 248 and Schedule 22 extend to Northern Ireland only.

(6) Section 251 extends to England and Wales and Scotland only.

(7) Section 252 extends to Northern Ireland only.

(8) Schedule 28 extends to Scotland only.

(9) Schedule 29 extends to Northern Ireland only.

(10) Any amendment, repeal or revocation made by Schedules 24 to 27 and 30 has the same extent as the provision subject to the amendment, repeal or revocation.

263. Commencement

(1) Part 1 comes into force in accordance with provision made by order by the Secretary of State, after consulting the Scottish Ministers and the Department of Finance and Personnel.

(2) Part 2, including Schedules 1 to 9, comes into force in accordance with provision made by order by the Secretary of State.

(3) Part 3, including Schedules 10 and 11, comes into force in accordance with provision made by order by the Scottish Ministers, after consulting the Secretary of State.

(4) Part 4, including Schedules 12 to 19, comes into force in accordance with provision made by order by the Department of Finance and Personnel, after consulting the Secretary of State.

(5) Part 5, excluding section 213(2) to (6) but including Schedule 20, comes into force in accordance with provision made by order by the Secretary of State, after consulting the Scottish Ministers and the Department of Finance and Personnel.

(6) Section 213(2) to (6) comes into force on the day on which this Act is passed.

(7) In Part 6—

    (a) sections 246 and 247(1) and Schedule 21 come into force in accordance with provision made by order by the Secretary of State, after consulting the Scottish Ministers and the Department of Finance and Personnel,

    (b) section 248(1) and Schedule 22 come into force in accordance with provision made by order by the Department of Finance and Personnel, after consulting the Secretary of State, and

    (c) sections 247(2) to (7) and 248(2) to (5) come into force on the day on which this Act is passed.

(8) In Part 7—

    (a) sections 249, 251, 253, 256 and 257 and Schedules 23, 25 and 26 come into force in accordance with provision made by order by the Secretary of State,

    (b) section 250 comes into force in accordance with provision made by order by the Secretary of State, after consulting the Scottish Ministers and the Department of Finance and Personnel,

    (c) section 252 comes into force in accordance with provision made by the Department of Finance and Personnel, after consulting the Secretary of State,

    (d) subject to paragraph (e), section 254(1) and Schedule 24 come into force in accordance with provision made by order by the Secretary of State,

    (e) the provisions of Schedule 24 listed in subsection (9), and section 254(1) so far as relating to those provisions, come into force in accordance with provision made by the Department of Finance and Personnel, after consulting the Secretary of State, and

    (f) sections 254(2) to (6) and 255 come into force on the day on which this Act is passed.

(9) The provisions are—
- (a) Part 2;
- (b) in Part 5, paragraphs 67 to 85, 87, 89 to 99 and 102 to 105;
- (c) Part 6;
- (d) Parts 9 and 10;
- (e) Part 15.

(10) In this Part—
- (a) sections 258, 259, 260 and 262, this section and section 264 come into force on the day on which this Act is passed,
- (b) section 261(1) and Schedule 27 and, except so far as relating to any Acts of the Scottish Parliament or any provision which extends to Northern Ireland only, section 261(4) and Schedule 30 come into force in accordance with provision made by order by the Secretary of State,
- (c) section 261(2) and Schedule 28 and, so far as relating to any Acts of the Scottish Parliament, section 261(4) and Schedule 30 come into force in accordance with provision made by order by the Scottish Ministers, after consulting the Secretary of State,
- (d) section 261(3) and Schedule 29 and, so far as relating to any provision which extends to Northern Ireland only, section 261(4) and Schedule 30 come into force in accordance with provision made by order by the Department of Finance and Personnel, after consulting the Secretary of State.

(11) The power to make an order under this section is exercisable by statutory instrument.

264. Short Title

This Act may be cited as the Civil Partnership Act 2004.

SCHEDULES

SCHEDULE 1

Sections 3(2) and 5(3)

PROHIBITED DEGREES OF RELATIONSHIP: ENGLAND AND WALES

Part 1

The Prohibitions

Absolute prohibitions

1 (1) Two people are within prohibited degrees of relationship if one falls within the list below in relation to the other.

Adoptive child
Adoptive parent
Child
Former adoptive child
Former adoptive parent
Grandparent
Grandchild

Parent
Parent's sibling
Sibling
Sibling's child

(2) In the list 'sibling' means a brother, sister, half-brother or half-sister.

Qualified prohibitions

2 (1) Two people are within prohibited degrees of relationship if one of them falls within the list below in relation to the other, unless—

    (a) both of them have reached 21 at the time when they register as civil partners of each other, and

    (b) the younger has not at any time before reaching 18 been a child of the family in relation to the other.

    Child of former civil partner
    Child of former spouse
    Former civil partner of grandparent
    Former civil partner of parent
    Former spouse of grandparent
    Former spouse of parent
    Grandchild of former civil partner
    Grandchild of former spouse

(2) 'Child of the family', in relation to another person, means a person who—

    (a) has lived in the same household as that other person, and

    (b) has been treated by that other person as a child of his family.

3 Two people are within prohibited degrees of relationship if one falls within column 1 of the table below in relation to the other, unless—

    (a) both of them have reached 21 at the time when they register as civil partners of each other, and

    (b) the persons who fall within column 2 are dead.

Relationship	Relevant deaths
Former civil partner of child	The child The child's other parent
Former spouse of child	The child The child's other parent
Parent of former civil partner	The former civil partner The former civil partner's other parent
Parent of former spouse	The former spouse The former spouse's other parent

Part 2

Special Provisions Relating to Qualified Prohibitions

Provisions relating to paragraph 2

4 Paragraphs 5 to 7 apply where two people are subject to paragraph 2 but intend to register as civil partners of each other by signing a civil partnership schedule.

5 (1) The fact that a notice of proposed civil partnership has been given must not be recorded in the register unless the registration authority—

    (a) is satisfied by the production of evidence that both the proposed civil partners have reached 21, and

    (b) has received a declaration made by each of the proposed civil partners—

        (i) specifying their affinal relationship, and

        (ii) declaring that the younger of them has not at any time before reaching 18 been a child of the family in relation to the other.

(2) Sub-paragraph (1) does not apply if a declaration is obtained under paragraph 7.

(3) A declaration under sub-paragraph (1)(b) must contain such information and must be signed and attested in such manner as may be prescribed by regulations.

(4) The fact that a registration authority has received a declaration under sub-paragraph (1)(b) must be recorded in the register.

(5) A declaration under sub-paragraph (1)(b) must be filed and kept by the registration authority.

6 (1) Sub-paragraph (2) applies if—

    (a) a registration authority receives from a person who is not one of the proposed civil partners a written statement signed by that person which alleges that a declaration made under paragraph 5 is false in a material particular, and

    (b) the register shows that such a statement has been received.

(2) The registration authority in whose area it is proposed that the registration take place must not issue a civil partnership schedule unless a High Court declaration is obtained under paragraph 7.

7 (1) Either of the proposed civil partners may apply to the High Court for a declaration that, given that—

    (a) both of them have reached 21, and

    (b) the younger of those persons has not at any time before reaching 18 been a child of the family in relation to the other,

there is no impediment of affinity to the formation of the civil partnership.

(2) Such an application may be made whether or not any statement has been received by the registration authority under paragraph 6.

8   Section 13 (objection to proposed civil partnership) does not apply in relation to a civil partnership to which paragraphs 5 to 7 apply, except so far as an objection to the issue of a civil partnership schedule is made under that section on a ground other than the affinity between the proposed civil partners.

Provisions relating to paragraph 3

9 (1) This paragraph applies where two people are subject to paragraph 3 but intend to register as civil partners of each other by signing a civil partnership schedule.

(2) The fact that a notice of proposed civil partnership has been given must not be recorded in the register unless the registration authority is satisfied by the production of evidence—

    (a) that both the proposed civil partners have reached 21, and

    (b) that the persons referred to in paragraph 3(b) are dead.

SCHEDULE 2

Section 4(2) and 5(3)

CIVIL PARTNERSHIPS OF PERSONS UNDER 18: ENGLAND AND WALES

Part 1

Appropriate Persons

1   Column 2 of the table specifies the appropriate persons (or person) to give consent to a child whose circumstances fall within column 1 and who intends to register as the civil partner of another—

Case	Appropriate persons
1 The circumstances do not fall within any of items 2 to 8.	Each of the following— (a) any parent of the child who has parental responsibility for him, and (b) any guardian of the child.
2 A special guardianship order is in force with respect to the child and the circumstances do not fall within any of items 3 to 7.	Each of the child's special guardians.
3 A care order has effect with respect to the child and the circumstances do not fall within item 5.	Each of the following— (a) the local authority designated in the order, and (b) each parent, guardian or special guardian (in so far as their parental responsibility has not been restricted under section 33(3) of the 1989 Act).
4 A residence order has effect with respect to the child and the circumstances do not fall within item 5.	Each of the persons with whom the child lives, or is to live, as a result of the order.
5 An adoption agency is authorised to place the child for adoption under section 19 of the 2002 Act.	Either— (a) the adoption agency, or (b) if a care order has effect with respect to the child, the local authority designated in the order.
6 A placement order is in force with respect to the child.	The local authority authorised by the placement order to place the child for adoption.
7 The child has been placed for adoption with prospective adopters.	The prospective adopters (in so far as their parental responsibility has not been restricted under section 25(4) of the 2002 Act), in addition to any person specified in relation to item 5 or 6.
8 The circumstances do not fall within any of items 2 to 7, but a residence order was in force with respect to the child immediately before he reached 16.	The persons with whom the child lived, or was to live, as a result of the order.

2   In the table—
'the 1989 Act' means the Children Act 1989 (c. 41) and 'guardian of a child', 'parental responsibility', 'residence order', 'special guardian', 'special guardianship order' and 'care order' have the same meaning as in that Act;

'the 2002 Act' means the Adoption and Children Act 2002 (c. 38) and 'adoption agency', 'placed for adoption', 'placement order' and 'local authority' have the same meaning as in that Act;

'appropriate local authority' means the local authority authorised by the placement order to place the child for adoption.

Part 2

Obtaining Consent: General

Consent of appropriate person unobtainable

3 (1) This paragraph applies if—
(a) a child and another person intend to register as civil partners of each other under any procedure other than the special procedure, and
(b) the registration authority to whom the child gives a notice of proposed civil partnership is satisfied that the consent of a person whose consent is required ('A') cannot be obtained because A is absent, inaccessible or under a disability.

(2) If there is any other person whose consent is also required, the registration authority must dispense with the need for A's consent.

(3) If no other person's consent is required—
(a) the Registrar General may dispense with the need for any consent, or
(b) the court may, on an application being made to it, consent to the child registering as the civil partner of the person mentioned in sub-paragraph (1)(a).

(4) The consent of the court under sub-paragraph (3)(b) has the same effect as if it had been given by A.

Consent of appropriate person refused

4 (1) This paragraph applies if—
(a) a child and another person intend to register as civil partners of each other under any procedure other than the special procedure, and
(b) any person whose consent is required refuses his consent.

(2) The court may, on an application being made to it, consent to the child registering as the civil partner of the person mentioned in sub-paragraph (1)(a).

(3) The consent of the court under sub-paragraph (2) has the same effect as if it had been given by the person who has refused his consent.

Declaration

5   If one of the proposed civil partners is a child and is not a surviving civil partner, the necessary declaration under section 8 must also—
(a) state in relation to each appropriate person—
(i) that that person's consent has been obtained,
(ii) that the need to obtain that person's consent has been dispensed with under paragraph 3, or

(iii) that the court has given consent under paragraph 3 or 4, or

(b) state that no person exists whose consent is required to a civil partnership between the child and another person.

Forbidding proposed civil partnership

6 (1) This paragraph applies if it has been recorded in the register that a notice of proposed civil partnership between a child and another person has been given.

(2) Any person whose consent is required to a child and another person registering as civil partners of each other may forbid the issue of a civil partnership schedule by giving any registration authority written notice that he forbids it.

(3) A notice under sub-paragraph (2) must specify—

(a) the name of the person giving it,

(b) his place of residence, and

(c) the capacity, in relation to either of the proposed civil partners, in which he forbids the issue of the civil partnership schedule.

(4) On receiving the notice, the registration authority must as soon as is practicable record in the register the fact that the issue of a civil partnership schedule has been forbidden.

(5) If the issue of a civil partnership schedule has been forbidden under this paragraph, the notice of proposed civil partnership and all proceedings on it are void.

(6) Sub-paragraphs (2) and (5) do not apply if the court has given its consent under paragraph 3 or 4.

Evidence

7 (1) This paragraph applies if, for the purpose of obtaining a civil partnership schedule, a person declares that the consent of any person or persons whose consent is required under section 4 has been given.

(2) The registration authority may refuse to issue the civil partnership schedule unless satisfied by the production of written evidence that the consent of that person or those persons has in fact been given.

Issue of civil partnership schedule

8 The duty in section 14(1) to issue a civil partnership schedule does not apply if its issue has been forbidden under paragraph 6.

9 If a proposed civil partnership is between a child and another person, the civil partnership schedule must contain a statement that the issue of the civil partnership schedule has not been forbidden under paragraph 6.

Part 3

Obtaining Consent: Special Procedure

Consent of appropriate person unobtainable or refused

10 (1) Sub-paragraph (2) applies if—

(a) a child and another person intend to register as civil partners of each other under the special procedure, and

(b) the Registrar General is satisfied that the consent of a person ('A') whose consent is required cannot be obtained because A is absent, inaccessible, or under a disability.

(2) If this sub-paragraph applies—

(a) the Registrar General may dispense with the need for A's consent (whether or not there is any other person whose consent is also required), or

(b) the court may, on application being made, consent to the child registering as the civil partner of the person mentioned in sub-paragraph (1)(a).

(3) The consent of the court under sub-paragraph (2)(b) has the same effect as if it had been given by A.

(4) Sub-paragraph (5) applies if—

(a) a child and another person intend to register as civil partners of each other under the special procedure, and

(b) any person whose consent is required refuses his consent.

(5) The court may, on application being made, consent to the child registering as the civil partner of the person mentioned in sub-paragraph (4)(a).

(6) The consent of the court under sub-paragraph (5) has the same effect as if it had been given by the person who has refused his consent.

Declaration

11 If one of the proposed civil partners is a child and is not a surviving civil partner, the necessary declaration under section 8 must also—

(a) state in relation to each appropriate person—

(i) that that person's consent has been obtained,

(ii) that the need to obtain that person's consent has been dispensed with under paragraph 10(2), or

(iii) that the court has given consent under paragraph 10(2) or (5), or

(b) state that no person exists whose consent is required to a civil partnership between the child and another person.

Forbidding proposed civil partnership

12 Paragraph 6 applies in relation to the special procedure as if—

(a) any reference to forbidding the issue of a civil partnership schedule were a reference to forbidding the Registrar General to give authority for the issue of his licence, and

(b) sub-paragraph (6) referred to the court giving its consent under paragraph 10(2) or (5).

Evidence

13 (1) This paragraph applies—

(a) if a child and another person intend to register as civil partners of each other under the special procedure, and

(b) the consent of any person ('A') is required to the child registering as the civil partner of that person.

(2) The person giving the notice (under section 21) of proposed civil partnership to the registration authority must produce to the authority such evidence as the Registrar General may require to satisfy him that A's consent has in fact been given.

(3) The power to require evidence under sub-paragraph (2) is in addition to the power to require evidence under section 22.

Issue of Registrar General's licence

14 The duty of the Registrar General under section 25(3)(b) to give authority for the issue of his licence does not apply if he has been forbidden to do so by virtue of paragraph 12.

Part 4

Provisions Relating to the Court

15 (1) For the purposes of Parts 2 and 3 of this Schedule, 'the court' means—
   (a) the High Court,
   (b) the county court of the district in which any applicant or respondent resides, or
   (c) a magistrates' court acting in the local justice area in which any applicant or respondent resides.
(2) Rules of court may be made for enabling applications under Part 2 or 3 of this Schedule—
   (a) if made to the High Court, to be heard in chambers;
   (b) if made to the county court, to be heard and determined by the district judge subject to appeal to the judge;
   (c) if made to a magistrates' court, to be heard and determined otherwise than in open court.
(3) Rules of court must provide that, where an application is made in consequence of a refusal to give consent, notice of the application is to be served on the person who has refused consent.

SCHEDULE 3

Section 5(2)

REGISTRATION BY FORMER SPOUSES ONE OF WHOM
HAS CHANGED SEX

Application of Schedule

1 This Schedule applies if—
   (a) a court—
      (i) makes absolute a decree of nullity granted on the ground that an interim gender recognition certificate has been issued to a party to the marriage, or
      (ii) (in Scotland) grants a decree of divorce on that ground,
      and, on doing so, issues a full gender recognition certificate (under section 5(1) of the Gender Recognition Act 2004 (c. 7)) to that party, and
   (b) the parties wish to register in England or Wales as civil partners of each other without being delayed by the waiting period.

The relevant period

2   For the purposes of this Schedule the relevant period is the period—
    (a) beginning with the issue of the full gender recognition certificate, and
    (b) ending at the end of 1 month from the day on which it is issued.

Modifications of standard procedure and procedures for house-bound and detained persons

3   If—
    (a) each of the parties gives a notice of proposed civil partnership during the relevant period, and
    (b) on doing so, each makes an election under this paragraph,
Chapter 1 of Part 2 applies with the modifications given in paragraphs 4 to 6.

4   (1) Omit—
    (a) section 10 (proposed civil partnership to be publicised);
    (b) section 11 (meaning of 'the waiting period');
    (c) section 12 (power to shorten the waiting period).
    (2) In section 14 (issue of civil partnership schedule), for subsection (1) substitute—
    '(1) As soon as the notices of proposed civil partnership have been given, the registration authority in whose area it is proposed that the registration take place must, at the request of one or both of the proposed civil partners, issue a document to be known as a "civil partnership schedule".'
    (3) For section 17 (period during which registration may take place) substitute—

'17 Period during which registration may take place

    (1) The proposed civil partners may register as civil partners by signing the civil partnership schedule at any time during the applicable period.
    (2) If they do not register as civil partners by signing the civil partnership schedule before the end of the applicable period—
    (a) the notices of proposed civil partnership and the civil partnership schedule are void, and
    (b) no civil partnership registrar may officiate at the signing of the civil partnership schedule by them.
    (3) The applicable period, in relation to two people registering as civil partners of each other, is the period of 1 month beginning with—
    (a) the day on which the notices of proposed civil partnership are given, or
    (b) if the notices are not given on the same day, the earlier of those days.'

5   In section 18 (house-bound persons), in subsection (3)—
    (a) treat the reference to the standard procedure as a reference to the standard procedure as modified by this Schedule, and
    (b) omit paragraph (c) (which provides for a 3 month registration period).

6   In section 19 (detained persons), in subsection (3)—
    (a) treat the reference to the standard procedure as a reference to the standard procedure as modified by this Schedule, and
    (b) omit paragraph (c) (which provides for a 3 month registration period).

Modified procedures for certain non-residents

7   (1) Sub-paragraphs (5) to (8) apply (in place of section 20) in the following three cases.
    (2) The first is where—
    (a) two people wish to register as civil partners of each other in England and Wales, and

229

(b) one of them ('A') resides in Scotland and the other ('B') resides in England or Wales.

(3) The second is where—

    (a) two people wish to register as civil partners of each other in England and Wales, and

    (b) one of them ('A') resides in Northern Ireland and the other ('B') resides in England or Wales.

(4) The third is where—

    (a) two people wish to register as civil partners of each other in England and Wales, and

    (b) one of them ('A') is a member of Her Majesty's forces who is serving outside the United Kingdom and the other ('B') resides in England or Wales.

(5) A is not required to give a notice of proposed civil partnership to a registration authority in England or Wales in order to register in England or Wales as B's civil partner.

(6) B may give a notice of proposed civil partnership and make the necessary declaration without regard to the requirement that would otherwise apply that A must reside in England or Wales.

(7) If, on giving such notice, B makes an election under this paragraph, Chapter 1 of Part 2 applies with the modifications given in paragraphs 4 to 6 and the further modifications in sub-paragraph (8).

(8) The further modifications are that—

    (a) the civil partnership schedule is not to be issued by a registration authority unless A or B produces to that registration authority a certificate of no impediment issued to A under the relevant provision;

    (b) the applicable period is the period of one month beginning with the day on which B's notice is given;

    (c) section 31 applies as if in subsections (1)(a) and (2)(c) for 'each notice' there were substituted 'B's notice'.

(9) 'The relevant provision' means—

    (a) if A resides in Scotland, section 97;

    (b) if A resides in Northern Ireland, section 150;

    (c) if A is a member of Her Majesty's forces who is serving outside the United Kingdom, section 239.

(10) 'Her Majesty's forces' has the same meaning as in the Army Act 1955 (3 & 4 Eliz. 2 c. 18).

SCHEDULE 4

Section 71

WILLS, ADMINISTRATION OF ESTATES AND FAMILY PROVISION

Part 1

Wills

1   Amend the Wills Act 1837 (c. 26) as follows.

2   After section 18A insert—

'18B Will to be revoked by civil partnership

(1) Subject to subsections (2) to (6), a will is revoked by the formation of a civil partnership between the testator and another person.

(2) A disposition in a will in exercise of a power of appointment takes effect despite the formation of a subsequent civil partnership between the testator and another person unless the property so appointed would in default of appointment pass to the testator's personal representatives.

(3) If it appears from a will—
   (a) that at the time it was made the testator was expecting to form a civil partnership with a particular person, and
   (b) that he intended that the will should not be revoked by the formation of the civil partnership,
   the will is not revoked by its formation.

(4) Subsections (5) and (6) apply if it appears from a will—
   (a) that at the time it was made the testator was expecting to form a civil partnership with a particular person, and
   (b) that he intended that a disposition in the will should not be revoked by the formation of the civil partnership.

(5) The disposition takes effect despite the formation of the civil partnership.

(6) Any other disposition in the will also takes effect, unless it appears from the will that the testator intended the disposition to be revoked by the formation of the civil partnership.

'18C Effect of dissolution or annulment of civil partnership on wills

(1) This section applies if, after a testator has made a will—
   (a) a court of civil jurisdiction in England and Wales dissolves his civil partnership or makes a nullity order in respect of it, or
   (b) his civil partnership is dissolved or annulled and the dissolution or annulment is entitled to recognition in England and Wales by virtue of Chapter 3 of Part 5 of the Civil Partnership Act 2004.

(2) Except in so far as a contrary intention appears by the will—
   (a) provisions of the will appointing executors or trustees or conferring a power of appointment, if they appoint or confer the power on the former civil partner, take effect as if the former civil partner had died on the date on which the civil partnership is dissolved or annulled, and
   (b) any property which, or an interest in which, is devised or bequeathed to the former civil partner shall pass as if the former civil partner had died on that date.

(3) Subsection (2)(b) does not affect any right of the former civil partner to apply for financial provision under the Inheritance (Provision for Family and Dependants) Act 1975.'

3   The following provisions—
   (a) section 15 of the Wills Act 1837 (c. 26) (avoidance of gifts to attesting witnesses and their spouses), and
   (b) section 1 of the Wills Act 1968 (c. 28) (restriction of operation of section 15),
   apply in relation to the attestation of a will by a person to whose civil partner there is given or made any such disposition as is described in section 15 of the 1837 Act as they apply in relation to a person to whose spouse there is given or made any such disposition.

4   In section 16 of the 1837 Act, after 'wife or husband' insert 'or civil partner'.

5   Except where a contrary intention is shown, it is presumed that if a testator—

(a) devises or bequeaths property to his civil partner in terms which in themselves would give an absolute interest to the civil partner, but

(b) by the same instrument purports to give his issue an interest in the same property,

the gift to the civil partner is absolute despite the purported gift to the issue.

Part 2

Administration of Estates and Family Provision

Public Trustee Act 1906 (c. 55)

6   In section 6(1), after 'widower, widow' (in both places) insert ', surviving civil partner'.

Administration of Estates Act 1925 (c. 23)

7   In section 46 (succession to real and personal estate on intestacy), for 'husband or wife' (in each place) substitute 'spouse or civil partner'.

8 (1) Amend section 47(1) (meaning of 'the statutory trusts') as follows.

(2) In paragraph (i), after 'or marry under that age' (in the first place) insert 'or form a civil partnership under that age'.

(3) In that paragraph, after 'or marry' (in the second place) insert ', or form a civil partnership,'.

(4) In paragraph (ii), after 'marries' insert ', or forms a civil partnership,'.

9   In section 47A, in subsection (1) and in the proviso to subsection (5), for 'husband or wife' substitute 'spouse or civil partner'.

10   In section 48(2), for 'husband or wife' (in each place) substitute 'spouse or civil partner'.

11   In section 51(3) (devolution of certain estates vested in infant who dies without having married and without issue), after 'without having been married' insert 'or having formed a civil partnership,'.

12   In section 55(1)(xviii) (which defines 'valuable consideration' as including marriage), after 'includes marriage,' insert 'and formation of a civil partnership,'.

Intestates' Estates Act 1952 (c. 64)

13 (1) Amend section 5 and Schedule 2 (rights of surviving spouse as respects the matrimonial home) as follows.

(2) For 'husband or wife' (in each place) substitute 'spouse or civil partner'.

(3) In section 5, after 'matrimonial' insert 'or civil partnership'.

(4) In the heading of each—

(a) after 'spouse' insert 'or civil partner', and

(b) after 'matrimonial' insert 'or civil partnership'.

Family Provision Act 1966 (c. 35)

14   In section 1(1) (fixed net sum payable to surviving spouse of person dying intestate), for 'husband or wife' substitute 'spouse or civil partner'.

Inheritance (Provision for Family and Dependants) Act 1975 (c. 63)

15 (1) Amend section 1 (application for financial provision from deceased person's estate) as follows.

(2) For subsection (1)(a) and (b) (application may be made by spouse or by former spouse who has not remarried) substitute—

'(a) the spouse or civil partner of the deceased;

(b) former spouse or former civil partner of the deceased, but not one who has formed a subsequent marriage or civil partnership;'.

(3) In subsection (1)(ba) (application may be made by person living as husband or wife of the deceased), after 'subsection (1A)' insert 'or (1B)'.

(4) In subsection (1)(d) (application may be made by child of the family), after 'marriage' (in each place) insert 'or civil partnership'.

(5) After subsection (1A) insert—

'(1B) This subsection applies to a person if for the whole of the period of two years ending immediately before the date when the deceased died the person was living—

(a) in the same household as the deceased, and

(b) as the civil partner of the deceased.'

(6) In subsection (2) (meaning of 'reasonable financial provision'), after paragraph (a) insert—

'(aa) in the case of an application made by virtue of subsection (1)(a) above by the civil partner of the deceased (except where, at the date of death, a separation order under Chapter 2 of Part 2 of the Civil Partnership Act 2004 was in force in relation to the civil partnership and the separation was continuing), means such financial provision as it would be reasonable in all the circumstances of the case for a civil partner to receive, whether or not that provision is required for his or her maintenance;'.

16 In section 2(1) (orders which may be made on an application), after paragraph (f) insert—

'(g) an order varying any settlement made—

(i) during the subsistence of a civil partnership formed by the deceased, or

(ii) in anticipation of the formation of a civil partnership by the deceased,

on the civil partners (including such a settlement made by will), the variation being for the benefit of the surviving civil partner, or any child of both the civil partners, or any person who was treated by the deceased as a child of the family in relation to that civil partnership.'

17 (1) Amend section 3(2) (application by spouse or former spouse: matters to which court is to have regard) as follows.

(2) For the words from the beginning to '1(1)(b) of this Act' substitute—

'This subsection applies, without prejudice to the generality of paragraph (g) of subsection (1) above, where an application for an order under section 2 of this Act is made by virtue of section 1(1)(a) or (b) of this Act.'

(3) The words from 'the court shall, in addition' to the end of paragraph (b) shall become a second sentence of the subsection and, in paragraph (a) of the sentence so formed, after 'duration of the marriage' insert 'or civil partnership'.

(4) The words from 'in the case of an application by the wife or husband' to the end shall become a third sentence of the subsection.

(5) At the end insert the following sentence—

'In the case of an application by the civil partner of the deceased, the court shall also, unless at the date of the death a separation order under Chapter 2 of Part 2 of the Civil Partnership Act 2004 was in force and the separation was continuing, have regard to the provision which the applicant might reasonably have expected to receive if on the day on which the deceased died the civil partnership, instead of being terminated by death, had been terminated by a dissolution order.'

18   In section 3(2A) (application by person living as husband or wife of deceased: matters to which court is to have regard), in paragraph (a), after 'wife' insert 'or civil partner'.

19   In section 6(3) and (10) (variation etc. of orders which cease on occurrence of specified event other than remarriage of former spouse), for '(other than the remarriage of a former wife or former husband)' substitute '(other than the formation of a subsequent marriage or civil partnership by a former spouse or former civil partner)'.

20   After section 14 insert—

'14A   Provision as to cases where no financial relief was granted in proceedings for the dissolution etc. of a civil partnership

(1)   Subsection (2) below applies where—

  (a)   a dissolution order, nullity order, separation order or presumption of death order has been made under Chapter 2 of Part 2 of the Civil Partnership Act 2004 in relation to a civil partnership,

  (b)   one of the civil partners dies within twelve months from the date on which the order is made, and

  (c)   either—

    (i)   an application for a financial provision order under Part 1 of Schedule 5 to that Act or a property adjustment order under Part 2 of that Schedule has not been made by the other civil partner, or

    (ii)   such an application has been made but the proceedings on the application have not been determined at the time of the death of the deceased.

(2)   If an application for an order under section 2 of this Act is made by the surviving civil partner, the court shall, notwithstanding anything in section 1 or section 3 of this Act, have power, if it thinks it just to do so, to treat the surviving civil partner as if the order mentioned in subsection (1)(a) above had not been made.

(3)   This section shall not apply in relation to a separation order unless at the date of the death of the deceased the separation order was in force and the separation was continuing.'

21   After section 15 insert—

'15ZA   Restriction imposed in proceedings for the dissolution etc. of a civil partnership on application under this Act

(1)   On making a dissolution order, nullity order, separation order or presumption of death order under Chapter 2 of Part 2 of the Civil Partnership Act 2004, or at any time after making such an order, the court, if it considers it just to do so, may, on the application of either of the civil partners, order that the other civil partner shall not on the death of the applicant be entitled to apply for an order under section 2 of this Act.

(2)   In subsection (1) above 'the court' means the High Court or, where a county court has jurisdiction by virtue of Part 5 of the Matrimonial and Family Proceedings Act 1984, a county court.

(3) In the case of a dissolution order, nullity order or presumption of death order ('the main order') an order may be made under subsection (1) above before (as well as after) the main order is made final, but if made before the main order is made final it shall not take effect unless the main order is made final.

(4) Where an order under subsection (1) above made in connection with a dissolution order, nullity order or presumption of death order has come into force with respect to a civil partner, then, on the death of the other civil partner, the court shall not entertain any application for an order under section 2 of this Act made by the surviving civil partner.

(5) Where an order under subsection (1) above made in connection with a separation order has come into force with respect to a civil partner, then, if the other civil partner dies while the separation order is in force and the separation is continuing, the court shall not entertain any application for an order under section 2 of this Act made by the surviving civil partner.'

22 After section 15A insert—

'15B Restriction imposed in proceedings under Schedule 7 to the Civil Partnership Act 2004 on application under this Act

(1) On making an order under paragraph 9 of Schedule 7 to the Civil Partnership Act 2004 (orders for financial provision, property adjustment and pension-sharing following overseas dissolution etc. of civil partnership) the court, if it considers it just to do so, may, on the application of either of the civil partners, order that the other civil partner shall not on the death of the applicant be entitled to apply for an order under section 2 of this Act.

(2) In subsection (1) above "the court" means the High Court or, where a county court has jurisdiction by virtue of Part 5 of the Matrimonial and Family Proceedings Act 1984, a county court.

(3) Where an order under subsection (1) above has been made with respect to one of the civil partners in a case where a civil partnership has been dissolved or annulled, then, on the death of the other civil partner, the court shall not entertain an application under section 2 of this Act made by the surviving civil partner.

(4) Where an order under subsection (1) above has been made with respect to one of the civil partners in a case where civil partners have been legally separated, then, if the other civil partner dies while the legal separation is in force, the court shall not entertain an application under section 2 of this Act made by the surviving civil partner.'

23 In section 16(1) (power to vary secured periodical payments orders)—
 (a) after 'the Matrimonial Causes Act 1973' insert 'or Schedule 5 to the Civil Partnership Act 2004', and
 (b) after 'that Act' insert 'of 1973 or Part 11 of that Schedule'.

24 In section 17(4) (meaning of 'maintenance agreement')—
 (a) for 'entered into a marriage' substitute 'formed a marriage or civil partnership',
 (b) after 'of the parties to that marriage' insert 'or of the civil partners', and
 (c) after 'marriage' (in the third and fourth places) insert 'or civil partnership'.

25 After section 18 insert—

'18A Availability of court's powers under this Act in applications under paragraphs 60 and 73 of Schedule 5 to the Civil Partnership Act 2004

(1) Where—
 (a) a person against whom a secured periodical payments order was made under Schedule 5 to the Civil Partnership Act 2004 has died and an application is made under paragraph 60 of that Schedule for the variation or discharge of that order or for the revival of the operation of any suspended provision of the order, or

   (b) a party to a maintenance agreement within the meaning of Part 13 of that Schedule has died, the agreement being one which provides for the continuation of payments under the agreement after the death of one of the parties, and an application is made under paragraph 73 of that Schedule for the alteration of the agreement under paragraph 69 of that Schedule,

the court shall have power to direct that the application made under paragraph 60 or 73 of that Schedule shall be deemed to have been accompanied by an application for an order under section 2 of this Act.

(2) Where the court gives a direction under subsection (1) above it shall have power, in the proceedings on the application under paragraph 60 or 73 of that Schedule, to make any order which the court would have had power to make under the provisions of this Act if the application under that paragraph had been made jointly with an application for an order under section 2 of this Act; and the court shall have power to give such consequential directions as may be necessary for enabling the court to exercise any of the powers available to the court under this Act in the case of an application for an order under section 2.

(3) Where an order made under section 15ZA(1) of this Act is in force with respect to a civil partner, the court shall not give a direction under subsection (1) above with respect to any application made under paragraph 60 or 73 of that Schedule by that civil partner on the death of the other civil partner.'

26 (1) Amend section 19 (effect, duration and form of orders) as follows.

(2) In subsection (2)(a), for 'former husband or former wife' substitute 'former spouse or former civil partner'.

(3) In subsection (2), after paragraph (b) insert 'or

   (c) an applicant who was the civil partner of the deceased in a case where, at the date of death, a separation order under Chapter 2 of Part 2 of the Civil Partnership Act 2004 was in force in relation to their civil partnership and the separation was continuing,'.

(4) In that subsection, in the words after paragraph (b), for 'on the remarriage of the applicant' onwards substitute 'on the formation by the applicant of a subsequent marriage or civil partnership, except in relation to any arrears due under the order on the date of the formation of the subsequent marriage or civil partnership.'

(5) In subsection (3), after 'section 15(1)' insert 'or 15ZA(1)'.

27 (1) Amend section 25 (interpretation) as follows.

(2) In subsection (1), in the definition of 'former wife' and 'former husband', for ' "former wife" or "former husband" ' substitute ' "former spouse" '.

(3) In that subsection, before that definition insert—

' "former civil partner" means a person whose civil partnership with the deceased was during the lifetime of the deceased either—

   (a) dissolved or annulled by an order made under the law of any part of the British Islands, or

   (b) dissolved or annulled in any country or territory outside the British Islands by a dissolution or annulment which is entitled to be recognised as valid by the law of England and Wales;'.

(4) In subsection (4)—

   (a) before 'wife' insert 'spouse,' and

   (b) in paragraph (b), for 'entered into a later marriage' substitute 'formed a subsequent marriage or civil partnership'.

(5) For subsection (5) substitute—

'(4A) For the purposes of this Act any reference to a civil partner shall be treated as including a reference to a person who in good faith formed a void civil partnership with the deceased unless either—

    (a) the civil partnership between the deceased and that person was dissolved or annulled during the lifetime of the deceased and the dissolution or annulment is recognised by the law of England and Wales, or

    (b) that person has during the lifetime of the deceased formed a subsequent civil partnership or marriage.

(5) Any reference in this Act to the formation of, or to a person who has formed, a subsequent marriage or civil partnership includes (as the case may be) a reference to the formation of, or to a person who has formed, a marriage or civil partnership which is by law void or voidable.

(5A) The formation of a marriage or civil partnership shall be treated for the purposes of this Act as the formation of a subsequent marriage or civil partnership, in relation to either of the spouses or civil partners, notwithstanding that the previous marriage or civil partnership of that spouse or civil partner was void or voidable.'

(6) After subsection (6) insert—

'(6A) Any reference in this Act to an order made under, or under any provision of, the Civil Partnership Act 2004 shall be construed as including a reference to anything which is deemed to be an order made (as the case may be) under that Act or provision.'

SCHEDULE 5

Section 72(1)

FINANCIAL RELIEF IN THE HIGH COURT OR A COUNTY COURT ETC.

Part 1

Financial Provision in Connection with Dissolution, Nullity or Separation

Circumstances in which orders under this Part may be made

1 (1) The court may make any one or more of the orders set out in paragraph 2(1)—

    (a) on making a dissolution, nullity or separation order, or

    (b) at any time afterwards.

(2) The court may make any one or more of the orders set out in paragraph 2(1)(d), (e) and (f)—

    (a) in proceedings for a dissolution, nullity or separation order, before making the order;

    (b) if proceedings for a dissolution, nullity or separation order are dismissed after the beginning of the trial, either straightaway or within a reasonable period after the dismissal.

(3) The power of the court to make an order under sub-paragraph (1) or (2)(a) in favour of a child of the family is exercisable from time to time.

(4) If the court makes an order in favour of a child under sub-paragraph (2)(b), it may from time to time make a further order in the child's favour of any of the kinds set out in paragraph 2(1)(d), (e) or (f).

The orders: periodical and secured periodical payments and lump sums

2 (1) The orders are—
   (a) an order that either civil partner must make to the other such periodical payments for such term as may be specified;
   (b) an order that either civil partner must secure to the other, to the satisfaction of the court, such periodical payments for such term as may be specified;
   (c) an order that either civil partner must pay to the other such lump sum or sums as may be specified;
   (d) an order that one of the civil partners must make—
      (i) to such person as may be specified for the benefit of a child of the family, or
      (ii) to a child of the family,
      such periodical payments for such term as may be specified;
   (e) an order that one of the civil partners must secure—
      (i) to such person as may be specified for the benefit of a child of the family, or
      (ii) to a child of the family,
      to the satisfaction of the court, such periodical payments for such term as may be specified;
   (f) an order that one of the civil partners must pay such lump sum as may be specified—
      (i) to such person as may be specified for the benefit of a child of the family, or
      (ii) to a child of the family.
(2) 'Specified' means specified in the order.

Particular provision that may be made by lump sum orders

3 (1) An order under this Part requiring one civil partner to pay the other a lump sum may be made for the purpose of enabling the other civil partner to meet any liabilities or expenses reasonably incurred by the other in maintaining—
   (a) himself or herself, or
   (b) a child of the family,
   before making an application for an order under this Part in his or her favour.
(2) An order under this Part requiring a lump sum to be paid to or for the benefit of a child of the family may be made for the purpose of enabling any liabilities or expenses reasonably incurred by or for the benefit of the child before making an application for an order under this Part to be met.
(3) An order under this Part for the payment of a lump sum may—
   (a) provide for its payment by instalments of such amount as may be specified, and
   (b) require the payment of the instalments to be secured to the satisfaction of the court.
(4) Sub-paragraphs (1) to (3) do not restrict the powers to make the orders set out in paragraph 2(1)(c) and (f).
(5) If the court—
   (a) makes an order under this Part for the payment of a lump sum, and
   (b) directs that—

     (i) payment of the sum or any part of it is to be deferred, or

     (ii) the sum or any part of it is to be paid by instalments,

it may provide for the deferred amount or the instalments to carry interest at such rate as may be specified from such date as may be specified until the date when payment of it is due.

(6) A date specified under sub-paragraph (5) must not be earlier than the date of the order.

(7) 'Specified' means specified in the order.

When orders under this Part may take effect

4 (1) If an order is made under paragraph 2(1)(a), (b) or (c) on or after making a dissolution or nullity order, neither the order nor any settlement made in pursuance of it takes effect unless the dissolution or nullity order has been made final.

(2) This paragraph does not affect the power of the court to give a direction under paragraph 76 (settlement of instrument by conveyancing counsel).

Restrictions on making of orders under this Part

5 The power to make an order under paragraph 2(1)(d), (e) or (f) is subject to paragraph 49(1) and (5) (restrictions on orders in favour of children who have reached 18).

Part 2

Property Adjustment on or after Dissolution, Nullity or Separation

Circumstances in which property adjustment orders may be made

6 (1) The court may make one or more property adjustment orders—

    (a) on making a dissolution, nullity or separation order, or

    (b) at any time afterwards.

(2) In this Schedule 'property adjustment order' means a property adjustment order under this Part.

Property adjustment orders

7 (1) The property adjustment orders are—

    (a) an order that one of the civil partners must transfer such property as may be specified, being property to which he is entitled—

       (i) to the other civil partner,

       (ii) to a child of the family, or

       (iii) to such person as may be specified for the benefit of a child of the family;

    (b) an order that a settlement of such property as may be specified, being property to which one of the civil partners is entitled, be made to the satisfaction of the court for the benefit of—

       (i) the other civil partner and the children of the family, or

       (ii) either or any of them;

    (c) an order varying for the benefit of—

       (i) the civil partners and the children of the family, or

       (ii) either or any of them,

     a relevant settlement;

(d) an order extinguishing or reducing the interest of either of the civil partners under a relevant settlement.

(2) The court may make a property adjustment order under sub-paragraph (1)(c) even though there are no children of the family.

(3) In this paragraph—

'pentitled' means entitled in possession or reversion,

'prelevant settlement' means, in relation to a civil partnership, a settlement made, during its subsistence or in anticipation of its formation, on the civil partners including one made by will or codicil, but not including one in the form of a pension arrangement (within the meaning of Part 4), and

'specified' means specified in the order.

When property adjustment orders may take effect

8 (1) If a property adjustment order is made on or after making a dissolution or nullity order, neither the property adjustment order nor any settlement made under it takes effect unless the dissolution or nullity order has been made final.

(2) This paragraph does not affect the power to give a direction under paragraph 76 (settlement of instrument by conveyancing counsel).

Restrictions on making property adjustment orders

9 The power to make a property adjustment order under paragraph 7(1)(a) is subject to paragraph 49(1) and (5) (restrictions on making orders in favour of children who have reached 18).

Part 3

Sale of Property Orders

Circumstances in which sale of property orders may be made

10 (1) The court may make a sale of property order—

(a) on making—

(i) under Part 1, a secured periodical payments order or an order for the payment of a lump sum, or

(ii) a property adjustment order, or

(b) at any time afterwards.

(2) In this Schedule 'sale of property order' means a sale of property order under this Part.

Sale of property orders

11 (1) A sale of property order is an order for the sale of such property as may be specified, being property in which, or in the proceeds of sale of which, either or both of the civil partners has or have a beneficial interest, either in possession or reversion.

(2) A sale of property order may contain such consequential or supplementary provisions as the court thinks fit.

(3) A sale of property order may in particular include—

(a) provision requiring the making of a payment out of the proceeds of sale of the property to which the order relates, and

(b) provision requiring any property to which the order relates to be offered for sale to a specified person, or class of persons.

(4) 'Specified' means specified in the order.

When sale of property orders may take effect

12 (1) If a sale of property order is made on or after the making of a dissolution or nullity order, it does not take effect unless the dissolution or nullity order has been made final.

(2) Where a sale of property order is made, the court may direct that—

(a) the order, or

(b) such provision of it as the court may specify,

is not to take effect until the occurrence of an event specified by the court or the end of a period so specified.

When sale of property orders cease to have effect

13 If a sale of property order contains a provision requiring the proceeds of sale of the property to which the order relates to be used to secure periodical payments to a civil partner, the order ceases to have effect—

(a) on the death of the civil partner, or

(b) on the formation of a subsequent civil partnership or marriage by the civil partner.

Protection of third parties

14 (1) Sub-paragraphs (2) and (3) apply if—

(a) a civil partner has a beneficial interest in any property, or in the proceeds of sale of any property, and

(b) another person ('A') who is not the other civil partner also has a beneficial interest in the property or the proceeds.

(2) Before deciding whether to make a sale of property order in relation to the property, the court must give A an opportunity to make representations with respect to the order.

(3) Any representations made by A are included among the circumstances to which the court is required to have regard under paragraph 20.

Part 4

Pension Sharing Orders on or after Dissolution or Nullity Order

Circumstances in which pension sharing orders may be made

15 (1) The court may make a pension sharing order—

(a) on making a dissolution or nullity order, or

(b) at any time afterwards.

(2) In this Schedule 'pension sharing order' means a pension sharing order under this Part.

Pension sharing orders

16 (1) A pension sharing order is an order which—
    (a) provides that one civil partner's—
        (i) shareable rights under a specified pension arrangement, or
        (ii) shareable state scheme rights,
        are to be subject to pension sharing for the benefit of the other civil partner, and
    (b) specifies the percentage value to be transferred.
(2) Shareable rights under a pension arrangement are rights in relation to which pension sharing is available under—
    (a) Chapter 1 of Part 4 of the Welfare Reform and Pensions Act 1999 (c. 30), or
    (b) corresponding Northern Ireland legislation.
(3) Shareable state scheme rights are rights in relation to which pension sharing is available under—
    (a) Chapter 2 of Part 4 of the 1999 Act, or
    (b) corresponding Northern Ireland legislation.
(4) In this Part 'pension arrangement' means—
    (a) an occupational pension scheme,
    (b) a personal pension scheme,
    (c) a retirement annuity contract,
    (d) an annuity or insurance policy purchased, or transferred, for the purpose of giving effect to rights under—
        (i) an occupational pension scheme, or
        (ii) a personal pension scheme, and
    (e) an annuity purchased, or entered into, for the purpose of discharging liability in respect of a pension credit under—
        (i) section 29(1)(b) of the 1999 Act, or
        (ii) corresponding Northern Ireland legislation.
(5) In sub-paragraph (4)—
    'occupational pension scheme' has the same meaning as in the Pension Schemes Act 1993 (c. 48);
    'personal pension scheme' has the same meaning as in the 1993 Act;
    'retirement annuity contract' means a contract or scheme approved under Chapter 3 of Part 14 of the Income and Corporation Taxes Act 1988 (c. 1).

Pension sharing orders: apportionment of charges

17 If a pension sharing order relates to rights under a pension arrangement, the court may include in the order provision about the apportionment between the civil partners of any charge under—
    (a) section 41 of the 1999 Act (charges in respect of pension sharing costs), or
    (b) corresponding Northern Ireland legislation.

Restrictions on making of pension sharing orders

18 (1) A pension sharing order may not be made in relation to a pension arrangement which—
    (a) is the subject of a pension sharing order in relation to the civil partnership, or
    (b) has been the subject of pension sharing between the civil partners.

(2) A pension sharing order may not be made in relation to shareable state scheme rights if—

    (a) such rights are the subject of a pension sharing order in relation to the civil partnership, or

    (b) such rights have been the subject of pension sharing between the civil partners.

(3) A pension sharing order may not be made in relation to the rights of a person under a pension arrangement if there is in force a requirement imposed by virtue of Part 6 which relates to benefits or future benefits to which that person is entitled under the pension arrangement.

When pension sharing orders may take effect

19 (1) A pension sharing order is not to take effect unless the dissolution or nullity order on or after which it is made has been made final.

(2) No pension sharing order may be made so as to take effect before the end of such period after the making of the order as may be prescribed by regulations made by the Lord Chancellor.

(3) The power to make regulations under sub-paragraph (2) is exercisable by statutory instrument which is subject to annulment in pursuance of a resolution of either House of Parliament.

Part 5

Matters to which Court is to have Regard Under Parts 1 to 4

General

20 The court in deciding—

    (a) whether to exercise its powers under—

        (i) Part 1 (financial provision on dissolution etc.),

        (ii) Part 2 (property adjustment orders),

        (iii) Part 3 (sale of property orders), or

        (iv) any provision of Part 4 (pension sharing orders) other than paragraph 17 (apportionment of charges), and

    (b) if so, in what way,

must have regard to all the circumstances of the case, giving first consideration to the welfare, while under 18, of any child of the family who has not reached 18.

Particular matters to be taken into account when exercising powers in relation to civil partners

21 (1) This paragraph applies to the exercise by the court in relation to a civil partner of its powers under—

    (a) Part 1 (financial provision on dissolution etc.) by virtue of paragraph 2(1)(a), (b) or (c),

    (b) Part 2 (property adjustment orders),

    (c) Part 3 (sale of property orders), or

    (d) Part 4 (pension sharing orders).

(2) The court must in particular have regard to—

(a) the income, earning capacity, property and other financial resources which each civil partner—

(i) has, or

(ii) is likely to have in the foreseeable future,

including, in the case of earning capacity, any increase in that capacity which it would in the opinion of the court be reasonable to expect a civil partner in the civil partnership to take steps to acquire;

(b) the financial needs, obligations and responsibilities which each civil partner has or is likely to have in the foreseeable future;

(c) the standard of living enjoyed by the family before the breakdown of the civil partnership;

(d) the age of each civil partner and the duration of the civil partnership;

(e) any physical or mental disability of either of the civil partners;

(f) the contributions which each civil partner has made or is likely in the foreseeable future to make to the welfare of the family, including any contribution by looking after the home or caring for the family;

(g) the conduct of each civil partner, if that conduct is such that it would in the opinion of the court be inequitable to disregard it;

(h) in the case of proceedings for a dissolution or nullity order, the value to each civil partner of any benefit which, because of the dissolution or annulment of the civil partnership, that civil partner will lose the chance of acquiring.

Particular matters to be taken into account when exercising powers in relation to children

22 (1) This paragraph applies to the exercise by the court in relation to a child of the family of its powers under—

(a) Part 1 (financial provision on dissolution etc.) by virtue of paragraph 2(1)(d), (e) or (f)),

(b) Part 2 (property adjustment orders), or

(c) Part 3 (sale of property orders).

(2) The court must in particular have regard to—

(a) the financial needs of the child;

(b) the income, earning capacity (if any), property and other financial resources of the child;

(c) any physical or mental disability of the child;

(d) the way in which the child was being and in which the civil partners expected the child to be educated or trained;

(e) the considerations mentioned in relation to the civil partners in paragraph 21(2)(a), (b), (c) and (e).

(3) In relation to the exercise of any of those powers against a civil partner ('A') in favour of a child of the family who is not A's child, the court must also have regard to—

(a) whether A has assumed any responsibility for the child's maintenance;

(b) if so, the extent to which, and the basis upon which, A assumed such responsibility and the length of time for which A discharged such responsibility;

(c) whether in assuming and discharging such responsibility A did so knowing that the child was not A's child;

(d) the liability of any other person to maintain the child.

Terminating financial obligations

23 (1) Sub-paragraphs (2) and (3) apply if, on or after the making of a dissolution or nullity order, the court decides to exercise its powers under—
    (a) Part 1 (financial provision on dissolution etc.) by virtue of paragraph 2(1)(a), (b) or (c),
    (b) Part 2 (property adjustment orders),
    (c) Part 3 (sale of property orders), or
    (d) Part 4 (pension sharing orders),
    in favour of one of the civil partners.

(2) The court must consider whether it would be appropriate to exercise those powers in such a way that the financial obligations of each civil partner towards the other will be terminated as soon after the making of the dissolution or nullity order as the court considers just and reasonable.

(3) If the court decides to make—
    (a) a periodical payments order, or
    (b) a secured periodical payments order,
in favour of one of the civil partners ('A'), it must in particular consider whether it would be appropriate to require the payments to be made or secured only for such term as would in its opinion be sufficient to enable A to adjust without undue hardship to the termination of A's financial dependence on the other civil partner.

(4) If—
    (a) on or after the making of a dissolution or nullity order, an application is made by one of the civil partners for a periodical payments or secured periodical payments order in that civil partner's favour, but
    (b) the court considers that no continuing obligation should be imposed on either civil partner to make or secure periodical payments in favour of the other,
the court may dismiss the application with a direction that the applicant is not entitled to make any future application in relation to that civil partnership for an order under Part 1 by virtue of paragraph 2(1)(a) or (b).

Part 6

Making of Part 1 Orders having Regard to Pension Benefits

Pension benefits to be included in matters to which court is to have regard

24 (1) The matters to which the court is to have regard under paragraph 21(2)(a) include any pension benefits under a pension arrangement or by way of pension which a civil partner has or is likely to have; and, accordingly, in relation to any pension benefits paragraph 21(2)(a)(ii) has effect as if 'in the foreseeable future' were omitted.

(2) The matters to which the court is to have regard under paragraph 21(2)(h) include any pension benefits which, because of the making of a dissolution or nullity order, a civil partner will lose the chance of acquiring.

(3) 'Pension benefits' means—
    (a) benefits under a pension arrangement, or
    (b) benefits by way of pension (whether under a pension arrangement or not).

Provisions applying where pension benefits taken into account in decision to make Part 1 order

25 (1) This paragraph applies if, having regard to any benefits under a pension arrangement, the court decides to make an order under Part 1.

(2) To the extent to which the Part 1 order is made having regard to any benefits under a pension arrangement, it may require the person responsible for the pension arrangement, if at any time any payment in respect of any benefits under the arrangement becomes due to the civil partner with pension rights, to make a payment for the benefit of the other civil partner.

(3) The Part 1 order must express the amount of any payment required to be made by virtue of sub-paragraph (2) as a percentage of the payment which becomes due to the civil partner with pension rights.

(4) Any such payment by the person responsible for the arrangement—

(a) discharges so much of his liability to the civil partner with pension rights as corresponds to the amount of the payment, and

(b) is to be treated for all purposes as a payment made by the civil partner with pension rights in or towards the discharge of that civil partner's liability under the order.

(5) If the civil partner with pension rights has a right of commutation under the arrangement, the Part 1 order may require that civil partner to exercise it to any extent.

(6) This paragraph applies to any payment due in consequence of commutation in pursuance of the Part 1 order as it applies to other payments in respect of benefits under the arrangement.

(7) The power conferred by sub-paragraph (5) may not be exercised for the purpose of commuting a benefit payable to the civil partner with pension rights to a benefit payable to the other civil partner.

(8) The powers conferred by sub-paragraphs (2) and (5) may not be exercised in relation to a pension arrangement which—

(a) is the subject of a pension sharing order in relation to the civil partnership, or

(b) has been the subject of pension sharing between the civil partners.

Pensions: lump sums

26 (1) This paragraph applies if the benefits which the civil partner with pension rights has or is likely to have under a pension arrangement include any lump sum payable in respect of that civil partner's death.

(2) The court's power under Part 1 to order a civil partner to pay a lump sum to the other civil partner includes the power to make by the order any provision in sub-paragraph (3) to (5).

(3) If the person responsible for the pension arrangement has power to determine the person to whom the sum, or any part of it, is to be paid, the court may require him to pay the whole or part of that sum, when it becomes due, to the other civil partner.

(4) If the civil partner with pension rights has power to nominate the person to whom the sum, or any part of it, is to be paid, the court may require the civil partner with pension rights to nominate the other civil partner in respect of the whole or part of that sum.

(5) In any other case, the court may require the person responsible for the pension arrangement in question to pay the whole or part of that sum, when it becomes due, for the benefit of the other civil partner instead of to the person to whom, apart from the order, it would be paid.

(6) Any payment by the person responsible for the arrangement under an order made under Part 1 made by virtue of this paragraph discharges so much of his liability in respect of the civil partner with pension rights as corresponds to the amount of the payment.

(7) The powers conferred by this paragraph may not be exercised in relation to a pension arrangement which—

(a) is the subject of a pension sharing order in relation to the civil partnership, or

(b) has been the subject of pension sharing between the civil partners.

Pensions: supplementary

27 If—

(a) a Part 1 order made by virtue of paragraph 25 or 26 imposes any requirement on the person responsible for a pension arrangement ('the first arrangement'),

(b) the civil partner with pension rights acquires rights under another pension arrangement ('the new arrangement') which are derived (directly or indirectly) from the whole of that civil partner's rights under the first arrangement, and

(c) the person responsible for the new arrangement has been given notice in accordance with regulations made by the Lord Chancellor,

the Part 1 order has effect as if it had been made instead in respect of the person responsible for the new arrangement.

Regulations

28 (1) The Lord Chancellor may by regulations—

(a) make provision, in relation to any provision of paragraph 25 or 26 which authorises the court making a Part 1 order to require the person responsible for a pension arrangement to make a payment for the benefit of the other civil partner, as to—

(i) the person to whom, and

(ii) the terms on which,

the payment is to be made;

(b) make provision, in relation to payment under a mistaken belief as to the continuation in force of a provision included by virtue of paragraph 25 or 26 in a Part 1 order, about the rights or liabilities of the payer, the payee or the person to whom the payment was due;

(c) require notices to be given in respect of changes of circumstances relevant to Part 1 orders which include provision made by virtue of paragraphs 25 and 26;

(d) make provision for the person responsible for a pension arrangement to be discharged in prescribed circumstances from a requirement imposed by virtue of paragraph 25 or 26;

(e) make provision about calculation and verification in relation to the valuation of—

      (i) benefits under a pension arrangement, or

      (ii) shareable state scheme rights (within the meaning of paragraph 16(3)),

     for the purposes of the court's functions in connection with the exercise of any of its powers under this Schedule.

(2) Regulations under sub-paragraph (1)(e) may include—

    (a) provision for calculation or verification in accordance with guidance from time to time prepared by a prescribed person, and

    (b) provision by reference to regulations under section 30 or 49(4) of the 1999 Act.

(3) The power to make regulations under paragraph 27 or this paragraph is exercisable by statutory instrument which is subject to annulment in pursuance of a resolution of either House of Parliament.

(4) 'Prescribed' means prescribed by regulations.

Interpretation of provisions relating to pensions

29 (1) In this Part 'the civil partner with pension rights' means the civil partner who has or is likely to have benefits under a pension arrangement.

(2) In this Part 'pension arrangement' has the same meaning as in Part 4.

(3) In this Part, references to the person responsible for a pension arrangement are to be read in accordance with section 26 of the Welfare Reform and Pensions Act 1999 (c. 30).

Part 7

Pension Protection Fund Compensation etc.

PPF compensation to be included in matters to which court is to have regard

30 (1) The matters to which a court is to have regard under paragraph 21(2)(a) include any PPF compensation to which a civil partner is or is likely to be entitled; and, accordingly, in relation to any PPF compensation paragraph 21(2)(a)(ii) has effect as if 'in the foreseeable future' were omitted.

(2) The matters to which a court is to have regard under paragraph 21(2)(h) include any PPF compensation which, because of the making of a dissolution or nullity order, a civil partner will lose the chance of acquiring entitlement to.

(3) In this Part 'PPF compensation' means compensation payable under—

    (a) Chapter 3 of Part 2 of the Pensions Act 2004 (pension protection), or

    (b) corresponding Northern Ireland legislation.

Assumption of responsibility by PPF Board in paragraph 25(2) cases

31 (1) This paragraph applies to an order under Part 1 so far as it includes provision made by virtue of paragraph 25(2) which—

    (a) imposed requirements on the trustees or managers of an occupational pension scheme for which the Board has assumed responsibility, and

    (b) was made before the trustees or managers received the transfer notice.

(2) From the time the trustees or managers of the scheme receive the transfer notice, the order has effect—

    (a) except in descriptions of case prescribed by regulations, with the modifications set out in sub-paragraph (3), and

(b) with such other modifications as may be prescribed by regulations.
(3) The modifications are that—
   (a) references in the order to the trustees or managers of the scheme have effect as references to the Board, and
   (b) references in the order to any pension or lump sum to which the civil partner with pension rights is or may become entitled under the scheme have effect as references to any PPF compensation to which that person is or may become entitled in respect of the pension or lump sum.

Assumption of responsibility by PPF Board in paragraph 25(5) cases

32 (1) This paragraph applies to an order under Part 1 if—
   (a) it includes provision made by virtue of paragraph 25(5) which requires the civil partner with pension rights to exercise his right of commutation under an occupational pension scheme to any extent, and
   (b) before the requirement is complied with the Board has assumed responsibility for the scheme.
(2) From the time the trustees or managers of the scheme receive the transfer notice, the order has effect with such modifications as may be prescribed by regulations.

Lump sums: power to modify paragraph 26 in respect of assessment period

33 Regulations may modify paragraph 26 in its application to an occupational pension scheme during an assessment period in relation to the scheme.

Assumption of responsibility by the Board not to affect power of court to vary order etc.

34 (1) This paragraph applies where the court makes, in relation to an occupational pension scheme—
   (a) a pension sharing order, or
   (b) an order including provision made by virtue of paragraph 25(2) or (5).
(2) If the Board subsequently assumes responsibility for the scheme, that does not affect—
   (a) the powers of the court under paragraph 51 to vary or discharge the order or to suspend or revive any provision of it;
   (b) on an appeal, the powers of the appeal court to affirm, reinstate, set aside or vary the order.

Regulations

35 Regulations may make such consequential modifications of any provision of, or made by virtue of, this Schedule as appear to the Lord Chancellor necessary or expedient to give effect to the provisions of this Part.
36 (1) In this Part 'regulations' means regulations made by the Lord Chancellor.
(2) A power to make regulations under this Part is exercisable by statutory instrument which is subject to annulment in pursuance of a resolution of either House of Parliament.

Interpretation

37 (1) In this Part—
   'assessment period' means—

(a) an assessment period within the meaning of Part 2 of the Pensions Act 2004 (pension protection), or

(b) an equivalent period under corresponding Northern Ireland legislation;

'the Board' means the Board of the Pension Protection Fund;

'the civil partner with pension rights' has the meaning given by paragraph 29(1);

'occupational pension scheme' has the same meaning as in the Pension Schemes Act 1993 (c. 48);

'transfer notice' has the same meaning as in—

(a) Chapter 3 of Part 2 of the 2004 Act, or

(b) corresponding Northern Ireland legislation.

(2) References in this Part to the Board assuming responsibility for a scheme are to the Board assuming responsibility for the scheme in accordance with—

(a) Chapter 3 of Part 2 of the 2004 Act (pension protection), or

(b) corresponding Northern Ireland legislation.

Part 8

Maintenance Pending Outcome of Dissolution, Nullity or Separation Proceedings

38 On an application for a dissolution, nullity or separation order, the court may make an order requiring either civil partner to make to the other for the other's maintenance such periodical payments for such term—

(a) beginning no earlier than the date on which the application was made, and

(b) ending with the date on which the proceedings are determined,

as the court thinks reasonable.

Part 9

Failure to Maintain: Financial Provision (and interim orders)

Circumstances in which orders under this Part may be made

39 (1) Either civil partner in a subsisting civil partnership may apply to the court for an order under this Part on the ground that the other civil partner ('the respondent')—

(a) has failed to provide reasonable maintenance for the applicant, or

(b) has failed to provide, or to make a proper contribution towards, reasonable maintenance for any child of the family.

(2) The court must not entertain an application under this paragraph unless—

(a) the applicant or the respondent is domiciled in England and Wales on the date of the application,

(b) the applicant has been habitually resident there throughout the period of 1 year ending with that date, or

(c) the respondent is resident there on that date.

(3) If, on an application under this paragraph, it appears to the court that—

(a) the applicant or any child of the family to whom the application relates is in immediate need of financial assistance, but

(b) it is not yet possible to determine what order, if any, should be made on the application, the court may make an interim order.

(4) If, on an application under this paragraph, the applicant satisfies the court of a ground mentioned in sub-paragraph (1), the court may make one or more of the orders set out in paragraph 41.

Interim orders

40 An interim order is an order requiring the respondent to make to the applicant, until the determination of the application, such periodical payments as the court thinks reasonable.

Orders that may be made where failure to maintain established

41 (1) The orders are—
(a) an order that the respondent must make to the applicant such periodical payments for such term as may be specified;
(b) an order that the respondent must secure to the applicant, to the satisfaction of the court, such periodical payments for such term as may be specified;
(c) an order that the respondent must pay to the applicant such lump sum as may be specified;
(d) an order that the respondent must make such periodical payments for such term as may be specified—
(i) to such person as may be specified, for the benefit of the child to whom the application relates, or
(ii) to the child to whom the application relates;
(e) an order that the respondent must secure—
(i) to such person as may be specified for the benefit of the child to whom the application relates, or
(ii) to the child to whom the application relates,
to the satisfaction of the court, such periodical payments for such term as may be specified;
(f) an order that the respondent must pay such lump sum as may be specified—
(i) to such person as may be specified for the benefit of the child to whom the application relates, or
(ii) to the child to whom the application relates.
(2) In this Part 'specified' means specified in the order.

Particular provision that may be made by lump sum orders

42 (1) An order under this Part for the payment of a lump sum may be made for the purpose of enabling any liabilities or expenses reasonably incurred in maintaining the applicant or any child of the family to whom the application relates before the making of the application to be met.
(2) An order under this Part for the payment of a lump sum may—
(a) provide for its payment by instalments of such amount as may be specified, and
(b) require the payment of the instalments to be secured to the satisfaction of the court.
(3) Sub-paragraphs (1) and (2) do not restrict the power to make an order by virtue of paragraph 41(1)(c) or (f).

Matters to which the court is to have regard on application under paragraph 39(1)(a)

43 (1) This paragraph applies if an application under paragraph 39 is made on the ground mentioned in paragraph 39(1)(a).

(2) In deciding—

(a) whether the respondent has failed to provide reasonable maintenance for the applicant, and

(b) what order, if any, to make under this Part in favour of the applicant,

the court must have regard to all the circumstances of the case including the matters mentioned in paragraph 21(2).

(3) If an application is also made under paragraph 39 in respect of a child of the family who has not reached 18, the court must give first consideration to the welfare of the child while under 18.

(4) Paragraph 21(2)(c) has effect as if for the reference in it to the breakdown of the civil partnership there were substituted a reference to the failure to provide reasonable maintenance for the applicant.

Matters to which the court is to have regard on application under paragraph 39(1)(b)

44 (1) This paragraph applies if an application under paragraph 39 is made on the ground mentioned in paragraph 39(1)(b).

(2) In deciding—

(a) whether the respondent has failed to provide, or to make a proper contribution towards, reasonable maintenance for the child of the family to whom the application relates, and

(b) what order, if any, to make under this Part in favour of the child,

the court must have regard to all the circumstances of the case.

(3) Those circumstances include—

(a) the matters mentioned in paragraph 22(2)(a) to (e), and

(b) if the child of the family to whom the application relates is not the child of the respondent, the matters mentioned in paragraph 22(3).

(4) Paragraph 21(2)(c) (as it applies by virtue of paragraph 22(2)(e)) has effect as if for the reference in it to the breakdown of the civil partnership there were substituted a reference to—

(a) the failure to provide, or

(b) the failure to make a proper contribution towards,

reasonable maintenance for the child of the family to whom the application relates.

Restrictions on making orders under this Part

45 The power to make an order under paragraph 41(1)(d), (e) or (f) is subject to paragraph 49(1) and (5) (restrictions on orders in favour of children who have reached 18).

Part 10

Commencement of Certain Proceedings and Duration of Certain Orders

Commencement of proceedings for ancillary relief, etc.

46 (1) Sub-paragraph (2) applies if an application for a dissolution, nullity or separation order has been made.

(2) Subject to sub-paragraph (3), proceedings for—
(a) an order under Part 1 (financial provision on dissolution etc.),
(b) a property adjustment order, or
(c) an order under Part 8 (maintenance pending outcome of dissolution, nullity or separation proceedings),
may be begun (subject to and in accordance with rules of court) at any time after the presentation of the application.

(3) Rules of court may provide, in such cases as may be prescribed by the rules, that—
(a) an application for any such relief as is mentioned in sub-paragraph (2) must be made in the application or response, and
(b) an application for any such relief which—
(i) is not so made, or
(ii) is not made until after the end of such period following the presentation of the application or filing of the response as may be so prescribed,
may be made only with the leave of the court.

Duration of periodical and secured periodical payments orders for a civil partner

47 (1) The court may specify in a periodical payments or secured periodical payments order in favour of a civil partner such term as it thinks fit, except that the term must not—
(a) begin before the date of the making of an application for the order, or
(b) extend beyond the limits given in sub-paragraphs (2) and (3).

(2) The limits in the case of a periodical payments order are—
(a) the death of either civil partner;
(b) where the order is made on or after the making of a dissolution or nullity order, the formation of a subsequent civil partnership or marriage by the civil partner in whose favour the order is made.

(3) The limits in the case of a secured periodical payments order are—
(a) the death of the civil partner in whose favour the order is made;
(b) where the order is made on or after the making of a dissolution or nullity order, the formation of a subsequent civil partnership or marriage by the civil partner in whose favour the order is made.

(4) In the case of an order made on or after the making of a dissolution or nullity order, sub-paragraphs (1) to (3) are subject to paragraphs 23(3) and 59(4).

(5) If a periodical payments or secured periodical payments order in favour of a civil partner is made on or after the making of a dissolution or nullity order, the court may direct that that civil partner is not entitled to apply under paragraph 51 for the extension of the term specified in the order.

(6) If—

(a) a periodical payments or secured periodical payments order in favour of a civil partner is made otherwise than on or after the making of a dissolution or nullity order, and

(b) the civil partnership is subsequently dissolved or annulled but the order continues in force,

the order ceases to have effect (regardless of anything in it) on the formation of a subsequent civil partnership or marriage by that civil partner, except in relation to any arrears due under it on the date of its formation.

Subsequent civil partnership or marriage

48 If after the making of a dissolution or nullity order one of the civil partners forms a subsequent civil partnership or marriage, that civil partner is not entitled to apply, by reference to the dissolution or nullity order, for—

(a) an order under Part 1 in that civil partner's favour, or

(b) a property adjustment order,

against the other civil partner in the dissolved or annulled civil partnership.

Duration of continuing orders in favour of children, and age limit on making certain orders in their favour

49 (1) Subject to sub-paragraph (5)—

(a) no order under Part 1,

(b) no property adjustment order made by virtue of paragraph 7(1)(a) (transfer of property), and

(c) no order made under Part 9 (failure to maintain) by virtue of paragraph 41,

is to be made in favour of a child who has reached 18.

(2) The term to be specified in a periodical payments or secured periodical payments order in favour of a child may begin with—

(a) the date of the making of an application for the order or a later date, or

(b) a date ascertained in accordance with sub-paragraph (7) or (8).

(3) The term to be specified in such an order—

(a) must not in the first instance extend beyond the date of the birthday of the child next following the child's reaching the upper limit of the compulsory school age unless the court considers that in the circumstances of the case the welfare of the child requires that it should extend to a later date, and

(b) must not in any event, subject to sub-paragraph (5), extend beyond the date of the child's 18th birthday.

(4) Sub-paragraph (3)(a) must be read with section 8 of the Education Act 1996 (c. 56) (which applies to determine for the purposes of any enactment whether a person is of compulsory school age).

(5) Sub-paragraphs (1) and (3)(b) do not apply in the case of a child if it appears to the court that—

(a) the child is, or will be, or, if an order were made without complying with either or both of those provisions, would be—

(i) receiving instruction at an educational establishment, or

(ii) undergoing training for a trade, profession or vocation,

whether or not the child also is, will be or would be in gainful employment, or

(b) there are special circumstances which justify the making of an order without complying with either or both of sub-paragraphs (1) and (3)(b).

(6) A periodical payments order in favour of a child, regardless of anything in the order, ceases to have effect on the death of the person liable to make payments under the order, except in relation to any arrears due under the order on the date of the death.

(7) If—

    (a) a maintenance calculation ('the current calculation') is in force with respect to a child, and

    (b) an application is made under this Schedule for a periodical payments or secured periodical payments order in favour of that child—

        (i) in accordance with section 8 of the Child Support Act 1991 (c. 48), and

        (ii) before the end of 6 months beginning with the making of the current calculation,

the term to be specified in any such order made on that application may be expressed to begin on, or at any time after, the earliest permitted date.

(8) 'The earliest permitted date' is whichever is the later of—

    (a) the date 6 months before the application is made, or

    (b) the date on which the current calculation took effect or, where successive maintenance calculations have been continuously in force with respect to a child, on which the first of those calculations took effect.

(9) If—

    (a) a maintenance calculation ceases to have effect by or under any provision of the 1991 Act, and

    (b) an application is made, before the end of 6 months beginning with the relevant date, for a periodical payments or secured periodical payments order in favour of a child with respect to whom that maintenance calculation was in force immediately before it ceased to have effect,

the term to be specified in any such order made on that application may begin with the date on which that maintenance calculation ceased to have effect or any later date.

(10) 'The relevant date' means the date on which the maintenance calculation ceased to have effect.

(11) In this paragraph 'maintenance calculation' has the same meaning as it has in the 1991 Act by virtue of section 54 of the 1991 Act as read with any regulations in force under that section.

Part 11

Variation, Discharge Etc. Of Certain Orders For Financial Relief

Orders etc. to which this Part applies

50 (1) This Part applies to the following orders—

    (a) a periodical payments order under Part 1 (financial provision on dissolution etc.) or Part 9 (failure to maintain);

    (b) a secured periodical payments order under Part 1 or 9;

    (c) an order under Part 8 (maintenance pending outcome of dissolution proceedings etc.);

    (d) an interim order under Part 9;

   (e) an order made under Part 1 by virtue of paragraph 3(3) or under Part 9 by virtue of paragraph 42(2) (lump sum by instalments);

   (f) a deferred order made under Part 1 by virtue of paragraph 2(1)(c) (lump sum for civil partner) which includes provision made by virtue of—

      (i) paragraph 25(2), or

      (ii) paragraph 26,

      (provision in respect of pension rights);

   (g) a property adjustment order made on or after the making of a separation order by virtue of paragraph 7(1)(b), (c) or (d) (order for settlement or variation of settlement);

   (h) a sale of property order;

   (i) a pension sharing order made before the dissolution or nullity order has been made final.

(2) If the court has made an order referred to in sub-paragraph (1)(f)(ii), this Part ceases to apply to the order on the death of either of the civil partners.

(3) The powers exercisable by the court under this Part in relation to an order are also exercisable in relation to any instrument executed in pursuance of the order.

Powers to vary, discharge, suspend or revive order

51 (1) If the court has made an order to which this Part applies, it may—

   (a) vary or discharge the order,

   (b) suspend any provision of it temporarily, or

   (c) revive the operation of any provision so suspended.

(2) Sub-paragraph (1) is subject to the provisions of this Part and paragraph 47(5).

Power to remit arrears

52 (1) If the court has made an order referred to in paragraph 50(1)(a), (b), (c) or (d), it may remit the payment of any arrears due under the order or under any part of the order.

(2) Sub-paragraph (1) is subject to the provisions of this Part.

Additional powers on discharging or varying a periodical or secured periodical payments order after dissolution of civil partnership

53 (1) Sub-paragraph (2) applies if, after the dissolution of a civil partnership, the court—

   (a) discharges a periodical payments order or secured periodical payments order made in favour of a civil partner, or

   (b) varies such an order so that payments under the order are required to be made or secured only for such further period as is determined by the court.

(2) The court may make supplemental provision consisting of any of the following—

   (a) an order for the payment of a lump sum in favour of one of the civil partners;

   (b) one or more property adjustment orders in favour of one of the civil partners;

   (c) one or more pension sharing orders;

   (d) a direction that the civil partner in whose favour the original order discharged or varied was made is not entitled to make any further application for—

      (i) a periodical payments or secured periodical payments order, or

(ii) an extension of the period to which the original order is limited by any variation made by the court.

(3) The power under sub-paragraph (2) is in addition to any power the court has apart from that sub-paragraph.

54 (1) An order for the payment of a lump sum under paragraph 53 may—

    (a) provide for the payment of it by instalments of such amount as may be specified, and

    (b) require the payment of the instalments to be secured to the satisfaction of the court.

(2) Sub-paragraphs (5) and (6) of paragraph 3 (interest on deferred instalments) apply where the court makes an order for the payment of a lump sum under paragraph 53 as they apply where it makes such an order under Part 1.

(3) If under paragraph 53 the court makes more than one property adjustment order in favour of the same civil partner, each of those orders must fall within a different paragraph of paragraph 7(1) (types of property adjustment orders).

(4) Part 3 (orders for the sale of property) and paragraph 76 (direction for settlement of instrument) apply where the court makes a property adjustment order under paragraph 53 as they apply where it makes any other property adjustment order.

(5) Paragraph 18 (restrictions on making of pension sharing order) applies in relation to a pension sharing order under paragraph 53 as it applies in relation to any other pension sharing order.

Variation etc. of periodical or secured periodical payments orders made in cases of failure to maintain

55 (1) An application for the variation under paragraph 51 of a periodical payments order or secured periodical payments order made under Part 9 in favour of a child may, if the child has reached 16, be made by the child himself.

(2) Sub-paragraph (3) applies if a periodical payments order made in favour of a child under Part 9 ceases to have effect—

    (a) on the date on which the child reaches 16, or

    (b) at any time after that date but before or on the date on which the child reaches 18.

(3) If, on an application made to the court for an order under this sub-paragraph, it appears to the court that—

    (a) the child is, will be or, if an order were made under this sub-paragraph, would be—

        (i) receiving instruction at an educational establishment, or

        (ii) undergoing training for a trade, profession or vocation,

        whether or not the child also is, will be or would be in gainful employment, or

    (b) there are special circumstances which justify the making of an order under this sub-paragraph;

the court may by order revive the order mentioned in sub-paragraph (2) from such date as it may specify.

(4) A date specified under sub-paragraph (3) must not be earlier than the date of the application under that sub-paragraph.

(5) If under sub-paragraph (3) the court revives an order it may exercise its power under paragraph 51 in relation to the revived order.

Variation etc. of property adjustment and pension sharing orders

56 The court must not exercise the powers conferred by this Part in relation to a property adjustment order falling within paragraph 7(1)(b), (c) or (d) (order for settlement or for variation of settlement) except on an application made in proceedings—

    (a) for the rescission of the separation order by reference to which the property adjustment order was made, or

    (b) for a dissolution order in relation to the civil partnership.

57 (1) In relation to a pension sharing order which is made at a time before the dissolution or nullity order has been made final—

    (a) the powers conferred by this Part (by virtue of paragraph 50(1)(i)) may be exercised—

        (i) only on an application made before the pension sharing order has or, but for paragraph (b), would have taken effect, and

        (ii) only if, at the time when the application is made, the dissolution or nullity order has not been made final, and

    (b) an application made in accordance with paragraph (a) prevents the pension sharing order from taking effect before the application has been dealt with.

(2) No variation of a pension sharing order is to be made so as to take effect before the order is made final.

(3) The variation of a pension sharing order prevents the order taking effect before the end of such period after the making of the variation as may be prescribed by regulations made by the Lord Chancellor.

(4) The power to make regulations under sub-paragraph (3) is exercisable by statutory instrument which is subject to annulment in pursuance of a resolution of either House of Parliament.

58 (1) Sub-paragraphs (2) and (3)—

    (a) are subject to paragraphs 53 and 54, and

    (b) do not affect any power exercisable by virtue of paragraph 50(e), (f), (g) or (i) or otherwise than by virtue of this Part.

(2) No property adjustment order or pension sharing order may be made on an application for the variation of a periodical payments or secured periodical payments order made (whether in favour of a civil partner or in favour of a child of the family) under Part 1.

(3) No order for the payment of a lump sum may be made on an application for the variation of a periodical payments or secured periodical payments order in favour of a civil partner (whether made under Part 1 or 9).

Matters to which court is to have regard in exercising powers under this Part

59 (1) In exercising the powers conferred by this Part the court must have regard to all the circumstances of the case, giving first consideration to the welfare, while under 18, of any child of the family who has not reached 18.

(2) The circumstances of the case include, in particular, any change in any of the matters to which the court was required to have regard when making the order to which the application relates.

(3) Sub-paragraph (4) applies in the case of—

(a) a periodical payments order, or

(b) a secured periodical payments order,

made on or after the making of a dissolution or nullity order.

(4) The court must consider whether in all the circumstances, and after having regard to any such change, it would be appropriate to vary the order so that payments under the order are required—

(a) to be made, or

(b) to be secured,

only for such further period as will in the opinion of the court be sufficient to enable the civil partner in whose favour the order was made to adjust without undue hardship to the termination of those payments.

(5) In considering what further period will be sufficient, the court must, if the civil partnership has been dissolved, take into account any proposed exercise by it of its powers under paragraph 53.

(6) If the civil partner against whom the order was made has died, the circumstances of the case also include the changed circumstances resulting from that civil partner's death.

Variation of secured periodical payments order where person liable has died

60 (1) This paragraph applies if the person liable to make payments under a secured periodical payments order has died.

(2) Subject to sub-paragraph (3), an application under this Part relating to the order (and to any sale of property order which requires the proceeds of sale of property to be used for securing those payments) may be made by—

(a) the person entitled to payments under the periodical payments order, or

(b) the personal representatives of the deceased person.

(3) No such application may be made without the leave of the court after the end of 6 months from the date on which representation in regard to the estate of that person is first taken out.

(4) The personal representatives of the person who has died are not liable for having distributed any part of the estate of the deceased after the end of the 6 month period on the ground that they ought to have taken into account the possibility that the court might allow an application under this paragraph to be made after that period by the person entitled to payments under the order.

(5) Sub-paragraph (4) does not affect any power to recover any part of the estate so distributed arising by virtue of the making of an order in pursuance of this paragraph.

(6) In considering for the purposes of sub-paragraph (3) the question when representation was first taken out—

(a) a grant limited to settled land or to trust property is to be disregarded, and

(b) a grant limited to real estate or to personal estate is to be disregarded unless a grant limited to the remainder of the estate has previously been made or is made at the same time.

Power to direct when variation etc. is to take effect

61 (1) If the court, in exercise of its powers under this Part, decides—

(a) to vary, or

(b) to discharge,

a periodical payments or secured periodical payments order, it may direct that the variation or discharge is not to take effect until the end of such period as may be specified in the order.

(2) Sub-paragraph (1) is subject to paragraph 47(1) and (6).

62 (1) If—

    (a) a periodical payments or secured periodical payments order in favour of more than one child ('the order') is in force,

    (b) the order requires payments specified in it to be made to or for the benefit of more than one child without apportioning those payments between them,

    (c) a maintenance calculation ('the calculation') is made with respect to one or more, but not all, of the children with respect to whom those payments are to be made, and

    (d) an application is made, before the end of the period of 6 months beginning with the date on which the calculation was made, for the variation or discharge of the order,

the court may, in exercise of its powers under this Part to vary or discharge the order, direct that the variation or discharge is to take effect from the date on which the calculation took effect or any later date.

(2) If—

    (a) an order ('the child order') of a kind prescribed for the purposes of section 10(1) of the Child Support Act 1991 (c. 48) is affected by a maintenance calculation,

    (b) on the date on which the child order became so affected there was in force a periodical payments or secured periodical payments order ('the civil partner's order') in favour of a civil partner having the care of the child in whose favour the child order was made, and

    (c) an application is made, before the end of the period of 6 months beginning with the date on which the maintenance calculation was made, for the civil partner's order to be varied or discharged,

the court may, in exercise of its powers under this Part to vary or discharge the civil partner's order, direct that the variation or discharge is to take effect from the date on which the child order became so affected or any later date.

(3) For the purposes of sub-paragraph (2), an order is affected if it ceases to have effect or is modified by or under section 10 of the 1991 Act.

(4) Sub-paragraphs (1) and (2) do not affect any other power of the court to direct that the variation of discharge of an order under this Part is to take effect from a date earlier than that on which the order for variation or discharge was made.

(5) In this paragraph 'maintenance calculation' has the same meaning as it has in the 1991 Act by virtue of section 54 of the 1991 Act as read with any regulations in force under that section.

Part 12

Arrears and Repayments

Payment of certain arrears unenforceable without the leave of the court

63 (1) This paragraph applies if any arrears are due under—
- (a) an order under Part 1 (financial provision on dissolution etc.),
- (b) an order under Part 8 (maintenance pending outcome of dissolution, nullity or separation proceedings), or
- (c) an order under Part 9 (failure to maintain),

and the arrears became due more than 12 months before proceedings to enforce the payment of them are begun.

(2) A person is not entitled to enforce through the High Court or any county court the payment of the arrears without the leave of that court.

(3) The court hearing an application for the grant of leave under this paragraph may—
- (a) refuse leave,
- (b) grant leave subject to such restrictions and conditions (including conditions as to the allowing of time for payment or the making of payment by instalments) as that court thinks proper, or
- (c) remit the payment of the arrears or of any part of them.

(4) An application for the grant of leave under this paragraph must be made in such manner as may be prescribed by rules of court.

Orders for repayment in certain cases of sums paid under certain orders

64 (1) This paragraph applies if—
- (a) a person ('R') is entitled to receive payments under an order listed in sub-paragraph (2), and
- (b) R's circumstances or the circumstances of the person ('P') liable to make payments under the order have changed since the order was made, or the circumstances have changed as a result of P's death.

(2) The orders are—
- (a) any order under Part 8 (maintenance pending outcome of dissolution, nullity or separation proceedings);
- (b) any interim order under Part 9;
- (c) any periodical payments order;
- (d) any secured periodical payments order.

(3) P or P's personal representatives may (subject to sub-paragraph (7)) apply for an order under this paragraph against R or R's personal representatives.

(4) If it appears to the court that, because of the changed circumstances or P's death, the amount received by R in respect of a relevant period exceeds the amount which P or P's personal representatives should have been required to pay, it may order the respondent to the application to pay to the applicant such sum, not exceeding the amount of the excess, as it thinks just.

(5) 'Relevant period' means a period after the circumstances changed or (as the case may be) after P's death.

(6) An order under this paragraph for the payment of any sum may provide for the

payment of that sum by instalments of such amount as may be specified in the order.

(7) An application under this paragraph—

    (a) may be made in proceedings in the High Court or a county court for—

        (i) the variation or discharge of the order listed in sub-paragraph (2), or

        (ii) leave to enforce, or the enforcement of, the payment of arrears under that order, but

    (b) if not made in such proceedings, must be made to a county court;

and accordingly references in this paragraph to the court are references to the High Court or a county court, as the circumstances require.

(8) The jurisdiction conferred on a county court by this paragraph is exercisable even though, because of the amount claimed in the application, the jurisdiction would not but for this sub-paragraph be exercisable by a county court.

Orders for repayment after cessation of order because of subsequent civil partnership etc.

65 (1) Sub-paragraphs (3) and (4) apply if—

    (a) a periodical payments or secured periodical payments order in favour of a civil partner ('R') has ceased to have effect because of the formation of a subsequent civil partnership or marriage by R, and

    (b) the person liable to make payments under the order ('P') (or P's personal representatives) has made payments in accordance with it in respect of a relevant period in the mistaken belief that the order was still subsisting.

(2) 'Relevant period' means a period after the date of the formation of the subsequent civil partnership or marriage.

(3) P (or P's personal representatives) is not entitled to bring proceedings in respect of a cause of action arising out of the circumstances mentioned in sub-paragraph (1)(a) and (b) against R (or R's personal representatives).

(4) But, on an application under this paragraph by P (or P's personal representatives) against R (or R's personal representatives), the court—

    (a) may order the respondent to pay to the applicant a sum equal to the amount of the payments made in respect of the relevant period, or

    (b) if it appears to the court that it would be unjust to make that order, may—

        (i) order the respondent to pay to the applicant such lesser sum as it thinks fit, or

        (ii) dismiss the application.

(5) An order under this paragraph for the payment of any sum may provide for the payment of that sum by instalments of such amount as may be specified in the order.

(6) An application under this paragraph—

    (a) may be made in proceedings in the High Court or a county court for leave to enforce, or the enforcement of, payment of arrears under the order in question, but

    (b) if not made in such proceedings, must be made to a county court;

and accordingly references in this paragraph to the court are references to the High Court or a county court, as the circumstances require.

(7) The jurisdiction conferred on a county court by this paragraph is exercisable even though, because of the amount claimed in the application, the jurisdiction would not but for this sub-paragraph be exercisable by a county court.

(8) Subject to sub-paragraph (9)—

(a) the designated officer for a magistrates' court to whom any payments under a payments order are required to be made is not liable for any act done by him in pursuance of the payments order after the date on which that order ceased to have effect because of the formation of a subsequent civil partnership or marriage by the person entitled to payments under it, and

(b) the collecting officer under an attachment of earnings order made to secure payments under a payments order is not liable for any act done by him after that date in accordance with any enactment or rule of court specifying how payments made to him in compliance with the attachment of earnings order are to be dealt with.

(9) Sub-paragraph (8) applies if (and only if) the act—

(a) was one which the officer would have been under a duty to do had the payments order not ceased to have effect, and

(b) was done before notice in writing of the formation of the subsequent civil partnership or marriage was given to him by or on behalf of—

(i) the person entitled to payments under the payments order,

(ii) the person liable to make payments under it, or

(iii) the personal representatives of either of them.

(10) In sub-paragraphs (8) and (9) 'payments order' means a periodical payments order or secured periodical payments order and 'collecting officer', in relation to an attachment of earnings order, means—

(a) the officer of the High Court,

(b) the district judge of a county court, or

(c) the designated officer for a magistrates' court,

to whom a person makes payments in compliance with the order.

Part 13

Consent Orders and Maintainence Agreements

Consent orders for financial relief

66 (1) Regardless of anything in the preceding provisions of this Schedule, on an application for a consent order for financial relief, the court may, unless it has reason to think that there are other circumstances into which it ought to inquire, make an order in the terms agreed on the basis only of such information supplied with the application as is required by rules of court.

(2) Sub-paragraph (1) applies to an application for a consent order varying or discharging an order for financial relief as it applies to an application for an order for financial relief.

(3) In this paragraph—

'consent order', in relation to an application for an order, means an order in the terms applied for to which the respondent agrees;

'order for financial relief' means an order under any of Parts 1, 2, 3, 4 and 9.

Meaning of 'maintenance agreement' and 'financial arrangements'

67 (1) In this Part 'maintenance agreement' means any agreement in writing between the civil partners in a civil partnership which—

(a) is made during the continuance or after the dissolution or annulment of the civil partnership and contains financial arrangements, or

(b) is a separation agreement which contains no financial arrangements but is made in a case where no other agreement in writing between the civil partners contains financial arrangements.

(2) In this Part 'financial arrangements' means provisions governing the rights and liabilities towards one another when living separately of the civil partners in a civil partnership (including a civil partnership which has been dissolved or annulled) in respect of—

(a) the making or securing of payments, or

(b) the disposition or use of any property,

including such rights and liabilities with respect to the maintenance or education of a child (whether or not a child of the family).

(3) 'Education' includes training.

Validity of maintenance agreements

68 If a maintenance agreement includes a provision purporting to restrict any right to apply to a court for an order containing financial arrangements—

(a) that provision is void, but

(b) any other financial arrangements contained in the agreement—

(i) are not void or unenforceable as a result, and

(ii) unless void or unenforceable for any other reason, are (subject to paragraphs 69 and 73) binding on the parties to the agreement.

Alteration of agreements by court during lives of parties

69 (1) Either party to a maintenance agreement may apply to the court or, subject to sub-paragraph (6), to a magistrates' court for an order under this paragraph if—

(a) the maintenance agreement is for the time being subsisting, and

(b) each of the parties to the agreement is for the time being domiciled or resident in England and Wales.

(2) The court may make an order under this paragraph if it is satisfied that—

(a) because of a change in the circumstances in the light of which—

(i) any financial arrangements contained in the agreement were made, or

(ii) financial arrangements were omitted from it,

the agreement should be altered so as to make different financial arrangements or so as to contain financial arrangements, or

(b) that the agreement does not contain proper financial arrangements with respect to any child of the family.

(3) In sub-paragraph (2)(a) the reference to a change in the circumstances includes a change foreseen by the parties when making the agreement.

(4) An order under this paragraph may make such alterations in the agreement—

(a) by varying or revoking any financial arrangements contained in it, or

(b) by inserting in it financial arrangements for the benefit of one of the parties to the agreement or of a child of the family,

as appear to the court to be just having regard to all the circumstances, including, if relevant, the matters mentioned in paragraph 22(3).

(5) The effect of the order is that the agreement is to be treated as if any alteration

made by the order had been made by agreement between the partners and for valuable consideration.

(6) The power to make an order under this paragraph is subject to paragraphs 70 and 71.

Restrictions on applications to and orders by magistrates' courts under paragraph 69

70 (1) A magistrates' court must not entertain an application under paragraph 69(1) unless—

(a) both the parties to the agreement are resident in England and Wales, and

(b) the court acts in, or is authorised by the Lord Chancellor to act for, a local justice area in which at least one of the parties is resident.

(2) A magistrates' court must not make any order on such an application other than—

(a) if the agreement includes no provision for periodical payments by either of the parties, an order inserting provision for the making by one of the parties of periodical payments for the maintenance of—

(i) the other party, or

(ii) any child of the family;

(b) if the agreement includes provision for the making by one of the parties of periodical payments, an order increasing or reducing the rate of, or terminating, any of those payments.

Provisions relating to periodical and secured periodical payments: duration

71 (1) If a court decides to make an order under paragraph 69 altering an agreement—

(a) by inserting provision for the making or securing by one of the parties to the agreement of periodical payments for the maintenance of the other party, or

(b) by increasing the rate of the periodical payments which the agreement provides shall be made by one of the parties for the maintenance of the other,

it may specify such term as it thinks fit as the term for which the payments or, as the case may be, the additional payments attributable to the increase are to be made under the altered agreement, except that the term must not extend beyond the limits in sub-paragraphs (2) and (3).

(2) The limits if the payments are not to be secured are—

(a) the death of either of the parties to the agreement, or

(b) the formation of a subsequent civil partnership or marriage by the party to whom the payments are to be made.

(3) The limits if the payments are to be secured are—

(a) the death of the party to whom the payments are to be made, or

(b) the formation of a subsequent civil partnership or marriage by that party.

(4) Sub-paragraph (5) applies if a court decides to make an order under paragraph 69 altering an agreement by—

(a) inserting provision for the making or securing by one of the parties to the agreement of periodical payments for the maintenance of a child of the family, or

(b) increasing the rate of the periodical payments which the agreement provides shall be made or secured by one of the parties for the maintenance of such a child.

(5) The court, in deciding the term for which under the agreement as altered by the order—

(a) the payments are to be made or secured for the benefit of the child, or

(b) the additional payments attributable to the increase are to be made or secured for the benefit of the child,

must apply paragraph 49(2) to (5) (age limits) as if the order in question were a periodical payments or secured periodical payments order in favour of the child.

Saving

72 Nothing in paragraphs 68 to 71 affects—

(a) any power of a court before which any proceedings between the parties to a maintenance agreement are brought under any other enactment (including a provision of this Schedule) to make an order containing financial arrangements, or

(b) any right of either party to apply for such an order in such proceedings.

Alteration of agreements by court after death of one party

73 (1) This paragraph applies if—

(a) a maintenance agreement provides for the continuation of payments under the agreement after the death of one of the parties, and

(b) that party ('A') dies domiciled in England and Wales.

(2) Subject to sub-paragraph (4), the surviving party or A's personal representatives may apply to the High Court or a county court for an order under paragraph 69.

(3) If a maintenance agreement is altered by a court on an application made under sub-paragraph (2), the same consequences follow as if the alteration had been made immediately before the death by agreement between the parties and for valuable consideration.

(4) An application under this paragraph may not, without the leave of the High Court or a county court, be made after the end of 6 months from the date on which representation in regard to A's estate is first taken out.

(5) A's personal representatives are not liable for having distributed any part of A's estate after the end of the 6 month period on the ground that they ought to have taken into account the possibility that a court might allow an application by virtue of this paragraph to be made by the surviving party after that period.

(6) Sub-paragraph (5) does not affect any power to recover any part of the estate so distributed arising by virtue of the making of an order in pursuance of this paragraph.

(7) Paragraph 60(6) applies for the purposes of sub-paragraph (4) as it applies for the purposes of paragraph 60(3).

Part 14

Miscellaneous and Supplementary

Avoidance of transactions intended to prevent or reduce financial relief

74 (1) This paragraph applies if proceedings for relief ('financial relief') are brought by one person ('A') against another ('B') under Part 1, 2, 4, 8, 9, or 11 (other than paragraph 60(2)), or paragraph 69.

(2) If the court is satisfied, on an application by A, that B is, with the intention of defeating A's claim for financial relief, about to—
   (a) make any disposition, or
   (b) transfer out of the jurisdiction or otherwise deal with any property,
it may make such order as it thinks fit for restraining B from doing so or otherwise for protecting the claim.

(3) If the court is satisfied, on an application by A, that—
   (a) B has, with the intention of defeating A's claim for financial relief, made a reviewable disposition, and
   (b) if the disposition were set aside, financial relief or different financial relief would be granted to A,
it make an order setting aside the disposition.

(4) If the court is satisfied, on an application by A in a case where an order has been obtained by A against B under any of the provisions mentioned in sub-paragraph (1), that B has, with the intention of defeating A's claim for financial relief, made a reviewable disposition, it may make an order setting aside the disposition.

(5) An application for the purposes of sub-paragraph (3) must be made in the proceedings for the financial relief in question.

(6) If the court makes an order under sub-paragraph (3) or (4) setting aside a disposition it must give such consequential directions as it thinks fit for giving effect to the order (including directions requiring the making of any payments or the disposal of any property).

75 (1) Any reference in paragraph 74 to defeating A's claim for financial relief is to—
   (a) preventing financial relief from being granted to A, or to A for the benefit of a child of the family,
   (b) reducing the amount of any financial relief which might be so granted, or
   (c) frustrating or impeding the enforcement of any order which might be or has been made at A's instance under any of those provisions.

(2) In paragraph 74 and this paragraph 'disposition'—
   (a) does not include any provision contained in a will or codicil, but
   (b) subject to paragraph (a), includes any conveyance, assurance or gift of property of any description (whether made by an instrument or otherwise).

(3) Any disposition made by B (whether before or after the commencement of the proceedings for financial relief) is a reviewable disposition for the purposes of paragraphs 74(3) and (4) unless it was made—
   (a) for valuable consideration (other than formation of a civil partnership), and
   (b) to a person who, at the time of the disposition, acted in relation to it in good faith and without notice of any intention on B's part to defeat A's claim for financial relief.

(4) If an application is made under paragraph 74 with respect to a disposition which took place less than 3 years before the date of the application or with respect to a disposition or other dealing with property which is about to take place and the court is satisfied—
   (a) in a case falling within paragraph 74(2) or (3), that the disposition or other dealing would (apart from paragraph 74) have the consequence of defeating A's claim for financial relief, or
   (b) in a case falling within paragraph 74(4), that the disposition has had the consequence of defeating A's claim for financial relief,

it is presumed, unless the contrary is shown, that the person who disposed of or is about to dispose of or deal with the property did so or, as the case may be, is about to do so, with the intention of defeating A's claim for financial relief.

Direction for settlement of instrument for securing payments or effecting property adjustment

76 (1) This paragraph applies if the court decides to make—
   (a) an order under Part 1 or 9 requiring any payments to be secured, or
   (b) a property adjustment order.
(2) The court may direct that the matter be referred to one of the conveyancing counsel of the court for him to settle a proper instrument to be executed by all necessary parties.
(3) If the order referred to in sub-paragraph (1) is to be made in proceedings for a dissolution, nullity or separation order, the court may, if it thinks fit, defer the making of the dissolution, nullity or separation order until the instrument has been duly executed.

Settlement, etc., made in compliance with a property adjustment order may be avoided on bankruptcy of settlor

77 The fact that—
   (a) a settlement, or
   (b) a transfer of property,
   had to be made in order to comply with a property adjustment order does not prevent the settlement or transfer from being a transaction in respect of which an order may be made under section 339 or 340 of the Insolvency Act 1986 (c. 45) (transfers at an undervalue and preferences).

Payments, etc., under order made in favour of person suffering from mental disorder

78 (1) This paragraph applies if—
   (a) the court makes an order under this Schedule requiring—
      (i) payments (including a lump sum payment) to be made, or
      (ii) property to be transferred,
      to a civil partner, and
   (b) the court is satisfied that the person in whose favour the order is made is incapable, because of mental disorder, of managing and administering his or her property and affairs.
(2) 'Mental disorder' has the same meaning as in the Mental Health Act 1983 (c. 20).
(3) Subject to any order, direction or authority made or given in relation to that person under Part 8 of the 1983 Act, the court may order the payments to be made or, as the case may be, the property to be transferred to such persons having charge of that person as the court may direct.

Appeals relating to pension sharing orders which have taken effect

79 (1) Sub-paragraphs (2) and (3) apply if an appeal against a pension sharing order is begun on or after the day on which the order takes effect.

(2) If the pension sharing order relates to a person's rights under a pension arrangement, the appeal court may not set aside or vary the order if the person responsible for the pension arrangement has acted to his detriment in reliance on the order taking effect.

(3) If the pension sharing order relates to a person's shareable state scheme rights, the appeal court may not set aside or vary the order if the Secretary of State has acted to his detriment in reliance on the taking effect of the order.

(4) In determining for the purposes of sub-paragraph (2) or (3) whether a person has acted to his detriment in reliance on the taking effect of the order, the appeal court may disregard any detriment which in its opinion is insignificant.

(5) Where sub-paragraph (2) or (3) applies, the appeal court may make such further orders (including one or more pension sharing orders) as it thinks fit for the purpose of putting the parties in the position it considers appropriate.

(6) Paragraph 19 only applies to a pension sharing order under this paragraph if the decision of the appeal court can itself be the subject of an appeal.

(7) In sub-paragraph (2), the reference to the person responsible for the pension arrangement is to be read in accordance with paragraph 29(3).

Interpretation

80 (1) References in this Schedule to—
    (a) periodical payments orders,
    (b) secured periodical payments orders, and
    (c) orders for the payment of a lump sum,
are references to such of the orders that may be made under Parts 1 and 9 (other than interim orders) as are relevant in the context of the reference in question.

(2) In this Schedule 'child of the family', in relation to two people who are civil partners of each other, means—
    (a) a child of both of them, and
    (b) any other child, other than a child placed with them as foster parents by a local authority or voluntary organisation, who has been treated by both the civil partners as a child of their family.

(3) In this Schedule 'the court' (except where the context otherwise requires) means—
    (a) the High Court, or
    (b) where a county court has jurisdiction by virtue of Part 5 of the Matrimonial and Family Proceedings Act 1984 (c. 42), a county court.

(4) References in this Schedule to a subsequent civil partnership include a civil partnership which is by law void or voidable.

(5) References in this Schedule to a subsequent marriage include a marriage which is by law void or voidable.

SCHEDULE 6

Section 72(3)

FINANCIAL RELIEF IN MAGISTRATES' COURTS ETC.

Part 1

Failure to Maintain etc.: Financial Provision

Circumstances in which orders under this Part may be made

1 (1) On an application to it by one of the civil partners, a magistrates' court may make any one or more of the orders set out in paragraph 2 if it is satisfied that the other civil partner—
   (a) has failed to provide reasonable maintenance for the applicant,
   (b) has failed to provide, or to make a proper contribution towards, reasonable maintenance for any child of the family,
   (c) has behaved in such a way that the applicant cannot reasonably be expected to live with the respondent, or
   (d) has deserted the applicant.

(2) The power of the court under sub-paragraph (1) is subject to the following provisions of this Schedule.

The orders: periodical and secured periodical payments and lump sums

2 (1) The orders are—
   (a) an order that the respondent must make to the applicant such periodical payments for such term as may be specified;
   (b) an order that the respondent must pay to the applicant such lump sum as may be specified;
   (c) an order that the respondent must make—
      (i) to the applicant for the benefit of a child of the family to whom the application relates, or
      (ii) to a child of the family to whom the application relates;
      such periodical payments for such term as may be specified;
   (d) an order that the respondent must pay such lump sum as may be specified—
      (i) to the applicant for the benefit of a child of the family to whom the application relates, or
      (ii) to such a child of the family to whom the application relates.

(2) The amount of a lump sum required to be paid under sub-paragraph (1)(b) or (d) must not exceed—
   (a) £1,000, or
   (b) such larger amount as the Lord Chancellor may from time to time by order fix for the purposes of this sub-paragraph.

(3) The power to make an order under sub-paragraph (2) is exercisable by statutory instrument which is subject to annulment in pursuance of a resolution of either House of Parliament.

(4) 'Specified' means specified in the order.

Particular provision that may be made by lump sum orders

3 (1) An order under this Part for the payment of a lump sum may be made for the purpose of enabling any liability or expenses reasonably incurred in maintaining the applicant or any child of the family to whom the application relates before the making of the order to be met.

(2) Sub-paragraph (1) does not restrict the power to make the orders set out in paragraph 2(1)(b) and (d).

Matters to which court is to have regard in exercising its powers under this Part—general

4   If an application is made for an order under this Part, the court, in deciding—
     (a) whether to exercise its powers under this Part, and
     (b) if so, in what way,
     must have regard to all the circumstances of the case, giving first consideration to the welfare while under 18 of any child of the family who has not reached 18.

Particular matters to be taken into account when exercising powers in relation to civil partners

5 (1) This paragraph applies in relation to the exercise by the court of its power to make an order by virtue of paragraph 2(1)(a) or (b).

(2) The court must in particular have regard to—
   (a) the income, earning capacity, property and other financial resources which each civil partner—
       (i) has, or
       (ii) is likely to have in the foreseeable future,
       including, in the case of earning capacity, any increase in that capacity which it would in the opinion of the court be reasonable to expect a civil partner in the civil partnership to take steps to acquire;
   (b) the financial needs, obligations and responsibilities which each civil partner has or is likely to have in the foreseeable future;
   (c) the standard of living enjoyed by the civil partners before the occurrence of the conduct which is alleged as the ground of the application;
   (d) the age of each civil partner and the duration of the civil partnership;
   (e) any physical or mental disability of either civil partner;
   (f) the contributions which each civil partner has made or is likely in the foreseeable future to make to the welfare of the family, including any contribution by looking after the home or caring for the family;
   (g) the conduct of each civil partner, if that conduct is such that it would in the opinion of the court be inequitable to disregard it.

Particular matters to be taken into account when exercising powers in relation to children

6 (1) This paragraph applies in relation to the exercise by the court of its power to make an order by virtue of paragraph 2(1)(c) or (d).

(2) The court must in particular have regard to—
   (a) the financial needs of the child;
   (b) the income, earning capacity (if any), property and other financial resources of the child;
   (c) any physical or mental disability of the child;

    (d) the standard of living enjoyed by the family before the occurrence of the conduct which is alleged as the ground of the application;

    (e) the way in which the child was being and in which the civil partners expected the child to be educated or trained;

    (f) the considerations mentioned in relation to the civil partners in paragraph 5(2)(a) and (b).

(3) In relation to the exercise of its power to make an order in favour of a child of the family who is not the respondent's child, the court must also have regard to—

    (a) whether the respondent has assumed any responsibility for the child's maintenance;

    (b) if so, the extent to which, and the basis on which, the respondent assumed that responsibility and the length of time during which the respondent discharged that responsibility;

    (c) whether in assuming and discharging that responsibility the respondent did so knowing that the child was not the respondent's child;

    (d) the liability of any other person to maintain the child.

Reconciliation

7 (1) If an application is made for an order under this Part—

    (a) the court, before deciding whether to exercise its powers under this Part, must consider whether there is any possibility of reconciliation between the civil partners, and

    (b) if at any stage of the proceedings on that application it appears to the court that there is a reasonable possibility of such a reconciliation, the court may adjourn the proceedings for such period as it thinks fit to enable attempts to be made to effect a reconciliation.

(2) If the court adjourns any proceedings under sub-paragraph (1), it may request—

    (a) an officer of the Children and Family Court Advisory and Support Service, or

    (b) any other person,

to attempt to effect a reconciliation between the civil partners.

(3) If any such request is made, the officer or other person—

    (a) must report in writing to the court whether the attempt has been successful, but

    (b) must not include in the report any other information.

Refusal of order in case more suitable for High Court

8 (1) If on hearing an application for an order under this Part a magistrates' court is of the opinion that any of the matters in question between the civil partners would be more conveniently dealt with by the High Court, the magistrates' court must refuse to make any order on the application.

(2) No appeal lies from a refusal under sub-paragraph (1).

(3) But, in any proceedings in the High Court relating to or comprising the same subject matter as an application in respect of which a magistrates' court has refused to make any order, the High Court may order the application to be reheard and determined by a magistrates' court acting for the same local justice area as the court which refused to make any order.

Part 2

Orders for Agreed Financial Provision

Orders for payments which have been agreed by the parties

9 (1) Either civil partner may apply to a magistrates' court for an order under this Part on the ground that that civil partner or the other civil partner has agreed to make such financial provision as may be specified in the application.

(2) On such an application, the court may order that the applicant or the respondent (as the case may be) is to make the financial provision specified in the application, if—

(a) it is satisfied that the applicant or the respondent (as the case may be) has agreed to make that provision, and

(b) it has no reason to think that it would be contrary to the interests of justice to do so.

(3) Sub-paragraph (2) is subject to paragraph 12.

Meaning of 'financial provision' and of references to specified financial provision

10 (1) In this Part 'financial provision' means any one or more of the following—

(a) the making of periodical payments by one civil partner to the other;

(b) the payment of a lump sum by one civil partner to the other;

(c) the making of periodical payments by one civil partner to a child of the family or to the other civil partner for the benefit of such a child;

(d) the payment by one party of a lump sum to a child of the family or to the other civil partner for the benefit of such a child.

(2) Any reference in this Part to the financial provision specified in an application or specified by the court is a reference—

(a) to the type of provision specified in the application or by the court,

(b) to the amount so specified as the amount of any payment to be made under the application or order, and

(c) in the case of periodical payments, to the term so specified as the term for which the payments are to be made.

Evidence to be produced where respondent not present etc.

11 (1) This paragraph applies if—

(a) the respondent is not present, or

(b) is not represented by counsel or a solicitor,

at the hearing of an application for an order under this Part.

(2) The court must not make an order under this Part unless there is produced to it such evidence as may be prescribed by rules of court of—

(a) the consent of the respondent to the making of the order,

(b) the financial resources of the respondent, and

(c) if the financial provision specified in the application includes or consists of provision in respect of a child of the family to be made by the applicant to the respondent for the benefit of the child or to the child, the financial resources of the child.

Exercise of powers in relation to children

12 (1) This paragraph applies if the financial provision specified in an application under this Part—

(a) includes, or

(b) consists of,

provision in respect of a child of the family.

(2) The court must not make an order under this Part unless it considers that the provision which the applicant or the respondent (as the case may be) has agreed to make in respect of the child provides for, or makes a proper contribution towards, the financial needs of the child.

Power to make alternative orders

13 (1) This paragraph applies if on an application under this Part the court decides—

(a) that it would be contrary to the interests of justice to make an order for the making of the financial provision specified in the application, or

(b) that any financial provision which the applicant or the respondent (as the case may be) has agreed to make in respect of a child of the family does not provide for, or make a proper contribution towards, the financial needs of that child.

(2) If the court is of the opinion—

(a) that it would not be contrary to the interests of justice to make an order for the making of some other financial provision specified by the court, and

(b) that, in so far as that other financial provision contains any provision for a child of the family, it provides for, or makes a proper contribution towards, the financial needs of that child,

then, if both the civil partners agree, the court may order that the applicant or the respondent (as the case may be) is to make that other financial provision.

Relationship between this Part and Part 1

14 (1) A civil partner who has applied for an order under Part 1 is not precluded at any time before the determination of the application from applying for an order under this Part.

(2) If—

(a) an order is made under this Part on the application of either civil partner, and

(b) either of them has also made an application for a Part 1 order,

the application for the Part 1 order is to be treated as if it had been withdrawn.

Part 3

Orders of Court where Civil Partners Living Apart by Agreement

Powers of court where civil partners are living apart by agreement

15 (1) If—

(a) the civil partners have been living apart for a continuous period exceeding 3 months, neither civil partner having deserted the other, and

(b) one of the civil partners has been making periodical payments for the benefit of the other civil partner or of a child of the family, the other civil partner may apply to a magistrates' court for an order under this Part.

(2) An application made under sub-paragraph (1) must specify the total amount of the payments made by the respondent during the period of 3 months immediately preceding the date of the making of the application.

(3) If on an application for an order under this Part the court is satisfied that the respondent has made the payments specified in the application, the court may make one or both of the orders set out in paragraph 16.

(4) Sub-paragraph (3) is subject to the provisions of this Schedule.

The orders that may be made under this Part

16 (1) The orders are—

    (a) an order that the respondent is to make to the applicant such periodical payments for such term as may be specified;

    (b) an order that the respondent is to make—

        (i) to the applicant for the benefit of a child of the family to whom the application relates, or

        (ii) to a child of the family to whom the application relates.

    such periodical payments for such term as may be specified.

(2) 'Specified' means specified in the order.

Restrictions on orders under this Part

17 The court in the exercise of its powers under this Part must not require—

    (a) the respondent to make payments whose total amount during any period of 3 months exceeds the total amount paid by him for the benefit of—

        (i) the applicant, or

        (ii) a child of the family,

    during the period of 3 months immediately preceding the date of the making of the application;

    (b) the respondent to make payments to or for the benefit of any person which exceed in amount the payments which the court considers that it would have required the respondent to make to or for the benefit of that person on an application under Part 1;

    (c) payments to be made to or for the benefit of a child of the family who is not the respondent's child, unless the court considers that it would have made an order in favour of that child on an application under Part 1.

Relationship with powers under Part 1

18 (1) Sub-paragraph (2) applies if on an application under this Part the court considers that the orders which it has the power to make under this Part—

    (a) would not provide reasonable maintenance for the applicant, or

    (b) if the application relates to a child of the family, would not provide, or make a proper contribution towards, reasonable maintenance for that child.

(2) The court—

    (a) must refuse to make an order under this Part, but

    (b) may treat the application as if it were an application for an order under Part 1.

Matters to be taken into consideration

19 Paragraphs 4 to 6 apply in relation to an application for an order under this Part as they apply in relation to an application for an order under Part 1, subject to the modification that for the reference in paragraph 5(2)(c) to the occurrence of the conduct which is alleged as the ground of the application substitute a reference to the living apart of the civil partners.

Part 4

Interim Orders

Circumstances in which interim orders may be made

20 (1) This paragraph applies if an application has been made for an order under Part 1, 2 or 3.

(2) A magistrates' court may make an interim order—

(a) at any time before making a final order on, or dismissing, the application, or

(b) on refusing (under paragraph 8) to make on order on the application.

(3) The High Court may make an interim order on ordering the application to be reheard by a magistrates' court (either after the refusal of an order under paragraph 8 or on an appeal made by virtue of paragraph 46).

(4) Not more than one interim order may be made with respect to an application for an order under Part 1, 2 or 3.

(5) Sub-paragraph (4) does not affect the power of a court to make an interim order on a further application under Part 1, 2 or 3.

Meaning of interim order

21 (1) An interim order is an order requiring the respondent to make such periodical payments as the court thinks reasonable—

(a) to the applicant,

(b) to any child of the family who is under 18, or

(c) to the applicant for the benefit of such a child.

(2) In relation to an interim order in respect of an application for an order under Part 2 by the civil partner who has agreed to make the financial provision specified in the application, sub-paragraph (1) applies as if—

(a) the reference to the respondent were a reference to the applicant, and

(b) the references to the applicant were references to the respondent.

When interim order may start

22 (1) An interim order may provide for payments to be made from such date as the court may specify, except that the date must not be earlier than the date of the making of the application for an order under Part 1, 2 or 3.

(2) Sub-paragraph (1) is subject to paragraph 27(7) and (8).

Payments which can be treated as having been paid on account

23 (1) If an interim order made by the High Court on an appeal made by virtue of paragraph 46 provides for payments to be made from a date earlier than the date of

the making of the order, the interim order may provide that payments made by the respondent under an order made by a magistrates' court are to be treated, to such extent and in such manner as may be provided by the interim order, as having been paid on account of any payment provided for by the interim order.

(2) In relation to an interim order in respect of an application for an order under Part 2 by the civil partner who has agreed to make the financial provision specified in the application, sub-paragraph (1) applies as if the reference to the respondent were a reference to the applicant.

When interim order ceases to have effect

24 (1) Subject to sub-paragraphs (2) and (3), an interim order made on an application for an order under Part 1, 2 or 3 ceases to have effect on the earliest of the following dates—

(a) the date, if any, specified for the purpose in the interim order;

(b) the date on which the period of 3 months beginning with the date of the making of the interim order ends;

(c) the date on which a magistrates' court either makes a final order on, or dismisses, the application.

(2) If an interim order made under this Part would, but for this sub-paragraph, cease to have effect under sub-paragraph (1)(a) or (b)—

(a) the magistrates' court which made the order, or

(b) in the case of an interim order made by the High Court, the magistrates' court by which the application for an order under Part 1, 2 or 3 is to be reheard,

may by order provide that the interim order is to continue in force for a further period.

(3) An order continued in force under sub-paragraph (2) ceases to have effect on the earliest of the following dates—

(a) the date, if any, specified for the purpose in the order continuing it;

(b) the date on which ends the period of 3 months beginning with—

(i) the date of the making of the order continuing it, or

(ii) if more than one such order has been made with respect to the application, the date of the making of the first such order;

(c) the date on which the court either makes a final order on, or dismisses, the application.

Supplementary

25 (1) An interim order made by the High Court under paragraph 20(3) on ordering an application to be reheard by a magistrates' court is to be treated for the purposes of—

(a) its enforcement, and

(b) Part 6 (variation etc. of orders),

as if it were an order of that magistrates' court (and not of the High Court).

(2) No appeal lies from the making of or refusal to make, the variation of or refusal to vary, or the revocation of or refusal to revoke, an interim order.

Part 5

Commencement and Duration of Orders Under Parts 1, 2 and 3

Duration of periodical payments order for a civil partner

26 (1) The court may specify in a periodical payments order made under paragraph 2(1)(a) or Part 3 in favour of a civil partner such term as it thinks fit, except that the term must not—
   (a) begin before the date of the making of the application for the order, or
   (b) extend beyond the death of either of the civil partners.

(2) If—
   (a) a periodical payments order is made under paragraph 2(1)(a) or Part 3 in favour of one of the civil partners, and
   (b) the civil partnership is subsequently dissolved or annulled but the order continues in force,
   the periodical payments order ceases to have effect (regardless of anything in it) on the formation of a subsequent civil partnership or marriage by that civil partner, except in relation to any arrears due under the order on the date of that event.

Age limit on making orders for financial provision for children and duration of such orders

27 (1) Subject to sub-paragraph (5), no order is to be made under paragraph 2(1)(c) or (d) or Part 3 in favour of a child who has reached 18.

(2) The term to be specified in a periodical payments order made under paragraph 2(1)(c) or Part 3 in favour of a child may begin with—
   (a) the date of the making of an application for the order or a later date, or
   (b) a date ascertained in accordance with sub-paragraph (7) or (8).

(3) The term to be specified in such an order—
   (a) must not in the first instance extend beyond the date of the birthday of the child next following his reaching the upper limit of the compulsory school age unless the court considers that in the circumstances of the case the welfare of the child requires that it should extend to a later date, and
   (b) must not in any event, subject to sub-paragraph (5), extend beyond the date of the child's 18th birthday.

(4) Sub-paragraph (3)(a) must be read with section 8 of the Education Act 1996 (c. 56) (which applies to determine for the purposes of any enactment whether a person is of compulsory school age).

(5) Sub-paragraphs (1) and (3)(b) do not apply in the case of a child if it appears to the court that—
   (a) the child is, or will be, or, if such an order were made without complying with either or both of those provisions, would be—
      (i) receiving instruction at an educational establishment, or
      (ii) undergoing training for a trade, profession or vocation,
   whether or not also the child is, will be or would be, in gainful employment, or
   (b) there are special circumstances which justify the making of the order without complying with either or both of sub-paragraphs (1) and (3)(b).

(6) Any order made under paragraph 2(1)(c) or Part 3 in favour of a child, regardless

of anything in the order, ceases to have effect on the death of the person liable to make payments under the order.

(7) If—

    (a) a maintenance calculation ('current calculation') is in force with respect to a child, and

    (b) an application is made for an order under paragraph 2(1)(c) or Part 3—

        (i) in accordance with section 8 of the Child Support Act 1991 (c. 48), and

        (ii) before the end of 6 months beginning with the making of the current calculation,

the term to be specified in any such order made on that application may be expressed to begin on, or at any time after, the earliest permitted date.

(8) 'The earliest permitted date' is whichever is the later of—

    (a) the date 6 months before the application is made, or

    (b) the date on which the current calculation took effect or, where successive maintenance calculations have been continuously in force with respect to a child, on which the first of those calculations took effect.

(9) If—

    (a) a maintenance calculation ceases to have effect by or under any provision of the 1991 Act, and

    (b) an application is made, before the end of 6 months beginning with the relevant date, for a periodical payments order under paragraph 2(1)(c) or Part 3 in favour of a child with respect to whom that maintenance calculation was in force immediately before it ceased to have effect,

the term to be specified in any such order, or in any interim order under Part 4, made on that application, may begin with the date on which that maintenance calculation ceased to have effect or any later date.

(10) 'The relevant date' means the date on which the maintenance calculation ceased to have effect.

(11) In this Schedule 'maintenance calculation' has the same meaning as it has in the 1991 Act by virtue of section 54 of the 1991 Act as read with any regulations in force under that section.

Application of paragraphs 26 and 27 to Part 2 orders

28 (1) Subject to sub-paragraph (3), paragraph 26 applies in relation to an order under Part 2 which requires periodical payments to be made to a civil partner for his own benefit as it applies in relation to an order under paragraph 2(1)(a).

(2) Subject to sub-paragraph (3), paragraph 27 applies in relation to an order under Part 2 for the making of financial provision in respect of a child of the family as it applies in relation to an order under paragraph 2(1)(c) or (d).

(3) If—

    (a) the court makes an order under Part 2 which contains provision for the making of periodical payments, and

    (b) by virtue of paragraph 14, an application for an order under Part 1 is treated as if it had been withdrawn,

the term which may be specified under Part 2 as the term for which the payments are to be made may begin with the date of the making of the application for the order under Part 1 or any later date.

Effect on certain orders of parties living together

29 (1) Sub-paragraph (2) applies if periodical payments are required to be made to a civil partner (whether for the civil partner's own benefit or for the benefit of a child of the family)—

(a) by an order made under Part 1 or 2, or

(b) by an interim order made under Part 4 (otherwise than on an application under Part 3).

(2) The order is enforceable even though—

(a) the civil partners are living with each other at the date of the making of the order, or

(b) if they are not living with each other at that date, they subsequently resume living with each other;

but the order ceases to have effect if after that date the parties continue to live with each other, or resume living with each other, for a continuous period exceeding 6 months.

(3) Sub-paragraph (4) applies if—

(a) an order is made under Part 1 or 2 which requires periodical payments to be made to a child of the family, or

(b) an interim order is made under Part 4 (otherwise than on an application under Part 3) which requires periodical payments to be made to a child of the family.

(4) Unless the court otherwise directs, the order continues to have effect and is enforceable even if—

(a) the civil partners are living with each other at the date of the making of the order, or

(b) if they are not living with each other at that date, they subsequently resume living with each other.

(5) An order made under Part 3, and any interim order made on an application for an order under that Part, ceases to have effect if the civil partners resume living with each other.

(6) If an order made under this Schedule ceases to have effect under—

(a) sub-paragraph (2) or (5), or

(b) a direction given under sub-paragraph (4),

a magistrates' court may, on an application made by either civil partner, make an order declaring that the order ceased to have effect from such date as the court may specify.

Part 6

Variation etc. of Orders

Power to vary, revoke, suspend or revive order

30 (1) If a magistrates' court has made an order for the making of periodical payments under Part 1, 2 or 3, the court may, on an application made under this Part—

(a) vary or revoke the order,

(b) suspend any provision of it temporarily, or

(c) revive any provision so suspended.

(2) If a magistrates' court has made an interim order under Part 4, the court may, on an application made under this Part—

(a) vary or revoke the order,

(b) suspend any provision of it temporarily, or

(c) revive any provision so suspended,

except that it may not by virtue of this sub-paragraph extend the period for which the order is in force.

Powers to order lump sum on variation

31 (1) If a magistrates' court has made an order under paragraph 2(1)(a) or (c) for the making of periodical payments, the court may, on an application made under this Part, make an order for the payment of a lump sum under paragraph 2(1)(b) or (d).

(2) If a magistrates' court has made an order under Part 2 for the making of periodical payments by a civil partner the court may, on an application made under this Part, make an order for the payment of a lump sum by that civil partner—

(a) to the other civil partner, or

(b) to a child of the family or to that other civil partner for the benefit of that child.

(3) Where the court has power by virtue of this paragraph to make an order for the payment of a lump sum—

(a) the amount of the lump sum must not exceed the maximum amount that may at that time be required to be paid under Part 1, but

(b) the court may make an order for the payment of a lump sum not exceeding that amount even if the person required to pay it was required to pay a lump sum by a previous order under this Schedule.

(4) Where—

(a) the court has power by virtue of this paragraph to make an order for the payment of a lump sum, and

(b) the respondent or the applicant (as the case may be) has agreed to pay a lump sum of an amount exceeding the maximum amount that may at that time be required to be paid under Part 1,

the court may, regardless of sub-paragraph (3), make an order for the payment of a lump sum of that amount.

Power to specify when order as varied is to take effect

32 An order made under this Part which varies an order for the making of periodical payments may provide that the payments as so varied are to be made from such date as the court may specify, except that, subject to paragraph 33, the date must not be earlier than the date of the making of the application under this Part.

33 (1) If—

(a) there is in force an order ('the order')—

(i) under paragraph 2(1)(c),

(ii) under Part 2 making provision of a kind set out in paragraph 10(1)(c) (regardless of whether it makes provision of any other kind mentioned in paragraph 10(1)(c)),

(iii) under paragraph 16(1)(b), or

(iv) which is an interim order under Part 4 under which the payments are to be made to a child or to the applicant for the benefit of a child,

(b) the order requires payments specified in it to be made to or for the benefit of more than one child without apportioning those payments between them,

(c) a maintenance calculation ('the calculation') is made with respect to one or more, but not all, of the children with respect to whom those payments are to be made, and

(d) an application is made, before the end of 6 months beginning with the date on which the calculation was made, for the variation or revocation of the order,

the court may, in exercise of its powers under this Part to vary or revoke the order, direct that the variation or revocation is to take effect from the date on which the calculation took effect or any later date.

(2) If—

    (a) an order ('the child order') of a kind prescribed for the purposes of section 10(1) of the Child Support Act 1991 is affected by a maintenance calculation,

    (b) on the date on which the child order became so affected there was in force an order ('the civil partner's order')—

        (i) under paragraph 2(1)(a),

        (ii) under Part 2 making provision of a kind set out in paragraph 10(1)(a) (regardless of whether it makes provision of any other kind mentioned in paragraph 10(1)(a)),

        (iii) under paragraph 16(1)(a), or

        (iv) which is an interim order under Part 4 under which the payments are to be made to the applicant (otherwise than for the benefit of a child), and

    (c) an application is made, before the end of 6 months beginning with the date on which the maintenance calculation was made, for the civil partner's order to be varied or revoked,

the court may, in exercise of its powers under this Part to vary or revoke the civil partner's order, direct that the variation or revocation is to take effect from the date on which the child order became so affected or any later date.

(3) For the purposes of sub-paragraph (2), an order is affected if it ceases to have effect or is modified by or under section 10 of the 1991 Act.

Matters to which court is to have regard in exercising powers under this Part

34 (1) In exercising the powers conferred by this Part the court must, so far as it appears to the court just to do so, give effect to any agreement which has been reached between the civil partners in relation to the application.

(2) If—

    (a) there is no such agreement, or

    (b) if the court decides not to give effect to the agreement,

the court must have regard to all the circumstances of the case, giving first consideration to the welfare while under 18 of any child of the family who has not reached 18.

(3) Those circumstances include any change in any of the matters—

    (a) to which the court was required to have regard when making the order to which the application relates, or

    (b) in the case of an application for the variation or revocation of an order made under Part 2 or on an appeal made by virtue of paragraph 46, to which the court would have been required to have regard if that order had been made under Part 1.

Variation of orders for periodical payments: further provisions

35 (1) The power of the court under paragraphs 30 to 34 to vary an order for the making of periodical payments includes power, if the court is satisfied that payment has not been made in accordance with the order, to exercise one of its powers under section 59(3)(a) to (d) of the Magistrates' Courts Act 1980 (c. 43).

(2) Sub-paragraph (1) is subject to paragraph 37.

36 (1) If—

(a) a magistrates' court has made an order under this Schedule for the making of periodical payments, and

(b) payments under the order are required to be made by any method of payment falling within section 59(6) of the 1980 Act (standing order, etc.),

an application may be made under this sub-paragraph to the court for the order to be varied as mentioned in sub-paragraph (2).

(2) Subject to sub-paragraph (4), if an application is made under sub-paragraph (1), a justices' clerk, after—

(a) giving written notice (by post or otherwise) of the application to the respondent, and

(b) allowing the respondent, within the period of 14 days beginning with the date of the giving of that notice, an opportunity to make written representations,

may vary the order to provide that payments under the order are to be made to the designated officer for the court.

(3) The clerk may proceed with an application under sub-paragraph (1) even if the respondent has not received written notice of the application.

(4) If an application has been made under sub-paragraph (1), the clerk may, if he considers it inappropriate to exercise his power under sub-paragraph (2), refer the matter to the court which, subject to paragraph 37, may vary the order by exercising one of its powers under section 59(3)(a) to (d) of the 1980 Act.

37 (1) Before varying the order by exercising one of its powers under section 59(3)(a) to (d) of the 1980 Act, the court must have regard to any representations made by the parties to the application.

(2) If the court does not propose to exercise its power under section 59(3)(c), (cc) or (d) of the 1980 Act, the court must, unless upon representations expressly made in that behalf by the person to whom payments under the order are required to be made it is satisfied that it is undesirable to do so, exercise its power under section 59(3)(b).

38 (1) Section 59(4) of the 1980 Act (power of court to order that account be opened) applies for the purposes of paragraphs 35 and 36(4) as it applies for the purposes of section 59.

(2) None of the powers of the court, or of a justices' clerk, conferred by paragraphs 35 to 37 and sub-paragraph (1) is exercisable in relation to an order under this Schedule for the making of periodical payments which is not a qualifying maintenance order (within the meaning of section 59 of the 1980 Act).

Persons who may apply under this Part

39 An application under paragraph 30, 31 or 36 may be made—

(a) if it is for the variation or revocation of an order under Part 1, 2, 3 or 4 for periodical payments, by either civil partner, and

(b) if it is for the variation of an order under paragraph 2(1)(c) or Part 2 or 3 for periodical payments to or in respect of a child, also by the child himself, if he has reached 16.

Revival of orders for periodical payments

40 (1) If an order made by a magistrates' court under this Schedule for the making of periodical payments to or in respect of a child (other than an interim order) ceases to have effect—

(a) on the date on which the child reaches 16, or

(b) at any time after that date but before or on the date on which he reaches 18,

the child may apply to the court which made the order for an order for its revival.

(2) If on such an application it appears to the court that—

(a) the child is, will be or (if an order were made under this sub-paragraph) would be receiving instruction at an educational establishment or undergoing training for a trade, profession or vocation, whether or not while in gainful employment, or

(b) there are special circumstances which justify the making of an order under this sub-paragraph,

the court may by order revive the order from such date as the court may specify, not being earlier than the date of the making of the application.

(3) Any order revived under this paragraph may be varied or revoked under paragraphs 30 to 34 in the same way as it could have been varied or revoked had it continued in being.

Variation of instalments of lump sum

41 If in the exercise of its powers under section 75 of the 1980 Act a magistrates' court orders that a lump sum required to be paid under this Schedule is to be paid by instalments, the court, on an application made by either the person liable to pay or the person entitled to receive that sum, may vary that order by varying—

(a) the number of instalments payable,

(b) the amount of any instalment payable, and

(c) the date on which any instalment becomes payable.

Supplementary provisions with respect to variation and revocation of orders

42 None of the following powers apply in relation to an order made under this Schedule—

(a) the powers of a magistrates' court to revoke, revive or vary an order for the periodical payment of money and the power of a justices' clerk to vary such an order under section 60 of the 1980 Act;

(b) the power of a magistrates' court to suspend or rescind certain other orders under section 63(2) of the 1980 Act.

Part 7

Arrears and Repayments

Enforcement etc. of orders for payment of money

43 Section 32 of the Domestic Proceedings and Magistrates' Courts Act 1978 (c. 22) applies in relation to orders under this Schedule as it applies in relation to orders under Part 1 of that Act.

Orders for repayment after cessation of order because of subsequent civil partnership etc.

44 (1) Sub-paragraphs (3) and (4) apply if—
   (a) an order made under paragraph 2(1)(a) or Part 2 or 3 has, under paragraph 26(2), ceased to have effect because of the formation of a subsequent civil partnership or marriage by the party ('R') in whose favour it was made, and
   (b) the person liable to make payments under the order ('P') made payments in accordance with it in respect of a relevant period in the mistaken belief that the order was still subsisting.

(2) 'Relevant period' means a period after the date of the formation of the subsequent civil partnership or marriage.

(3) No proceedings in respect of a cause of action arising out of the circumstances mentioned in sub-paragraph (1)(a) and (b) is maintainable by P (or P's personal representatives) against R (or R's personal representatives).

(4) But on an application made under this paragraph by P (or P's personal representatives) against R (or R's personal representatives) the court—
   (a) may order the respondent to pay to the applicant a sum equal to the amount of the payments made in respect of the relevant period, or
   (b) if it appears to the court that it would be unjust to make that order, may—
      (i) order the respondent to pay to the applicant such lesser sum as it thinks fit, or
      (ii) dismiss the application.

(5) An order under this paragraph for the payment of any sum may provide for the payment of that sum by instalments of such amount as may be specified in the order.

(6) An application under this paragraph—
   (a) may be made in proceedings in the High Court or a county court for leave to enforce, or the enforcement of, the payment of arrears under an order made under paragraph 2(1)(a) or Part 2 or 3, but
   (b) if not made in such proceedings, must be made to a county court,
   and accordingly references in this paragraph to the court are references to the High Court or a county court, as the circumstances require.

(7) The jurisdiction conferred on a county court by this paragraph is exercisable by a county court even though, because of the amount claimed in an application under this paragraph, the jurisdiction would not but for this sub-paragraph be exercisable by a county court.

(8) Subject to sub-paragraph (9)—
   (a) the designated officer for a magistrates' court to whom any payments under an order made under paragraph 2(1)(a), or Part 2 or 3, are required to be made is not liable for any act done by him in pursuance of the order after the date on

285

which that order ceased to have effect because of the formation of a subsequent civil partnership or marriage by the person entitled to payments under it, and

(b) the collecting officer under an attachment of earnings order made to secure payments under the order under paragraph 2(1)(a), or Part 2 or 3, is not liable for any act done by him after that date in accordance with any enactment or rule of court specifying how payments made to him in compliance with the attachment of earnings order are to be dealt with.

(9) Sub-paragraph (8) applies if (but only if) the act—

(a) was one which he would have been under a duty to do had the order under paragraph 2(1)(a) or Part 2 or 3 not ceased to have effect, and

(b) was done before notice in writing of the formation of the subsequent civil partnership or marriage was given to him by or on behalf of—

(i) the person entitled to payments under the order,

(ii) the person liable to make payments under it, or

(iii) the personal representatives of either of them.

(10) In this paragraph 'collecting officer', in relation to an attachment of earnings order, means—

(a) the officer of the High Court, or

(b) the officer designated by the Lord Chancellor,

to whom a person makes payments in compliance with the order.

Part 8

Supplementary

Restrictions on making of orders under this Schedule: welfare of children

45 If—

(a) an application is made by a civil partner for an order under Part 1, 2 or 3, and

(b) there is a child of the family who is under 18,

the court must not dismiss or make a final order on the application until it has decided whether to exercise any of its powers under the Children Act 1989 (c. 41) with respect to the child.

Constitution of courts, powers of High Court and county court in relation to orders and appeals

46 The following provisions of the Domestic Proceedings and Magistrates' Courts Act 1978 (c. 22) apply in relation to an order under this Schedule relating to a civil partnership as they apply in relation to an order under Part 1 of that Act relating to a marriage—

(a) section 28 (powers of the High Court and a county court in relation to certain orders),

(b) section 29 (appeals), and

(c) section 31 (constitution of courts).

Provisions as to jurisdiction and procedure

47 (1) Subject to section 2 of the Family Law Act 1986 (c. 55) and section 70 of the Magistrates' Courts Act 1980 (c. 43) and any determination of the Lord Chancellor,

a magistrates' court has jurisdiction to hear an application for an order under this Schedule if it acts in, or is authorised by the Lord Chancellor to act for, a local justice area in which either the applicant or the respondent ordinarily resides at the date of the making of the application.

(2) Any jurisdiction conferred on a magistrates' court by this Schedule is exercisable even if any party to the proceedings is not domiciled in England and Wales.

Meaning of 'child of the family'

48 In this Schedule 'child of the family', in relation to two people who are civil partners of each other, means—

(a) a child of both of them, and

(b) any other child, other than a child placed with them as foster parents by a local authority or voluntary organisation, who has been treated by both the civil partners as a child of their family.

SCHEDULE 7

Section 72(4)

FINANCIAL RELIEF IN ENGLAND AND WALES AFTER OVERSEAS DISSOLUTION ETC. OF A CIVIL PARTNERSHIP

Part 1

Financial Relief

Part applies where civil partnership has been dissolved etc. overseas

1 (1) This Part of this Schedule applies where—

(a) a civil partnership has been dissolved or annulled, or the civil partners have been legally separated, by means of judicial or other proceedings in an overseas country, and

(b) the dissolution, annulment or legal separation is entitled to be recognised as valid in England and Wales.

(2) This Part of this Schedule applies even if the date of the dissolution, annulment or legal separation is earlier than the date on which the Part comes into force.

(3) In this Schedule 'overseas country' means a country or territory outside the British Islands.

(4) In this Part of this Schedule 'child of the family' means—

(a) a child of both of the civil partners, and

(b) any other child, other than a child placed with them as foster parents or by a local authority or voluntary organisation, who has been treated by both the civil partners as a child of their family.

Either civil partner may make application for financial relief

2 (1) Either of the civil partners may make an application to the court for an order under paragraph 9 or 13.

(2) The rights conferred by sub-paragraph (1) are subject to—

    (a) paragraph 3 (civil partner may not apply after forming subsequent civil partnership etc.), and

    (b) paragraph 4 (application may not be made until leave to make it has been granted).

(3) An application for an order under paragraph 9 or 13 must be made in a manner prescribed by rules of court.

No application after formation of subsequent civil partnership or marriage

3 (1) If—

    (a) the civil partnership has been dissolved or annulled, and

    (b) after the dissolution or annulment, one of the civil partners forms a subsequent civil partnership or marriage,

    that civil partner shall not be entitled to make, in relation to the civil partnership, an application for an order under paragraph 9 or 13.

(2) The reference in sub-paragraph (1) to the forming of a subsequent civil partnership or marriage includes a reference to the forming of a civil partnership or marriage which is by law void or voidable.

Leave of court required for making of application

4 (1) No application for an order under paragraph 9 or 13 shall be made unless the leave of the court has been obtained in accordance with rules of court.

(2) The court shall not grant leave under this paragraph unless it considers that there is substantial ground for the making of an application for such an order.

(3) The court may grant leave under this paragraph notwithstanding that an order has been made by a court in a country outside England and Wales requiring the other civil partner to make any payment, or transfer any property, to the applicant or to a child of the family.

(4) Leave under this paragraph may be granted subject to such conditions as the court thinks fit.

Interim orders for maintenance

5 (1) Where—

    (a) leave is granted under paragraph 4, and

    (b) it appears to the court that the civil partner who applied for leave, or any child of the family, is in immediate need of financial assistance,

    the court may, subject to sub-paragraph (4), make an interim order for maintenance.

(2) An interim order for maintenance is one requiring the other civil partner to make—

    (a) to the applicant, or

    (b) to the child,

    such periodical payments as the court thinks reasonable for such term as the court thinks reasonable.

(3) The term must be one—

    (a) beginning not earlier than the date of the grant of leave, and

    (b) ending with the date of the determination of the application made under the leave.

(4) If it appears to the court that the court will, in the event of an application being made under the leave, have jurisdiction to entertain the application only under paragraph 7(4), the court shall not make an interim order under this paragraph.

(5) An interim order under this paragraph may be made subject to such conditions as the court thinks fit.

Paragraphs 7 and 8 apply where application made for relief under paragraph 9 or 13

6 Paragraphs 7 and 8 apply where—
   (a) one of the civil partners has been granted leave under paragraph 4, and
   (b) acting under the leave, that civil partner makes an application for an order under paragraph 9 or 13.

Jurisdiction of the court

7 (1) The court shall have jurisdiction to entertain the application only if one or more of the following jurisdictional requirements is satisfied.

(2) The first requirement is that either of the civil partners—
   (a) was domiciled in England and Wales on the date when the leave was applied for, or
   (b) was domiciled in England and Wales on the date when the dissolution, annulment or legal separation took effect in the overseas country in which it was obtained.

(3) The second is that either of the civil partners—
   (a) was habitually resident in England and Wales throughout the period of one year ending with the date when the leave was applied for, or
   (b) was habitually resident in England and Wales throughout the period of one year ending with the date on which the dissolution, annulment or legal separation took effect in the overseas country in which it was obtained.

(4) The third is that either or both of the civil partners had, at the date when the leave was applied for, a beneficial interest in possession in a dwelling-house situated in England or Wales which was at some time during the civil partnership a civil partnership home of the civil partners.

(5) In sub-paragraph (4) 'possession' includes receipt of, or the right to receive, rents and profits, but here 'rent' does not include mortgage interest.

Duty of the court to consider whether England and Wales is appropriate venue for application

8 (1) Before deciding the application, the court must consider whether in all the circumstances of the case it would be appropriate for an order of the kind applied for to be made by a court in England and Wales.

(2) If the court is not satisfied that it would be appropriate, the court shall dismiss the application.

(3) The court must, in particular, have regard to the following matters—
   (a) the connection which the civil partners have with England and Wales;
   (b) the connection which the civil partners have with the country in which the civil partnership was dissolved or annulled or in which they were legally separated;
   (c) the connection which the civil partners have with any other country outside England and Wales;

(d) any financial benefit which, in consequence of the dissolution, annulment or legal separation—
   (i) the applicant, or
   (ii) a child of the family,
   has received, or is likely to receive, by virtue of any agreement or the operation of the law of a country outside England and Wales;
(e) in a case where an order has been made by a court in a country outside England and Wales requiring the other civil partner—
   (i) to make any payment, or
   (ii) to transfer any property,
   for the benefit of the applicant or a child of the family, the financial relief given by the order and the extent to which the order has been complied with or is likely to be complied with;
(f) any right which the applicant has, or has had, to apply for financial relief from the other civil partner under the law of any country outside England and Wales and, if the applicant has omitted to exercise that right, the reason for that omission;
(g) the availability in England and Wales of any property in respect of which an order under this Schedule in favour of the applicant could be made;
(h) the extent to which any order made under this Schedule is likely to be enforceable;
(i) the length of time which has elapsed since the date of the dissolution, annulment or legal separation.

Orders for financial provision, property adjustment and pension sharing

9 (1) Sub-paragraphs (2) and (3) apply where one of the civil partners has made an application for an order under this paragraph.
(2) If the civil partnership has been dissolved or annulled, the court may on the application make any one or more of the orders which it could make under Part 1, 2 or 4 of Schedule 5 (financial provision, property adjustment and pension sharing) if a dissolution order or nullity order had been made in respect of the civil partnership under Chapter 2 of Part 2 of this Act.
(3) If the civil partners have been legally separated, the court may on the application make any one or more of the orders which it could make under Part 1 or 2 of Schedule 5 (financial provision and property adjustment) if a separation order had been made in respect of the civil partners under Chapter 2 of Part 2 of this Act.
(4) Where under sub-paragraph (2) or (3) the court makes—
   (a) an order which, if made under Schedule 5, would be a secured periodical payments order,
   (b) an order for the payment of a lump sum, or
   (c) an order which, if made under that Schedule, would be a property adjustment order,
   then, on making that order or at any time afterwards, the court may make any order which it could make under Part 3 of Schedule 5 (sale of property) if the order under sub-paragraph (2) or (3) had been made under that Schedule.
(5) The powers under sub-paragraphs (2) to (4) are subject to paragraph 11.

Matters to which court is to have regard in exercising its powers under paragraph 9

10 (1) The court, in deciding—
   (a) whether to exercise its powers under paragraph 9, and
   (b) if so, in what way,
   must act in accordance with this paragraph.
(2) The court must have regard to all the circumstances of the case, giving first consideration to the welfare, while under 18, of any child of the family who has not reached 18.
(3) The court, in exercising its powers under paragraph 9 in relation to one of the civil partners—
   (a) must in particular have regard to the matters mentioned in paragraph 21(2) of Schedule 5, and
   (b) shall be under duties corresponding to those imposed by sub-paragraphs (2) and (3) of paragraph 23 of that Schedule (duties to consider termination of financial obligations) where it decides to exercise under paragraph 9 powers corresponding to the powers referred to in those sub-paragraphs.
(4) The matters to which the court is to have regard under sub-paragraph (3)(a), so far as relating to paragraph 21(2)(a) of Schedule 5 (regard to be had to financial resources), include—
   (a) any benefits under a pension arrangement which either of the civil partners has or is likely to have, and
   (b) any PPF compensation to which a civil partner is or is likely to be entitled,
(whether or not in the foreseeable future).
(5) The matters to which the court is to have regard under sub-paragraph (3)(a), so far as relating to paragraph 21(2)(h) of Schedule 5 (regard to be had to benefits that cease to be acquirable), include—
   (a) any benefits under a pension arrangement which, because of the dissolution or annulment of the civil partnership, one of the civil partners will lose the chance of acquiring, and
   (b) any PPF compensation which, because of the making of the dissolution or nullity order, a civil partner will lose the chance of acquiring entitlement to.
(6) The court, in exercising its powers under paragraph 9 in relation to a child of the family, must in particular have regard to the matters mentioned in paragraph 22(2) of Schedule 5.
(7) The court, in exercising its powers under paragraph 9 against a civil partner ('A') in favour of a child of the family who is not A's child, must also have regard to the matters mentioned in paragraph 22(3) of Schedule 5.
(8) Where an order has been made by a court outside England and Wales for—
   (a) the making of payments, or
   (b) the transfer of property,
   by one of the civil partners, the court in considering in accordance with this paragraph the financial resources of the other civil partner, or of a child of the family, shall have regard to the extent to which that order has been complied with or is likely to be complied with.
(9) In this paragraph—
   (a) 'pension arrangement' has the same meaning as in Part 4 of Schedule 5,
   (b) references to benefits under a pension arrangement include any benefits by way of pension, whether under a pension arrangement or not, and

(c) 'PPF compensation' has the same meaning as in Part 7 of Schedule 5.

Restriction of powers under paragraph 9 where jurisdiction depends on civil partnership home in England or Wales

11 (1) Sub-paragraphs (2) to (4) apply where the court has jurisdiction to entertain an application for an order under paragraph 9 only because a dwelling-house which was a civil partnership home of the civil partners is situated in England or Wales.

(2) The court may make under paragraph 9 any one or more of the following orders (but no other)—

   (a) an order that one of the civil partners shall pay to the other a specified lump sum;

   (b) an order that one of the civil partners shall pay to a child of the family, or to a specified person for the benefit of a child of the family, a specified lump sum;

   (c) an order that one of the civil partners shall transfer that civil partner's interest in the dwelling-house, or a specified part of that interest—

      (i) to the other,

      (ii) to a child of the family, or

      (iii) to a specified person for the benefit of a child of the family;

   (d) an order that a settlement of the interest of one of the civil partners in the dwelling-house, or a specified part of that interest, be made to the satisfaction of the court for the benefit of any one or more of—

      (i) the other civil partner and the children of the family, or

      (ii) either or any of them;

   (e) an order varying for the benefit of any one or more of—

      (i) the civil partners and the children of the family, or

      (ii) either or any of them,

   a relevant settlement so far as that settlement relates to an interest in the dwelling-house;

   (f) an order extinguishing or reducing the interest of either of the civil partners under a relevant settlement so far as that interest is an interest in the dwelling-house;

   (g) an order for the sale of the interest of one of the civil partners in the dwelling-house.

(3) Where under paragraph 9 the court makes just one order for the payment of a lump sum by one of the civil partners, the amount of the lump sum must not exceed the amount specified in sub-paragraph (5).

(4) Where under paragraph 9 the court makes two or more orders each of which is an order for the payment of a lump sum by the same civil partner, the total of the amounts of the lump sums must not exceed the amount specified in sub-paragraph (5).

(5) That amount is—

   (a) if the interest of the paying civil partner in the dwelling-house is sold in pursuance of an order made under sub-paragraph (2)(g), the amount of the proceeds of sale of that interest after deducting from those proceeds any costs incurred in the sale of that interest;

   (b) if that interest is not so sold, the amount which in the opinion of the court represents the value of that interest.

(6) Where the interest of one of the civil partners in the dwelling-house is held jointly or in common with any other person or persons—

    (a) the reference in sub-paragraph (2)(g) to the interest of one of the civil partners shall be construed as including a reference to the interest of that other person, or the interest of those other persons, in the dwelling-house, and

    (b) the reference in sub-paragraph (5)(a) to the amount of the proceeds of a sale ordered under sub-paragraph (2)(g) shall be construed as a reference to that part of those proceeds which is attributable to the interest of that civil partner in the dwelling-house.

(7) In sub-paragraph (2)—

'relevant settlement' means a settlement made, during the subsistence of the civil partnership or in anticipation of its formation, on the civil partners, including one made by will or codicil;

'specified' means specified in the order.

Consent orders under paragraph 9

12 (1) On an application for a consent order under paragraph 9, the court may make an order in the terms agreed on the basis only of the prescribed information furnished with the application.

(2) Sub-paragraph (1) does not apply if the court has reason to think that there are other circumstances into which it ought to inquire.

(3) Sub-paragraph (1) applies to an application for a consent order varying or discharging an order under paragraph 9 as it applies to an application for such an order.

(4) Sub-paragraph (1) applies despite paragraph 10.

(5) In this paragraph—

'consent order', in relation to an application for an order, means an order in the terms applied for to which the respondent agrees;

'prescribed' means prescribed by rules of court.

Orders for transfers of tenancies of dwelling-houses

13 (1) This paragraph applies if—

    (a) an application is made by one of the civil partners for an order under this paragraph, and

    (b) one of the civil partners is entitled, either in his own right or jointly with the other civil partner, to occupy a dwelling-house in England or Wales by virtue of a tenancy which is a relevant tenancy within the meaning of Schedule 7 to the Family Law Act 1996 (c. 27).

(2) The court may make in relation to that dwelling-house any order which it could make under Part 2 of that Schedule (order transferring tenancy or switching statutory tenants) if it had power to make a property adjustment order under Part 2 of Schedule 5 to this Act with respect to the civil partnership.

(3) The provisions of paragraphs 10, 11 and 14(1) of Schedule 7 to the Family Law Act 1996 (payments by transferee, pre-transfer liabilities and right of landlord to be heard) apply in relation to any order under this paragraph as they apply to any order under Part 2 of that Schedule.

Application to orders under paragraphs 5 and 9 of provisions of Schedule 5

14 (1) The following provisions of Schedule 5 apply in relation to an order made under paragraph 5 or 9 of this Schedule as they apply in relation to a like order made under that Schedule—

  (a) paragraph 3(1) to (3) and (7) (lump sums);

  (b) paragraph 11(2) to (4), 12(2), 13 and 14 (orders for sale);

  (c) paragraphs 17, 18 and 19(2) and (3) (pension sharing);

  (d) paragraphs 25 and 26 (orders under Part 1 relating to pensions);

  (e) paragraphs 31 to 37 (orders under Part 1 relating to pensions where Board has assumed responsibility for scheme);

  (f) paragraphs 47(1) to (4) and (6) and 49 (duration of orders);

  (g) paragraphs 50 to 54 and 57 to 62, except paragraph 50(1)(g) (variation etc. of orders);

  (h) paragraphs 63 to 65 (arrears and repayments);

  (i) paragraphs 76 to 79 (drafting of instruments, bankruptcy, mental disorder, and pension-sharing appeals).

  (2) Sub-paragraph (1)(d) does not apply where the court has jurisdiction to entertain an application for an order under paragraph 9 only because a dwelling-house which was a civil partnership home of the civil partners is situated in England or Wales.

  (3) Paragraph 27 of Schedule 5 (change of pension arrangement under which rights are shared) applies in relation to an order made under paragraph 9 of this Schedule - by virtue of sub-paragraph (1)(d) above as it applies to an order made under Part 1 of Schedule 5 by virtue of paragraph 25 or 26 of that Schedule.

  (4) The Lord Chancellor may by regulations make for the purposes of this Schedule - provision corresponding to any provision which may be made by him under paragraph 28(1) to (3) of Schedule 5 (supplementary provision about orders relating to pensions under Part 1 of that Schedule).

  (5) The power to make regulations under this paragraph is exercisable by statutory instrument which is subject to annulment in pursuance of a resolution of either House of Parliament.

Avoidance of transactions designed to defeat claims under paragraphs 5 and 9

15 (1) Sub-paragraphs (2) and (3) apply where one of the civil partners ('A') is granted leave under paragraph 4 to make an application for an order under paragraph 9.

  (2) If the court is satisfied, on application by A, that the other civil partner ('B') is, with the intention of defeating a claim by A, about to—

  (a) make any disposition, or

  (b) transfer out of the jurisdiction, or otherwise deal with, any property,

  it may make such order as it thinks fit for restraining B from doing so or otherwise for protecting the claim.

  (3) If the court is satisfied, on application by A—

  (a) that the other civil partner ('B') has, with the intention of defeating a claim by A, made a reviewable disposition, and

  (b) that, if the disposition were set aside—

    (i) financial relief under paragraph 5 or 9, or

    (ii) different financial relief under paragraph 5 or 9,

    would be granted to A,

it may make an order setting aside the disposition.

(4) If—

    (a) an order under paragraph 5 or 9 has been made by the court at the instance of one of the civil partners ('A'), and

    (b) the court is satisfied, on application by A, that the other civil partner ('B') has, with the intention of defeating a claim by A, made a reviewable disposition,

the court may make an order setting aside the disposition.

(5) Where the court has jurisdiction to entertain an application for an order under paragraph 9 only under paragraph 7(4), it shall not make any order under sub-paragraph (2), (3) or (4) in respect of any property other than the dwelling-house concerned.

(6) Where the court makes an order under sub-paragraph (3) or (4) setting aside a disposition, it shall give such consequential directions as it thinks fit for giving effect to the order (including directions requiring the making of any payments or the disposal of any property).

(7) For the purposes of sub-paragraphs (3) and (4), but subject to sub-paragraph (8), any disposition made by B is a 'reviewable disposition' (whether made before or after the commencement of A's application under that sub-paragraph).

(8) A disposition made by B is not a reviewable disposition for those purposes if made for valuable consideration (other than formation of a civil partnership) to a person who, at the time of the disposition, acted in relation to it in good faith and without notice of any intention on the part of B to defeat A's claim.

(9) A reference in this paragraph to defeating a claim by one of the civil partners is a reference to—

    (a) preventing financial relief being granted, or reducing the amount of financial relief which might be granted, under paragraph 5 or 9 at the instance of that civil partner, or

    (b) frustrating or impeding the enforcement of any order which might be, or has been, made under paragraph 5 or 9 at the instance of that civil partner.

Presumptions for the purposes of paragraph 15

16 (1) Sub-paragraph (3) applies where—

    (a) an application is made under paragraph 15(2) or (3) by one of the civil partners with respect to—

        (i) a disposition which took place less than 3 years before the date of the application, or

        (ii) a disposition or other dealing with property which is about to take place, and

    (b) the court is satisfied that the disposition or other dealing would (apart from paragraph 15 and this paragraph of this Schedule) have the consequence of defeating a claim by the applicant.

(2) Sub-paragraph (3) also applies where—

    (a) an application is made under paragraph 15(4) by one of the civil partners with respect to a disposition which took place less than 3 years before the date of the application, and

    (b) the court is satisfied that the disposition has had the consequence of defeating a claim by the applicant.

(3) It shall be presumed, unless the contrary is shown, that the person who—

    (a) disposed of, or

(b) is about to dispose of or deal with the property,

did so, or (as the case may be) is about to do so, with the intention of defeating the applicant's claim.

(4) A reference in this paragraph to defeating a claim by one of the civil partners has the meaning given by paragraph 15(9).

Part 2

Steps to Prevent Avoidance Prior to Application for Leave Under Paragraph 4

Prevention of transactions intended to defeat prospective claims under paragraphs 5 and 9

17 (1) If it appears to the court, on application by one of the persons ('A') who formed a civil partnership—

(a) that the civil partnership has been dissolved or annulled, or that the civil partners have been legally separated, by means of judicial or other proceedings in an overseas country,

(b) that A intends to apply for leave to make an application for an order under paragraph 9 as soon as he or she has been habitually resident in England and Wales for the period of one year, and

(c) that the other civil partner ('B') is, with the intention of defeating A's claim, about to—

(i) make any disposition, or

(ii) transfer out of the jurisdiction, or otherwise deal with, any property,

the court may make such order as it thinks fit for restraining B from taking such action as is mentioned in paragraph (c).

(2) Sub-paragraph (1) applies even if the date of the dissolution, annulment or legal separation is earlier than the date on which that sub-paragraph comes into force.

(3) Sub-paragraph (4) applies where—

(a) an application is made under sub-paragraph (1) with respect to—

(i) a disposition which took place less than 3 years before the date of the application, or

(ii) a disposition or other dealing with property which is about to take place, and

(b) the court is satisfied that the disposition or other dealing would (apart from this paragraph of this Schedule) have the consequence of defeating a claim by the applicant.

(4) It shall be presumed, unless the contrary is shown, that the person who—

(a) disposed of, or

(b) is about to dispose of or deal with the property,

did so, or (as the case may be) is about to do so, with the intention of defeating the applicant's claim.

(5) A reference in this paragraph to defeating a person's claim is a reference to preventing financial relief being granted, or reducing the amount of financial relief which might be granted, under paragraph 5 or 9 at the instance of that person.

Part 3

Supplementary

Paragraphs 15 to 17: meaning of 'disposition' and saving

18 (1) In paragraphs 15 to 17 'disposition' does not include any provision contained in a will or codicil but, with that exception, includes any conveyance, assurance or gift of property of any description, whether made by an instrument or otherwise.

(2) The provisions of paragraphs 15 to 17 are without prejudice to any power of the High Court to grant injunctions under section 37 of the Supreme Court Act 1981 (c. 54).

Interpretation of Schedule

19 In this Schedule—

'the court' means the High Court or, where a county court has jurisdiction by virtue of Part 5 of the Matrimonial and Family Proceedings Act 1984 (c. 42), a county court;

'dwelling-house' includes—

(a) any building, or part of a building, which is occupied as a dwelling, and

(b) any yard, garden, garage or outhouse belonging to, and occupied with, the dwelling-house;

'overseas country' has the meaning given by paragraph 1(3).

SCHEDULE 8

Section 81

HOUSING AND TENANCIES

Law of Property Act 1925 (c. 20)

1 (1) Amend section 149(6) (which includes provision for a lease determinable on mar-riage of the lessee to take effect as a lease for 90 years determinable by notice after the lessee's marriage) as follows.

(2) After 'or on the marriage of the lessee,' insert 'or on the formation of a civil partnership between the lessee and another person,'.

(3) For 'after the death or marriage (as the case may be) of the original lessee, or of the survivor of the original lessees,' substitute 'after (as the case may be) the death or marriage of, or the formation of a civil partnership by, the original lessee or the survivor of the original lessees,'.

Landlord and Tenant Act 1954 (c. 56)

2 In paragraph 1(e) of Schedule 3 (grounds for possession: premises required as resi-dence for landlord or family member), for the words from 'as a residence' to 'spouse, and' substitute 'as a residence for—

  (i)   himself,
  (ii) any son or daughter of his over eighteen years of age,
  (iii) his father or mother, or
  (iv) the father, or mother, of his spouse or civil partner,
and'.

Leasehold Reform Act 1967 (c. 88)

3   In section 1(1ZC)(c) (which refers to section 149(6) of the Law of Property Act 1925), after 'terminable after a death or marriage' insert 'or the formation of a civil partnership'.

4   In section 1B (which refers to a tenancy granted so as to become terminable by notice after a death or marriage), for 'a death or marriage' substitute 'a death, a marriage or the formation of a civil partnership'.

5 (1) Amend section 3(1) (meaning of 'long tenancy') as follows.

(2) In the words describing section 149(6) of the Law of Property Act 1925, after 'terminable after a death or marriage' insert 'or the formation of a civil partnership'.

(3) In the proviso (exclusion of certain tenancies terminable by notice after death or marriage)—

    (a) for 'a death or marriage' substitute 'a death, a marriage or the formation of a civil partnership', and

    (b) in paragraph (a), after 'marriage of' insert ', or the formation of a civil partnership by,'.

6 (1) Amend section 7 (rights of members of family succeeding to tenancy on death) as follows.

(2) In subsection (7) ('family member'), for 'wife or husband' (in each place) substitute 'spouse or civil partner'.

(3) In subsection (8) (surviving spouse's rights on intestacy)—

    (a) in paragraph (a), for 'wife or husband' substitute 'spouse or civil partner', and

    (b) in paragraph (b), for 'husband or wife' substitute 'spouse or civil partner'.

7   In section 18(3) (members of landlord's family whose residential rights exclude enfranchisement or extension), for 'wife or husband' (in each place) substitute 'spouse or civil partner'.

Caravan Sites Act 1968 (c. 52)

8   In section 3(2) ('occupier' includes surviving spouse of deceased occupier), for 'or widower' (in each place) substitute ', widower or surviving civil partner'.

Rent (Agriculture) Act 1976 (c. 80)

9 (1) Amend section 3 (protected occupiers by succession) as follows.

(2) For subsection (2) (succession by surviving spouse) substitute—

    '(2) Where the original occupier was a person who died leaving a surviving partner who was residing in the dwelling-house immediately before the original occupier's death then, after the original occupier's death, if the surviving partner has, in relation to the dwelling-house, a relevant licence or tenancy, the surviving partner shall be a protected occupier of the dwelling-house.'

(3) In subsection (3) (succession by other family members)—

(a) for 'surviving spouse' substitute 'surviving partner',

(b) for 'his' (in each place) substitute 'the original occupier's', and

(c) for 'him' substitute 'the original occupier'.

(4) After subsection (3) insert—

'(3A) In subsections (2) and (3) above "surviving partner" means surviving spouse or surviving civil partner.'

10 (1) Amend section 4 (statutory tenants and tenancies) as follows.

(2) For subsection (3) (surviving spouse's statutory tenancy) substitute—

'(3) If the original occupier was a person who died leaving a surviving partner who was residing in the dwelling-house immediately before the original occupier's death then, after the original occupier's death, unless the surviving partner is a protected occupier of the dwelling-house by virtue of section 3(2) above, the surviving partner shall be the statutory tenant if and so long as he occupies the dwelling-house as his residence.'

(3) In subsection (4) (statutory tenancy for other family members)—

(a) for 'surviving spouse' substitute 'surviving partner',

(b) for 'his' (in each place) substitute 'the original occupier's', and

(c) for 'him' substitute 'the original occupier'.

(4) For subsection (5A) (references to original occupier's spouse include person living with occupier as his or her wife or husband) substitute—

'(5ZA) In subsections (3) and (4) above "surviving partner" means surviving spouse or surviving civil partner.

(5A) For the purposes of subsection (3) above—

(a) a person who was living with the original occupier as his or her husband or wife shall be treated as the spouse of the original occupier, and

(b) a person who was living with the original occupier as if they were civil partners shall be treated as the civil partner of the original occupier,

and, subject to subsection (5B) below, "surviving spouse" and "surviving civil partner" in subsection (5ZA) above shall be construed accordingly.'

11 In section 31(3)(c) (power of Secretary of State and National Assembly for Wales to require information about occupiers of housing accommodation associated with agricultural or forestry land), after 'who has been married to' insert ', or has been the civil partner of,'.

12 In paragraph 1 of Case 9 in Part 1 of Schedule 4 (discretionary grounds for possession: dwelling required as residence for member of landlord's family), after 'husband' (in each place) insert 'or civil partner'.

Rent Act 1977 (c. 42)

13 (1) In Part 1 of Schedule 1 (statutory tenants by succession), amend paragraph 2 (succession by surviving spouse) as follows.

(2) In sub-paragraph (1), after 'surviving spouse' insert ', or surviving civil partner,'.

(3) For sub-paragraph (2) substitute—

'(2) For the purposes of this paragraph—

(a) a person who was living with the original tenant as his or her wife or husband shall be treated as the spouse of the original tenant, and

(b) a person who was living with the original tenant as if they were civil partners shall be treated as the civil partner of the original tenant.'

(4) In sub-paragraph (3), for the words after 'the county court' substitute 'shall for the purposes of this paragraph be treated (according to whether that one of them is of the opposite sex to, or of the same sex as, the original tenant) as the surviving spouse or the surviving civil partner.'

14 In Schedule 15 (grounds for possession), in Case 9 in Part 1 (dwelling required as residence for landlord or member of his family), for 'wife or husband' substitute 'spouse or civil partner'.

Protection from Eviction Act 1977 (c. 43)

15 In section 4(2)(b) (special provisions for agricultural employees: 'occupier' includes surviving spouse of former tenant), for 'widow or widower' (in each place) substitute 'surviving spouse or surviving civil partner'.

Housing Act 1980 (c. 51)

16 In section 54(2) (protected shorthold tenancy etc. may not be assigned except in pursuance of certain orders), after paragraph (c) insert ', or
(d) Part 2 of Schedule 5, or paragraph 9(2) or (3) of Schedule 7, to the Civil Partnership Act 2004 (property adjustment orders in connection with civil partnership proceedings or after overseas dissolution of civil partnership, etc.).'

17 In section 76(3) (which amends provisions of the Rent (Agriculture) Act 1976 replaced by this Schedule), for 'sections 3(2) and (3)(a) and 4(3) and (4)(a)' substitute 'sections 3(3)(a) and 4(4)(a)'.

Housing Act 1985 (c. 68)

18 In sections 39(2)(b) and 160(2)(b) (meaning of 'qualifying person' in definition of 'exempted disposal'), after 'the spouse or a former spouse' insert ', or the civil partner or a former civil partner,'.

19 In section 39(3) (disposals exempt if in pursuance of certain orders), after paragraph (d) insert ', or
(e) Part 2 or 3 of Schedule 5, or paragraph 9 of Schedule 7, to the Civil Partnership Act 2004 (property adjustment orders, or orders for the sale of property, in connection with civil partnership proceedings or after overseas dissolution of civil partnership, etc.).'

20 In section 87(a) (entitlement of tenant's spouse to succeed to secure tenancy), after 'spouse' insert 'or civil partner'.

21 (1) Amend section 88 (cases where secure tenant is a successor) as follows.
(2) In subsection (1)(d), for '(2) and (3)' substitute '(2) to (3)'.
(3) After subsection (2) insert—
'(2A) A tenant to whom the tenancy was assigned in pursuance of an order under Part 2 of Schedule 5, or paragraph 9(2) or (3) of Schedule 7, to the Civil Partnership Act 2004 (property adjustment orders in connection with civil partnership proceedings or after overseas dissolution of civil partnership, etc.) is a successor only if the other civil partner was a successor.'

22 (1) Amend section 89 (succession to periodic secured tenancy) as follows.
(2) In subsection (2)(a) (tenant's spouse is preferred successor), after 'spouse' insert 'or civil partner'.

(3) In subsection (3)(a), after 'parents)' in sub-paragraph (iii) insert ', or

(iv) Part 2 of Schedule 5, or paragraph 9(2) or (3) of Schedule 7, to the Civil Partnership Act 2004 (property adjustment orders in connection with civil partnership proceedings or after overseas dissolution of civil partnership, etc.)'.

23 In section 90(3)(a) (secure tenancy for term certain does not cease to be secure tenancy if vested under certain orders), after sub-paragraph (iii) insert—

'(iv) Part 2 of Schedule 5, or paragraph 9(2) or (3) of Schedule 7, to the Civil Partnership Act 2004 (property adjustment orders in connection with civil partnership proceedings or after overseas dissolution of civil partnership, etc.), or'.

24 In section 91(3)(b) (assignments not prohibited if in pursuance of certain orders), after 'parents)' in sub-paragraph (iii) insert ', or

(iv) Part 2 of Schedule 5, or paragraph 9(2) or (3) of Schedule 7, to the Civil Partnership Act 2004 (property adjustment orders in connection with civil partnership proceedings or after overseas dissolution of civil partnership, etc.)'.

25 In section 99B(2)(e) (subsection applies to assignees in pursuance of certain orders), after 'parents)' in sub-paragraph (iii) insert ', or

(iv) Part 2 of Schedule 5, or paragraph 9(2) or (3) of Schedule 7, to the Civil Partnership Act 2004 (property adjustment orders in connection with civil partnership proceedings or after overseas dissolution of civil partnership, etc.)'.

26 In section 101(3)(c) (assignees in pursuance of certain orders are qualifying successors), after 'parents)' in sub-paragraph (iii) insert ', or

(iv) Part 2 of Schedule 5, or paragraph 9(2) or (3) of Schedule 7, to the Civil Partnership Act 2004 (property adjustment orders in connection with civil partnership proceedings or after overseas dissolution of civil partnership, etc.)'.

27 (1) Amend sections 113 and 186 (meaning of 'member of a person's family' in Parts 3 and 4) as follows.

(2) In subsection (1)(a)—

(a) after 'spouse' insert 'or civil partner', and

(b) after 'live together as husband and wife' insert 'or as if they were civil partners'.

(3) In subsection (2)(a), after 'a relationship by marriage' insert 'or civil partnership'.

28 In section 123(2)(a) (family members with whom right to buy may be exercised), after 'is his spouse' insert ', is his civil partner'.

29 In section 130(3) (persons whose receipt of discount results in reduction of subsequent discount)—

(a) in paragraph (b), after 'spouse' insert ', or civil partner,' and

(b) in paragraph (c), after 'deceased spouse' insert ', or deceased civil partner,'.

30 In section 160(3) (right to buy: disposals in pursuance of certain orders are exempted), after paragraph (d) insert ', or

(e) Part 2 or 3 of Schedule 5, or paragraph 9 of Schedule 7, to the Civil Partnership Act 2004 (property adjustment orders, or orders for the sale of property, in connection with civil partnership proceedings or after overseas dissolution of civil partnership, etc.).'

31 In section 171B(4)(b) (persons who become tenants in pursuance of certain orders are qualifying successors), after sub-paragraph (iv) insert 'or

(v) an order under Part 2 of Schedule 5, or a property adjustment order under paragraph 9(2) or (3) of Schedule 7, to the Civil Partnership Act 2004 (property adjustment orders in connection with civil partnership proceedings or after overseas dissolution of civil partnership, etc.),'.

32 In section 554(2A) (grant by registered social landlords to former owner-occupier of defective dwelling), for paragraph (b) substitute—

'(b) is the spouse or civil partner, or a former spouse or former civil partner, or the surviving spouse or surviving civil partner, of a person falling within paragraph (a); or'.

33 In Part 1 of Schedule 2 (secure tenancies: grounds for possession if court considers possession reasonable), in ground 2A (violence by member of a couple)—

(a) for 'a married couple or' substitute 'a married couple, a couple who are civil partners of each other,' and

(b) after 'as husband or wife' insert 'or a couple living together as if they were civil partners'.

34 In paragraphs 2, 5 and 5A of Schedule 4 (qualifying period for right to buy and discount)—

(a) after 'deceased spouse' in paragraph (c) of each of those paragraphs insert ', or deceased civil partner,' and

(b) after 'spouse' (in each other place) insert 'or civil partner'.

35 (1) Amend Schedule 6A (redemption of landlord's share) as follows.

(2) In paragraph 1(2)(a) (meaning of 'excluded disposal'), after 'spouse' insert 'or civil partner'.

(3) In paragraph 1(2)(c) (disposals excluded if in pursuance of certain orders), after sub-paragraph (iv) insert 'or

(v) Part 2 or 3 of Schedule 5, or paragraph 9 of Schedule 7, to the Civil Partnership Act 2004 (property adjustment orders, or orders for the sale of property, in connection with civil partnership proceedings or after overseas dissolution of civil partnership, etc.),'.

(4) In paragraphs 4(3)(b) and 12(1), (2) and (3)(d), for 'qualifying spouse' substitute 'qualifying partner'.

(5) In paragraph 12(2) (which will define 'qualifying partner'), for paragraph (c) and the words after that paragraph substitute—

'(c) he—

(i) is the spouse, the civil partner, a former spouse, a former civil partner, the surviving spouse, the surviving civil partner, a surviving former spouse or a surviving former civil partner of the person who immediately before that time was entitled to the interest to which this paragraph applies or, as the case may be, the last remaining such interest, or

(ii) is the surviving spouse, the surviving civil partner, a surviving former spouse or a surviving former civil partner of a person who immediately before his death was entitled to such an interest.'

Agricultural Holdings Act 1986 (c. 5)

36 (1) In sections 35(2) and 49(3) (interpretation respectively of sections 36 to 48, and sections 49 to 58, etc.), amend the definition of 'close relative' as follows.

(2) In paragraph (a), for 'or husband' substitute ', husband or civil partner'.

(3) In paragraph (d), after 'marriage' (in each place) insert 'or civil partnership'.

37 In section 36 (eligible person may apply for new tenancy on death of tenant), after subsection (4) insert—

'(4A) In the case of the deceased's civil partner the reference in subsection (3)(a) above to the relative's agricultural work shall be read as a reference to agricultural work carried out by either the civil partner or the deceased (or both of them).'

38 In section 50 (eligible person may apply for new tenancy on retirement of tenant), after subsection (3) insert—

'(3A) In the case of the civil partner of the retiring tenant the reference in subsection (2)(a) above to the relative's agricultural work shall be read as a reference to agricultural work carried out by either the civil partner or the retiring tenant (or both of them).'

39 (1) Amend Schedule 6 (eligibility to apply for new tenancy under Part 4) as follows.

(2) In paragraph 1(2) (control of body corporate by deceased's close relative)—

(a) after 'or his spouse' insert 'or his civil partner', and

(b) after 'together' insert 'or he and his civil partner together'.

(3) In paragraph 1 (preliminary), after sub-paragraph (3) insert—

'(4) Any reference in this Schedule to the civil partner of a close relative of the deceased does not apply in relation to any time when the relative's civil partnership is subject to—

(a) a separation order under Chapter 2 of Part 2 of the Civil Partnership Act 2004, or

(b) a dissolution order, nullity order or presumption of death order that is a conditional order under that Chapter.'

(4) In paragraph 6(2) (no disregard of occupation by relative under tenancy granted by his spouse), after 'spouse' insert 'or civil partner'.

(5) In paragraph 9(1)(a) (occupation by spouse of relative treated as occupation by relative), after 'spouse' insert ', or civil partner,'.

(6) In paragraph 9(2) (cases involving joint occupation by spouse, or controlled body, and another)—

(a) for the words from 'joint occupation of land' to 'sub-paragraphs' substitute 'joint occupation of land by—

(a) his spouse or civil partner or a body corporate, and

(b) any other person or persons,

sub-paragraphs', and

(b) after 'spouse' (in the second place) insert 'or civil partner,'.

(7) In paragraph 10(3)(a) (meaning of 'connected person'), after 'spouse' insert 'or civil partner'.

(8) In the italic heading before each of paragraphs 9 and 10, after 'spouse' insert ', civil partner'.

Landlord and Tenant Act 1987 (c. 31)

40 (1) Amend section 4 (meaning of 'relevant disposal' for purposes of tenants' rights of first refusal) as follows.

(2) In subsection (2)(c) (disposals in pursuance of certain orders not relevant disposals), after sub-paragraph (vi) insert—

'(vii) Part 2 of Schedule 5, or paragraph 9(2) or (3) of Schedule 7, to the Civil Partnership Act 2004 (property adjustment orders in connection with civil partnership proceedings or after overseas dissolution of a civil partnership, etc.), or

(viii) Part 3 of Schedule 5, or paragraph 9(4) of Schedule 7, to the Civil Partnership Act 2004 (orders for the sale of property in connection with civil partnership proceedings or after overseas dissolution of a civil partnership, etc.) where the order includes provision requiring the property concerned to be offered for sale to a person or class of persons specified in the order;'.

(3) In subsection (5)(a)—
    (a) after 'spouse' insert 'or civil partner', and
    (b) after 'live together as husband and wife' insert 'or as if they were civil partners'.

(4) In subsection (6)(a), after 'a relationship by marriage' insert 'or civil partnership'.

Housing Act 1988 (c. 50)

41 (1) Amend section 17 (succession to assured periodic tenancy by spouse) as follows.

(2) In subsection (1), after 'spouse' (in each place) insert 'or civil partner'.

(3) For subsection (4) substitute—
    '(4) For the purposes of this section—
        (a) a person who was living with the tenant as his or her wife or husband shall be treated as the tenant's spouse, and
        (b) a person who was living with the tenant as if they were civil partners shall be treated as the tenant's civil partner.'

(4) In subsection (5), for the words after 'the county court' substitute 'shall for the purposes of this section be treated (according to whether that one of them is of the opposite sex to, or of the same sex as, the tenant) as the tenant's spouse or the tenant's civil partner.'

42 In section 82(1)(b) (after disposal by housing action trust, legal assistance may be given to surviving spouse of pre-disposal tenant), for 'or widower' substitute ', widower or surviving civil partner'.

43 (1) Amend Schedule 2 (assured tenancies: grounds for possession) as follows.

(2) In Part 1 (cases where court must order possession), in paragraph (b) of Ground 1 (landlord previously resident or requiring premises as residence for himself or his spouse), for 'his or his spouse's' substitute 'his, his spouse's or his civil partner's'.

(3) In Part 2 (cases where court may order possession), in Ground 14A (violence by member of a couple)—
    (a) for 'a married couple or' substitute 'a married couple, a couple who are civil partners of each other,' and
    (b) after 'as husband or wife' insert 'or a couple living together as if they were civil partners'.

44 (1) Amend paragraph 3 of Schedule 3 (agricultural worker condition where dwelling occupied by surviving spouse or family member of previous qualifying occupier) as follows.

(2) In sub-paragraphs (1)(c)(i), (3)(a) and (6), for 'widow or widower' substitute 'surviving partner'.

(3) For sub-paragraph (2) substitute—
    '(2) For the purposes of sub-paragraph (1)(c)(i) above and sub-paragraph (3) below—
        (a) "surviving partner" means widow, widower or surviving civil partner; and
        (b) a surviving partner of the previous qualifying occupier of the dwelling-

house is a qualifying surviving partner if that surviving partner was residing in the dwelling-house immediately before the previous qualifying occupier's death.'

(4) For sub-paragraph (5) (person living as wife or husband with previous occupier) substitute—

'(5) For the purposes of sub-paragraph (2)(a) above—

(a) a person who, immediately before the previous qualifying occupier's death, was living with the previous occupier as his or her wife or husband shall be treated as the widow or widower of the previous occupier, and

(b) a person who, immediately before the previous qualifying occupier's death, was living with the previous occupier as if they were civil partners shall be treated as the surviving civil partner of the previous occupier.'

45 (1) Amend paragraph 4 of Schedule 11 (exempted disposals by housing action trusts) as follows.

(2) In sub-paragraph (2)(b) (meaning of 'qualifying person' in definition of 'exempted disposal'), after 'the spouse or a former spouse' insert ', or the civil partner or a former civil partner,'.

(3) In sub-paragraph (4) (disposals in pursuance of certain orders), after paragraph (d) insert ', or

(e) Part 2 or 3 of Schedule 5, or paragraph 9 of Schedule 7, to the Civil Partnership Act 2004 (property adjustment orders, or orders for the sale of property, in connection with civil partnership proceedings or after overseas dissolution of civil partnership, etc.).'

Local Government and Housing Act 1989 (c. 42)

46 In paragraph 5(1)(c) of Schedule 10 (long residential tenancies: grounds for possession: premises required as residence for landlord or family member), for the words from 'as a residence' to 'mother and,' substitute 'as a residence for—

(i) himself,

(ii) any son or daughter of his over eighteen years of age,

(iii) his father or mother, or

(iv) the father, or mother, of his spouse or civil partner,

and,'.

Leasehold Reform, Housing and Urban Development Act 1993 (c. 28)

47 (1) Amend section 7 (meaning of 'long lease') as follows.

(2) In subsection (1)(b) (which refers to section 149(6) of the Law of Property Act 1925), after 'terminable after a death or marriage' insert 'or the formation of a civil partnership'.

(3) In subsection (2) (exclusion of certain leases terminable by notice after death or marriage)—

(a) for 'a death or marriage' substitute 'a death, a marriage or the formation of a civil partnership', and

(b) in paragraph (a), after 'marriage of' insert ', or the formation of a civil partnership by,'.

48 In section 10(5) (members of family of resident landlord), for 'wife or husband' (in each place) substitute 'spouse or civil partner'.

Agricultural Tenancies Act 1995 (c. 8)

49 In section 7(3) (which refers to section 149(6) of the Law of Property Act 1925), after 'marriage of' insert ', or formation of a civil partnership by,'.

Housing Act 1996 (c. 52)

50 (1) Amend section 15 (relevant and exempted disposals) as follows.

(2) In subsection (5)(b) (meaning of 'qualifying person' in the definition of 'exempted disposal'), after 'the spouse or a former spouse' insert ', or the civil partner or a former civil partner,'.

(3) In subsection (6) (disposals in pursuance of certain orders are exempt), after paragraph (d) insert '; or

(e) Part 2 or 3 of Schedule 5, or paragraph 9 of Schedule 7, to the Civil Partnership Act 2004 (property adjustment orders, or orders for the sale of property, in connection with civil partnership proceedings or after overseas dissolution of civil partnership, etc.).'

51 (1) Amend sections 62 and 140 (meaning of 'member of a person's family' in Part 1 and in Chapter 1 of Part 5) as follows.

(2) In subsection (1)(a)—

(a) after 'spouse' insert 'or civil partner', and

(b) after 'live together as husband and wife' insert 'or as if they were civil partners'.

(3) In subsection (2)(a), after 'a relationship by marriage' insert 'or civil partnership'.

52 In section 132 (introductory tenancies: cases where tenant is successor), after subsection (2) insert—

'(2A) A tenant to whom the tenancy was assigned in pursuance of an order under Part 2 of Schedule 5, or paragraph 9(2) or (3) of Schedule 7, to the Civil Partnership Act 2004 (property adjustment orders in connection with civil partnership proceedings or after overseas dissolution of civil partnership, etc.) is a successor only if the other civil partner was a successor.'

53 (1) Amend section 133 (succession to introductory tenancy) as follows.

(2) In subsection (2)(a) (spouse of deceased tenant is preferred successor), after 'spouse' insert 'or civil partner'.

(3) In subsection (3)(a) (tenancy ceases to be introductory on vesting otherwise than in pursuance of certain orders), after 'parents)' in sub-paragraph (iii) insert ', or

(iv) Part 2 of Schedule 5, or paragraph 9(2) or (3) of Schedule 7, to the Civil Partnership Act 2004 (property adjustment orders in connection with civil partnership proceedings or after overseas dissolution of civil partnership, etc.)'.

54 In section 134(2)(a) (introductory tenancy may not be assigned except in pursuance of certain orders), after 'parents)' in sub-paragraph (iii) insert ', or

(iv) Part 2 of Schedule 5, or paragraph 9(2) or (3) of Schedule 7, to the Civil Partnership Act 2004 (property adjustment orders in connection with civil partnership proceedings or after overseas dissolution of civil partnership, etc.)'.

55 In section 143H(5)(a) (two or more successors to demoted tenancy), for 'spouse or (if the tenant has no spouse)' substitute 'spouse or civil partner or (if the tenant has neither spouse nor civil partner)'.

56 In section 143I(3) (tenancy does not cease to be demoted tenancy if vested pursuant to certain orders), after paragraph (c) insert—

'(d) Part 2 of Schedule 5, or paragraph 9(2) or (3) of Schedule 7, to the Civil

Partnership Act 2004 (property adjustment orders in connection with civil partnership proceedings or after overseas dissolution of civil partnership, etc.).'

57 For paragraphs (a) and (b) of section 143J(5) (successor by assignment to secure tenancy terminated by demotion order) substitute—

'(a) the tenancy was assigned—

(i) in proceedings under section 24 of the Matrimonial Causes Act 1973 (property adjustment orders in connection with matrimonial proceedings) or section 17(1) of the Matrimonial and Family Proceedings Act 1984 (property adjustment orders after overseas divorce, etc.), or

(ii) in proceedings under Part 2 of Schedule 5, or paragraph 9(2) or (3) of Schedule 7, to the Civil Partnership Act 2004 (property adjustment orders in connection with civil partnership proceedings or after overseas dissolution of civil partnership, etc.),

(b) where the tenancy was assigned as mentioned in paragraph (a)(i), neither he nor the other party to the marriage was a successor, and

(c) where the tenancy was assigned as mentioned in paragraph (a)(ii), neither he nor the other civil partner was a successor.'

58 In section 143K(2) (demoted tenancy may be assigned only in pursuance of certain orders), after paragraph (c) insert—

'(d) Part 2 of Schedule 5, or paragraph 9(2) or (3) of Schedule 7, to the Civil Partnership Act 2004 (property adjustment orders in connection with civil partnership proceedings or after overseas dissolution of civil partnership, etc.).'

59 (1) Amend section 143P (meaning of 'member of another's family') as follows.

(2) In subsection (1)(a), after 'spouse' insert 'or civil partner'.

(3) In subsection (3)(a), after 'marriage' insert 'or civil partnership'.

60 In section 160 (cases where provisions about allocations do not apply), in each of subsections (2)(e) and (3)(d) (cases where secure or introductory tenancy vests etc. in pursuance of certain orders), after sub-paragraph (iii) insert ', or

(iv) Part 2 of Schedule 5, or paragraph 9(2) or (3) of Schedule 7, to the Civil Partnership Act 2004 (property adjustment orders in connection with civil partnership proceedings or after overseas dissolution of civil partnership, etc.).'

61 (1) Amend section 178 (meaning of 'associated person' in Part 7) as follows.

(2) In subsection (1), after paragraph (a) insert—

'(aa) they are or have been civil partners of each other;'.

(3) In subsection (1), after paragraph (e) insert—

'(ea) they have entered into a civil partnership agreement between them (whether or not that agreement has been terminated);'.

(4) In subsection (3), after the definition of 'child' insert—

' "civil partnership agreement" has the meaning given by section 73 of the Civil Partnership Act 2004;'.

(5) In subsection (3), for the definition of 'cohabitants' substitute—

' "cohabitants" means—

(a) a man and a woman who, although not married to each other, are living together as husband and wife, or

(b) two people of the same sex who, although not civil partners of each other, are living together as if they were civil partners;

and "former cohabitants" shall be construed accordingly;'.

(6) In subsection (3), in each of paragraphs (a) and (b) of the definition of 'relative', for 'spouse or former spouse' substitute 'spouse, civil partner, former spouse or former civil partner'.

(7) In paragraph (b) of that definition, for 'affinity' substitute 'marriage or civil partnership'.

Housing Grants, Construction and Regeneration Act 1996 (c. 53)

62 In section 30(6)(a) (power to provide for financial position of others to be taken into account in means-testing applicant for grant), after 'his spouse,' insert 'his civil partner,'.

63 (1) In section 54(3) (disposals in pursuance of certain orders are exempt) as it has effect by virtue of Article 11(2) of the 2002 Order (saving for certain purposes of repealed provisions), after paragraph (d) insert '; or

(e) Part 2 or 3 of Schedule 5, or paragraph 9 of Schedule 7, to the Civil Partnership Act 2004 (property adjustment orders, or orders for the sale of property, in connection with civil partnership proceedings or after overseas dissolution of civil partnership, etc.).'

(2) In sub-paragraph (1) 'the 2002 Order' means the Regulatory Reform (Housing Assistance) (England and Wales) Order 2002 (S.I. 2002/1860).

Commonhold and Leasehold Reform Act 2002 (c. 15)

64 In section 76(2)(c) (which refers to section 149(6) of the Law of Property Act 1925), after 'terminable after a death or marriage' insert 'or the formation of a civil partnership'.

65 In section 77(1) ('long lease': exclusion of certain leases terminable by notice after death or marriage)—

(a) for 'a death or marriage' substitute 'a death, a marriage or the formation of a civil partnership', and

(b) in paragraph (a), after 'marriage of' insert ', or the formation of a civil partnership by,'.

66 In paragraph 3(8) of Schedule 6 (members of freeholder's family whose occupation of premises excludes premises from right to manage), after 'spouse' (in each place) insert 'or civil partner'.

SCHEDULE 9

Section 82

FAMILY HOMES AND DOMESTIC VIOLENCE

Part 1

Amendments of the Family Law Act 1996 (c. 27)

1 (1) Amend section 30 (rights concerning matrimonial home where one spouse has no estate, etc.) as follows.

(2) In subsection (1)—
    (a) in paragraph (a)—
        (i) after 'one spouse' insert 'or civil partner ("A")', and
        (ii) for 'that spouse' substitute 'A'.
    (b) in paragraph (b), after 'other spouse' insert 'or civil partner ("B")'.
(3) In subsection (2)—
    (a) for 'the spouse not so entitled' substitute 'B',
    (b) for '("matrimonial home rights")' substitute '("home rights")', and
    (c) in paragraph (a), for 'the other spouse' substitute 'A'.
(4) In subsection (3)—
    (a) for 'a spouse' and for 'that spouse' substitute 'B', and
    (b) for 'the other spouse' (in both places) substitute 'A'.
(5) In subsection (4)—
    (a) for 'A spouse's' substitute 'B's',
    (b) in paragraph (a), for 'by the other spouse as the other spouse's' substitute 'by A as A's', and
    (c) in paragraph (b)—
        (i) for 'the spouse occupies the dwelling-house as that spouse's' substitute 'B occupies the dwelling-house as B's', and
        (ii) for 'by the other spouse as the other spouse's' substitute 'by A as A's'.
(6) In subsection (5)—
    (a) for 'a spouse ("the first spouse")' substitute 'B', and
    (b) in paragraph (b), for 'the other spouse ("the second spouse")' substitute 'A',
    (c) for 'the second spouse' substitute 'A', and
    (d) for 'the first spouse against the second spouse' substitute 'B against A'.
(7) In subsection (6)—
    (a) for 'a spouse' substitute 'B', and
    (b) for 'the other spouse' (in both places) substitute 'A'.
(8) In subsection (7), for the words from first 'which' to the end substitute 'which—
    (a) in the case of spouses, has at no time been, and was at no time intended by them to be, a matrimonial home of theirs; and
    (b) in the case of civil partners, has at no time been, and was at no time intended by them to be, a civil partnership home of theirs.'
(9) In subsection (8)—
    (a) for 'A spouse's matrimonial home rights' substitute 'B's home rights',
    (b) in paragraph (a), after 'marriage' insert 'or civil partnership', and
    (c) in paragraph (b), for 'the other spouse' substitute 'A'.
(10) In subsection (9)—
    (a) for 'a spouse' (in both places) substitute 'a person', and
    (b) for 'matrimonial home rights' substitute 'home rights'.
(11) In the heading to section 30, for 'matrimonial home where one spouse' substitute 'home where one spouse or civil partner' and, in the preceding cross-heading, after 'matrimonial' insert 'or civil partnership'.
2 (1) Amend section 31 (effect of matrimonial home rights as charge on dwelling-house) as follows.
(2) In subsection (1) for 'marriage, one spouse' substitute 'marriage or civil partnership, A'.

(3) In subsection (2) for 'The other spouse's matrimonial home rights' substitute 'B's home rights'.

(4) In subsection (3)—

    (a) in paragraph (a), for 'the spouse so entitled' substitute 'A', and

    (b) in paragraph (b), after 'marriage' insert 'or of the formation of the civil partnership'.

(5) In subsection (4)—

    (a) for 'a spouse's matrimonial home rights' substitute 'B's home rights',

    (b) for 'the other spouse' substitute 'A', and

    (c) for 'either of the spouses' substitute 'A or B'.

(6) In subsection (5) for 'the other spouse' substitute 'A'.

(7) In subsection (7) for 'the spouses' substitute 'A and B'.

(8) In subsection (8)—

    (a) for 'a spouse's matrimonial home rights' substitute 'B's home rights',

    (b) in paragraph (a), for 'the other spouse' substitute 'A', and

    (c) in paragraph (b), after 'marriage' insert 'or civil partnership'.

(9) In subsection (9)—

    (a) in paragraph (a), for 'a spouse's matrimonial home rights' substitute 'B's home rights', and

    (b) for 'the other spouse' (in both places) substitute 'A'.

(10) In subsection (10)—

    (a) for 'a spouse' and for 'that spouse' substitute 'A', and

    (b) in paragraph (b), for 'a spouse's matrimonial home rights' substitute 'B's home rights'.

(11) For subsection (12)(a) substitute—

    '(a) B's home rights are a charge on the estate of A or of trustees of A, and'.

(12) In the heading to section 31, for 'matrimonial home rights' substitute 'home rights'.

3   For section 32 (further provisions relating to matrimonial home rights) substitute—

'32 Further provisions relating to home rights

    Schedule 4 (provisions supplementary to sections 30 and 31) has effect.'

4 (1) Amend section 33 (occupation orders where applicant has estate or interest etc. or has matrimonial home rights) as follows.

(2) In subsection (1)(a)(ii), for 'matrimonial home rights' substitute 'home rights'.

(3) After subsection (2) insert—

    '(2A) If a civil partnership agreement (as defined by section 73 of the Civil Partnership Act 2004) is terminated, no application under this section may be made by virtue of section 62(3)(eza) by reference to that agreement after the end of the period of three years beginning with the day on which it is terminated.'

(4) In subsection (3)(e)—

    (a) for 'matrimonial home rights' substitute 'home rights', and

    (b) after 'spouse' insert 'or civil partner'.

(5) In subsection (4), for 'matrimonial home rights' substitute 'home rights'.

(6) In subsection (5)—

    (a) for 'matrimonial home rights' substitute 'home rights',

    (b) after 'is the other spouse' insert 'or civil partner',

(c) after 'during the marriage' insert 'or civil partnership',

(d) in paragraph (a), after 'spouse' insert 'or civil partner', and

(e) in paragraph (b), after 'marriage' insert 'or civil partnership'.

(7) In the heading to section 33, for 'matrimonial home rights' substitute 'home rights'.

5   In section 34 (effect of order under section 33 where rights are charge on dwelling-house), in subsection (1)—

(a) for 'a spouse's matrimonial home rights' substitute 'B's home rights', and

(b) for 'the other spouse' (in each place) substitute 'A'.

6 (1) Amend section 35 (one former spouse with no existing right to occupy) as follows.

(2) In subsection (1)(a) and (b), after 'former spouse' insert 'or former civil partner'.

(3) For subsection (1)(c) substitute—

'(c) the dwelling-house—

(i)   in the case of former spouses, was at any time their matrimonial home or was at any time intended by them to be their matrimonial home, or

(ii) in the case of former civil partners, was at any time their civil partnership home or was at any time intended by them to be their civil partnership home.'

(4) In subsection (2), after 'former spouse' (in both places) insert 'or former civil partner'.

(5) In subsection (6)(f), after 'marriage' insert 'or civil partnership'.

(6) After subsection (6)(g)(i), insert—

'(ia) for a property adjustment order under Part 2 of Schedule 5 to the Civil Partnership Act 2004;=.

(7) In subsection (9)(a), after 'former spouses' insert 'or former civil partners'.

(8) In subsections (11) and (12), after 'former spouse' insert 'or former civil partner'.

(9) For subsection (13)(a) and (b) substitute—

'(a) as if he were B (the person entitled to occupy the dwelling-house by virtue of that section); and

(b) as if the respondent were A (the person entitled as mentioned in subsection (1)(a) of that section).'

(10) In the heading to section 35, after 'former spouse' insert 'or former civil partner'.

7   In section 36 (one cohabitant or former cohabitant with no existing right to occupy), for subsection (13)(a) and (b) substitute—

'(a) as if he were B (the person entitled to occupy the dwelling-house by virtue of that section); and

(b) as if the respondent were A (the person entitled as mentioned in subsection (1)(a) of that section).'

8 (1) Amend section 37 (neither spouse entitled to occupy) as follows.

(2) After subsection (1) insert—

'(1A) This section also applies if—

(a) one civil partner or former civil partner and the other civil partner or former civil partner occupy a dwelling-house which is or was the civil partnership home; but

(b) neither of them is entitled to remain in occupation—

(i)by virtue of a beneficial estate or interest or contract; or (ii)by virtue of any enactment giving him the right to remain in occupation.'

(3) In subsection (3)(b), for 'spouses' substitute 'parties'.

(4) In the heading to section 37, after 'spouse' insert 'or civil partner'.

9   In section 42 (non-molestation orders), after subsection (4) insert—

'(4ZA) If a civil partnership agreement (as defined by section 73 of the Civil Partnership Act 2004) is terminated, no application under this section may be made by virtue of section 62(3)(eza) by reference to that agreement after the end of the period of three years beginning with the day on which it is terminated.'

10 (1) In section 44 (evidence of agreement to marry), after subsection (2) insert—

'(3) Subject to subsection (4), the court shall not make an order under section 33 or 42 by virtue of section 62(3)(eza) unless there is produced to it evidence in writing of the existence of the civil partnership agreement (as defined by section 73 of the Civil Partnership Act 2004).

(4) Subsection (3) does not apply if the court is satisfied that the civil partnership agreement was evidenced by—

(a) a gift by one party to the agreement to the other as a token of the agreement, or

(b) a ceremony entered into by the parties in the presence of one or more other persons assembled for the purpose of witnessing the ceremony.'

(2) In the heading to section 44, after 'marry' insert 'or form a civil partnership'.

11   In section 49 (variation and discharge of orders), in subsection (3)—

(a) for 'a spouse's matrimonial home rights' substitute 'B's home rights are, under section 31,', and

(b) for 'the other spouse' (in each place) substitute 'A'.

12 (1) Amend section 54 (dwelling-house subject to mortgage) as follows.

(2) In subsections (3)(a) and (4), for 'matrimonial home rights' substitute 'home rights'.

(3) In subsection (5), after 'spouse, former spouse' insert ', civil partner, former civil partner'.

13 (1) Amend section 62 (meaning of 'cohabitants', 'relevant child' and 'associated persons') as follows.

(2) In subsection (1)—

(a) in paragraph (a), for 'two persons who, although not married to each other, are living together as husband and wife or (if of the same sex) in an equivalent relationship;' substitute 'two persons who are neither married to each other nor civil partners of each other but are living together as husband and wife or as if they were civil partners;', and

(b) in paragraph (b), after 'have subsequently married each other' insert 'or become civil partners of each other'.

(3) After subsection (3)(a) insert—

'(aa) they are or have been civil partners of each other;'.

(4) After subsection (3)(e) insert—

'(eza) they have entered into a civil partnership agreement (as defined by section 73 of the Civil Partnership Act 2004) (whether or not that agreement has been terminated);'.

14 (1) Amend section 63 (interpretation of Part 4) as follows.

(2) In subsection (1), after the definition of 'health' insert—

' "home rights" has the meaning given by section 30;'.

(3) Omit the definition of 'matrimonial home rights' in that subsection.

(4) In the definition of relative in that subsection—

    (a) in paragraphs (a) and (b), for 'spouse or former spouse' substitute 'spouse, former spouse, civil partner or former civil partner',

    (b) in paragraph (b), for 'by affinity)' substitute 'by marriage or civil partnership)', and

    (c) after 'were married to each other' insert 'or were civil partners of each other'.

(5) After subsection (2)(i) insert—

'(j) Schedules 5 to 7 to the Civil Partnership Act 2004.'

15 (1) Amend Schedule 4 (provisions supplementary to sections 30 and 31) as follows.

(2) In paragraph 2, after 'spouse' (in both places) insert 'or civil partner'.

(3) In paragraph 3(1) and (3), after 'spouse' insert 'or civil partner'.

(4) In paragraph 4(1), for 'spouse's matrimonial home rights' substitute 'spouse's or civil partner's home rights'.

(5) For paragraphs 4(1)(a) to (c) substitute—

    '(a) in the case of a marriage—

        (i) by the production of a certificate or other sufficient evidence, that either spouse is dead,

        (ii) by the production of an official copy of a decree or order of a court, that the marriage has been terminated otherwise than by death, or

        (iii) by the production of an order of the court, that the spouse's home rights constituting the charge have been terminated by the order, and

    (b) in the case of a civil partnership—

        (i) by the production of a certificate or other sufficient evidence, that either civil partner is dead,

        (ii) by the production of an official copy of an order or decree of a court, that the civil partnership has been terminated otherwise than by death, or

        (iii) by the production of an order of the court, that the civil partner's home rights constituting the charge have been terminated by the order.'

(6) In paragraph 4(2)—

    (a) in paragraph (a)—

        (i) after 'marriage' insert 'or civil partnership', and

        (ii) after 'spouse' insert 'or civil partner', and

    (b) in paragraph (b), after 'spouse' insert 'or civil partner'.

(7) In paragraph 4(3), after 'spouse' insert 'or civil partner'.

(8) In the heading to paragraph 4, after 'marriage' insert 'or civil partnership'.

(9) In paragraph 5(1), for 'spouse entitled to matrimonial home rights' substitute 'spouse or civil partner entitled to home rights'.

(10) In paragraph 5(2)—

    (a) for 'matrimonial home rights' substitute 'home rights', and

    (b) in paragraph (a), after 'spouse' insert 'or civil partner'.

(11) In the heading to paragraph 5, for 'matrimonial home rights' substitute 'home rights'.

(12) In paragraph 6, after 'spouse' (in both places) insert 'or civil partner'.

16 (1) Amend Schedule 7 (transfer of certain tenancies on divorce etc. or on separation of cohabitants) as follows.

(2) In paragraph 1, before the definition of 'cohabitant' insert—

' "civil partner", except in paragraph 2, includes (where the context requires) former civil partner;'.

(3) In paragraph 2(1), after 'spouse' (in both places) insert 'or civil partner'.

(4) For paragraph 2(2) substitute—

'(2) The court may make a Part II order—

(a) on granting a decree of divorce, a decree of nullity of marriage or a decree of judicial separation or at any time thereafter (whether, in the case of a decree of divorce or nullity of marriage, before or after the decree is made absolute), or

(b) at any time when it has power to make a property adjustment order under Part 2 of Schedule 5 to the Civil Partnership Act 2004 with respect to the civil partnership.'

(5) Omit 'or' at the end of paragraph 4(a) and insert—

'(aa) in the case of civil partners, a civil partnership home; or'.

(6) In paragraph 5(a), after 'spouses' insert ', civil partners'.

(7) In paragraph 6—

(a) after 'spouse' (in the first place) insert ', a civil partner', and

(b) after 'spouse' (in the second place) insert ', civil partner'.

(8) In paragraph 7(1) and (2), after 'spouse' (in each place) insert ', civil partner'.

(9) For paragraph 7(3) to (4) substitute—

'(3) If the spouse, civil partner or cohabitant so entitled is a successor within the meaning of Part 4 of the Housing Act 1985—

(a) his former spouse (or, in the case of judicial separation, his spouse),

(b) his former civil partner (or, if a separation order is in force, his civil partner), or

(c) his former cohabitant,

is to be deemed also to be a successor within the meaning of that Part.

(3A) If the spouse, civil partner or cohabitant so entitled is a successor within the meaning of section 132 of the Housing Act 1996—

(a) his former spouse (or, in the case of judicial separation, his spouse),

(b) his former civil partner (or, if a separation order is in force, his civil partner), or

(c) his former cohabitant,

is to be deemed also to be a successor within the meaning of that section.

(4) If the spouse, civil partner or cohabitant so entitled is for the purposes of section 17 of the Housing Act 1988 a successor in relation to the tenancy or occupancy—

(a) his former spouse (or, in the case of judicial separation, his spouse),

(b) his former civil partner (or, if a separation order is in force, his civil partner), or

(c) his former cohabitant,

is to be deemed to be a successor in relation to the tenancy or occupancy for the purposes of that section.'

(10) In paragraph 7(5)(a), after 'spouse' insert ', civil partner'.

(11) Omit paragraph 7(6).

(12) In paragraph 8(1) and (2)(a) and (b), after 'spouse' insert ', civil partner'.

(13) In paragraph 8(3), after 'surviving spouse' insert 'or surviving civil partner'.

(14) In paragraphs 9(1), (2)(a) and (b) and (3) (in both places) and 10(1) (in both places), after 'spouse' insert ', civil partner'.

(15) In paragraph 11(1), after 'spouses' insert ', civil partners'.

(16) In paragraph 11(2), after 'spouse' insert ', civil partner'.

(17) For paragraph 12 and the heading preceding it, substitute—

'Date when order made between spouses or civil partners takes effect

12 The date specified in a Part II order as the date on which the order is to take effect must not be earlier than—

    (a) in the case of a marriage in respect of which a decree of divorce or nullity has been granted, the date on which the decree is made absolute;

    (b) in the case of a civil partnership in respect of which a dissolution or nullity order has been made, the date on which the order is made final.'

(18) For paragraph 13 and the heading preceding it substitute—

'Effect of remarriage or subsequent civil partnership

13 (1) If after the grant of a decree dissolving or annulling a marriage either spouse remarries or forms a civil partnership, that spouse is not entitled to apply, by reference to the grant of that decree, for a Part II order.

(2) If after the making of a dissolution or nullity order either civil partner forms a subsequent civil partnership or marries, that civil partner is not entitled to apply, by reference to the making of that order, for a Part II order.

(3) In sub-paragraphs (1) and (2)—

    (a) the references to remarrying and marrying include references to cases where the marriage is by law void or voidable, and

    (b) the references to forming a civil partnership include references to cases where the civil partnership is by law void or voidable.'

(19) In paragraph 15(1)—

    (a) after 'spouse' insert 'or civil partner', and

    (b) for 'spouse's matrimonial home rights' substitute 'spouse's or civil partner's home rights'.

(20) In paragraph 15(2), after 'spouse' insert ', civil partner'.

Part 2

Consequential Amendments

Land Compensation Act 1973 (c. 26)

17 (1) Amend section 29A (spouses having statutory rights of occupation) as follows.

(2) In subsection (1)—

    (a) for 'one spouse ("A")' substitute 'one spouse or civil partner ("A")', and

    (b) for 'the other spouse ("B") acquires matrimonial home rights' substitute 'the other spouse or civil partner ("B") acquires home rights'.

(3) In subsection (2) for 'matrimonial home rights' substitute 'home rights'.

(4) In the heading to section 29A, after 'spouses' insert 'and civil partners'.

Housing Act 1985 (c. 68)

18 (1) Amend section 85 (extended discretion of court in certain proceedings for possession) as follows.

(2) In subsection (5)—

    (a) in paragraph (a) for 'tenant's spouse or former spouse, having matrimonial home rights' substitute 'tenant's spouse or former spouse, or civil partner or former civil partner, having home rights',

    (b) after 'the spouse or former spouse' insert ', or the civil partner or former civil partner,', and

    (c) for 'those matrimonial home rights' substitute 'those home rights'.

(3) In subsection (5A)—

    (a) in paragraph (a), for 'former spouse of the tenant' substitute 'former spouse or former civil partner of the tenant', and

    (b) in paragraph (b) and in the words following paragraph (c) after 'former spouse,' insert 'former civil partner,'.

19 In section 99B (persons qualifying for compensation) in subsection (2)(f), after 'spouse, former spouse,' insert 'civil partner, former civil partner,'.

20 In section 101 (rent not to be increased on account of tenant's improvements) in subsection (3)(d), after 'spouse, former spouse,' insert 'civil partner, former civil partner,'.

Insolvency Act 1986 (c. 45)

21 (1) Amend section 336 (rights of occupation etc. of bankrupt's spouse) as follows.

(2) In subsection (1), for 'matrimonial home rights' substitute 'home rights'.

(3) In subsection (2)—

    (a) for 'a spouse's matrimonial home rights' substitute 'a spouse's or civil partner's home rights', and

    (b) after 'the other spouse' (in each place) insert 'or civil partner'.

(4) In subsection (4)(b) and (c) after 'spouse or former spouse' insert 'or civil partner or former civil partner'.

(5) In the heading to section 336 after 'spouse' insert 'or civil partner'.

22 (1) Amend section 337 (rights of occupation of bankrupt) as follows.

(2) In subsection (2), for 'spouse (if any) has matrimonial home rights' substitute 'spouse or civil partner (if any) has home rights'.

(3) In subsection (3)—

    (a) in paragraph (a), for 'matrimonial home rights' substitute 'home rights', and

    (b) in paragraph (c), after 'spouse' insert 'or civil partner'.

Housing Act 1988 (c. 50)

23 (1) Amend section 9 (extended discretion of court in possession claims) as follows.

(2) In subsection (5)—

    (a) for 'tenant's spouse or former spouse, having matrimonial home rights' substitute 'tenant's spouse or former spouse, or civil partner or former civil partner, having home rights',

    (b) after 'the spouse or former spouse' insert ', or the civil partner or former civil partner', and

    (c) for 'those matrimonial home rights' substitute 'those home rights'.

(3) In subsection (5A)—

    (a) for 'former spouse of the tenant' substitute 'former spouse or former civil partner of the tenant',

    (b) for 'cohabitant, former cohabitant or former spouse' (in both places) substitute 'former spouse, former civil partner, cohabitant or former cohabitant'.

Commonhold and Leasehold Reform Act 2002 (c. 15)

24 (1) Amend section 61 (matrimonial rights) as follows.

(2) For 'matrimonial home rights (within the meaning of section 30(2) of the Family Law Act 1996 (c. 27) (matrimonial home))' substitute 'home rights (within the meaning of section 30(2) of the Family Law Act 1996 (c. 27) (rights in respect of matrimonial or civil partnership home))'.

(3) In the heading to section 61 for 'Matrimonial' substitute 'Home'.

Part 3

Transitional Provision

25 (1) Any reference (however expressed) in any enactment, instrument or document (whether passed or made before or after the passing of this Act)—

    (a) to rights of occupation under, or within the meaning of, the Matrimonial Homes Act 1983 (c. 19), or

    (b) to matrimonial home rights under, or within the meaning of, Part 4 of the Family Law Act 1996 (c. 27),

is to be construed, so far as is required for continuing the effect of the enactment, instrument or document, as being or as the case requires including a reference to home rights under, or within the meaning of, Part 4 of the 1996 Act as amended by this Schedule.

(2) Any reference (however expressed) in Part 4 of the 1996 Act or in any other enactment, instrument or document (including any enactment amended by this Schedule) to home rights under, or within the meaning of, Part 4 of the 1996 Act is to be construed as including, in relation to times, circumstances and purposes before the commencement of this Schedule, references to rights of occupation under, or within the meaning of, the 1983 Act and to matrimonial home rights under, or within the meaning of, Part 4 of the 1996 Act without the amendments made by this Schedule.

. . .

SCHEDULE 20

Section 213

MEANING OF OVERSEAS RELATIONSHIP: SPECIFIED RELATIONSHIPS

A relationship is specified for the purposes of section 213 (meaning of 'overseas relationship') if it is registered in a country or territory given in the first column of the table and fits the description given in relation to that country or territory in the second column—

Country or territory	Description
Belgium	cohabitation légale (statutory cohabitation)
Belgium	marriage
Canada: Nova Scotia	domestic partnership
Canada: Quebec	civil union
Denmark	registreret partnerskab (registered partnership)
Finland	rekisteröity parisuhde (registered partnership)
France	pacte civile de solidarité (civil solidarity pact)
Germany	Lebenspartnerschaft (life partnership)
Iceland	staðfesta samvist (confirmed cohabitation)
Netherlands	geregistreerde partnerschap (registered partnership)
Netherlands	marriage
Norway	registrert partnerskap (registered partnership)
Sweden	registrerat partnerskap (registered partnership)
United States of America: Vermont	civil union

SCHEDULE 21

Section 247

REFERENCES TO STEPCHILDREN ETC. IN EXISTING ACTS

1 The Declinature Act 1681 (c. 79) (Senators of College of Justice not to sit in causes of persons related to them).
2 Section 21 of the Small Landholders (Scotland) Act 1911 (c. 49) (assignment of holding).
3 Section 68(2)(e) of the Marriage Act 1949 (c. 76) (solemnisation of marriages of stepchildren of servicemen in naval, military and air force chapels etc.).
4 Section 7(7) of the Leasehold Reform Act 1967 (c. 88) (rights of members of family succeeding to tenancy on death: member of another's family).
5 Section 18(3) of that Act (residential rights and exclusion of enfranchisement or extension: adult member of another's family).
6 Section 2(2) of the Employers' Liability (Compulsory Insurance) Act 1969 (c. 57) (employees to be covered).
7 Section 27(5) of the Parliamentary and other Pensions Act 1972 (c. 48) (pensions for dependants of Prime Minister or Speaker).
8 Section 184(5) of the Consumer Credit Act 1974 (c. 39) (associates).
9 Section 1(5) of the Fatal Accidents Act 1976 (c. 30) (right of action for wrongful act causing death: who are dependants).
10 The definition of 'relative' in section 31(1) of the Credit Unions Act 1979 (c. 34) (interpretation, etc.).

11 Section 32(3) of the Estate Agents Act 1979 (c. 38) ('associate': meaning of relative).

12 Section 13(1) of the Administration of Justice Act 1982 (c. 53) (deduction of relationships).

13 Section 12(5) of the Mental Health Act 1983 (c. 20) (general provisions as to medical recommendations: persons who may not give recommendations).

14 Section 25C(10) of that Act (supervision applications: meaning of 'close relative').

15 Section 5(3) of the Mobile Homes Act 1983 (c. 34) (interpretation: member of another's family).

16 Section 153(4) of the Companies Act 1985 (c. 6) (transactions not prohibited by section 151).

17 Section 203(1) of that Act (notification of family and corporate interests: person interested in shares).

18 Section 327(2) of that Act (extension of section 323 to spouses and children).

19 Section 328(8) of that Act (extension of section 324 to spouses and children).

20 Section 346(2) of that Act ('connected persons').

21 Section 430E(8) of that Act (associates).

22 Section 742A(6) of that Act (meaning of 'offer to the public').

23 Section 74(4)(a) of the Bankruptcy (Scotland) Act 1985 (c. 66) (meaning of 'associate').

24 Section 113(2) of the Housing Act 1985 (c. 68) (members of a person's family).

25 Section 186(2) of that Act (members of a person's family).

26 Section 105(2) of the Housing Associations Act 1985 (c. 69) (members of a person's family).

27 Section 20(6) of the Airports Act 1986 (c. 31) (powers of investment and disposal in relation to public airport companies).

28 Section 435(8) of the Insolvency Act 1986 (c. 45) (meaning of 'associate').

29 Section 70(2)(a) and (c), (3)(a) and (4) of the Building Societies Act 1986 (c. 53) (interpretation).

30 Section 83(2)(c) of the Housing (Scotland) Act 1987 (c. 26) (members of a person's family).

31 Section 4(6) of the Landlord and Tenant Act 1987 (c. 31) (relevant disposals).

32 Section 52(2)(a) of the Companies Act 1989 (c. 40) (meaning of 'associate').

33 The definition of 'relative' in section 105(1) of the Children Act 1989 (c. 41) (interpretation).

34 Paragraph 1(2) of Schedule 2 to the Broadcasting Act 1990 (c. 42) (restrictions on the holding of licences).

35 Section 11(1) of the Agricultural Holdings (Scotland) Act 1991 (c. 55) (bequest of lease).

36 Section 77(3)(c) of the Friendly Societies Act 1992 (c. 40) (information on appointed actuary to be annexed to balance sheet).

37 The definitions of 'son' and 'daughter' in section 119A(2) of that Act (meaning of 'associate').

38 Paragraph 2(1) of Schedule 5 to the Charities Act 1993 (c. 10) (meaning of 'connected person' for purposes of section 36(2)).

39 Section 10(5) of the Leasehold Reform, Housing and Urban Development Act 1993 (c. 28) (premises with a resident landlord: adult member of another's family).

40 Section 61(2) of the Crofters (Scotland) Act 1993 (c. 44) (member of family).

41 Section 2 of the Criminal Law (Consolidation) (Scotland) Act 1995 (c. 39) (intercourse with stepchild).

42 Section 161(1) of the Employment Rights Act 1996 (c. 18) (domestic servants).

43 The definition of 'relative' in section 63(1) of the Family Law Act 1996 (c. 27) (interpretation of Part 4 of the 1996 Act).

44 Section 62(2) of the Housing Act 1996 (c. 52) (members of a person's family: Part 1).

45 Section 140(2) of that Act (members of a person's family: Chapter 1).

46 Section 143P(3) of that Act (members of a person's family: Chapter 1A).

47 The definition of 'relative' in section 178(3) of that Act (meaning of associated person).

48 Section 422(4)(b) of the Financial Services and Markets Act 2000 (c. 8) (controller).

49 Paragraph 16(2) of Schedule 11 to that Act (offers of securities).

50 Section 108(2)(c) of the Housing (Scotland) Act 2001 (asp 10) (meaning of certain terms).

51 Section 1(3) of the Mortgage Rights (Scotland) Act 2001 (asp 11) (application to suspend enforcement of standard security).

52 Paragraph 3(8) of Schedule 6 to the Commonhold and Leasehold Reform Act 2002 (c. 15) (premises excluded from right to manage).

53 Section 127(6) of the Enterprise Act 2002 (c. 40) (associated persons).

. . .

SCHEDULE 23

Section 249

IMMIGRATION CONTROL AND FORMATION OF CIVIL PARTNERSHIPS

Part 1

Introduction

Application of Schedule

1 (1) This Schedule applies if—
   (a) two people wish to register as civil partners of each other, and
   (b) one of them is subject to immigration control.

(2) For the purposes of this Schedule a person is subject to immigration control if—
   (a) he is not an EEA national, and
   (b) under the Immigration Act 1971 (c. 77) he requires leave to enter or remain in the United Kingdom (whether or not leave has been given).

(3) 'EEA national' means a national of a State which is a contracting party to the Agreement on the European Economic Area signed at Oporto on 2nd May 1992 (as it has effect from time to time).

The qualifying condition

2 (1) For the purposes of this Schedule the qualifying condition, in relation to a person subject to immigration control, is that the person—

   (a) has an entry clearance granted expressly for the purpose of enabling him to form a civil partnership in the United Kingdom,

   (b) has the written permission of the Secretary of State to form a civil partnership in the United Kingdom, or

   (c) falls within a class specified for the purpose of this paragraph by regulations made by the Secretary of State.

(2) 'Entry clearance' has the meaning given by section 33(1) of the Immigration Act 1971.

(3) Section 25 of the Asylum and Immigration (Treatment of Claimants, etc.) Act 2004 (c. 19) (regulations about applications for permission to marry) applies in relation to the permission referred to in sub-paragraph (1)(b) as it applies in relation to permission to marry under sections 19(3)(b), 21(3)(b) and 23(3)(b) of that Act.

Part 2

England and Wales

Application of this part

3   This Part of this Schedule applies if the civil partnership is to be formed in England and Wales by signing a civil partnership schedule.

Procedure for giving notice of proposed civil partnership

4 (1) Each notice of proposed civil partnership under Chapter 1 of Part 2 of this Act—

   (a) must be given to a registration authority specified for the purposes of this paragraph by regulations made by the Secretary of State, and

   (b) must be delivered to the relevant individual in person by the two proposed civil partners.

(2) 'The relevant individual' means such employee or officer or other person provided by the specified registration authority as is determined in accordance with regulations made by the Secretary of State for the purposes of this sub-paragraph.

(3) Regulations under sub-paragraph (2) may, in particular, describe a person by reference to the location or office where he works.

(4) Before making any regulations under this paragraph the Secretary of State must consult the Registrar General.

Declaration

5   The necessary declaration under section 8 must include a statement that the person subject to immigration control fulfils the qualifying condition (and the reason why).

Recording of notice

6 (1) The fact that a notice of proposed civil partnership has been given must not be recorded in the register unless the registration authority is satisfied by the production of specified evidence that the person fulfils the qualifying condition.

(2) 'Specified evidence' means such evidence as may be specified in guidance issued by the Registrar General.

Supplementary

7 (1) Part 2 of this Act has effect in any case where this Part of this Schedule applies subject to any necessary modification.

(2) In particular section 52 has effect as if the matters proof of which is not necessary in support of the civil partnership included compliance with this Part of this Schedule.

(3) An expression used in this Part of this Schedule and in Chapter 1 of Part 2 of this Act has the same meaning as in that Chapter.

. . .

Part 5

Regulations

17 Any power to make regulations under this Schedule is exercisable by statutory instrument which is subject to annulment in pursuance of a resolution of either House of Parliament.

SCHEDULE 24

Section 254

SOCIAL SECURITY, CHILD SUPPORT AND TAX CREDITS

Part 1

Amendments of the Child Support Act 1991 (c. 48)

1 In section 8 (role of the courts with respect to maintenance for children), after subsection (11)(e) insert—
'(ea) Schedule 5, 6 or 7 to the Civil Partnership Act 2004; or'.

2 In section 15 (powers of inspectors), in subsection (7)—
(a) after 'married' insert 'or is a civil partner', and
(b) after 'spouse' insert 'or civil partner'.

3 In section 55 (meaning of 'child'), in subsection (2)—
(a) in paragraph (a), after 'married' insert 'or a civil partner',
(b) in paragraph (b), after 'marriage' insert ', or been a party to a civil partnership,', and
(c) in paragraph (c), after 'granted' insert 'or has been a party to a civil partnership in respect of which a nullity order has been made'.

4 For paragraph 6(5)(b) (as originally enacted) of Schedule 1 (maintenance assessments) substitute—
'(b) where the absent parent—
(i) is living together in the same household with another adult of the opposite sex (regardless of whether or not they are married),
(ii) is living together in the same household with another adult of the same sex who is his civil partner, or

    (iii) is living together in the same household with another adult of the same sex
          as if they were civil partners,
  income of that other adult,'.
5 After paragraph 6(5) (as originally enacted) of that Schedule insert—
   '(5A) For the purposes of this paragraph, two adults of the same sex are to be
        regarded as living together in the same household as if they were civil partners if,
        but only if, they would be regarded as living together as husband and wife were
        they instead two adults of the opposite sex.'
6 In paragraph 10C of that Schedule (as substituted by section 1(3) of, and Schedule 1
   to, the Child Support, Pensions and Social Security Act 2000 (c. 19)), for sub-
   paragraph (5) substitute—
   '(5) In sub-paragraph (4)(a), "couple" means—
     (a) a man and a woman who are married to each other and are members of the
         same household,
     (b) a man and a woman who are not married to each other but are living
         together as husband and wife,
     (c) two people of the same sex who are civil partners of each other and are
         members of the same household, or
     (d) two people of the same sex who are not civil partners of each other but are
         living together as if they were civil partners.
   (6) For the purposes of this paragraph, two people of the same sex are to be regarded
        as living together as if they were civil partners if, but only if, they would be
        regarded as living together as husband and wife were they instead two people of
        the opposite sex.'

. . .

Part 3

Amendments of the Social Security Contributions and Benefits Act 1992 (c. 4)

13 In section 20 (descriptions of contributory benefits), in subsection (1)(f)(ii), after
    'spouse' insert 'or civil partner.'
14 In section 30A (incapacity benefit: entitlement), in subsection (2)(b)(ii), after
    'spouse' insert 'or deceased civil partner'.
15 In section 30B (incapacity benefit: rate), in subsection (3)(a), after 'people' insert 'or
    civil partners'.
16 (1) Amend section 36 (bereavement payment) as follows.
    (2) In subsection (1), after 'spouse' (in each place) insert 'or civil partner'.
    (3) For subsection (2) substitute—
        '(2) A bereavement payment shall not be payable to a person if—
          (a) that person and a person of the opposite sex to whom that person was not
              married were living together as husband and wife at the time of the spouse's
              or civil partner's death, or
          (b) that person and a person of the same sex who was not his or her civil
              partner were living together as if they were civil partners at the time of the
              spouse's or civil partner's death.'
17 In section 36A (cases in which sections 37 to 41 apply), in subsection (2), after
    'spouse' insert 'or civil partner'.

18 (1) Amend section 37 (widowed mother's allowance) as follows.

(2) In subsection (3), after 'remarries' insert 'or forms a civil partnership'.

(3) After subsection (4)(b) insert 'or

    (c) for any period during which she and a woman who is not her civil partner are living together as if they were civil partners.'

19 (1) Amend section 38 (widow's pension) as follows.

(2) In subsection (2), after 'remarries' insert 'or forms a civil partnership'.

(3) After subsection (3)(c) insert 'or

    (d) for any period during which she and a woman who is not her civil partner are living together as if they were civil partners.'

20 (1) Amend section 39A (widowed parent's allowance) as follows.

(2) After 'spouse' (in each place other than subsections (2)(b) and (4)), insert 'or civil partner'.

(3) After 'spouse's' (in each place) insert 'or civil partner's'.

(4) In subsection (2), after paragraph (b) insert 'or

    (c) the surviving civil partner is a woman who—

        (i) was residing together with the deceased civil partner immediately before the time of the death, and

        (ii) is pregnant as the result of being artificially inseminated before that time with the semen of some person, or as a result of the placing in her before that time of an embryo, of an egg in the process of fertilisation, or of sperm and eggs.'

(5) In subsection (4), after 'remarries' insert 'or forms a civil partnership'.

(6) After subsection (4) insert—

'(4A) The surviving civil partner shall not be entitled to the allowance for any period after she or he forms a subsequent civil partnership or marries, but, subject to that, the surviving civil partner shall continue to be entitled to it for any period throughout which she or he—

    (a) satisfies the requirements of subsection (2)(a) or (b) above; and

    (b) is under pensionable age.'

(7) After subsection (5)(b) insert 'or

    (c) for any period during which the surviving spouse or civil partner and a person of the same sex who is not his or her civil partner are living together as if they were civil partners.'

21 (1) Amend section 39B (bereavement allowance where no dependent children) as follows.

(2) After 'spouse' (in each place) other than subsection (4), insert 'or civil partner'.

(3) After 'spouse's' (in each place) insert 'or civil partner's'.

(4) In subsection (4), after 'remarries' insert 'or forms a civil partnership'.

(5) After subsection (4) insert—

'(4A) The surviving civil partner shall not be entitled to the allowance for any period after she or he forms a subsequent civil partnership or marries, but, subject to that, the surviving civil partner shall continue to be entitled to it until—

    (a) she or he attains pensionable age, or

    (b) the period of 52 weeks mentioned in subsection (3) above expires,

whichever happens first.'

(6) After subsection (5)(b) insert 'or

    (c) for any period during which the surviving spouse or civil partner and a person of the same sex who is not his or her civil partner are living together as if they were civil partners.'

22 In section 39C (rate of widowed parent's allowance and bereavement allowance)—
   (a) after 'spouse' (in each place) insert 'or civil partner', and
   (b) in subsection (5), after 'spouse's' insert 'or civil partner's'.

23 In section 46 (modifications of section 45 for calculating the additional pension in certain benefits)—
   (a) after 'under pensionable age', in subsection (2), insert 'or by virtue of section 39C(1) above or section 48A(4), 48B(2) or 48BB(5) below in a case where the deceased civil partner died under pensionable age',
   (b) after 'spouse', in paragraph (b)(i) of the definition of 'N' in subsection (2), insert 'or civil partner', and
   (c) after 'spouse' (in each place) in subsection (3), insert 'or civil partner'.

24 (1) Amend section 48 (use of former spouse's contributions) as follows.
(2) In subsection (1)—
   (a) for 'married' substitute 'in a relevant relationship',
   (b) for 'marriage' substitute 'relationship', and
   (c) after 'spouse' insert 'or civil partner'.
(3) In subsection (2), for 'marriage' substitute 'relevant relationship'.
(4) For subsection (3) substitute—
   '(3) Where a person has been in a relevant relationship more than once, this section applies only to the last relevant relationship and the references to his relevant relationship and his former spouse or civil partner shall be construed accordingly.
   (4) In this section, "relevant relationship" means a marriage or civil partnership.'

25 (1) Amend section 48A (category B retirement pension for married person) as follows.
(2) After subsection (2) insert—
   '(2A) A person who—
      (a) has attained pensionable age, and
      (b) on attaining that age was a civil partner or forms a civil partnership after attaining that age,
shall be entitled to a Category B retirement pension by virtue of the contributions of the other party to the civil partnership ("the contributing civil partner") if the following requirement is met.
(2B) The requirement is that the contributing civil partner—
      (a) has attained pensionable age and become entitled to a Category A retirement pension, and
      (b) satisfies the conditions specified in Schedule 3, Part 1, paragraph 5.'
(3) In subsections (3) and (4), after 'spouse' insert 'or contributing civil partner'.
(4) In subsection (4A), for 'widow or widower' substitute 'widow, widower or surviving civil partner'.
(5) In subsection (5), after 'spouse's' insert 'or contributing civil partner's'.
(6) Section 48A (as amended by this paragraph) does not confer a right to a Category B retirement pension on a person by reason of his or her forming a civil partnership with a person who was born before 6th April 1950.

26 (1) Amend section 48B (category B retirement pension for widows and widowers) as follows.

(2) After subsection (1) insert—

'(1A) A person ("the pensioner") who attains pensionable age on or after 6th April 2010 and whose civil partner died—

(a) while they were civil partners of each other, and

(b) after the pensioner attained pensionable age,

shall be entitled to a Category B retirement pension by virtue of the contributions of the civil partner if the civil partner satisfied the conditions specified in Schedule - 3, Part 1, paragraph 5.'

(3) In subsection (2), after 'subsection (1)' insert 'or (1A)'.

(4) In subsection (3), after 'spouse' (in each place) insert 'or civil partner'.

27 (1) Amend section 48BB (category B retirement pension: entitlement by reference to benefits under section 39A or 39B) as follows.

(2) After 'spouse' (in each place) insert 'or civil partner'.

(3) After 'spouse's' (in each place) insert 'or civil partner's'.

(4) In subsections (1)(b) and (3)(b), for 'remarried' substitute 'following that death married or formed a civil partnership'.

28 (1) Amend section 51 (category B retirement pension for widowers) as follows.

(2) After subsection (1) insert—

'(1A) A civil partner shall be entitled to a Category B retirement pension if—

(a) his or her civil partner has died and they were civil partners of each other at the time of that death,

(b) they were both over pensionable age at the time of that death, and

(c) before that death the deceased civil partner satisfied the contribution conditions for a Category A retirement pension in Schedule 3, Part 1, paragraph 5.'

(3) In subsection (2)—

(a) for 'man's' substitute 'person's', and

(b) after 'wife' insert 'or deceased civil partner'.

(4) In subsection (3), after '2002' insert 'or a surviving civil partner'.

(5) In subsection (4)—

(a) for 'man' substitute 'person', and

(b) after 'pension' insert 'under this section'.

(6) Section 51 (as amended by this paragraph) does not confer a right to a Category B retirement pension on a person who attains pensionable age on or after 6th April 2010.

29 In section 51A (special provision for married people), in subsection (1)—

(a) after 'person' insert 'or civil partner', and

(b) after 'marriage' insert 'or civil partnership'.

30 In section 52 (special provision for surviving spouses), in subsection (1), after 'spouse' insert 'or civil partner'.

31 In section 60 (complete or partial failure to satisfy contributions conditions), in subsection (2)—

(a) after 'married' insert 'or a civil partner', and

(b) for 'widow or widower' substitute 'widow, widower or surviving civil partner'.

32 In section 61A (contributions paid in error), in subsection (3)—

(a) after 'spouse' insert 'or civil partner', and

(b) in paragraph (b), for 'widows or widowers' substitute 'widows, widowers or surviving civil partners'.

33 In section 62 (graduated retirement benefit), after subsection (1)(aa) insert—

'(ab) for extending section 37 of that Act (increase of woman's retirement pension by reference to her late husband's graduated retirement benefit) to civil partners and their late civil partners and for that section (except subsection (5)) so to apply as it applies to women and their late husbands;'.

34 In section 77 (guardian's allowance)—

(a) in subsection (6)(a)(ii), after 'spouses' insert 'or civil partners', and

(b) in subsection (8)(a), after 'divorce' insert 'or the civil partnership of the child's parents has been dissolved'.

35 In section 82 (short-term benefit: increase for adult dependants)—

(a) in subsection (3)(a) and (b), after 'husband' insert 'or civil partner',

(b) in subsection (3)(b), for 'his' substitute 'her husband's or civil partner's', and

(c) in subsection (4)(a), after 'spouse' insert 'or civil partner'.

36 In section 83A (pension increase for spouse)—

(a) in subsection (1), for 'married pensioner' substitute 'pensioner who is married or a civil partner', and

(b) in subsections (2) and (3), after 'spouse' (in each place) insert 'or civil partner'.

37 (1) Amend section 85 (pension increase: person with care of children) as follows.

(2) Omit subsection (1).

(3) After subsection (1) insert—

'(1A) Subject to subsections (2A) and (4) below, the weekly rate of a Category A retirement pension shall be increased by the amount specified in relation to that pension in Schedule 4, Part 4, column (3) for any period during which a person who is neither the spouse nor civil partner of the pensioner nor a child has the care of a child or children in respect of whom the pensioner is entitled to child benefit.'

(4) In subsection (2)—

(a) for 'the following provisions' substitute 'subsections (3) and (4) below', and

(b) for 'pension to which this section applies' substitute 'Category C retirement pension payable by virtue of section 78(1) above'.

(5) After subsection (2) insert—

'(2A) Subsection (1A) above does not apply if the pensioner is a person whose spouse or civil partner is entitled to a Category B retirement pension, or to a Category C retirement pension by virtue of section 78(2) above or in such other cases as may be prescribed.'

(6) In subsection (4), after 'subsection' insert '(1A) or'.

38 In section 113 (general provisions as to disqualification and suspension), in subsection (1), for 'wife or husband,' substitute 'wife, husband or civil partner,'.

39 In section 114 (persons maintaining dependants etc.)—

(a) in subsection (2), for 'wife' substitute 'wife, civil partner', and

(b) in subsection (3)(a), after 'spouse' insert 'or civil partner'.

40 After subsection (1)(a) of section 121 (treatment of certain marriages) insert—

'(aa) for a voidable civil partnership which has been annulled, whether before or after the date when the regulations come into force, to be treated for the purposes of the provisions to which this subsection applies as if it had been a valid civil partnership which was dissolved at the date of annulment;'.

41 (1) Amend section 122 (interpretation of Parts 1 to 6 and supplementary provisions) as follows.

(2) In subsection (1), in the definition of 'relative' after 'by marriage' insert 'or civil partnership'.

(3) After subsection (1) insert—

'(1A) For the purposes of Parts 1 to 5 and this Part of this Act, two people of the same sex are to be regarded as living together as if they were civil partners if, but only if, they would be regarded as living together as husband and wife were they instead two people of the opposite sex.'

42 In section 124 (income support), in subsection (1)(c), (f) and (g), for 'married or unmarried couple' substitute 'couple'.

43 In section 126 (trade disputes), in subsection (3)(b), (c) and (d), for 'married or unmarried couple' substitute 'couple'.

44 In section 127 (effect of return to work), for 'married or unmarried couple' (in each place) substitute 'couple'.

45 In section 132 (couples), in subsection (1), for 'married or unmarried couple' substitute 'couple'.

46 (1) Amend section 137 (interpretation of Part 7 and supplementary provisions) as follows.

(2) In paragraphs (a), (b) and (c) of the definition of 'family' in subsection (1), for 'married or unmarried couple' substitute 'couple'.

(3) After the definition of 'child' in subsection (1) insert—

' "couple" means—

(a) a man and woman who are married to each other and are members of the same household;

(b) a man and woman who are not married to each other but are living together as husband and wife otherwise than in prescribed circumstances;

(c) two people of the same sex who are civil partners of each other and are members of the same household; or

(d) two people of the same sex who are not civil partners of each other but are living together as if they were civil partners otherwise than in prescribed circumstances;'.

(4) Omit the definitions of 'married couple' and 'unmarried couple' in subsection (1).

(5) After subsection (1) insert—

'(1A) For the purposes of this Part, two people of the same sex are to be regarded as living together as if they were civil partners if, but only if, they would be regarded as living together as husband and wife were they instead two people of the opposite sex.'

47 In section 143 (meaning of 'person responsible for child'), in subsection (5), after 'spouses' insert 'or civil partners'.

48 (1) Amend section 145A (entitlement after death of child) as follows.

(2) In subsection (2)—

(a) in paragraph (a), after 'couple' insert 'or civil partnership' and after 'to whom he was married' insert 'or who was his civil partner',

(b) in paragraph (b), after 'couple' insert 'or a cohabiting same-sex couple', and

(c) for 'married couple or unmarried couple' substitute 'couple or partnership'.

(3) Before the definition of 'married couple' in subsection (5) insert—

' "civil partnership" means two people of the same sex who are civil partners of each other and are neither—

    (a) separated under a court order, nor

    (b) separated in circumstances in which the separation is likely to be permanent,

"cohabiting same-sex couple" means two people of the same sex who are not civil partners of each other but are living together as if they were civil partners,'.

(4) After subsection (5) insert—

    '(6) For the purposes of this section, two people of the same sex are to be regarded as living together as if they were civil partners if, but only if, they would be regarded as living together as husband and wife were they instead two people of the opposite sex.'

49 (1) Amend section 150 (interpretation of Part 10) as follows.

(2) In the definition of 'war widow's pension' in subsection (2)—

    (a) after 'any widow's' insert 'or surviving civil partner's', and

    (b) after 'widow' insert 'or surviving civil partner'.

(3) For subsection (3) substitute—

    '(3) In this Part of this Act, "couple" has the meaning given by section 137(1) above.'

50 In section 171ZL (entitlement to statutory adoption pay), in subsection (4)(b)—

    (a) after 'married couple' insert 'or civil partnership', and

    (b) after 'spouse' (in each place) insert 'or civil partner'.

51 (1) Amend Schedule 4A (additional pension) as follows.

(2) In paragraph 1(2), after 'under pensionable age,' insert 'or by virtue of section 39C(1), 48A(4) or 48B(2) above, in a case where the deceased civil partner died under pensionable age,'.

(3) In paragraph 1(4)(a) and (b), (5), (6) and (7)(a) and (b), after 'spouse' insert 'or civil partner'.

52 (1) Amend Schedule 7 (industrial injuries benefits) as follows.

(2) For paragraph 4(3)(a) of Part 1 substitute—

    '(a) a beneficiary is one of two persons who are—

        (i) spouses or civil partners residing together,

        (ii) a man and woman who are not married to each other but are living together as if they were husband and wife, or

        (iii) two people of the same sex who are not civil partners of each other but are living together as if they were civil partners, and'.

(3) In paragraph 5(2)(a)(ii) of Part 1, after 'spouses' insert 'or civil partners'.

(4) In Part 1—

    (a) in paragraph 6(1), (3) and (4), after 'spouse' (in each place) insert 'or civil partner', and

    (b) in paragraph 6(4)(a), after 'spouse's' insert 'or civil partner's'.

(5) In paragraph 15 of Part 6—

    (a) in sub-paragraph (2), after 'remarries' insert 'or forms a civil partnership', and

    (b) at the end of sub-paragraph (3), insert 'or is living together with a person of the same sex as if they were civil partners'.

53 (1) Amend Schedule 8 (industrial injuries and diseases: old cases) as follows.

(2) In paragraph 6(4)(d), and the substituted paragraph (d) in paragraph 6(5), after 'spouse' (in each place) insert 'or civil partner'.

(3) After paragraph 8(1) insert—

'(1A) Any reference in this Schedule to a member of a person's family within the meaning of the Workmen's Compensation Act 1925 is to be read as including a civil partner of his.'

54 In Schedule 9 (exclusions from entitlement to child benefit), in paragraph 3, after 'married' insert 'or is a civil partner'.

Part 4

Amendments of the Social Security Administration Act 1992 (c. 5)

55 In section 2AA (full entitlement to certain benefits conditional on work-focused interview for partner), in subsection (7), for the definition of 'couple' substitute—
' "couple" has the meaning given by section 137(1) of the Contributions and Benefits Act;'.

56 In section 3 (late claims for bereavement benefit where death is difficult to establish)—

(a) after 'spouse' (in each place) insert 'or civil partner', and

(b) after 'spouse's' (in each place) insert 'or civil partner's'.

57 (1) Amend section 15A (payment out of benefit of sums in respect of mortgage interest etc.) as follows.

(2) In subsection (4)—

(a) in paragraph (a) of the definition of 'partner', for 'to whom the borrower is married' substitute 'who is married to, or a civil partner of, the borrower', and

(b) in paragraph (b) of that definition, for 'to whom the borrower is not married but who lives together with the borrower as husband and wife' substitute 'who is neither married to, nor a civil partner of, the borrower but who lives together with the borrower as husband and wife or as if they were civil partners'.

(3) After subsection (4A) insert—

'(4B) For the purposes of this section, two people of the same sex are to be regarded as living together as if they were civil partners if, but only if, they would be regarded as living together as husband and wife were they instead two people of the opposite sex.'

58 (1) Amend section 71 (overpayments—general) as follows.

(2) In subsection (9), for 'married or unmarried couple' substitute 'couple'.

(3) After subsection (11) insert—

'(12) In this section, "couple" has the meaning given by section 137(1) of the Contributions and Benefits Act.'

59 In section 73 (overlapping benefits—general), in subsections (2)(b) and (d) and (5)(b) and (d), for 'wife or husband' substitute 'wife, husband or civil partner'.

60 In section 74A (payment of benefit where maintenance payments collected by Secretary of State), in subsection (5)—

(a) after the definition of 'child maintenance' insert—
' "couple" has the meaning given by section 137(1) of the Contributions and Benefits Act;',

(b) in the definition of 'family', for 'married or unmarried couple' (in each place) substitute 'couple', and

(c) omit the definitions of 'married couple' and 'unmarried couple'.

61 (1) Amend section 78 (recovery of social fund awards) as follows.

(2) In subsection (3)(b), for 'married or unmarried couple' substitute 'couple'.

(3) For subsection (5) substitute—

'(5) In this section "couple" has the meaning given by section 137(1) of the Contributions and Benefits Act.'

(4) In subsection (6)—

(a) in paragraph (a), after 'wife' insert 'or civil partner', and

(b) in paragraph (b), after 'husband' insert 'or civil partner'.

62 In section 105 (failure to maintain—general), in subsection (4), after 'spouse' insert 'or civil partner'.

63 (1) Amend section 107 (recovery of expenditure on income support: additional amounts and transfer of orders) as follows.

(2) In subsection (1)(b), after 'wife' insert 'or civil partner'.

(3) In subsection (15), after paragraph (a)(ii) of the definition of 'maintenance order' insert—

'(iii) any order under Schedule 7 to the Civil Partnership Act 2004 for the making of periodical payments or for the payment of a lump sum;'.

64 In section 109B (power to require information), in subsection (5)(a), for 'married, his spouse' substitute 'married or is a civil partner, his spouse or civil partner'.

65 In section 139 (arrangement for community charge benefits), in subsection (11), in the definition of 'war widow's pension'—

(a) after 'any widow's' insert 'or surviving civil partner's', and

(b) after 'widow' insert 'or surviving civil partner'.

66 In section 156 (up-rating under section 150 of pensions increased under section 52(3) of the Contributions and Benefits Act)—

(a) in subsection (1), after 'spouse' insert 'or civil partner', and

(b) in subsections (2) and (3), after 'spouse's' (in each place) insert 'or civil partner's'.

. . .

Part 7

Amendments of the Jobseekers Act 1995 (c. 18)

118 In section 1 (the jobseeker's allowance), in subsection (4), in the definition of 'a joint-claim couple', for 'married or unmarried couple' substitute 'couple'.

119 In section 3 (the income-based conditions), in subsection (1)(dd) and (e), for 'married or unmarried couple' substitute 'couple'.

120 In section 15 (effect on other claimants), in subsection (2)(b), for 'married or unmarried couple' substitute 'couple'.

121 In section 15A (trade disputes: joint-claim couples), in subsection (5)(c), for 'married or unmarried couple' substitute 'couple'.

122 In section 23 (recovery of sums in respect of maintenance), in subsection (1), after 'spouse' insert 'or civil partner'.

123 In section 31 (termination of awards), in subsections (1) and (2), for 'married or unmarried couple' substitute 'couple'.

124 (1) Amend section 35 (interpretation) as follows.

(2) After the definition of 'contribution-based jobseeker's allowance' in subsection (1) insert—

' "couple" means—

   (a) a man and woman who are married to each other and are members of the same household;

   (b) a man and woman who are not married to each other but are living together as husband and wife otherwise than in prescribed circumstances;

   (c) two people of the same sex who are civil partners of each other and are members of the same household; or

   (d) two people of the same sex who are not civil partners of each other but are living together as if they were civil partners otherwise than in prescribed circumstances;'.

(3) In paragraphs (a), (b) and (c) of the definition of 'family' in subsection (1), for 'married or unmarried couple' substitute 'couple'.

(4) Omit the definitions of 'married couple' and 'unmarried couple' in subsection (1).

(5) After subsection (1) insert—

'(1A) For the purposes of this Act, two people of the same sex are to be regarded as living together as if they were civil partners if, but only if, they would be regarded as living together as husband and wife were they instead two people of the opposite sex.'

125 In Schedule 1 (supplementary provisions), in paragraph 9C(1), for 'married or unmarried couple' substitute 'couple'.

Part 8

Amendments of the Child Support Act 1995 (c. 34)

126 (1) Amend subsection (7) of section 10 (the child maintenance bonus) as follows.

(2) After the definition of 'child maintenance' insert—

' "couple" means—

   (a) a man and woman who are married to each other and are members of the same household;

   (b) a man and woman who are not married to each other but are living together as husband and wife otherwise than in prescribed circumstances;

   (c) two people of the same sex who are civil partners of each other and are members of the same household; or

   (d) two people of the same sex who are not civil partners of each other but are living together as if they were civil partners otherwise than in prescribed circumstances;'.

(3) In the definition of 'family' for 'married or unmarried couple' (in each place) substitute 'couple'.

(4) Omit the definitions of 'married couple' and 'unmarried couple'.

127 After section 10(7) insert—

'(7A) For the purposes of this section, two people of the same sex are to be regarded as living together as if they were civil partners if, but only if, they would be regarded as living together as husband and wife were they instead two people of the opposite sex.'

. . .

Part 11

Amendments of the Social Security Act 1998 (c. 14)

138 (1) Amend section 72 (power to reduce child benefit for lone parents) as follows.

(2) In subsection (2), after 'spouse' (in each place) insert 'or civil partner'.

(3) After subsection (2) insert—

'(3) For the purpose of this section, a parent is to be regarded as living with another person as his civil partner if, but only if, he would be regarded as living with the other person as his spouse, were they instead two people of the opposite sex.'

. . .

Part 13

Amendments of the State Pension Credit Act 2002 (c. 16)

140 In sections 2(5)(a) and (8)(b), 3(1)(b), 4(1), 5, 6(3)(c)(ii) and 9(4)(a), (b) and (d), for 'married or unmarried couple' substitute 'couple'.

141 In section 2(5)(b), for 'such a couple' substitute 'a couple'.

142 (1) Amend subsection (1) of section 17 (other interpretation provisions) as follows.

(2) After the definition of 'the Contributions and Benefits Act' insert—

' "couple" means—

    (a) a man and woman who are married to each other and are members of the same household;

    (b) a man and woman who are not married to each other but are living together as husband and wife otherwise than in prescribed circumstances;

    (c) two people of the same sex who are civil partners of each other and are members of the same household; or

    (d) two people of the same sex who are not civil partners of each other but are living together as if they were civil partners otherwise than in prescribed circumstances;'.

(3) In the definition of 'foreign war widow's or widower's pension' for 'widow or widower' (in each place) substitute 'widow, widower or surviving civil partner'.

(4) Omit the definitions of 'married couple' and 'unmarried couple'.

(5) In the definition of 'war widow's or widower's pension'—

    (a) in paragraph (a), for 'any widow's or widower's' substitute 'any widow's, widower's or surviving civil partner's', and

    (b) in paragraph (b), for 'widow or widower' substitute 'widow, widower or surviving civil partner'.

143 After section 17(1) insert—

'(1A) For the purposes of this Act, two people of the same sex are to be regarded as living together as if they were civil partners if, but only if, they would be regarded as living together as husband and wife were they instead two people of the opposite sex.'

Part 14

Amendments of the Tax Credits Act 2002 (c. 21)

144 (1) Amend section 3 (claims) as follows.

(2) In subsection (3)(a), for 'married couple or unmarried couple' substitute 'couple'.

(3) For subsections (5) and (6) substitute—

'(5A) In this Part "couple" means—

    (a) a man and woman who are married to each other and are neither—

        (i) separated under a court order, nor

        (ii) separated in circumstances in which the separation is likely to be permanent,

    (b) a man and woman who are not married to each other but are living together as husband and wife,

    (c) two people of the same sex who are civil partners of each other and are neither—

        (i) separated under a court order, nor

        (ii) separated in circumstances in which the separation is likely to be permanent, or

    (d) two people of the same sex who are not civil partners of each other but are living together as if they were civil partners.'

145 In sections 4(1)(g), 11(6)(b) and (c), 17(10)(b), 24(2) and 32(6), for 'married couple or an unmarried couple' (in each place) substitute 'couple'.

146 In sections 4(1)(g) and 17(10)(b), for 'the married couple or unmarried couple' substitute 'the couple'.

147 (1) Renumber section 48 (interpretation) as subsection (1) of that section.

(2) In subsection (1), after the definition of 'child' insert—

' "couple" has the meaning given by section 3(5A),',

and omit the definitions of 'married couple' and 'unmarried couple'.

(3) After subsection (1) insert—

'(2) For the purposes of this Part, two people of the same sex are to be regarded as living together as if they were civil partners if, but only if, they would be regarded as living together as husband and wife were they instead two people of the opposite sex.'

. . .

SCHEDULE 25

Section 256

AMENDMENT OF CERTAIN ENACTMENTS RELATING TO PENSIONS

Fire Services Act 1947 (c. 41)

1 In section 26 (firemen's pension scheme), in subsections (1) and (2A), for 'widows,' substitute 'surviving spouses, surviving civil partners,'.

House of Commons Members' Fund Act 1948 (c. 36)

2   In section 4 (provision for cases of special hardship), in subsection (1)(b), for 'widowers' substitute 'widowers, surviving civil partners'.

Parliamentary and other Pensions Act 1972 (c. 48)

3   In section 27 (pensions for dependants of Prime Minister or Speaker), in subsection (2)(a)(i), for 'widow or widower' substitute 'widow, widower or surviving civil partner'.

Theatres Trust Act 1976 (c. 27)

4   In section 3 (employment of staff), in subsection (d)(iii) (power to secure pensions and gratuities payable to or in respect of officers and servants), for 'widow,' substitute 'surviving spouse, surviving civil partner,'.

SCHEDULE 26

Section 257

AMENDMENT OF CERTAIN ENACTMENTS RELATING TO THE
ARMED FORCES

Greenwich Hospital Act 1865 (c. 89)

1   In section 5 (power to appoint pensions to officers, etc.), after 'widows' insert 'or surviving civil partners'.

Navy and Marines (Property of Deceased) Act 1865 (c. 111)

2   In section 4 (disposal of residue belonging to deceased person in civil service of navy), after 'widow' insert 'or surviving civil partner'.

Pensions Commutation Act 1871 (c. 36)

3 (1)   In section 4 (power to Treasury to commute pensions), in subsection (2)—
   (a) after 'marries' insert 'or forms a civil partnership', and
   (b) after 'widow' insert 'or surviving civil partner'.
(2)   In section 4(3), for 'wife' substitute 'wife, civil partner'.

Greenwich Hospital Act 1883 (c. 32)

4   In section 2 (power to grant pensions, allowances, and gratuities), in subsection (1), after 'widows' insert 'or surviving civil partners'.

Pensions and Yeomanry Pay Act 1884 (c. 55)

5   In section 4 (distribution of money not exceeding £5,000 without requiring probate), after 'widower' insert 'surviving civil partner'.

Regimental Debts Act 1893 (c. 5)

6   In section 10 (application of residue undisposed of), in subsection (2), for 'widows' substitute 'widows, surviving civil partners'.

7   In section 24 (application of Act to cases of insanity), in paragraph (a), for 'wife or husband' substitute 'wife, husband or civil partner'.

Naval Medical Compassionate Fund Act 1915 (c. 28)

8   In section 1 (power by Order in Council to regulate fund), in subsection (1)(f), for 'widows, widowers' substitute 'widows, widowers, surviving civil partners'.

Naval and Military War Pensions, &c., (Administrative Expenses) Act 1917 (c. 14)

9 (1) In section 5 (alteration of purposes for which voluntary funds may be applied in certain cases)—
   (a) after 'wives,' (in each place) insert 'civil partners,', and
   (b) after 'widows,' (in each place) insert 'surviving civil partners,'.

(2) In section 6 (power of Secretary of State to accept and administer gifts for assisting disabled officers and men), after 'widows,' insert 'surviving civil partners,'.

War Pensions (Administrative Provisions) Act 1919 (c. 53)

10   In section 8 (appeals to Pensions Appeal Tribunals), in subsection (1), for 'the motherless child or' substitute 'surviving civil partner or the orphan,'.

War Pensions Act 1920 (c. 23)

11   In section 7 (restoration of forfeited pensions), in subsection (2), after 'wife,' insert 'civil partner,'.

12   In section 8 (statutory right of widow or dependant to a pension), for 'widow' substitute 'widow, surviving civil partner'.

Admiralty Pensions Act 1921 (c. 39)

13   In section 2 (restoration of forfeited pension), in subsection (2), after 'wife,' insert 'civil partner,'.

Greenwich Hospital Act 1942 (c. 35)

14 (1) In section 1 (extension of powers to grant pensions to persons employed for the purposes of Greenwich Hospital), in subsection (1)(a) and (b) for 'widows' substitute 'widows, surviving civil partners'.

(2) In section 1(2), for 'spouses' substitute 'spouses, civil partners'.

Pensions Appeal Tribunals Act 1943 (c. 39)

15   In section 1 (appeals against rejection of war pension claims made in respect of members of the naval, military or air forces), in subsection (4)(ii)—
   (a) after 'widower,' insert 'surviving civil partner,',
   (b) for 'husband' substitute 'husband, civil partner',
   (c) after 'marriage' insert 'or civil partnership', and
   (d) after 'place' insert 'or been formed'.

Greenwich Hospital Act 1947 (10 & 11 Geo. 6 c. 5)

16   In section 2 (extension of power to grant pensions, etc.), in subsection (1), after 'widows' insert 'and surviving civil partners'.

Polish Resettlement Act 1947 (c. 19)

17   In section 1 (power to apply Royal Warrant as to pensions etc. to certain Polish forces), in subsection (1), after 'widows,' insert 'surviving civil partners,'.

18   In section 2 (allowances from the Assistance Board), in subsection (2)(c)—
      (a) for 'of men' substitute 'or civil partners of persons',
      (b) for 'woman' substitute 'person',
      (c) for 'of a man' substitute 'or civil partner of a person', and
      (d) for 're-married' substitute 'subsequently married or formed a civil partnership'.

Naval Forces (Enforcement of Maintenance Liabilities) Act 1947 (c. 24)

19   (1) Amend section 1 (deduction from pay in respect of liabilities for maintenance, etc.) as follows.

(2) In subsection (1), in paragraphs (a), (aa) and (b) after 'wife' insert 'or civil partner'.

(3) In subsection (2A), after paragraph (a) insert—
      '(aa) if, in proceedings in connection with the dissolution or annulment of a civil partnership, an order has been made for the payment of any periodical or other sum in respect of the maintenance of the person who, if the civil partnership had subsisted, would have been the civil partner of any such person as is mentioned in subsection (1) above, references in this section to that person's civil partner include references to the person in whose favour the order was made; and'.

Royal Patriotic Fund Corporation Act 1950 (c. 10)

20   In section 1 (extension of objects of soldiers' effects fund), in subsection (1)—
      (a) for 'widows or children' substitute 'widows, surviving civil partners or children', and
      (b) after 'widows,' insert 'surviving civil partners,'.

Reserve and Auxiliary Forces (Protection of Civil Interests) Act 1951 (c. 65)

21   In section 23(1) (interpretation of Part 2)—
      (a) in paragraph (a) of the definition of 'dependant', for 'wife' substitute 'spouse or civil partner', and
      (b) in the definition of 'statutory tenancy', for 'widow' substitute 'surviving spouse or surviving civil partner'.

22   In paragraph (a) of section 25(6) (meaning of 'dependant'), for 'wife' substitute 'spouse or civil partner'.

23   In section 27(5) (interpretation of section), for 'wife' (in each place) substitute 'spouse or civil partner'.

24   In section 38(5) (interpretation of section), for 'wife' (in each place) substitute 'spouse or civil partner'.

25   (1) Amend section 46 (general provisions as to payments to make up civil remuneration) as follows.

(2) In subsection (2), for 'wife' substitute 'spouse or civil partner'.

(3) In subsection (3)—
    (a) the words from 'a widow entitled to a widow's pension' to the end of paragraph (iv) become paragraph (a) of the subsection (so that paragraphs (i) to (iv) become sub-paragraphs of that paragraph (a)),
    (b) in that paragraph (a), for 'widow entitled to a widow's pension' substitute 'surviving spouse entitled to a surviving spouse's pension',
    (c) in sub-paragraph (iv) of that paragraph (a), at the end insert 'or', and
    (d) before 'there may' insert the following paragraph—
    '(b) a surviving civil partner entitled to a surviving civil partner's pension by virtue of any of those provisions,'.

26 In section 52(2)(a) ('service pay' includes marriage etc. allowances), after 'marriage,' insert 'civil partnership,'.

27 (1) Amend Schedule 3 (financial provisions consequential on treating a person dying on service as alive and the converse) as follows.

(2) In paragraph 1(3), for 'widow' substitute 'surviving spouse, surviving civil partner'.

(3) In paragraph 2(4), for 'wife' (in each place) substitute 'spouse, civil partner'.

Army Act 1955 (3 & 4 Eliz. 2 c. 18)

28 (1) Section 150 (enforcement of maintenance and affiliation orders by deduction from pay) is amended as follows.

(2) In subsection (1)(a) and (aa), after 'wife' insert 'or civil partner'.

(3) In subsection (5), after 'marriage had subsisted;' insert—
    'references to a civil partner include, in relation to an order made in proceedings in connection with the dissolution or annulment of a civil partnership, references to a person who would have been the civil partner of the defendant if the civil partnership had subsisted.'

29 In section 151 (deductions from pay for maintenance of wife or child), in subsection (1)—
    (a) after 'wife' (in the first place) insert 'or civil partner', and
    (b) for 'wife' (in the second place) substitute 'wife, civil partner'.

Air Force Act 1955 (3 & 4 Eliz. 2 c. 19)

30 (1) Section 150 (enforcement of maintenance and affiliation orders by deduction from pay) is amended as follows.

(2) In subsection (1)(a) and (aa), after 'wife' insert 'or civil partner'.

(3) In subsection (5), after 'marriage had subsisted;' insert—
    'references to a civil partner include, in relation to an order made in proceedings in connection with the dissolution or annulment of a civil partnership, references to a person who would have been the civil partner of the defendant if the civil partnership had subsisted.'

31 In section 151 (deductions from pay for maintenance of wife or child), in subsection (1)—
    (a) after 'wife' (in the first place) insert 'or civil partner', and
    (b) for 'wife' (in the second place) substitute 'wife, civil partner'.

Naval Discipline Act 1957 (c. 53)

32 (1) Section 101 (service of proceedings for maintenance etc.) is amended as follows.

(2) In subsection (5)(a) and (b), after 'wife' insert 'or civil partner'.

(3) In subsection (5A), after paragraph (a) insert—

'(aa) references to the civil partner of a person include, in relation to an order made in proceedings in connection with the dissolution or annulment of a civil partnership, references to a person who would have been his civil partner if the civil partnership had subsisted; and'.

Courts-Martial (Appeals) Act 1968 (c. 20)

33 In section 48A (appeals on behalf of deceased persons), in subsection (3)(a), for 'widow or widower' substitute 'widow, widower or surviving civil partner'.

SCHEDULE 27

Section 261(1)

MINOR AND CONSEQUENTIAL AMENDMENTS: GENERAL

Explosive Substances Act 1883 (c. 3)

1 In section 6 (inquiry by Attorney-General, and apprehension of absconding witnesses), in subsection (2), for 'husband or wife' (in both places) substitute 'spouse or civil partner'.

Partnership Act 1890 (c. 39)

2 In section 2 (rules for determining existence of partnership), in rule (3)(c), after 'widow' insert ', widower, surviving civil partner'.

Law of Distress Amendment Act 1908 (c. 53)

3 In section 4(1) (exclusion of certain goods), after 'husband or wife', insert 'or civil partner'.

Census Act 1920 (c. 41)

4 In the Schedule (matters in respect of which particulars may be required), in paragraph 5 after 'as to marriage' insert 'or civil partnership'.

Trustee Act 1925 (c. 19)

5 (1) Amend section 31(2)(i) (trust on reaching 18 or marrying under that age of accumulations during infancy) as follows.

(2) In sub-paragraph (a)—

(a) after 'marries under that age' insert 'or forms a civil partnership under that age', and

(b) for 'or until his marriage' substitute ', or until his marriage or his formation of a civil partnership,'.

(3) In sub-paragraph (b), after 'marriage' insert ', or formation of a civil partnership,'.

(4) In the words after that sub-paragraph, after 'marriage' insert 'or formation of a civil partnership'.

6 In section 33(1)(ii)(a) and (b) (trust to maintain principal beneficiary and his spouse

and issue on failure of protective trust under paragraph (i)), for 'wife or husband' substitute 'spouse or civil partner'.

Law of Property Act 1925 (c. 20)

7   In section 205(1)(xxi) (which defines 'valuable consideration' as including marriage), after 'includes marriage' insert ', and formation of a civil partnership,'.

Judicial Proceedings (Regulation of Reports) Act 1926 (c. 61)

8   (1) Amend section 1 (restriction on publication of reports of judicial proceedings) as follows.

(2) In subsection (1)(b), for 'or for restitution of conjugal rights' substitute 'or for the dissolution or annulment of a civil partnership or for the separation of civil partners'.

(3) Omit subsection (5).

Population (Statistics) Act 1938 (c. 12)

9   In the Schedule (particulars which may be required), in paragraph 2—

(a) in paragraph (a), for 'or divorced;' substitute ', divorced, a civil partner or former civil partner, and, if a former civil partner, whether the civil partnership ended on death or dissolution;', and

(b) in paragraph (b), after 'surviving spouse' insert 'or civil partner'.

Landlord and Tenant (Requisitioned Land) Act 1942 (c. 13)

10   In section 13(1) (definition of 'member of the family'), after 'the wife or husband of the tenant,' insert 'the civil partner of the tenant,'.

Limitation (Enemies and War Prisoners) Act 1945 (c. 16)

11   In section 2 (interpretation), in the definition of 'statute of limitation', after the entry relating to the Matrimonial Causes Act 1973 insert—
'section 51(2) of the Civil Partnership Act 2004,'.

Statistics of Trade Act 1947 (c. 39)

12   In section 10 (information from persons entering or leaving the UK by air), in subsection (1), after 'marriage' insert 'or civil partnership'.

Marriage Act 1949 (c. 76)

13   (1) Amend section 1 (marriages within prohibited degrees) as follows.

(2) In subsection (1), for the words from 'between a man' to 'the said Part I,' substitute 'between a person and any person mentioned in the list in Part 1 of Schedule 1'.

(3) In subsection (2), for the words from 'between a man' to 'the said Part II,' substitute 'between a person and any person mentioned in the list in Part 2 of Schedule 1'.

(4) In subsection (4), for the words from 'between a man' to 'the said Part III' substitute 'between a person and any person mentioned in the list in Part 3 of Schedule 1'.

(5) In subsection (5) for paragraphs (a) to (d) substitute—
'(a) in the case of a marriage between a person and the parent of a former spouse of that person, after the death of both the former spouse and the former spouse's other parent;
(b) in the case of a marriage between a person and the parent of a former civil partner of that person, after the death of both the former civil partner and the former civil partner's other parent;
(c) in the case of a marriage between a person and the former spouse of a child of that person, after the death of both the child and the child's other parent;
(d) in the case of a marriage between a person and the former civil partner of a child of that person, after the death of both the child and the child's other parent.'
(6) Omit subsections (6) to (8).

14 In section 27 (notice of marriage), in subsection (3), for 'the name and surname, marital status, occupation, place of residence and nationality of each of the persons to be married' substitute 'the name and surname, occupation, place of residence and nationality of each of the persons to be married, whether either of them has previously been married or formed a civil partnership and, if so, how the marriage or civil partnership ended'.

15 In section 28A (power to require evidence), for subsection (3) substitute—
'(3) "Specified evidence", in relation to a person, means such evidence as may be specified in guidance issued by the Registrar General—
(a) of the person's name and surname,
(b) of the person's age,
(c) as to whether the person has previously been married or formed a civil partnership and, if so, as to the ending of the marriage or civil partnership, and
(d) of the person's nationality.'

16 In section 78(1) (interpretation), in the definition of 'child', after ' "child" ' insert ', except where used to express a relationship,'.

17 For Schedule 1 (kindred and affinity) substitute—

'SCHEDULE 1

KINDRED AND AFFINITY

Part 1

Prohibited degrees: Kindred

1 (1) The list referred to in section 1(1) is—
Adoptive child
Adoptive parent
Child
Former adoptive child
Former adoptive parent
Grandparent
Grandchild
Parent

Parent's sibling
Sibling
Sibling's child

(2) In the list 'sibling' means a brother, sister, half-brother or half-sister.

Part 2

Degrees of affinity referred to in section 1(2) and (3)

2 The list referred to in section 1(2) is as follows—
Child of former civil partner
Child of former spouse
Former civil partner of grandparent
Former civil partner of parent
Former spouse of grandparent
Former spouse of parent
Grandchild of former civil partner
Grandchild of former spouse

Part 3

Degrees of affinity referred to in section 1(4) and (5)

3 The list referred to in section 1(4) is as follows—
Parent of former spouse
Parent of former civil partner
Former spouse of child
Former civil partner of child.'

Maintenance Orders Act 1950 (c. 37)

18 (1) Amend section 16 (application of Part 2) as follows.

(2) After subsection (2)(a)(viii) insert—
'(ix) Part 1, 8 or 9 of Schedule 5 to the Civil Partnership Act 2004, Schedule 6 to that Act or paragraph 5 or 9 of Schedule 7 to that Act;'.

(3) After subsection (2)(b)(ix) insert—
'(x) an order made on an application under Schedule 11 to the Civil Partnership Act 2004;'.

(4) After subsection (2)(c)(ix) insert—
'(x) Part 1, 7 or 8 of Schedule 15 to the Civil Partnership Act 2004, Schedule 16 to that Act or paragraph 5 or 9 of Schedule 17 to that Act;'.

Births and Deaths Registration Act 1953 (c. 20)

19 In section 41 (interpretation), in the definition of 'relative', after 'by marriage' insert 'or civil partnership'.

Pharmacy Act 1954 (c. 61)

20 In section 17(c) (benevolent fund: distressed relatives eligible for relief), for 'widows,' substitute 'surviving spouses, surviving civil partners,'.

Registration of Births, Deaths and Marriages (Special Provisions) Act 1957 (c. 58)

21 In section 1 (records of deaths, births and marriages among armed forces and service civilians and their families overseas), in subsection (1), for 'and marriages solemnised,' substitute 'marriages solemnised and civil partnerships formed,'.

Maintenance Orders Act 1958 (c. 39)

22 (1) Amend section 4 (variation of orders registered in magistrates' courts) as follows.

(2) In each of subsections (5A) and (5B) (application of section 60(4) to (11) of the Magistrates' Courts Act 1980), for 'and section 15(2) of the Children Act 1989' substitute ', section 15(2) of the Children Act 1989 and paragraph 42 of Schedule 6 to the Civil Partnership Act 2004'.

(3) In subsection (6B) (no application may be made for variation under the Act of certain registered orders), after '1984' insert 'or under Schedule 7 to the Civil Partnership Act 2004'.

Offices, Shops and Railway Premises Act 1963 (c. 41)

23 In section 2 (exception for premises in which only employer's relatives or outworkers work), in subsection (1), after 'wife' insert ', civil partner'.

Industrial and Provident Societies Act 1965 (c. 12)

24 (1) Amend section 23 (nomination to property in society) as follows.

(2) In subsection (2), for 'husband, wife,' substitute 'spouse, civil partner,'.

(3) After subsection (6) insert—

'(7) The formation of a civil partnership by a member of a society revokes any nomination made by him before the formation of the civil partnership; but if any property of that member has been transferred by an officer of the society in pursuance of the nomination in ignorance of a civil partnership formed by the nominator after the date of the nomination—

(a) the receipt of the nominee shall be a valid discharge to the society, and

(b) the society shall be under no liability to any other person claiming the property.'

25 In section 25 (provision for intestacy), in subsection (2), after 'widower' insert ', surviving civil partner'.

Criminal Appeal Act 1968 (c. 19)

26 In section 44A (appeals in cases of death), in subsection (3)(a), after 'widower' insert 'or surviving civil partner'.

Theft Act 1968 (c. 60)

27 (1) Amend section 30 (husband and wife) as follows.

(2) In subsections (4) and (5), after 'wife or husband' in each place except paragraph (a)(ii) to the proviso to subsection (4) insert 'or civil partner'.

(3) At the end of paragraph (a)(ii) to the proviso insert 'or

(iii) an order (wherever made) is in force providing for the separation of that person and his or her civil partner.',

and omit 'or' at the end of paragraph (a)(i) to the proviso.

(4)   For the heading to section 30 substitute 'Spouses and civil partners'.

28   In section 31 (effect on civil proceedings and rights), in subsection (1)—
   (a) for 'wife or husband' substitute 'spouse or civil partner', and
   (b) for 'married after the making of the statement or admission) against the wife or husband' substitute 'married or became civil partners after the making of the statement or admission) against the spouse or civil partner'.

Domestic and Appellate Proceedings (Restriction of Publicity) Act 1968 (c. 63)

29   (1)   Amend section 2 (restriction of publicity for certain matrimonial etc. proceedings) as follows.

(2)   In subsection (1), after paragraph (d) insert—
   '(da) proceedings under Part 9 of Schedule 5 to the Civil Partnership Act 2004 (provision corresponding to the provision referred to in paragraph (c) above);
   (db) proceedings under section 58 of the 2004 Act (declarations as to subsistence etc. of civil partnership);'.

(3)   In subsection (3), after '(1)(d)' insert 'or (db)'.

Civil Evidence Act 1968 (c. 64)

30   In section 14 (privilege against incrimination of self or spouse)—
   (a) in subsection (1)(b), for 'husband or wife' substitute 'spouse or civil partner', and
   (b) in the heading, after 'spouse' insert 'or civil partner'.

Gaming Act 1968 (c. 65)

31   In Schedule 2 (grant, renewal, cancellation and transfer of licences), in paragraph 35A(8)(a) for 'wife or husband' substitute 'spouse or civil partner'.

Medicines Act 1968 (c. 67)

32   In section 114 (supplementary provisions as to rights of entry and related rights), in subsection (4), for 'married) the husband or wife' substitute 'married or a civil partner) the spouse or civil partner'.

Employers' Liability (Compulsory Insurance) Act 1969 (c. 57)

33   In section 2(2)(a) (persons whom employer is not required to insure) after 'husband, wife,' insert 'civil partner,'.

Administration of Justice Act 1970 (c. 31)

34   In Schedule 8 (meaning of 'maintenance order' in Part 2 of the Act and in the Maintenance Orders Act 1958), after paragraph 14 insert—
   '15. An order for periodical or other payments made under Schedule 5, 6 or 7 to the Civil Partnership Act 2004.'

Attachment of Earnings Act 1971 (c. 32)

35   In Schedule 1 (maintenance orders to which the 1971 Act applies), after paragraph 14 insert—
   '15 An order made under Schedule 5 to the Civil Partnership Act 2004 (financial relief in the High Court or a county court etc.), for periodical or other payments.

16 An order made under Schedule 6 to the 2004 Act (financial relief in magistrates' courts etc.), for maintenance or other payments to or in respect of a civil partner or child.'

Criminal Damage Act 1971 (c. 48)

36 In section 9 (evidence in connection with offences under the 1971 Act)—
    (a) for 'wife or husband' substitute 'spouse or civil partner', and
    (b) for 'married after the making of the statement or admission) against the wife or husband' substitute 'married or became civil partners after the making of the statement or admission) against the spouse or civil partner'.

Immigration Act 1971 (c. 77)

37 In section 5(4) (members of another's family for purposes of deportation)—
    (a) in paragraph (a), after 'his wife' insert 'or civil partner,' and
    (b) in paragraph (b), after 'her husband' insert 'or civil partner,'.

Local Government Act 1972 (c. 70)

38 In section 95 (pecuniary interests for purposes of section 94), after subsection (3) insert—
    '(4) In the case of civil partners living together the interest of one civil partner, shall, if known to the other, be deemed for the purpose of section 94 above to be also an interest of the other.'
39 In section 96 (general notices and recording of disclosures for purposes of section 94), in subsection (1), after 'spouse' (in each place) insert 'or civil partner'.

Matrimonial Causes Act 1973 (c. 18)

40 In section 11 (grounds on which marriage is void), at the end of paragraph (b) insert 'or a civil partner'.
41 (1) Amend section 14 (marriages governed by foreign law or celebrated abroad under English law) as follows.
(2) In subsection (1), at the beginning insert 'Subject to subsection (3)'.
(3) After subsection (2) insert—
    '(3) No marriage is to be treated as valid by virtue of subsection (1) if, at the time when it purports to have been celebrated, either party was already a civil partner.'
42 In section 24A (orders for sale of property), in subsection (5), after 're-marriage of' insert ', or formation of a civil partnership by,'.
43 (1) Amend section 28 (duration of continuing financial provision orders in favour of party to marriage, and effect of remarriage) as follows.
(2) In subsection (1)(a) and (b) after 'remarriage of' insert ', or formation of a civil partnership by,'.
(3) In subsection (2)—
    (a) after 'remarriage of' insert ', or formation of a civil partnership by,', and
    (b) after 'the remarriage' insert 'or formation of the civil partnership'.

(4) In subsection (3), after 'remarries whether at any time before or after the commencement of this Act', insert 'or forms a civil partnership'.

(5) In the heading to section 28, after 'remarriage' insert 'or formation of civil partnership'.

44 In section 35 (alteration of agreements by court during lives of parties), in subsection (4)(a) and (b), after 'remarriage of' insert ', or formation of a civil partnership by,'.

45 (1) Amend section 38 (orders for repayment in certain cases of sums paid after cessation of order by reason of remarriage) as follows.

(2) In subsection (1)—

    (a) in paragraph (a), after 'remarriage of', insert ', or formation of a civil partnership by,', and

    (b) in paragraph (b), after 'remarriage' insert 'or formation of the civil partnership'.

(3) In subsection (6)—

    (a) in paragraph (a), after 'remarriage of' insert ', or formation of a civil partnership by,' and

    (b) in the words following paragraph (b), after 'had remarried' insert 'or formed a civil partnership'.

(4) In the heading to section 38, after 'remarriage' insert 'or formation of civil partnership'.

46 In section 52 (interpretation), after subsection (3), insert—

    '(3A) References in this Act to the formation of a civil partnership by a person include references to a civil partnership which is by law void or voidable.'

Fair Trading Act 1973 (c. 41)

47 In section 30 (offences in connection with exercise of powers under section 29), in subsection (6) for 'married) the husband or wife' substitute 'married or a civil partner) the spouse or civil partner'.

Slaughterhouses Act 1974 (c. 3)

48 In section 10 (temporary continuance of licence on death), for 'his personal representative, or of his widow or any other member of his family, until the expiration of two months from his death,' substitute 'the deceased's personal representative, or widow or widower or surviving civil partner or any other member of the deceased's family, until the end of two months from the deceased's death,'.

Health and Safety at Work etc. Act 1974 (c. 37)

49 In section 20 (powers of inspectors), in subsection (7), for 'husband or wife' substitute 'spouse or civil partner'.

Consumer Credit Act 1974 (c. 39)

50 In section 165 (obstruction of authorised officers), in subsection (3), for 'married) the husband or wife' substitute 'married or a civil partner) the spouse or civil partner'.

51 (1) Amend section 184 (associates) as follows.

(2) For subsection (1) substitute—

    '(1) A person is an associate of an individual if that person is—

        (a) the individual's husband or wife or civil partner,

        (b) a relative of—

    (i)   the individual, or
    (ii) the individual's husband or wife or civil partner, or
    (c) the husband or wife or civil partner of a relative of—
        (i)   the individual, or
        (ii) the individual's husband or wife or civil partner.'
(3) In subsection (2), after 'husband or wife' insert 'or civil partner'.
(4) In subsection (5)—
    (a) omit the word 'and' immediately before 'references',
    (b) for 'or wife;' substitute 'or wife, and references to a civil partner include a former civil partner;', and
    (c) for 'had been a child born to him in wedlock' substitute 'were the legitimate child of the relationship in question'.

Friendly Societies Act 1974 (c. 46)

52 (1) Amend section 66 (power of member to nominate person to receive sums payable on his death) as follows.
(2) In subsection (5)(a), for 'husband, wife,' substitute 'spouse, civil partner,'.
(3) After subsection (7) insert—
    '(7A) The formation of a civil partnership by a member of the society or branch revokes any nomination previously made by that member under this section.'

Rehabilitation of Offenders Act 1974 (c. 53)

53 In section 7 (limitations on rehabilitation under the 1974 Act, etc.), in subsection (2)(c), after 'the marriage of any minor,' insert 'or the formation of a civil partnership by any minor,'.

Sex Discrimination Act 1975 (c. 65)

54 In section 82(5) (general interpretation: meaning of 'near relative')
    (a) after 'wife or husband' (in both places) insert 'or civil partner', and
    (b) for 'by affinity)' substitute 'by marriage or civil partnership)'.

Race Relations Act 1976 (c. 74)

55 In section 78(5) (general interpretation: meaning of 'near relative')—
    (a) after 'wife or husband' (in both places) insert 'or civil partner', and
    (b) for 'by affinity)' substitute 'by marriage or civil partnership)'.

Criminal Law Act 1977 (c. 45)

56 In section 2 (exemptions from liability for conspiracy), in subsection (2)(a), after 'spouse' insert 'or civil partner'.

Domestic Proceedings and Magistrates' Courts Act 1978 (c. 22)

57 In section 4 (duration of orders for financial provision for a party to a marriage), in subsection (2)—
    (a) after 'remarriage of' insert ', or formation of a civil partnership by,', and
    (b) after 'the remarriage' insert 'or formation of the civil partnership'.

58 (1) Amend section 35 (orders for repayment in certain cases of sums paid after cessation of order by reason of remarriage) as follows.

(2) In subsection (1)—

    (a) in paragraph (a), after 'remarriage of' insert ', or formation of a civil partnership by,', and

    (b) in paragraph (b), after 'that remarriage' insert 'or the formation of that civil partnership'.

(3) In subsection (7)—

    (a) in paragraph (a), after 'remarriage of' insert ', or formation of a civil partnership by,', and

    (b) in the words following paragraph (b)—

        (i) after 'the remarriage' insert 'or the formation of that civil partnership', and

        (ii) after 'had remarried' insert 'or formed a civil partnership'. (4) In the heading to section 35, after 'remarriage' insert 'or formation of civil partnership'.

Interpretation Act 1978 (c. 30)

59 At the appropriate place in Schedule 1 (words and expressions defined) insert—

    ' "Civil partnership" means a civil partnership which exists under or by virtue of the Civil Partnership Act 2004 (and any reference to a civil partner is to be read accordingly).'

Protection of Children Act 1978 (c. 37)

60 In section 1A (marriage and other relationships), in subsections (1)(a) and (2)(a) after 'were married' insert 'or civil partners of each other'.

Credit Unions Act 1979 (c. 34)

61 (1) Amend section 31(1) (interpretation) as follows.

(2) After the definition of 'charitable' insert—

    ' "civil partner" includes former civil partner;'.

(3) In the definition of 'relative'—

    (a) in paragraphs (a), (b) and (c), after 'spouse' insert 'or civil partner', and

    (b) in the words following paragraph (c), for 'a child born in wedlock' substitute 'the legitimate child of the relationship in question'.

Estate Agents Act 1979 (c. 38)

62 In section 27 (obstruction and personation of authorised officers), in subsection (4), for 'husband or wife' substitute 'spouse or civil partner'.

63 (1) Amend section 32 (associates) as follows.

(2) In subsection (2), after 'spouse' insert 'or civil partner'.

(3) In subsection (3)—

    (a) omit the word 'and' immediately before 'references',

    (b) for 'reputed spouse;' substitute 'reputed spouse, and references to a civil partner include a former civil partner;', and

    (c) for 'had been a child born to him in wedlock' substitute 'were the legitimate child of the relationship in question'.

Magistrates' Courts Act 1980 (c. 43)

64 In section 59 (orders for periodical payments: means of payment), in subsection (7)(b), after 'Domestic Proceedings and Magistrates' Courts Act 1978' insert 'or Schedule 6 to the Civil Partnership Act 2004'.

65 (1) Amend section 65 (meaning of family proceedings) as follows.

(2) After subsection (1)(c) insert—
'(ca) Schedule 2 to the Civil Partnership Act 2004;'.

(3) After subsection (1)(ee) insert—
'(ef) paragraphs 69 to 72 of Schedule 5 to the Civil Partnership Act 2004;'.

(4) After subsection (1)(j) insert—
'(ja) Schedule 6 to the Civil Partnership Act 2004;'.

Disused Burial Grounds (Amendment) Act 1981 (c. 18)

66 In section 9 (interpretation), in the definition of 'relative', for 'husband or wife' substitute 'spouse or civil partner'.

Forgery and Counterfeiting Act 1981 (c. 45)

67 In section 5 (offences relating to money orders, share certificates, passports, etc.), in subsection (5)(l)—
(a) after 'adoptions, marriages' insert ', civil partnerships', and
(b) for 'register marriages' substitute 'issue certified copies relating to such entries'.

Supreme Court Act 1981 (c. 54)

68 In section 18(1) (restrictions on appeals to Court of Appeal), before paragraph (g) insert—
'(fa) from a dissolution order, nullity order or presumption of death order under Chapter 2 of Part 2 of the Civil Partnership Act 2004 that has been made final, by a party who, having had time and opportunity to appeal from the conditional order on which that final order was founded, has not appealed from the conditional order;'.

69 (1) Amend section 72 (withdrawal of privilege against incrimination of self or spouse in certain proceedings) as follows.

(2) In subsection (1), after 'spouse' insert 'or civil partner'.

(3) In subsection (3), for 'married after the making of the statement or admission) against the spouse' substitute 'married or became civil partners after the making of the statement or admission) against the spouse or civil partner'.

70 In paragraph 3 of Schedule 1 (business assigned to Family Division of High Court), after sub-paragraph (h) insert—
'(i) all civil partnership causes and matters (whether at first instance or on appeal);
(j) applications for consent to the formation of a civil partnership by a minor or for a declaration under paragraph 7 of Schedule 1 to the Civil Partnership Act 2004;
(k) applications under section 58 of that Act (declarations relating to civil partnerships).'

British Nationality Act 1981 (c. 61)

71 In section 3(6)(a) (registration as British citizen of minor whose parents' marriage has terminated etc.), after 'marriage' insert 'or civil partnership'.

72 In section 6(2) (naturalisation of person married to British citizen), after 'is married to a British citizen' insert 'or is the civil partner of a British citizen'.

73 In section 10(2)(b) (registration as British citizen after pre–1983 renunciation of citizenship), after 'has been married to' insert ', or has been the civil partner of,'.

74 In section 12(5) (renunciation: persons who have married deemed of full age), after 'has been married' insert ', or has formed a civil partnership,'.

75 In section 17(6)(a) (registration as British overseas territories citizen of minor whose parents' marriage has terminated etc.), after 'marriage' insert 'or civil partnership'.

76 In section 18(2) (naturalisation of person married to a British overseas territories citizen), after 'is married to such a citizen' insert 'or is the civil partner of such a citizen'.

77 In section 22(2)(b) (naturalisation as British overseas territories citizen after pre–1983 renunciation of citizenship), after 'has been married to' insert ', or has been the civil partner of,'.

78 (1) Amend paragraphs 4(d) and 8(d) of Schedule 1 (requirements for naturalisation under sections 6(2) and 18(2)) as follows.

(2) In the paragraph (f) set out in each of those provisions, after 'to whom the applicant is married' insert ', or of whom the applicant is the civil partner,'.

Forfeiture Act 1982 (c. 34)

79 In section 3 (application for financial provision not affected by forfeiture rule), in subsection (2), for paragraph (b) and the word 'and' immediately preceding it substitute—

(b) 'sections 31(6) and 36(1) of the Matrimonial Causes Act 1973 (variation by court in England and Wales of periodical payments orders and maintenance agreements in respect of marriages);

(c) paragraphs 60(2) and 73(2) of Schedule 5 to the Civil Partnership Act 2004 (variation by court in England and Wales of periodical payments orders and maintenance agreements in respect of civil partnerships); and

(d) section 13(4) of the Family Law (Scotland) Act 1985 (variation etc. of periodical allowances in respect of marriages and civil partnerships).'

Representation of the People Act 1983 (c. 2)

80 (1) Amend section 14 (service qualification) as follows.

(2) In subsection (1)(d), for 'wife or husband' substitute 'spouse or civil partner'.

(3) For subsection (1)(e) substitute—

'(e) is the spouse or civil partner of a person mentioned in paragraph (b) or paragraph (c) above and is residing outside the United Kingdom to be with his or her spouse or civil partner,'.

81 In section 16 (contents of service declaration), for 'wife or husband' substitute 'spouse or civil partner'.

82 In section 59 (supplemental provisions as to members of forces and service voters), in subsection (3)(b), for 'by him and any wife of his or, as the case may be, by her and any husband of hers,' substitute 'by that person and any spouse or civil partner of that person'.

83 In section 61 (other voting offences), in subsection (4), for 'husband, wife,' substitute 'spouse, civil partner,'.

84 In section 141 (duty to answer relevant questions), in subsections (1)(a)(i) and (2)(a), for 'husband or wife,' substitute 'spouse or civil partner,'.

85 (1) Amend Schedule 1 (parliamentary elections rules) as follows.

(2) In rule 11(4), for 'wife or husband' substitute 'spouse or civil partner'.

(3) In rule 35(2), for 'husband (wife),' (in both places) substitute 'spouse, civil partner,'.

(4) In rule 39(3)(b), for 'husband, wife,' substitute 'spouse, civil partner,'.

(5) In rule 44(2)(b), for 'wives or husbands' substitute 'spouses or civil partners'.

Mental Health Act 1983 (c. 20)

86 In—
(a) section 12 (general provisions as to medical recommendations), in subsection (5), in the words following paragraph (e), and
(b) section 25C (supervision applications: supplementary), in subsection (10),
after 'husband, wife' insert ', civil partner'.

Mobile Homes Act 1983 (c. 34)

87 In section 3(3) (succession to agreements to which Act applies), for 'or widower' (in each place) substitute ', widower or surviving civil partner'.

88 In section 5(3) (meaning of 'member of another's family')—
(a) after 'spouse,' insert 'civil partner,'
(b) in paragraph (a), after 'marriage' insert 'or civil partnership', and
(c) in the words after paragraph (b), after 'as husband and and wife' insert 'or as if they were civil partners'.

Dentists Act 1984 (c. 24)

89 In section 41(4) (family or representatives may carry on deceased dentist's business for three years), for 'his widow' (in each place) substitute 'his surviving spouse or his surviving civil partner'.

Matrimonial and Family Proceedings Act 1984 (c. 42)

90 (1) Amend section 12 (applications for financial relief after overseas divorce etc.) as follows.

(2) In subsection (2) (no application may be made after remarriage), for 'remarries' substitute 'forms a subsequent marriage or civil partnership,'.

(3) For subsection (3) substitute—
'(3) The reference in subsection (2) above to the forming of a subsequent marriage or civil partnership includes a reference to the forming of a marriage or civil partnership which is by law void or voidable.'

91 In section 32 (meaning of 'family business' etc.), after the definition of 'family proceedings' insert—
' "civil partnership cause" means an action for the dissolution or annulment of a civil partnership or for the legal separation of civil partners;'.

92 After section 36 insert—

'**36A Jurisdiction of county courts in civil partnership causes and matters**

(1) The Lord Chancellor may by order—
   (a) designate any county court as a civil partnership proceedings county court, and
   (b) designate, as a court of trial, any county court designated as a civil partnership proceedings county court.

(2) In this Part of this Act "civil partnership proceedings county court" means a county court designated under subsection (1)(a) above.

(3) A civil partnership proceedings county court shall have jurisdiction to hear and determine any civil partnership cause, subject to subsection (4) below.

(4) A civil partnership proceedings county court shall have jurisdiction to try a civil partnership cause only if it is designated under subsection (1)(b) above as a court of trial.

(5) The jurisdiction conferred by this section on a civil partnership proceedings county court shall be exercisable throughout England and Wales, but rules of court may provide for a civil partnership cause pending in one such court to be heard and determined—
   (a) partly in that court and partly in another such court, or
   (b) in another such court.

(6) Every civil partnership cause shall be commenced in a civil partnership proceedings county court.

(7) Every civil partnership cause shall be heard and determined in a civil partnership proceedings county court unless, or except to the extent, it is transferred to the High Court under—
   (a) section 39 below, or
   (b) section 41 of the County Court Act 1984 (transfer to High Court by order of High Court).

(8) The Lord Chancellor may by order designate a civil partnership proceedings county court as a court for the exercise of jurisdiction in civil partnership matters under Schedule 7 to the Civil Partnership Act 2004.

(9) The power to make an order under subsection (1) or (8) above shall be exercisable by statutory instrument.

36B Jurisdiction of civil partnership proceedings county courts as respects financial relief and protection of children

(1) Subject to subsection (2) below, a civil partnership proceedings county court shall have the following jurisdiction—
   (a) a jurisdiction to exercise any power exercisable under—
      (i) section 63 of the Civil Partnership Act 2004 (restrictions on making of orders affecting children), or
      (ii) Schedule 5 to that Act (financial relief in the courts), other than Part 12 (arrears and repayments) and paragraph 73 (alteration of maintenance agreements by court after death of one party),
      in connection with any application or order pending in, or made by, a civil partnership proceedings county court;
   (b) a jurisdiction to exercise any power exercisable under—
      (i) Part 9 of that Schedule (failure to maintain: financial provision (and interim orders)), or
      (ii) paragraphs 69 to 71 of that Schedule (alteration of maintenance agreements by court during lives of parties);
   (c) if designated under section 36A(8) above, jurisdiction to exercise any power under Schedule 7 to that Act.

(2) Any proceedings for the exercise of a power which a civil partnership proceedings county court has jurisdiction to exercise by virtue of subsection (1) above shall be commenced in such civil partnership proceedings county court as may be prescribed by rules of court.

(3) Nothing in this section shall affect the jurisdiction of a magistrates' court under paragraphs 69 to 71 of Schedule 5 to the Civil Partnership Act 2004.

36C Consideration of agreements or arrangements

Where rules of court make provision for the purposes of section 43 of the Civil Partnership Act 2004 with respect to any power exercisable by the court on an application made under that section before an application is made for a dissolution or separation order, the rules shall confer jurisdiction to exercise the power on civil partnership proceedings county courts.

36D Assignment of circuit judges to civil partnership proceedings

The jurisdiction conferred by the preceding provisions of this Part of this Act on civil partnership proceedings county courts, so far as it exercisable by judges of such courts, shall be exercised by such Circuit judges as the Lord Chancellor may direct.'

93   For section 38(3) (transfer of family proceedings from High Court to county court) substitute—
    '(3) Proceedings transferred under this section shall be transferred to such county court as the High Court directs, subject to subsections (3A) and (3B) below.
    (3A) Where a matrimonial cause or matter within the jurisdiction of a divorce county court only is transferred under this section, it shall be transferred to such divorce county court as the High Court directs.
    (3B) Where a civil partnership cause or matter within the jurisdiction of a civil partnership proceedings county court only is transferred under this section, it shall be transferred to such civil partnership proceedings county court as the High Court directs.'
94   In section 39(2) (family proceedings transferable to the High Court), for 'or divorce county court' (in each place) substitute ', divorce county court or civil partnership proceedings county court'.
95   In section 40(4)(b) (enforcement in High Court of orders of divorce county court), after 'a divorce county court' insert 'or a civil partnership proceedings county court'.
96   (1) Amend section 42 (county court proceedings in principal registry of Family Division) as follows.
    (2) In subsection (1)—
        (a) after 'Sections 33 to 35' insert 'and 36A to 36C',
        (b) after 'section 34(2)' insert 'or 36B(2)', and
        (c) after 'divorce county court' insert 'or civil partnership proceedings county court'.
    (3) After that subsection insert—
        '(1A) Subsection (2) below applies to—
            (a) the jurisdiction in matrimonial causes or matters conferred by sections 33, 34 and 35 above on divorce county courts, and
            (b) the jurisdiction in civil partnership causes or matters conferred by sections 36A, 36B and 36C above on civil partnership proceedings county courts.'
    (4) In subsection (2), for the words from the beginning to 'on divorce county courts' substitute 'A jurisdiction to which this subsection applies'.
    (5) For the words in subsection (2) after paragraph (b) substitute the following new subsection—

'(2A) Rules of court may make provision—

    (a) for treating, for any purposes specified in the rules, matrimonial causes and matters pending in the registry with respect to which the jurisdiction mentioned in subsection (1A)(a) above is exercisable as pending in a divorce county court,

    (b) for treating, for any purposes specified in the rules, civil partnership causes and matters pending in the registry with respect to which the jurisdiction mentioned in subsection (1A)(b) above is exercisable as pending in a civil partnership proceedings county court, and

    (c) for the application of section 74(3) of the Solicitors Act 1974 (costs) with respect to proceedings treated as mentioned in paragraph (a) or (b) above.'

(6) In subsection (3), for 'subsection (2)' substitute 'subsection (2A)'.

(7) After subsection (3) insert—

'(3A) Where, by virtue of rules under subsection (2A) above, a civil partnership cause or matter is pending in the registry as in a civil partnership proceedings county court, any ancillary or related proceedings which could be taken in a civil partnership proceedings county court and which are not of a description excluded by the rules from the operation of this subsection may be taken and dealt with in the registry as in a civil partnership proceedings county court.'

(8) After subsection (4) insert—

'(4ZA) The principal registry shall be treated as a civil partnership proceedings county court—

    (a) for the purposes of any provision to be made by rules of court under section 36A(5) above;

    (b) for the purpose of any provision to be made under section 36B(2) above prescribing the county court in which any proceedings are to be commenced; and

    (c) for the purpose of any transfer of family proceedings under section 38 or 39 above between the High Court and a civil partnership proceedings county court.'

(9) In subsection (4A), after 'in any matrimonial cause or matter' insert ', or in any civil partnership cause or matter,'.

(10) In subsection (5), for paragraphs (a) and (b) substitute—

'(a) as regards service of process—

    (i) as if proceedings commenced in the principal registry in a matrimonial cause or matter had been commenced in a divorce county court, and

    (ii) as if proceedings commenced in that registry in a civil partnership cause or matter had been commenced in a civil partnership proceedings county court; and

(b) as regards enforcement of orders—

    (i) as if orders made in that registry in the exercise of the family jurisdiction conferred by sections 33, 34 and 35 above on divorce county courts were orders made by such a court, and

    (ii) as if orders made in that registry in the exercise of the family jurisdiction conferred by sections 36A, 36B and 36C above on civil partnership proceedings county courts were orders made by such a court.'

(11) After that subsection insert—
    '(5A) For the purposes of subsection (3A) above, proceedings—
        (a) are "ancillary" to a civil partnership cause if they are connected with the cause, and
        (b) are "related" to a civil partnership cause if they are for protecting or otherwise relate to any rights, or the exercise of any rights, of—
            (i) the civil partners as civil partners, or
            (ii) any children of the family.'

Police and Criminal Evidence Act 1984 (c. 60)

97 (1) Amend section 80 (compellability of accused's spouse) as follows.
(2) In subsections (2), (2A) and (3), for 'wife or husband' (in each place) substitute 'spouse or civil partner'.
(3) After subsection (5) insert—
    '(5A) In any proceedings a person who has been but is no longer the civil partner of the accused shall be compellable to give evidence as if that person and the accused had never been civil partners.'
(4) In the heading to section 80, after 'accused's spouse' insert 'or civil partner'.
98 In section 80A (rule where accused's spouse not compellable)—
    (a) for 'wife or husband' substitute 'spouse or civil partner', and
    (b) in the heading, after 'spouse' insert 'or civil partner'.

Companies Act 1985 (c. 6)

99 In section 203 (notification of family and corporate interests), in subsection (1), after 'spouse' insert 'or civil partner'.
100 (1) Amend section 327 (extension of section 323 to spouses and children) as follows.
(2) In subsection (1)—
    (a) in paragraph (a), after 'wife or husband' insert 'or civil partner', and
    (b) in the words following paragraph (b), after 'as the case may be,' insert 'civil partner or'.
(3) In the heading to section 327, after 'spouses' insert ', civil partners'.
101 (1) Amend section 328 (extension of section 324 to spouses and children) as follows.
(2) In subsections (1)(a) and (2)(a), after 'wife or husband' insert 'or civil partner'.
(3) In subsection (3)—
    (a) in paragraph (a), after 'spouse' insert 'or civil partner', and
    (b) in paragraph (b), after 'spouse' insert 'or civil partner' and after 'wife, husband,' insert 'civil partner,'.
(4) In the heading to section 328, after 'spouses' insert ', civil partners'.
102 In section 346 (connected persons) in subsection (2)—
    (a) in paragraph (a), after 'spouse,' insert 'civil partner,',
    (b) in paragraph (c) after 'spouse' (in both places) insert 'or civil partner'.
103 In section 430E (associates), in subsection (8) after 'spouse' insert 'or civil partner'.
104 (1) Amend section 742A (meaning of 'offer to the public') as follows.
(2) In subsection (3)(a)(iii), after 'widower' insert 'or surviving civil partner'.
(3) In subsection (6)(a), after 'spouse' insert 'or civil partner'.

105 In Schedule 7 (matters to be dealt with in directors' report), in paragraph 2B(3), after 'spouse' insert 'or civil partner'.

Enduring Powers of Attorney Act 1985 (c. 29)

106 In section 3 (scope of authority etc. of attorney under enduring power), in subsection (5)(a), for 'or marriage' substitute ', marriage or the formation of a civil partnership'.
107 In Schedule 1 (notification prior to registration of instrument creating power of attorney), in paragraph 2(1)—
   (a) in paragraph (a), after 'wife' insert 'or civil partner', and
   (b) in paragraph (e), after 'widower' insert 'or surviving civil partner'.
108 Paragraphs 106 and 107 apply in relation to the exercise of powers under enduring powers of attorney created before the passing of this Act as well as in relation to those created on or after its passing.

Food and Environment Protection Act 1985 (c. 48)

109 In Schedule 2 (officers and their powers), in paragraph 2A(4), after 'spouse' insert 'or civil partner'.

Child Abduction and Custody Act 1985 (c. 60)

110 In section 24A (power to order disclosure of child's whereabouts), in subsection (2), after 'spouse' insert 'or civil partner'.

Airports Act 1986 (c. 31)

111 In section 20 (powers of investment and disposal in relation to public airport companies), in subsection (6)(b), after 'widowers' insert ', civil partners, surviving civil partners'.

Insolvency Act 1986 (c. 45)

112 In section 215 (proceedings under sections 213, 214), in subsection (3)(b), after 'marriage' insert 'or the formation of a civil partnership'.
113 In section 283A (bankrupt's home ceasing to form part of estate), in subsection (1)—
   (a) in paragraph (b), after 'spouse' insert 'or civil partner', and
   (b) in paragraph (c), after 'spouse' insert 'or former civil partner'.
114 In section 313 (charge on bankrupt's home), in subsection (1), after 'former spouse' insert 'or by his civil partner or former civil partner'.
115 In section 313A (low value home: application for sale, possession or charge), in subsection (1)—
   (a) in paragraph (a)(ii), after 'spouse' insert 'or civil partner', and
   (b) in paragraph (a)(iii), after 'spouse' insert 'or former civil partner'.
116 In section 329 (debts to spouse), in subsection (1), after 'spouse' (in each place) insert 'or civil partner'.
117 In section 332 (saving for bankrupt's home), in subsection (1), after 'former spouse' insert 'or by his civil partner or former civil partner'.
118 In section 335A (rights under trusts of land), in subsection (2)(b)—

(a) for 'bankrupt's spouse or former spouse' substitute 'bankrupt's spouse or civil partner or former spouse or former civil partner', and

(b) in sub-paragraphs (i) and (ii), for 'spouse or former spouse' substitute 'spouse, civil partner, former spouse or former civil partner'.

119 In section 339 (transactions at an undervalue), in subsection (3)(b), after 'marriage' insert 'or the formation of a civil partnership'.

120 In section 366 (inquiry into bankrupt's dealings and property), in subsection (1)(a), after 'former spouse' insert 'or civil partner or former civil partner'.

121 In section 423 (transactions defrauding creditors), in subsection (1)(b), after 'marriage' insert 'or the formation of a civil partnership'.

122 (1) Amend section 435 (meaning of 'associate') as follows.

(2) For subsection (2) substitute—

'(2) A person is an associate of an individual if that person is—

    (a) the individual's husband or wife or civil partner,

    (b) a relative of—

        (i) the individual, or

        (ii) the individual's husband or wife or civil partner, or

    (c) the husband or wife or civil partner of a relative of—

        (i) the individual, or

        (ii) the individual's husband or wife or civil partner.'

(3) In subsection (3), after 'husband or wife' insert 'or civil partner'.

(4) In subsection (8), at the end insert 'and references to a civil partner include a former civil partner'.

Building Societies Act 1986 (c. 53)

123 In section 70 (interpretation), in—

    (a) subsection (2)(a) and (c), and

    (b) subsection (4),

after 'spouse' (in each place) insert 'or civil partner'.

Family Law Act 1986 (c. 55)

124 In section 33 (power to order disclosure of child's whereabouts), in subsection (2), after 'spouse' insert 'or civil partner'.

125 In section 50 (non-recognition of divorce or annulment in another jurisdiction no bar to remarriage), for the words from 're-marrying' to the end substitute 'forming a subsequent marriage or civil partnership in that part of the UK or cause the subsequent marriage or civil partnership of either party (wherever it takes place) to be treated as invalid in that part.'

Consumer Protection Act 1987 (c. 43)

126 In section 47 (savings for certain privileges), in subsection (2), after 'spouse' insert 'or civil partner'.

Criminal Justice Act 1988 (c. 33)

127 In section 160A (marriage and other relationships), in subsections (1)(a) and (2)(a), after 'were married' insert 'or civil partners of each other'.

Companies Act 1989 (c. 40)

128 In section 52 (meaning of 'associate'), in subsection (2)(a) after 'spouse' insert 'or civil partner'.

Children Act 1989 (c. 41)

129 (1) Amend section 8 (residence, contact and other orders with respect to children) as follows.

(2) After subsection (4)(b) insert—
'(ba) Schedule 5 to the Civil Partnership Act 2004;'.

(3) After subsection (4)(e) insert—
'(ea) Schedule 6 to the Civil Partnership Act 2004;'.

130 In section 48 (powers to assist in discovery of children who may be in need of emergency protection), in subsection (2), after 'spouse' insert 'or civil partner'.

131 In section 50 (recovery of abducted children etc.), in subsection (11), after 'spouse' insert 'or civil partner'.

132 In section 98 (self-incrimination), in subsections (1) and (2), after 'spouse' insert 'or civil partner'.

Local Government and Housing Act 1989 (c. 42)

133 In section 19 (members' interests) in subsection (7), after 'spouse' insert 'or civil partner'.

134 In section 69 (companies subject to local authority influence), in subsection (6)(c), after 'spouse' insert 'or civil partner'.

Opticians Act 1989 (c. 44)

135 In section 29(1) (family or representatives may use deceased optician's title for three years), in paragraphs (b) and (d), for 'his widow' substitute 'his surviving spouse or his surviving civil partner'.

Food Safety Act 1990 (c. 16)

136 In section 43 (continuance of registration or licence on death) in subsection (2), for the words from 'the deceased's personal representative' to 'his death' substitute 'the deceased's personal representative, or widow or widower or surviving civil partner or any other member of the deceased's family, until the end of—
(a) the period of three months beginning with the deceased's death'.

Courts and Legal Services Act 1990 (c. 41)

137 In section 10 (family proceedings in magistrates' courts and related matters), in subsection (1), after 'Domestic Proceedings and Magistrates' Courts Act 1978' insert 'or Schedule 6 to the Civil Partnership Act 2004'.

138 In section 58A (conditional fee agreements: supplementary), omit 'and' at the end of subsection (2)(f) and insert—
'(fa) Chapter 2 of Part 2 of the Civil Partnership Act 2004 (proceedings for dissolution etc. of civil partnership);
(fb) Schedule 5 to the 2004 Act (financial relief in the High Court or a county court etc.);

(fc) Schedule 6 to the 2004 Act (financial relief in magistrates' courts etc.);

(fd) Schedule 7 to the 2004 Act (financial relief in England and Wales after overseas dissolution etc. of a civil partnership); and'.

Broadcasting Act 1990 (c. 42)

139 In paragraph 1(2) of Part 1 of Schedule 2 (restrictions on the holding of licences)—

(a) in paragraphs (a) and (d), after 'husband or wife' (in each place) insert 'or civil partner', and

(b) at the end insert 'and references to a civil partner shall include a former civil partner'.

Local Government Finance Act 1992 (c. 14)

140 (1) In section 9(1)(a) (joint and several liability for council tax of married couple resident in same dwelling), after 'is married to' insert ', or is the civil partner of,'.

(2) After section 9(3) insert—

'(4) For the purposes of this section two persons are civil partners of each other if they are of the same sex and either—

(a) they are civil partners of each other; or

(b) they are not civil partners of each other but are living together as if they were civil partners.'

(3) In section 18(1)(b) (power to make regulations to deal with death of a person liable for council tax as a spouse under section 9), after 'spouse' insert 'or civil partner'.

Friendly Societies Act 1992 (c. 40)

141 In section 77 (information on appointed actuary to be annexed to balance sheet), in subsection (3)(a), after 'spouse' insert 'or civil partner'.

142 In section 119A (meaning of 'associate'), in subsection (1)(a), after 'wife or husband' insert 'or civil partner'.

143 In Schedule 2 (the activities of a friendly society), in Head A, in class II—

(a) in the second column (description), after 'Marriage' insert ', civil partnership', and

(b) in the third column (nature of business), after 'sum on marriage' insert 'or on the formation of a civil partnership'.

Trade Union and Labour Relations Act 1992 (c. 52)

144 In section 23 (restriction on enforcement of awards against certain property), in subsection (3)(b) for 'the wife' substitute 'the spouse or civil partner'.

145 In section 241 (intimidation or annoyance by violence or otherwise), in subsection (1)(a), for 'wife' substitute 'spouse or civil partner'.

146 In section 292 (death of employee or employer), in subsection (3)(b), after 'widow,' insert 'surviving civil partner,'.

Charities Act 1993 (c. 10)

147 In Schedule 5 (meaning of 'connected person' for purposes of section 36(2)) in paragraph 1(e) after 'spouse' insert 'or civil partner'.

Pension Schemes Act 1993 (c. 48)

148 In section 101E(1)(b) after 'or widower' insert 'or surviving civil partner'.

Pension Schemes (Northern Ireland) Act 1993 (c. 49)

149 In section 97E(1)(b) after 'or widower' insert 'or surviving civil partner'.

Disability Discrimination Act 1995 (c. 50)

150 (1) In section 23 (exemption for small dwellings), amend subsection (7) as follows.
(2) In the definition of 'near relative'—
    (a) after 'spouse' insert 'or civil partner', and
    (b) for 'by affinity)' substitute 'by marriage or civil partnership)'.
(3) For the definition of 'partner' substitute—
    ' "partner" means the other member of a couple consisting of—
        (a) a man and a woman who are not married to each other but are living together as husband and wife, or
        (b) two people of the same sex who are not civil partners of each other but are living together as if they were civil partners.'

Employment Rights Act 1996 (c. 18)

151 In section 57A (time off for dependants), in subsection (3)(a), after 'spouse' insert 'or civil partner'.

Family Law Act 1996 (c. 27)

152 (1) Amend section 64 (provision for separate representation for children) as follows.
(2) Omit 'or' at the end of subsection (1)(c).
(3) At the end of subsection (1)(d) insert 'or
    (e) Schedule 5 or 6 to the Civil Partnership Act 2004.'

Trusts of Land and Appointment of Trustees Act 1996 (c. 47)

153 In paragraph 3 of Schedule 1 (family charges), after 'in consideration of marriage' insert 'or the formation of a civil partnership'.

Civil Procedure Act 1997 (c. 12)

154 In section 7 (power of courts to make orders for preserving evidence etc.), in subsection (7), after 'spouse' insert 'or civil partner'.

National Minimum Wage Act 1998 (c. 39)

155 In section 14 (powers of officers), in subsection (2), for 'married, the person's spouse' substitute 'married or a civil partner, the person's spouse or civil partner'.

Access to Justice Act 1999 (c. 22)

156 In Schedule 2 (community legal service: excluded services), in paragraph 2(3)(d), after 'Domestic Proceedings and Magistrates' Courts Act 1978' insert 'or Schedule 6 to the Civil Partnership Act 2004'.

Welfare Reform and Pensions Act 1999 (c. 30)

157 (1) Amend section 23 (supply of pension information in connection with divorce etc.) as follows.

(2) After subsection (1)(a)(i) insert—

'(ia) financial relief under Schedule 5 or 7 to the Civil Partnership Act 2004 (England and Wales powers in relation to domestic and overseas dissolution of civil partnerships etc.),'.

(3) In subsection (1)(a)(ii)—

(a) after '1984' insert 'or Schedule 11 to the 2004 Act', and

(b) at the end, omit 'or'.

(4) In subsection (1)(a)(iii) for '(corresponding Northern Ireland powers);' substitute '(Northern Ireland powers corresponding to those mentioned in sub-paragraph (i)), or

(iv) financial relief under Schedule 15 or 17 to the 2004 Act (Northern Ireland powers corresponding to those mentioned in sub-paragraph (ia));'.

(5) In subsection (1)(b), for 'or (iii)' substitute '(ia), (iii) or (iv)'.

158 (1) Amend section 24 (charges by pension arrangements in relation to earmarking orders) as follows.

(2) After paragraph (a) insert—

'(aa) an order under Part 1 of Schedule 5 to the Civil Partnership Act 2004 (financial provision orders in connection with dissolution of civil partnerships etc.) so far as it includes provision made by virtue of Part 6 of that Schedule (powers to include provision about pensions),'.

(3) At the end of paragraph (b) omit 'or' and after paragraph (c) insert ', or

(d) an order under Part 1 of Schedule 15 to the 2004 Act so far as it includes provision made by virtue of Part 5 of that Schedule (Northern Ireland powers corresponding to those mentioned in paragraph (aa)).'

159 (1) Amend section 28 (activation of pension sharing) as follows.

(2) After subsection (1)(a) insert—

'(aa) a pension sharing order under Schedule 5 to the Civil Partnership Act 2004,'.

(3) After subsection (1)(d) insert—

'(da) an order under Schedule 7 to the 2004 Act (financial relief in England and Wales after overseas dissolution etc. of a civil partnership) corresponding to such an order as is mentioned in paragraph (aa),'.

(4) In subsection (1)(f)—

(a) at the end of sub-paragraph (i) insert 'or between persons who are civil partners of each other', and

(b) at the end of sub-paragraph (iii) insert 'or (as the case may be) on the grant, in relation to the civil partnership, of decree of dissolution or of declarator of nullity'.

(5) In subsection (1)(g), after 'divorce etc.)' insert 'or under Schedule 11 to the 2004 Act (financial provision in Scotland after overseas proceedings)'.

(6) In subsection (1)(h) for 'Northern Ireland legislation, and' substitute 'the Matrimonial Causes (Northern Ireland) Order 1978 (S.I. 1978/1045 (N.I. 15)),'.

(7) After subsection (1)(i) insert—

'(j) a pension sharing order under Schedule 15 to the 2004 Act, and

(k) an order under Schedule 17 to the 2004 Act (financial relief in Northern Ireland after overseas dissolution etc. of a civil partnership) corresponding to such an order as is mentioned in paragraph (j).'

(8) In subsection (7)(a), omit 'matrimonial'.

(9) In subsection (8)—

   (a) in paragraph (a), after 'divorce' insert ', dissolution', and

   (b) at the end of paragraph (b) insert 'or, where the order is under Schedule 11 to the 2004 Act, the date of disposal of the application under paragraph 2 of that Schedule'.

(10) In subsection (9)—

   (a) omit 'matrimonial', and

   (b) in paragraphs (a) and (b)(i), after 'divorce' insert ', dissolution'.

160 (1) Amend section 34 ('implementation period') as follows.

(2) In subsection (1)(b)(i), omit 'matrimonial'.

(3) In subsection (2)—

   (a) omit 'matrimonial', and

   (b) in paragraph (b), after 'divorce' insert ', dissolution'.

161 (1) Amend section 48 (activation of benefit sharing) as follows.

(2) After subsection (1)(a) insert—

'(aa) a pension sharing order under Schedule 5 to the Civil Partnership Act 2004,'.

(3) After subsection (1)(d) insert—

'(da) an order under Schedule 7 to the 2004 Act (financial relief in England and Wales after overseas dissolution etc. of a civil partnership) corresponding to such an order as is mentioned in paragraph (aa),'.

(4) In subsection (1)(f)—

   (a) at the end of sub-paragraph (i) insert 'or between persons who are civil partners of each other', and

   (b) at the end of sub-paragraph (iii) insert 'or (as the case may be) on the grant, in relation to the civil partnership, of decree of dissolution or of declarator of nullity'.

(5) In subsection (1)(g), after 'divorce etc.)' insert 'or under Schedule 11 to the 2004 Act (financial provision in Scotland after overseas proceedings)'.

(6) In subsection (1)(h) for 'Northern Ireland legislation, and' substitute 'the Matrimonial Causes (Northern Ireland) Order 1978 (S.I. 1978/1045 (N.I. 15)),'.

(7) After subsection (1)(i) insert—

'(j) a pension sharing order under Schedule 15 to the 2004 Act, and

   (k) an order under Schedule 17 to the 2004 Act (financial relief in Northern Ireland after overseas dissolution etc. of a civil partnership) corresponding to such an order as is mentioned in paragraph (j).'

(8) In subsection (6)(a), omit 'matrimonial'.

(9) In subsection (7)—

   (a) in paragraph (a), after 'divorce' insert ', dissolution', and

   (b) at the end of paragraph (b) insert 'or, where the order is under Schedule 11 to the 2004 Act, the date of disposal of the application under paragraph 2 of that Schedule'.

(10) In subsection (8)—

   (a) omit 'matrimonial', and

   (b) in paragraphs (a) and (b)(i), after 'divorce' insert ', dissolution'.

Immigration and Asylum Act 1999 (c. 33)

162 After section 24 insert—

'24A Duty to report suspicious civil partnerships

(1) Subsection (3) applies if—
   (a) a registration authority to whom a notice of proposed civil partnership has been given under section 8 of the Civil Partnership Act 2004,
   (b) any person who, under section 8 of the 2004 Act, has attested a declaration accompanying such a notice,
   (c) a district registrar to whom a notice of proposed civil partnership has been given under section 88 of the 2004 Act, or
   (d) a registrar to whom a civil partnership notice has been given under section 139 of the 2004 Act,
   has reasonable grounds for suspecting that the civil partnership will be a sham civil partnership.
(2) Subsection (3) also applies if—
   (a) two people register as civil partners of each other under Part 2, 3 or 4 of the 2004 Act in the presence of the registrar, and
   (b) before, during or immediately after they do so, the registrar has reasonable grounds for suspecting that the civil partnership will be, or is, a sham civil partnership.
(3) The person concerned must report his suspicion to the Secretary of State without delay and in such form and manner as may be prescribed by regulations.
(4) The regulations are to be made—
   (a) in relation to England and Wales, by the Registrar General for England and Wales with the approval of the Chancellor of the Exchequer;
   (b) in relation to Scotland, by the Secretary of State after consulting the Registrar General of Births, Deaths and Marriages for Scotland;
   (c) in relation to Northern Ireland, by the Secretary of State after consulting the Registrar General in Northern Ireland.
(5) 'Sham civil partnership' means a civil partnership (whether or not void)—
   (a) formed between a person ("A") who is neither a British citizen nor a national of an EEA State other than the United Kingdom and another person (whether or not such a citizen or such a national), and
   (b) formed by A for the purpose of avoiding the effect of one or more provisions of United Kingdom immigration law or the immigration rules.
(6) 'The registrar' means—
   (a) in relation to England and Wales, the civil partnership registrar acting under Part 2 of the 2004 Act;
   (b) in relation to Scotland, the authorised registrar acting under Part 3 of the 2004 Act;
   (c) in relation to Northern Ireland, the registrar acting under Part 4 of the 2004 Act.'

163 In section 166 (regulations and orders), in subsection (6)(b) after '24(3)' insert ', 24A(3)'.

Representation of the People Act 2000 (c. 2)

164 (1) Amend Schedule 4 (absent voting in Great Britain) as follows.
(2) In paragraph 3(3)(c), for 'his spouse,' (in both places) substitute 'his spouse or civil partner,'.
(3) In paragraph 6(6), for 'husband, wife,' substitute 'spouse, civil partner,'.

Financial Services and Markets Act 2000 (c. 8)

165 In section 422 (controller), in subsection (4)(a), after 'spouse' insert 'or civil partner'.
166 In Schedule 11 (offers of securities), in paragraph 16(2), after 'wife, husband, widow, widower' insert ', civil partner, surviving civil partner,'.

Land Registration Act 2002 (c. 9)

167 In section 125 (privilege against self-incrimination), in subsection (2), after 'spouse' insert 'or civil partner'.

Enterprise Act 2002 (c. 40)

168 In section 127 (associated persons), in subsections (4)(a) and (c) and (6), after 'spouse' (in each place) insert ', civil partner'.
169 In section 222 (bodies corporate: accessories), in subsection (10), after 'spouse' in paragraphs (a), (c), (d) and (e) (in each place) insert 'or civil partner'.

Licensing Act 2003 (c. 17)

170 In section 101 (minimum of 24 hours between event periods), in subsection (3)(a) and (d), after 'spouse' insert 'or civil partner'.

Local Government Act 2003 (c. 26)

171 In paragraph 2(1)(a) of Schedule 4 (spouse of employee of the Valuation Tribunal Service disqualified for appointment as member of the Service), after 'is married to' insert 'or is the civil partner of'.

Courts Act 2003 (c. 39)

172 In section 76 (further provision about scope of Family Procedure Rules), in subsection (2)(b), after 'divorce county court' insert 'or civil partnership proceedings county court (within the meaning of Part 5 of the Matrimonial and Family Proceedings Act 1984)'.

Sexual Offences Act 2003 (c. 42)

173 (1) Amend section 23 (sections 16 to 19: marriage exception) as follows.
(2) At the end of subsection (1)(b) insert 'or civil partners of each other'.
(3) In subsection (2), for 'were lawfully married at the time' substitute 'were at the time lawfully married or civil partners of each other'.
(4) In the heading to section 23 for 'marriage exception' substitute 'exception for spouses and civil partners'.
174 (1) Amend section 28 (sections 25 and 26: marriage exception) as follows.
(2) At the end of subsection (1)(b) insert 'or civil partners of each other'.
(3) In subsection (2), for 'were lawfully married at the time' substitute 'were at the time lawfully married or civil partners of each other'.
(4) In the heading to section 28 for 'marriage exception' substitute 'exception for spouses and civil partners'.
175 (1) Amend section 43 (sections 38 and 41: marriage exception) as follows.
(2) At the end of subsection (1)(b) insert 'or civil partners of each other'.

(3) In subsection (2), for 'were lawfully married at the time' substitute 'were at the time lawfully married or civil partners of each other'.

(4) In the heading to section 43 for 'marriage exception' substitute 'exception for spouses and civil partners'.

. . .

SCHEDULE 30

Section 261(4)

REPEALS AND REVOCATIONS

Family provision

Short title and chapter	Extent of repeal
Inheritance (Provision for Family and Dependants) Act 1975 (c. 63)	In section 3(2), 'and,' immediately following paragraph (b).

Housing and tenancies

Short title and chapter	Extent of repeal
Housing Act 1980 (c. 51)	In section 54(2)(b), 'or' at the end.
Housing Act 1985 (c. 68)	In each of sections 39(3)(c), 89(3)(a)(ii), 90(3)(a)(ii), 91(3)(b)(ii), 99B(2)(e)(ii), 101(3)(c)(ii) and 160(3)(c), and paragraph 1(2)(c)(iii) of Schedule 6A, 'or' at the end.
Landlord and Tenant Act 1987 (c. 31)	In section 4(2)(c)(v), 'or' at the end.
Housing Act 1988 (c. 50)	In paragraph 4(4)(c) of Schedule 11, 'or' at the end.
Housing Act 1996 (c. 52)	In sections 15(6)(c), 133(3)(a)(ii), 134(2)(a)(ii) and 160(2)(e)(ii) and (3)(d)(ii), 'or' at the end.

Family homes and domestic violence

Short title and chapter	Extent of repeal
Family Law Act 1966 (c. 27)	In section 63(1), the definition of 'matrimonial home rights'. In Schedule 7, 'or' at the end of paragraph 4(a) and paragraph 7(6). In Schedule 8, paragraphs 48(3), 53(2)(b) and 59(2)(b), and 'and' immediately preceding paragraphs 53(2)(b) and 59(2)(b).

Family homes and domestic violence

Short title and chapter	Extent of repeal
Family Law Act 1966 (c. 27)	In section 63(1), the definition of 'matrimonial home rights'. In Schedule 7, 'or' at the end of paragraph 4(a) and paragraph 7(6). In Schedule 8, paragraphs 48(3), 53(2)(b) and 59(2)(b), and 'and' immediately preceding paragraphs 53(2)(b) and 59(2)(b).

Family homes and domestic violence: Northern Ireland

Title and number	Extent of revocation
Family Homes and Domestic Violence (Northern Ireland) Order 1998 (S.I. 1998/1071 (N.I. 6))	In Article 2(2), the definition of 'matrimonial home rights'. In Schedule 2, 'or' at the end of paragraph 4(1)(a).

Discrimination

Short title and chapter	Extent of repeal
Sex Discrimination Act 1975 (c. 27)	Section 1(4).
Sex Discrimination (Northern Ireland) Order 1976 (S.I. 1976/1042 (N.I. 15))	Article 3(4).

Social security, child support and tax credits

Short title and chapter	Extent of repeal or revocation
Child Support Act 1991 (c. 48)	In section 8(11), 'or' at the end of paragraph (e).
Child Support (Northern Ireland) Order 1991 (S.I. 1991/2628 (N.I. 23))	In Article 10(11), 'or' at the end of sub-paragraph (dd).
Social Security Contributions and Benefits Act 1992 (c. 4)	In section 37(4) 'or' at the end of paragraph (a). In section 38(3), 'or' at the end of paragraph (b). In section 39A(2) and (5), 'or' at the end of paragraph (a). In section 39B(5), 'or' at the end of paragraph (a). Section 85(1). In section 137(1), the definitions of 'married couple' and 'unmarried couple'.

Short title and chapter	Extent of repeal or revocation
Social Security Administration Act 1992 (c. 5)	In section 74A(5), the definitions of 'married couple' and 'unmarried couple'.
Social Security Contributions and Benefits (Northern Ireland) Act 1992 (c. 7)	In section 37(4), 'or' at the end of paragraph (a). In section 38(3), 'or' at the end of paragraph (b). In section 39A(2) and (5), 'or' at the end of paragraph (a). In section 39B(5), 'or' at the end of paragraph (a). Section 85(1). In section 133(1), the definitions of 'married couple' and 'unmarried couple'.
Social Security Administration (Northern Ireland) Act 1992 (c. 8)	In section 72A(5), the definitions of 'married couple' and 'unmarried couple'.
Jobseekers Act 1995 (c. 18)	In section 35(1), the definitions of 'married couple' and 'unmarried couple'.
Child Support Act 1995 (c. 34)	In section 10(7), the definitions of 'married couple' and 'unmarried couple'.
Child Support (Northern Ireland) Order 1995 (S.I. 1995/2702 (N.I. 13))	In Article 4(7), the definitions of 'married couple' and 'unmarried couple'.
Jobseekers (Northern Ireland) Order 1995 (S.I. 1995/2705 (N.I. 15))	In Article 2(2), the definitions of 'married couple' and 'unmarried couple'.
State Pension Credit Act 2002 (c. 16)	In section 17(1), the definitions of 'married couple' and 'unmarried couple'.
Tax Credits Act 2002 (c. 21)	In section 48(1), the definitions of 'married couple' and 'unmarried couple', and 'and' at the end of the definition of 'tax year'.
State Pension Credit Act (Northern Ireland) 2002 (c. 14 (N.I.))	In section 17(1), the definitions of 'married couple' and 'unmarried couple'.

Minor and consequential amendments: general

Short title and chapter	Extent of repeal
Judicial Proceedings (Regulation of Reports) Act 1926 (c. 61)	Section 1(5).
Marriage Act 1949 (c. 76)	Section 1(6) to (8).
Theft Act 1968 (c. 60)	In section 30(4), 'or' at the end of paragraph (a)(i) to the proviso.
Consumer Credit Act 1974 (c. 39)	In section 184(5), 'and' immediately before 'references'.
Estate Agents Act 1979 (c. 38)	In section 32(3), 'and' immediately before 'references'.
Courts and Legal Services Act 1990 (c. 41)	In section 58A, 'and' at the end of subsection (2)(f).
Family Law Act 1996 (c. 27)	In section 64, 'or' at the end of subsection (1)(c).

Short title and chapter	Extent of repeal
Welfare Reform and Pensions Act 1999 (c. 30)	At the end of section 23(1)(a)(ii), 'or'. At the end of section 24(b), 'or'. In sections 28(7)(a) and (9), 34(1)(b)(i) and (2) and 48(6)(a) and (8) 'matrimonial'.
Gender Recognition Act 2004 (c. 7)	In Schedule 4, paragraph 2.

Consequential amendments: Scotland

Short title and chapter	Extent of repeal
Damages (Scotland) Act 1976 (c. 13)	In Schedule 1, 'and' at the end of paragraph 1(e).
Family Law (Scotland) Act 1985 (c. 37)	In section 10(2), first 'matrimonial'.
Adults with Incapacity (Scotland) Act 2000 (asp 4)	In section 87, in subsection (1), in the definition of 'nearest relative', ', subject to subsection (2),' and subsections (2) and (3).

Minor and consequential amendments: Northern Ireland

Title and number	Extent of revocation
Welfare Reform and Pensions (Northern Ireland) Order 1999 (S.I. 1999/3147 (N.I. 11))	At the end of Article 22(b), 'or'. In Article 31(1)(b)(i) and (2), 'matrimonial'.

APPENDIX 2

Useful Web References

http://www.csa.gov.uk	Child Support Agency website
http://www.dwp.gov.uk	Information in relation to the state pension and social security benefits
http://www.flba.co.uk	Family Law Bar Association: barristers specializing in family law
http://www.hmso.gov.uk	Full texts of primary and subordinate legislation and draft legislation
http://www.lagla.org.uk	Association of lesbian and gay lawyers
http://www.sfla.co.uk	'Resolution': solicitors specializing in family law

Index

References are to Paragraph Numbers

Index